YORK NOTES COM

The Long 18th Century

Literature from 1660 to 1790

Penny Pritchard

Longman
is an imprint of

PEARSON

  York Press

Harlow, England • London • New York • Boston • San Francisco • Toronto
Sydney • Tokyo • Singapore • Hong Kong • Seoul • Taipei • New Delhi
Cape Town • Madrid • Mexico City • Amsterdam • Munich • Paris • Milan

YORK PRESS
322 Old Brompton Road, London SW5 9JH

PEARSON EDUCATION LIMITED
Edinburgh Gate, Harlow CM20 2JE. United Kingdom
Tel: +44 (0)1279 623623   Fax: +44 (0)1279 431059
Website: www.pearsoned.co.uk

First edition published in Great Britain in 2010

© Librairie du Liban *Publishers* 2010

The right of Penny Pritchard to be identified as author of this work has been
asserted by her in accordance with the Copyright, Designs and Patents Act 1988.

ISBN 978–1–4082–0473–3

British Library Cataloguing in Publication Data
A CIP catalogue record for this book can be obtained from the British Library

Library of Congress Cataloging in Publication Data
Pritchard, Penny.
  The long 18th century : literature from 1660 to 1790 / Penny Pritchard.
    p. cm. -- (York notes companions)
  Includes bibliographical references and index.
  ISBN 978-1-4082-0473-3 (pbk. : alk. paper) 1. English literature--18th
century--History and criticism--Handbooks, manuals, etc. 2. Literature and
society-- Great Britain--History--18th century. I. Title.
  PR441.P75 2010
  820.9'005--dc22
                                   2010006009

10 9 8 7 6 5 4 3 2 1
14 13 12 11 10

Phototypeset by Carnegie Book Production, Lancaster
Printed in Malaysia, CTP-KHL

Contents

Part One
Introduction

Almost every day, the long eighteenth century seems to be getting longer. And wider. It's all a matter of where to draw the artificial boundaries between the stages of time over which human culture continues to change. This volume offers just one version of a period of history many refer to as the 'long eighteenth century', especially as it relates to the literature and culture of England.

This version of the long eighteenth century begins in 1660, when a particularly momentous historical event offers a convenient place to begin this story. The Restoration of Charles II marks a point when the nation – or, at least, some of the most powerful and influential individuals alive at the time – decided to 'restore' to England a form of national government which combined monarchical rule with an elected parliament. The cultural impact of the Restoration, and how authors anticipated its effect on the country's future, is widely evident in contemporary literature. So, too, are authors' meaningful reflections on previous periods of English history, and how depictions of that history could be refashioned to suit new ideas about England's national culture.

Looking back to the beginning of the long eighteenth century, it is worth noting that the Restoration of Charles II in 1660 itself presents the culmination of ongoing political debates from earlier periods in English history, notably the period of religious and civil unrest which erupted into civil war from about 1642. The long eighteenth century starts to get a little bit longer, in other words, as soon as we seek to understand specific events in relation to cultural developments over time. In Part Two, a more detailed overview of such events is provided to give a fuller sense of this period's rich, but necessarily complex, cultural history as a whole.

A Cultural Overview

Different strands of religious, economic, political, artistic and social issues are woven together throughout this volume to give a broad understanding of the long eighteenth century. It would not be an exaggeration to say that religion plays a fundamental role in all of the momentous cultural events of the period (the English Civil War, the Restoration and even the Industrial Revolution), but each event also has its political, economic and – vital to our understanding of the period's literature – its artistic dimension.

We must also consider precisely what it is we mean by the term 'literature' (the primary focus of artistic consideration in this volume). Several decades of critical debate about the *kinds* of writing that scholars should study in order to understand the past have questioned the formal boundaries that have long existed between 'history' and 'literature'. There is no doubt that the imaginative writing of the past (poetry, fictional narratives, essays and so on) help us to understand past cultures, but so, too, do other forms of extant writing (including, but not restricted to, private correspondence, household accounts, ecclesiastical records, menus, legislation and so on). The increasingly recognised value of these alternative sources of cultural history, sometimes referred to as 'historicism', is one that is taken for granted in this volume although the principal subjects for discussion here are works of imaginative literature in the traditional sense.

This book is intended to help students gain a better understanding of the long eighteenth century but also invites its readers to think about the ways in which we study the past, and past literature, in order to understand our own culture. The period between 1660 and 1790 witnessed the acquisition of many aspects of daily life that we now take for granted as 'modern'. This is a cultural feature of the period which makes its study especially interesting to social historians and others keen to explore what 'modernity' really means. Indeed, the end of our period is also frequently described as the culmination of the 'Early Modern Period' of English history. Already apparent, in the last stages of our long eighteenth century, are some of the social and economic developments that enable further profound cultural changes to be wrought by England's Industrial Revolution from early in the nineteenth century. Such developments include the much-improved social status of the mercantile and middle classes and the huge growth of urban centres of population.

In late 1688, another momentous event in English political history occurred when the Roman Catholic King James II abdicated from the throne and was replaced by his Protestant son-in-law and daughter, William III and Mary II. Although this event did not incur the devastating losses of life that took place in the country between 1642 and 1649, it is still referred to as a 'revolution' because of its profound impact in shaping the structure and balance of political power in English government. The roots of the 'Glorious Revolution' (as it is sometimes called) go back to the Protestant Reformation which began during the reign of Henry VIII. The Bill of Rights brought in under William and Mary (and further ratified by the passage of the 1701 Act of Settlement) stipulated that no Roman Catholic could succeed to the English throne. Though under government review, at the time of writing this legislation remains in force.

Moving beyond the topic of English government and monarchy to consider other important aspects of the long eighteenth century, the period's 'boundaries' remain fluid. Consider, for example, England's enormous economic expansion through the acquisition of colonial territories and global trade during this period. This version of the long eighteenth century might instead begin in 1632, when Charles I granted a licence to a group of London merchants to undertake the transportation of enslaved people from West Africa to labour on plantation colonies in the Caribbean. Indeed, a discussion of the long

3

eighteenth century which does proper justice to the history of England's participation in the international slave trade might not end until full legislation abolished the trade in 1833. The *full* extent of England's history as a leading colonial empire might not end until 1947, when India achieved independence.

Both the beginning and the end of the long eighteenth century, therefore, should and do remain subject to scholarly debate. The period formally covered by this volume ends in the year after the French Revolution – just after the point when many literary scholars discern the beginning of the Romantic period with the publication of the *Lyrical Ballads* of Wordsworth and Coleridge in 1798. An extensive consideration of the profound impact of these events on English literature and culture is the subject of the *Romantic Literature* volume in this series. Inevitably and usefully, however, there are points of overlap between the long eighteenth century and the periods which come before and after it in chronological order.

Texts, Writers and Contexts

Literary genre, as we now conceive of it, is itself the product of social and critical consensus, and therefore subject to debate. The six chapters in Part Three provide a detailed overview of four literary genres during the course of this period: drama, satire, poetry and novels. There is analysis of individual literary texts and explanation of the dominant themes which extend across specific considerations of genre. The closer analysis of a single text in each Extended Commentary will help readers to further their understanding of how genre, culture and literature really interact in this period.

Most new readers of eighteenth-century literature are surprised to find that all of its best-known authors – including Alexander Pope, Jonathan Swift, Daniel Defoe and Samuel Johnson – published copious works of literature in both verse and prose (the latter in forms ranging from essays and fiction to pamphlets and literary criticism). Others such as Dryden also translated or adapted Classical works of literature into

English prose and poetry, and some (including Henry Fielding) wrote plays.

Though many of the period's best-known texts are given full consideration in Part Three, the versatility of certain authors means that their names pop up in other, sometimes unexpected, places. In addition, this volume tries to balance its discussion and analysis of familiar texts (e.g. Pope's *Rape of the Lock* or Samuel Richardson's *Clarissa*) with lesser known works (e.g. George Crabbe's poem *The Village* or Eliza Haywood's 'novella' *Fantomina*). It is worth noting, at this point, that the key criteria for the selection of less familiar texts in this volume is their current popularity with undergraduate students and their 'usefulness' in uncovering a specific cultural aspect of the long eighteenth century. The range of texts on offer is intended to convey effectively the key themes and cultural concepts of this volume. At the same time, and equally importantly, it provides tried-and-tested suggestions for further reading in primary texts.

The advent of one of the most important genres in English literary culture, the novel, is associated with this period; different strands of its development over the course of the long eighteenth century are considered in two of Part Three's chapters. The lengthy consideration of the novel reflects not only the prevalence of the genre itself – from late eighteenth- to twenty-first-century literary culture – but the complexity of how the novel developed over this period. This volume assumes that novels are, essentially, long(ish) works of prose fiction which often depict the development of an individual human being over a period of time. This loose definition in itself reflects some of the ongoing critical debates about what novels are.

A cultural period of nearly one and a half centuries necessarily witnesses enormous diversity in its output of poetry, the subject of two more chapters in Part Three. As was also the case during the Renaissance, readers in the long eighteenth century looked to poetry as perhaps the highest form of literary expression. The writing of poetry was also seen, particularly in the earlier decades of the period, as a suitably genteel and learned recreational pursuit for gentlemen and the proper channel through which to commemorate or glorify public institutions. By the end of the period, however, some of the most notable and popular works of poetry anticipate not only the subject matter, but many of the aesthetic and artistic concerns of the Romantic period. These include, increasingly, an inward and very personalised sense of poetic perception. None of these transitions occurred quickly, however, and detailed discussion of key texts and subjects across the period helps to illuminate these developments over time.

The beginning of the long eighteenth century coincides with the rejuvenation of English theatre after a period of relative inactivity. This is not only apparent in the extensive number of new plays which were staged in Restoration London (and, progressively, elsewhere in the kingdom). The period benefited from the introduction of movable stage scenery and – most significant of all – the presence of females on the stage. Now best remembered for the witty repartee and lively plots of its comedies of social manners, English drama during the long eighteenth century constantly reinvented itself to meet the changing demands and tastes of its audience. Perhaps more than any other genre, drama reflects the changing moral standards that were progressively applied to popular literature over the course of this cultural period.

Also covered by Part Three is satire – a literary form which extends across both prose and poetry and occupies such a predominant cultural role during the course of the long eighteenth century that it merits consideration as a genre in its own right. Satire is neither 'invented' nor confined to this cultural period but, in the long eighteenth century, it constitutes a way of perceiving external reality equally as vital as that presented by novels, plays or poems (all of which, in this period, contain elements of satire).

Critical Theories, Debates and Resources

One of the most rewarding ways that students can explore cultural and literary developments is not to focus merely on a single literary text, or even a single genre, but to consider how certain themes or debates run right through a period of time, like a bright thread in a piece of woven fabric. How and why, for example, did the depiction of women and sexuality change over the course of the long eighteenth century? How did the enormous expansion of the print trade affect the quality and content of 'popular' literature? Questions such as these often emerge, quite rightly, from the reading of primary texts but deserve further investigation in their own right. It is therefore intentional that some of the material in Part Four, which looks at critical theories and debates across the main genres, overlaps with, and extends, thematic and contextual ideas first raised in relation to specific texts or genres in Part Three.

The topics in each chapter of Part Four could easily command book-length consideration, or even multiple-book consideration (and have done so). It is only possible here to provide a general 'bill of fare' which touches on the principal areas of critical study, theories and debates that have interested scholars over the past few decades. The subjects on offer are selected as four of the most prevalent (and therefore useful) thematic areas for undergraduate study.

Lists of anthologies and websites are provided in Part Five to give students a truly useful resource for further independent investigation. In addition, Part Five offers an extensive list of annotated suggestions for further reading on the subject, together with a detailed timeline of key literary and historical events during the long eighteenth century.

Penny Pritchard

Part Two
A Cultural Overview

During the long eighteenth century, English men and women followed traditional and time-honoured principles of deference and obedience to one's 'superiors' in the social hierarchy. Age almost always prevailed over youth, and male over female, at every level of the class system. Regarding the third traditional element of this social hierarchy (whereby aristocrats prevailed over commoners), it is harder to generalise. Put another way, English social hierarchies did not remain *unchanged* over the course of 130 years, but it is difficult to pinpoint the precise nature and extent of the changes. One of the most influential studies of the social history of this period is Lawrence Stone's *The Family, Sex and Marriage in England 1500–1800* (1979). Stone's historical perspective is obviously much longer than ours; his fascinating study charts the increasing 'iconographic and literary evidence for a new interest in the self, and for recognition of the uniqueness of the individual' during this period. In other words, Stone's model of English history in this period is a broadly 'progressive' one, moving discernibly towards what we recognise as characteristic features of 'modern' social values such as the recognition of the status of the individual within society.

Notwithstanding its 'progression', Stone stresses how traditional principles of social deference and obedience in the period found open expression in the elaborate rituals of doffing of hats in the presence of superiors; the giving of the wall when passing in the [often very narrow] street; the meticulous ordering of official processions such as funerals, by which every rank was allotted his appropriate place; [and in] the socially graded arrangements for seating in churches.[1]

Stone's examples are particularly valuable because they illustrate how eighteenth-century social deference might be observed across a broad, though still highly stratified, spectrum of class. Although it was unlikely for widely disparate members of English society (that is, the very lowest and highest social ranks) to meet frequently, the church and the public street were among the few sites of public assembly where such meetings might take place. Keith Thomas has similarly noted that in 'rural parishes it was common for the congregation to rise when the local gentleman and his family entered the church and for communion to be taken in order of social precedence'.[2]

Among the nobler ranks of society, social precedence could be taken very seriously indeed. Anecdotal evidence provided by Thomas (taken from archival records of contemporary law trials) chronicles that

[i]n 1673 Lord Cholmondeley killed a carter for his 'insolence' in not allowing his coach precedence on the highway. In 1699 Lord Wharton and Lord Cheyne fought a duel after a dispute as to which of them should sit on the right hand of the chairman of the Buckinghamshire quarter sessions.[3]

Such archaic modes of aristocratic behaviour were probably not the norm during the eighteenth century but were clearly still in evidence. Perhaps, it might be argued, the extremely zealous way that some aristocrats guarded their social precedence itself reveals that social mobility was in fact changing, and that competition and class hostility are the natural by-products of a society that feels threatened by such changes. As Thomas argues:

A system which required the constant acknowledgement of superiority was bound to generate competition, particularly among equals. In the early modern period, when social mobility was upsetting traditional hierarchies, the need to assert one's superiority was felt intensely, by the old-established and the parvenu alike.[4]

This is a useful point with which to begin our detailed consideration of the long eighteenth century's culture and society because it acknowledges that change incurs responses on both sides of the social equation (both for those whose status quo is threatened, and those wishing to assert their own, more recently acquired, status). Relations between the older and newer orders of England's social elite changed dramatically over the course of the period as the nature of their economic, religious or political influence over each other and society continued to change. Different aspects of this relationship are further considered below, as they relate to the following historical survey of the period.

The Restoration: Variations on a Theme

The English Restoration is documented extensively through contemporary literature and art. It is widely known that Charles II was restored to the throne of England on 29 May 1660 (his thirtieth birthday), riding into London in a ceremonious parade of fittingly lavish proportions. The event, declared a 'national day of thanksgiving', was a magnificent 'public relations exercise' calculated to take full advantage of the wave of popular support enjoyed by the restored monarch. In a contemporary diary entry, John Evelyn described it thus: 'with a Triumph of above 20000 horse and foote ... The wayes straw'd with flowers, the bells ringing, the streetes hung with Tapissry, fountaines running with wine'.

Beyond the day of celebration which returned him to the throne, Charles II himself is a charismatic figure who looms large in the public imagination of English history. The clothes would have helped; the tall, bewigged and elegantly dressed King was an aesthetic triumph as well as a public symbol of all that was noble and manly in the English status quo. His passion for culture, recreation and beautiful women is too widely documented to need much elaboration here but it should suffice to say that the popular image of Restoration culture finds its greatest manifestation in the body and bearing of its King, and vice versa. This subject is given further consideration in relation to the poetry of both John Dryden and John Wilmot, the second Earl of Rochester, in Part Three: 'Poetry and History'.

Historical surveys of the Restoration period and culture can sometimes read like an extended version of the seventeenth-century 'public relations exercise' previously described. The Commonwealth* period which precedes it can be seen as an austere and, predictably, puritanical regime; often noted is the period's suppression of certain traditions and pastimes (the bans on playing of games on the Sabbath, celebration of Easter and Christmas as holidays, the closing of the theatres). In dramatic contrast to the sombre and gloomy Commonwealth period, the Restoration is depicted as an explosion of colour, festivity and aristocratic grandeur for English culture. It is an enormously attractive, but not resoundingly accurate, depiction of what the period must have been like for many people living in England at the time.

It fails to do justice, for one thing, to a dimension of everyday experience that was central to the lives of many (perhaps most) of the English population, but that is now much less frequently regarded. Religion was an emotional and psychological cornerstone for English life in the seventeenth and eighteenth centuries; the English Revolution had been fought on many fronts but religion remained its primary and driving force. From the time of the Reformation onwards, English Protestants had divided along religious lines. The majority chose to remain within the established (Anglican) Church and defend the

---

* 'Commonwealth', in this context, is used here to refer to the period of republican government over England, Scotland and Wales (and subsequently Ireland) from 30 January 1649 until the monarchical restoration of 1660, including the period from 1653 when Oliver Cromwell served as Lord Protector (effectively, as a king-like ruler) until his death in 1658. As its name suggests, the term 'Interregnum' refers to the same period of time but is employed to denote the cultural context of those who celebrated the Restoration as the 'rightful' return of civil and executive authority in the monarch.

institutional authority of its bishops under any circumstances. Other English Protestants felt the spiritual need to reform their modes of worship beyond what was accepted – or even demanded – by the state church. Whether these diverse groups of Protestants are described as 'Puritans', 'Nonconformists', dissenters, or by the different names of their separate denominations and sects (including but not restricted to Presbyterians, Congregationalists, Baptists and Quakers), it should be noted that they sometimes shared little more than a religious conviction, as Protestant Christians, to worship God in the way they saw fit. The seemingly conflicting demands of spiritual conviction and religious toleration, within the wider Protestant Christian community of England, needs to remain at or near the centre of our cultural understanding of the long eighteenth century.

Protestant Nonconformity

By opting out of the Anglican Church it is highly unlikely that most English Nonconformists intended to reject the authority of their monarch. Half a century earlier, numerous Puritans – suffering what they considered to be intolerable restraints on their religious liberties under James I – had migrated to the American colonies. Their purpose, however, was to establish an *English* colonial settlement there under James I's jurisdiction. By the time of the English Civil War, however, many of the devout Parliamentarians who rejected the absolutist monarchy of Charles I also did so on religious grounds; the deeply held differences between Royalists (or 'Cavaliers') and Parliamentarians needs to be seen as a matter of *both* religious and political difference.

As the head of the Church of England, the King was (to devout Anglicans) God's representative on earth; to them, the execution of Charles I in January 1649 was an aberration against God as well as mankind. Equally, many English Nonconformists saw the end of absolute monarchy as the greatest manifestation of God's blessing on their ambitious project for religious, social and political reform. The religious and political antagonism between Royalists and

Parliamentarians is just as evident after 1660 when the balance of power shifts again. As a gruesome but wholly symbolic gesture in January 1661, the embalmed remains of the late Lord Protector Oliver Cromwell (who had died in 1658) were removed from Westminster Abbey. Several days later, on the twelfth anniversary of the beheading of Charles I, Cromwell was one of three dead regicides* whose bodies were dragged to Tyburn and hanged before subsequently being beheaded. Cromwell's head remained on public display for over twenty years.

Beyond this 'gesture', Charles II's 'Cavalier Parliament' (the first parliament to meet after the Restoration) actively sought to redress what they saw as an eleven-year insult to their political and religious authority through a series of vicious legislative measures aimed towards Protestant Nonconformists. These measures are sometimes known as the Clarendon Code and take their name from the Earl of Clarendon, Edward Hyde (1609–74) who served as Charles's Lord Chancellor for the first seven years of the Restoration period.

Put simply, the Clarendon Code imposed severe restrictions on the civil liberties of Nonconformists which made it difficult or impossible (without incurring hefty fines or imprisonment) to hold any positions of public authority, or to serve as ministers or teachers. It also outlawed, briefly, congregational worship outside of the Anglican Church itself (although limited numbers of Nonconformist ministers were allowed, after 1672, to apply for licences under Charles's Declaration of Indulgence).

After 1660: Suppression and Civil Liberty

The plight of English Nonconformists offers a rather different view of the English Restoration. In the previous section, it has been suggested that the Restoration in 1660 might be seen as a culmination of the

---

* The other regicides were Cromwell's son-in-law Henry Ireton (1611–51) who married Cromwell's eldest daughter, Bridget, in 1646, and possibly also John Bradshaw (1602–59), a judge at the trial of Charles I. The bodies were first hanged from the gallows at Tyburn for a day before being beheaded and their heads left on public display.

period of civil unrest which began in England around 1642. One way that the Restoration brought civil and religious unrest to an end was through ruthless suppression (as seen in the Clarendon Code); Charles also tried, unsuccessfully, to close down the coffee houses which had gained a popular foothold in English culture during the late Interregnum because they were potential sites for public debate about state authority. Charles used his royal prerogative (that is, passed into law without parliamentary ratification) to introduce the Licensing Act of 1662, which prohibited the publication of any literary work without prior licensed consent from the state-authorised Stationers' Company. In charge of operations was Licenser of the Press, Sir Roger L'Estrange (1616–1704), an ebullient and devoted Royalist who zealously exercised his authority from the time of the Act's passage until its expiration in 1679. The Act was renewed in 1685, the year that Charles died and was succeeded by his brother James, and then remained in place for another decade before its final expiry during the reign of William III.[5]

It should be clear by now that we need to put aside oversimplified versions of historical narrative, such as those which either reflect negatively on the Interregnum or that suggest that England's Civil War and Interregnum period represent a 'triumph' of democracy and civil protest over royal absolutism. This is a fascinating area of scholarly debate over a period of history which, although it occurs just before our period, continues to exercise a profound impact on the decades which follow.[6] By beginning this investigation in 1660, we are necessarily focused upon a consideration of what was being 'restored' – whether for better or for worse – to English culture and society. Although virtually all periods of history reveal dramatic social change, this volume would like to plead a special case for the causes and effects of the English Civil War. As Kevin Sharpe observes:

> [N]one could deny that the civil war was the greatest fissure, and only violent revolution, in the English body politic, nor that it produced a vibrant political discourse of passion, ideological fervor, and theoretical sophistication.[7]

The English Civil War certainly inspired a level of social and ideological revolution unprecedented in English history; it also killed more Englishmen as a proportion of the population than any military conflict before or since.[8] There is little question that both of these factors, as well as the period of republican government and legislative change that followed in the Interregnum, would have exercised a dramatic impact across all of English society. At the same time, it is worth remembering that the vast majority of England's population in 1660 still lived in rural villages and hamlets, gaining their livelihoods from agriculture and farming. It is probably also the case that at least half of England's rural population were functionally illiterate and had little access to printed matter such as newsbooks or pamphlets (although it remains notoriously difficult to assess rates and qualities of reading competency in this period of English history, for a whole host of reasons).[9]

All of these observations are offered to help us query the true and practical extent of the Restoration's immediate impact on the majority of England's populace. An elite minority of the population read – and wrote – books, and had first-hand experience of the profound changes in English government from 1660, but it is on their accounts that we largely depend for our cultural understanding of the period. A relatively small audience of sophisticated London gentry (including the King himself) avidly attended the Restoration theatre and probably thoroughly enjoyed the striking parallels between its use of elaborate costumes, plot intrigues and witty sexual dalliance, and those which featured within the equally dramatic realm of courtly life. In the sparkling wit and sexually charged dialogue of the English comedy of manners, such as the plays of Aphra Behn, we have retained at least some nuances of that vividly entertaining world.

Two momentous events from this early part of the English Restoration are indelibly retained in the public memory. The Great Plague of 1665 was in fact the last of a number of outbreaks of bubonic plague throughout British history. The infection spread to England via Holland; it was aided by the exceptionally hot summer of 1665 as well as the early efforts of London's wealthier inhabitants to escape the plague (thus spreading it into the surrounding countryside as they went). Early civil measures taken to counteract the spread of the disease proved ineffectual or worse; these included certificates of health required for travel or entry to towns (which could be forged or bought with bribes) and, in London, the mass slaughter of dogs and cats as the suspected carriers and spreaders of the infection. The true cause, not to be discovered for several centuries, was the fleas which lived on rats; by killing the city's dog and cat population, the authorities inadvertently helped to increase London's rats, and therefore its population of plague-infected fleas.

Approximately 100,000 Londoners are thought to have died by the end of the year. Infection, however, was not isolated to the capital: rural towns and villages also suffered. By November 1666, Eyam in Derbyshire had lost three-quarters of its population of 350 inhabitants. Eyam isolated its infection and prevented its spread to neighbouring villages through a rigorous system of quarantine: this village's plague experiences are movingly chronicled in the diary of William Mompesson, the village's Anglican minister.

It seems strangely ironic that London's Great Fire in 1666 probably helped to prevent the recurrence of the bubonic plague in the city. The famous fire which began in the early morning of 2 September in Pudding Lane was fuelled by the combined factors of a strong east wind and the tinder-dry condition of the wood and thatch (after another hot summer) that comprised the vast majority of London's housing materials. Closely-built houses, and the combustible nature of many of the materials contained in warehouses and storerooms near where the fire began, aided its rapid spread. Over four days and nights, the fire destroyed more than 13,000 homes as well as most of the public buildings in its path (including, famously, the Norman-style St Paul's Cathedral). In an entry for 16 March 1667, Samuel Pepys notes in his diary: 'smoke remaining, coming out of some cellars, from the late great Fire, now above six months since'.[10] As is well known, the fire did not directly claim many lives but it left hundreds of thousands homeless and bereft of their livelihoods and possessions.

It would be inaccurate to suggest that the dramatic story of London's Great Fire concerned only the inhabitants of the city itself. The task of rebuilding London out of brick and stone tells another story, one in which a vast array of migrant workers and industries in Britain and abroad supplied the labour and materials. The project to rebuild London after 1666 marks the point at which the city began to expand its population in earnest. This volume explores in detail how London's expansion, and expanding literary interest in the city centre as both a place of urban sophistication and a potential source of moral corruption and danger, are profoundly significant aspects of how England develops during the course of the long eighteenth century.

After 1666: The Exclusion Crisis

Many notable features of Charles II's reign still have the power to capture our imagination. The passage of several centuries might now make these appear as a rapid succession of events although, in reality, most significant cultural developments occur over extended periods of years. While the landscape of London was almost completely destroyed by fire over the course of only four days and nights, its rebuilding took several decades. Sir Christopher Wren's new building of St Paul's Cathedral offers a convincing example of this. The old building was still in use until 1668 when it was found to be structurally unsound and demolition began. After that, disputes over proposed new designs continued for nine years before building works actually started in 1675; the cathedral itself was finally completed in 1710.

Charles had been on the throne for nearly two decades when the political tensions which flared into the Popish Plot and the Exclusion Crisis* came to the fore. These particular events are discussed further in

---

* The Popish Plot of 1678 was an early key event in the Exclusion Crisis. It concerned an assassination plot – probably entirely false – in which Titus Oates had accused a large number of prominent Roman Catholics of conspiring to murder Charles II. Anti-Catholic hysteria during this period was further fuelled by the openly professed Roman Catholic faith of Charles's proposed successor, his brother James, the Duke of York. Members of Parliament made several failed attempts to pass a Bill excluding James from succession, but Charles exercised his royal prerogative to overturn their efforts until the Bill's final defeat in the House of Lords in 1681.

relation to Dryden's *Absalom and Achitophel* (1681) in Part Three: 'Poetry and History'; it is worth noting here, however, that the period's political tensions centre, once again, on the issues of state religion and the extent of royal authority. Charles's failure to produce a legitimate heir for the throne of England, coupled with the fact that James, the Duke of York (his brother and likely successor) had by now openly converted to the Catholic faith, were strong factors which added to some people's growing sense of unease about the probable return of a Catholic monarch to the English throne.

The possibility was a strong one: both Charles and James had much sympathy for the religion of their mother and the French court which had given them both support and protection after their father's execution. Charles's Portuguese wife, Catherine of Braganza, and James's second wife, Mary of Modena, were Roman Catholics; James's conversion in 1667 was made public in 1673. More significantly, and not to be revealed until his death, was the fact that Charles had secretly signed the Treaty of Dover with his first cousin, King Louis XIV, in 1670. In it, he agreed (in exchange for funds) to convert to Roman Catholicism at an unspecified future date and to support the civil and religious liberties of Roman Catholics both at home (with the 1672 Declaration of Indulgence) and abroad (by fighting with the French against the Protestant Dutch in the Third Anglo-Dutch War). Charles's secret treaty with France meant that, as his reign progressed, he was less obliged to defer to Parliament's demands in order to seek revenue. During and after the Exclusion Crisis, two short-lived meetings of Parliament took place in 1679 and 1680; the third Exclusion Parliament convened for only one week in Oxford in March 1681, and after this Parliament did not meet again during Charles's lifetime.

Whigs versus Tories

As is discussed in relation to Dryden's poem *Absalom and Achitophel* in Part Three: 'Poetry and History', anti-Catholic feelings ran high during this period and coalesced around the parliamentary ministers led by Shaftesbury. On the other side of the political divide – whether they were Roman Catholics or not – staunch Royalists were less concerned about James's Catholicism than the possibility of another monarch less sympathetic to their interests and more likely to make concessions to dissenters (many of whom were still viewed, only two decades after Cromwell's death, as religious zealots and troublemakers).

One verbal manifestation of fear and hostility, often witnessed in both the playground and Parliament, is name-calling between opposing parties. The origins of two particular names, whose significance to our understanding of the long eighteenth century is hard to exaggerate, find their cultural legacy in the Exclusion Crisis and its aftermath. 'Whig' and 'Tory' were, originally, terms of abuse not directly related to English parliamentary politics at all, but came to be adopted to the extent that their original meanings are now less familiar than these later associations. As used in England prior to about 1679 or 1680, the term 'Tories' originally referred to bands of hardened and violent Irish outlaws who had wreaked havoc in Ireland for centuries. As a long-exploited colonial territory under English rule, Ireland's stereotyped depiction as a lawless land of endemic poverty and criminality was well established by this period. Robert Willman observes that it was unlikely that the Irish Tories

> ever offered a serious threat to the English establishment in Ireland. It ranged from menacing demands for charity … to highway robbery and occasional murder, but its chief victims were Irish peasants and petty traders; the Tories only occasionally ever bothered the gentry, who were better equipped to look after themselves and were often, in fact, on good terms with Tory leaders.[11]

The term was used as a pejorative description of the Royalist supporters of James, thereby also reflecting the anti-Catholic fear of the 'Whig' opposition. The term 'Whig' (a shortened form of 'Whiggamaire') had originally referred to Scottish rebels who had violently resisted English rule in Scotland.[12] It is clear that, once established within the context of English politics and culture, both terms continued to shift their meanings and, significantly, their pejorative connotations. 'Paradoxically', Willman also notes, '"Tory" owes its survival less to the Whigs than to the Tories themselves', since Royalists such as the vehement polemicist Sir Roger L'Estrange had begun to use it in print as a term of self-reference before the Whigs' widely circulated propaganda related to the Exclusion Crisis had adopted the term.[13]

The original religious associations of pro- and anti-Catholic feeling in 'Tory' and 'Whig' were, gradually, subsumed into more complex social and political divisions of identity and affiliation. As the political divisions within English society become broadly stabilised into the 'Whig' and 'Tory' ministries who served, first during the reign of William and Mary, and subsequently Queen Anne, the opposing parties also come to represent divided economic interests.[14] Tories are *generally* associated with the landed gentry (that is, those whose wealth was derived from property); Whigs are *generally* associated with the interests of City finance, trade and overseas expansion.

This broad distinction can help us to understand some political debates: for example, many Tories were reluctant to support and fund King William's keen efforts to engage in a war with France because they saw it as unrelated to English interests while his Whig supporters encouraged the war effort for the advantages it brought to English trading interests abroad. Hard and fast divisions are rarely accurate, however, and political affiliations are notoriously subject to change. Sir Robert Harley was a moderate Tory statesman who supported the French war during the reign of Queen Anne (and bankrolled Defoe to provide propaganda to this purpose in his *Review* periodical between 1704 and 1711) although he had previously supported the Whig party.

The omnipresence – if not always the relevance – of Whig versus Tory politics becomes all too apparent to readers of this period's literature. Certain authors are more clearly associated with the interests of one party (Pope, Fielding and Johnson as Tories, for example) but distinctions become more problematic as the period progresses and many authors, then as now, actively chose to distance themselves and their writing from contemporary politics. Moreover, while some authors did engage in controversial and sometimes polemic political debates in the press, most remained acutely aware that they needed to temper their opinions in order to avoid censorship or, in extreme cases, arrest and possible imprisonment.

After the Licensing Act expired in 1695, authors (as well as printers and booksellers associated with a particular publication) could still be prosecuted under charges of seditious libel. The publication of Defoe's inflammatory pamphlet *The Shortest Way with the Dissenters* (1702) led to his imprisonment in Newgate and several sessions in the public pillory on just such charges (as well as his first bankruptcy). Further legislation which censored literature during this period included Walpole's 1737 Licensing Act, intended to scrutinise specific genres (such as contemporary drama) for containing what was deemed to be subversive or anti-government sentiment.

Beyond political divisions or state censorship, authors who expressed inflammatory or offensive opinions during this period could also expect violent reprisals from offended readers. It is widely reported that, following the first publication of *The Dunciad* in 1728, Pope only went out when accompanied by his Great Dane, Bounce, and a pair of loaded pistols in his pocket; a less well-known author, Whig journalist John Tutchin, died in 1707 as a direct result of severe beatings sustained in response to the polemical opinions he expressed in his periodical *The Observator*. Such anecdotes help to indicate how fragile and deeply subjective the notion of 'freedom of the press' could be during the eighteenth century.

The Glorious Revolution

James II's succession in 1685 was short lived; along with the two Protestant daughters who succeeded him on the throne but had no surviving children, James represents the effectual end of the English Stuart monarchy.* James's abdication was warmly welcomed by William's many Whig supporters. The Jacobite uprisings of 1715 and 1745 indicate that popular support for the Stuart succession remained intact long after 1688; these events witnessed the separate attempts of James II's son and grandson (the 'Old Pretender' and 'Young Pretender') to reclaim the throne of England that their Stuart ancestry made rightfully theirs (but from which their Roman Catholic religion barred them).

The accession of William and Mary is referred to as the 'Glorious Revolution' because it incurred no bloodshed (although it is unlikely that many of James's supporters and England's extant Roman Catholic population would have described it in these terms). The Dutch King William of Orange was no friend to Roman Catholics although he was both the nephew and son-in-law of James II (his Protestant wife was also his first cousin).† He was, however, a shrewd military and strategic ruler on the international stage who had little interest in matters of English domestic concern; what the English throne offered him was the useful opportunity to consolidate Protestant forces in the European arena against the French. William left his wife Mary largely in charge of England during the earlier years of their reign (most notably when he defeated her father's attempts to regain his crown at the Irish Battle of the Boyne in 1690).

After Mary's death from smallpox in December 1694, William divided his time between his English affairs (centred at Hampton Court) and the Netherlands. His death in 1702, following a hunting accident, was not widely mourned in the English press. It seems ironic, then, that the English populace have William and his relative indifference for English politics to thank for several important aspects of legislation which were passed in the 1689 Declaration of Rights. From the

---

* James's daughters became Queen Mary (1662–94, who ruled England with her husband, William, from 1688) and Queen Anne (1665–1714, who ruled from 1702). They were the only surviving children of his first wife, Anne Hyde (1637–71). James's abdication occurred when his Protestant daughter Mary and her Dutch husband, William of Orange (1650–1702), arrived in England to claim the English throne that James's ministers had offered to them.

† William III of Orange was the son of the English Charles I's eldest daughter, Mary Stuart (sister to Charles II and James II); his wife, Mary II, was James's eldest daughter by his first wife, Anne Hyde.

beginning of his reign, William and his supporters were engaged in maintaining the Protestant balance of power in Europe. William agreed to many of Parliament's demands to limit his monarchical powers in order that, in exchange, he had regular opportunities to canvas Parliament for war revenues; the result is the restricted powers of the English monarch and the regular convening of Parliament that remain largely unchanged today.

William's reign, and that of his sister-in-law Anne after him, witnessed the early stages of a sustained period of economic expansion through new forms of investment and financial speculation – with some significant setbacks, such as the South Sea Bubble (now widely recognised as the first stock market crash, see Part Four: 'Trade, Colonial Expansion and Slavery') – and periodic but sustained warfare in Europe. This political 'stability' (albeit one marked by extensive growth and war) was subsequently aided by the smooth monarchical succession of four King Georges between 1714 and 1830. Extending beyond our period, this royal succession stands in direct contrast to the periods of political uncertainty and tension which characterised most of the monarchical transitions in the earlier part of the long eighteenth century (from Charles II to James II, James II to William and Mary, and from Anne to George I).

Another aspect of this broad sense of 'stability' in the earlier part of the eighteenth century is Sir Robert Walpole's lengthy period of ministerial office. Walpole dominated English political life from 1715 (in the dual roles of First Lord of the Treasury and Chancellor of the Exchequer) until his resignation in 1742. Sometimes referred to as Britain's first Prime Minister (as the recipient of George II's gift of 10 Downing Street in 1735), Walpole was undoubtedly a powerful and charismatic politician although accusations of bribery and corruption darkened his latter years in office; his manipulative relationship with the popular press and his refusal to tolerate satirical comment on his ministry are also widely acknowledged in contemporary literature.

By the second decade of the eighteenth century, England was well on the way to establishing its position as a global military and economic presence of the first order. The impact of these economic changes on everyday life in England was becoming as evident in material surroundings as in the (increasingly available) 'news from abroad'. England's consumption of imported products – coffee, tea, chocolate, sugar, rum and tobacco, manufactured goods including fabrics and furniture, materials such as ivory and precious metals – increased at an exponential rate during the eighteenth century. So, too, did demand for reading materials; the size and diversity of popular literature expanded rapidly to meet a growing public of readers with specific tastes and preferences. The expansion and diversification of the periodical press, the 'rise' of the novel, and the birth of literary criticism, all derive from this period.

If many of these products were once within the reach of only England's wealthier consumers, they started to become accessible to a much wider social and economic spectrum. At the same time, England's 'middling orders' – the wide band of individuals at neither the top nor bottom ends of the social scale – were growing considerably in numbers and wealth (and therefore purchasing power). As Keith Wrightson argues, it was, specifically, the trading, manufacturing and professional activities of *this* part of the social spectrum that contributed most to this period of expansion and change:

> [T]hey included people as various as merchants, lawyers, medical practitioners, clothiers, ironmongers, mining engineers, shipmasters and what [Roy] Porter calls 'an anthill of petty traders, horse dealers, builders, innkeepers and manufacturers who excelled in turning a penny for themselves'.[15]

As is equally the case today, the purchase and consumption of imported goods or 'luxury' products brought with it questions for some eighteenth-century consumers about ethical trade. For example, authors such as William Cowper expressed concerns about the exploitation of trading partners in a global – but hardly equal – commercial market more than two centuries ago. Corresponding with England's economic and commercial expansion is a widely increasing sense (in contemporary poetry and periodicals, especially) that material 'luxury' is itself a corrupt and corrupting force within English society. This is expressed by Goldsmith and Smollett, among others, but arguably forms part of the wider cultural response to England's changing national identity as it becomes, in time, the largest imperial and economic force in Europe.

By the third quarter of the eighteenth century, the intolerable burden of taxation that England imposed on its American colonies (without parliamentary representation) led to a war for independence that interrogated many of the principles of freedom and justice held dear by English men and women. Due to restrictions of space and the timeframe of this volume, literature pertaining to the American and French Revolutions must necessarily remain beyond this discussion; it is worth observing, however, that the revolutionary spirit that, differently, inspired the bid for American political independence and French republicanism had a profound impact on a number of English authors writing in the last decades of the eighteenth century. This impact would coalesce, during the following decades, in the writing of Wollstonecraft, Blake, Wordsworth and Coleridge, but its first stirrings are discernable in the distinct social conscience and calls for reform heard in the late eighteenth century in authors such as William Cowper.

Cowper's poem *The Task* (1785) (discussed in Part Three: 'Pastoral and Anti-pastoral Poetry') reflects a wide range of social concerns, from the corrupting powers of material wealth within England's domestic realm to the cost in lives and human suffering with which that wealth was acquired. The transatlantic slave trade (discussed in Part Four: 'Political and Social Satire'), contributed enormously to England's eighteenth-century economic success story; some of the earliest English voices against the slave trade, in the press, also begin to be heard in this period.

These are not all of the underlying social and economic tensions, highly prevalent in contemporary literature, which lie just underneath the seemingly 'stable' surface of mid- and late eighteenth-century English culture. The spectre of abject poverty and desolation hanging over England's rural landscape – seen in contemporary poems such as Goldsmith's *The Deserted Village* (1770) and Crabbe's *The Village* (1783) and discussed in Part Three: 'Pastoral and Anti-pastoral Poetry'

– was no literary flight of fancy. Wide-scale abuse of the electoral system (in the form of bribery and corruption) was evident in the 'rotten boroughs' and 'pocket boroughs' of its rural constituencies, as addressed by both Samuel Johnson and George Crabbe. The nature of the English rural landscape itself was being refashioned to accommodate the rapid increase in enclosures (legislation enabled common land to be converted into private property). Enclosures meant that agricultural estates could expand significantly in terms of size and efficiency, but the poorer rural population (who, previously, had maintained some independence by virtue of the common land) became increasingly dependent on wealthy landowners for their survival. The economic migration of the rural poor, either to the swelling urban centres or abroad to its colonial territories, was yet another aspect of England's shifting domestic landscape.

History and Historiography in the Long Eighteenth Century

The previous discussion of Whigs and Tories addressed the use of the terms during and after the Exclusion Crisis and their subsequent use in eighteenth-century political culture. There is another, completely different, context in which we must now contend with the important notion of Whig and Tory politics. This relates to the manner in which we interpret periods of history (such as the long eighteenth century) and how certain *versions* of history can be put forward in preference to others. There is, of course, no definitive 'true' version of past events; the discussion and study of variations between different versions are known as 'historiography'. In this context, it should be recognised that the vast majority of the historical surveys of the long eighteenth century (at least, those undertaken since the 1960s) imply a certain cultural perspective and sense of priority that merit, at least, our acknowledgement. These *versions* of the history of the long eighteenth century have, in fact, been widely described as 'Whig' models of history, for reasons that are now considered.

'Whig' models of the eighteenth century imply a notion of the period's cultural progress or refinement as it moves further away from older, more 'repressive' forms of government (such as absolute monarchy), state censorship and more 'hierarchical and stratified' versions of class structure. Such 'progress' may also take the myriad form of everything from increased social mobility, to an expanding print culture (expressing a wider form of democratic freedom), the opening-up of new sites of public assembly and debate such as the coffee house or club, the advent of parliamentary reform, the expansion of free trade, the cultural ascendance of economic individualism, and so on.

The previous paragraph's observations concerning progress are not intended as rejections of Whig models of history *per se* (indeed, it might well be argued that this volume is decidedly Whiggish in its leanings). It is always valuable, however, to recognise how any historical model neglects or underestimates certain aspects of a wider historical narrative. One of the best-known recent discussions of this subject is offered by Jonathan Clark. Clark's revisionist historiography of the long eighteenth century does not dismiss or deny the indisputable material growth and expansion of Britain (as an economic and imperial force, or in terms of its expanded population). He does, however, point to the relative neglect by Whig historians of the religious dimension of a culture 'in which all moved, whether Anglican, Roman Catholic or Dissenter'.[16] This neglect, Clark notes, is most apparent in relation to the established and majority religion:

> The Anglican Church in particular, its politics, its theology, its social theory, its relation to popular religion – all were dismissed from History syllabi in most universities, and with them went all forms of social history of a non-positivist kind.[17]

Clark also notes a Whig tendency in many historians' reduction of the past to matters of economic or sociological change, thus missing the fundamental cultural differences that separate the eighteenth century's deferential and traditional society from our own 'modern' one. In tracing aspects of our own modernity in the eighteenth century, we find its beginnings in the many forms of 'progress' that Whig histories – including this book – uncover. In doing so, however, do we not risk losing sight of what makes eighteenth-century culture different from our own?

It is perhaps inevitable that we try to understand the past by comparing it to our modern culture. Clark, however, is also surely right when he suggests that historians – whether they are conscious of it or not – tend to have an agenda, a motivating reason for tracing the emergence of a particular theme through a period of history as it 'progresses' or 'deteriorates'. The bias of any particular historical approach, combined with the essential richness and diversity of culture itself, means that we always tend to find what we are looking for. This can be particularly apparent in the analysis of specific themes (for example, gender studies or postcolonial studies as discussed in Part Four).

Such studies, however, can greatly enrich our understanding of any historical period when they are taken in conjunction with other studies, thus building together a pluralist, rather than a specialist, version of the long eighteenth century. That is very much the intention of this volume. Lawrence Lipking argues:

> Any long view of the development of eighteenth-century studies must come to terms with the way that scholars partly invent the periods and subjects that they study. Every age makes its own past, projecting its own preoccupations back into time … Very likely they are offering singular definitions of something that makes sense only in the plural. There are enough eighteenth centuries to satisfy everyone.[18]

It is sincerely hoped that, in the following pages, readers may discover a few more eighteenth centuries – longer and shorter, Whig and Tory, ancient and modern – to satisfy themselves.

Notes

1   Lawrence Stone, *The Family, Sex and Marriage in England 1500–1800*, abr. edn (London: Penguin Books, 1979), p. 150.

2   Keith Thomas, *The Ends of Life: Roads to Fulfilment in Early Modern England* (Oxford: Oxford University Press, 2009), p. 151.

3   Ibid., p. 150.

4   Ibid., p. 151.

5   See J. Walker, 'The Censorship of the Press during the Reign of Charles II', *History*, 35 (1950), pp. 219–38; and F. S. Siebert, *Freedom of the Press in England 1476–1776* (Urbana: University of Illinois Press, 1965).

6   Useful sources on the Civil War are Kevin Sharpe, *Politics and Ideas in Early Stuart England* (London: Pinter, 1989); and Christopher Hill, *Puritanism and Revolution* (London: Panther, 1968).

7   Kevin Sharpe, 'Religion, Rhetoric, and Revolution in Seventeenth-century England', *Huntington Library Quarterly*, 57:3 (Summer 1994), p. 255.

8   Robert Thomas, *Civil Society and the English Civil War* (London: Libertarian Alliance, 1992), p. 3.

9   For an interesting and detailed discussion of seventeenth-century literature in England, and the problems of its analysis, see David Cressy, 'Literacy in Seventeenth-century England: More Evidence', *Journal of Interdisciplinary History*, 8:1 (Summer 1977), pp. 141–50.

10   Diary extract cited on the website www.pepys.info/fire.html.

11   Robert Willman, 'The Origins of "Whig" and "Tory" in English Political Language', *Historical Journal*, 17:2 (June 1974), p. 252.

12   Willman notes that the use of 'Whig' as a pejorative term in its English coinage is less easy to understand than its 'Tory' counterpart: ibid., pp. 253–4.

13   Ibid., p. 261.

14   On this subject, see W. A. Speck, *Stability and Strife : England 1714–1760* (London: Edward Arnold, 1977), pp. 143–8.

15   Keith Wrightson, *Earthly Necessities: Economic Lives in Early Modern Britain, 1470–1750* (London: Penguin Books, 2002), p. 289. Wrightson's work, as well as Roy Porter's *English Society in the Eighteenth Century* (London: Penguin, 1982), are excellent introductory sources to the (extremely wide) scholarly study of eighteenth-scentury social and economic practice.

16   J. C. D. Clark, *English Society 1688–1832: Ideology, Social Structure and Political Practice during the Ancien Regime* (Cambridge: Cambridge University Press, 1985), p. 43.

17   Ibid., p. 9.

18   Lawrence Lipking, 'Inventing the Eighteenth Centuries: A Long View', in Leo Damrosch (ed.), *The Profession of Eighteenth-century Literature: Reflections on an Institution* (Madison and London: University of Wisconsin Press, 1992), p. 7.

Part Three
Texts, Writers and Contexts

Poetry and History: Dryden, Johnson and Rochester

History repeats itself. Every cultural age, including our own, is self-defined through comparison with the past. In the process, we reveal our common humanity. The three principal poems under discussion here share the direct evocation of much older literary forms, yet their authors were keenly aware of the precise cultural and political moment in which they lived and wrote.

The word 'political' is used advisedly in the previous sentence, invoking notions of public authority and power as they apply to English culture during the long eighteenth century. Its literature – in particular, its poetry – is firmly established within a political context from its beginning, marked by Charles II's restoration in 1660. Yesterday's political events, however, are tomorrow's history; all of these poems explore how earlier historical models provide interpretative material from which contemporary readers may glean a better understanding of their own culture. The historical model in question may relate to personal experience (such as one's sexual history), an ongoing period of time (such as the reign of Charles II) or a general survey of 'mankind, from China to Peru'. The variations in these historical models foreground important questions about how authors draw parallels between specific political issues and universal truths concerning human nature.

Historical comparison between ancient and contemporary modes of experience is also evident in these poems' literary models. Dryden's

Absalom and Achitophel (1681) derives from the Bible story in which Absalom (the illegitimate son of King David) rebels against his father, while Johnson's *The Vanity of Human Wishes* (1749) is an 'Imitation of the Tenth Satire of Juvenal'.* Rochester's *Imperfect Enjoyment* (1680), the subject of this chapter's Extended Commentary, derives from both the Classical tradition as well as a contemporary vogue for poems on the theme of male impotence.†

The (Sexual) Body Politic and the Court: Rochester and Dryden

Despite his frequent focus on 'personal' subjects – often related to sexual activity and genitalia – Rochester's canon as a whole confounds the assumption that his verse does not address wider political questions. On the contrary, the overtly sexual nature of much of Rochester's verse brings profound cultural resonance to the concept of the 'body politic', in which the monarch represents the corporeal head of an organised system of government. During the Restoration period, the concept is powerfully addressed through the political philosophy of Thomas Hobbes.[1] Questions about the notion of kingly authority are deeply embedded into the political consciousness of late seventeenth-century England; Charles II's failure to produce a legitimate heir – despite fathering more than a dozen illegitimate ones with his many mistresses – divided political loyalties as older anxieties concerning the possible succession of a Roman Catholic monarch (Charles's brother James, Duke of York) were renewed. Only a few decades later, the public imagination was once again centred on the body and being of a Stuart monarch – this time Queen Anne – as the potential source of political stability, though here it was within the context of its procreative function as well as its royal authority.

---

*   The verse satires of Roman poet Juvenal (*c.* AD 60–*c.* 136) vividly depict scenes in which the poet berates human vice in all he surveys. The story of Absalom and Achitophel occurs in 2 Samuel 13–18, although Dryden's poem also draws on other Biblical references.

†   John Wilmot is generally referred to by his title, second Earl of Rochester.

Rochester's thematic focus on sexual desire and its lack – through premature ejaculation, (im)potence and so on – thus relates directly to the nation's political state *as well* as the primary subject. Best known for his explicit sexual language, Rochester merits at least equal credit for 'turning sex into a problem of thought (and thought of sex)'.[2] The concept of the body politic helps us to understand that his verse addresses the *united* realms of public and private experience.

Rochester was a first-hand witness and participant in the sexual exploits of the Restoration court. His well-known contempt for conventional authority certainly extended as far as the King; his manuscript verses exchange subtlety for the mocking and privileged irreverence of the courtly elite:

> In the Isle of Britain long since famous grown
> For breeding the best cunts in all Christendom,
> There now does live – ah, let him long survive –
> The easiest king and the best bred man alive ...
> Peace is his aim, his gentleness is such,
> And love he loves, for he loves fucking much.
> Nor are his high desires above his strength
> His sceptre and his prick are of an equal length.[3]

Given the rather striking version of nationalism that Rochester offers here, the parallels between his and Dryden's portrait of 'the best bred man alive' might at first be overlooked. Irresponsible sexual promiscuity is explicitly associated with Rochester's Charles, while, as we shall see, Dryden's depiction necessarily confines its inferences to the subtler ambiguity of word play. Though he receives God's personal blessing in *Absalom and Achitophel*'s final lines, Dryden's 'Idol Monarch' bears more than a passing resemblance to Rochester's 'good and gracious King ... Who never said a foolish thing,/ Nor ever did a wise one'.[4]

The obvious but profound differences between Dryden's and Rochester's verse reflects the poets' differing motivations for writing. Frank Ellis's lively biography of Rochester sums up the relationship between this sneering young aristocrat and the man, now nearing 50, whom King Charles appointed as Poet Laureate in 1668 and historiographer royal in 1670:

> For Rochester, Dryden was a cadet … son of a younger son, ineluctably a commoner. But an educated commoner and deservedly the poet laureate, a *rara avis*, an owl that could sing and worse yet an owl with social ambitions. Dryden had married the daughter of an earl, and taken a mistress from the stage exactly as the king, Charles Sackville, Lord Buckhurst, and John Wilmot, earl of Rochester, had done. For Dryden, Rochester was obviously a dilettante [who] dabbled in verse which circulated in manuscript … but published nothing.[5]

The luxury of publishing nothing was unavailable to John Dryden. He first gained recognition for his plays but his later career as Poet Laureate, in which *Absalom and Achitophel* appeared, closely follows the fortunes of the Stuart monarchy. Dryden's depiction of the dangerous upheavals which marked the period during and after the Popish Plot makes clear his desire for a political stability, founded in kingly authority, which would run for 'mighty years in long succession'. The true brilliance of *Absalom and Achitophel* is the manner in which Dryden reconciles – in terms that would be acceptable to his reading public – this notion of kingly authority with (the common knowledge of) Charles's sexual promiscuity.

Absalom and Achitophel: Allegory and Patronage

The original Biblical story shares with Dryden's narrative the central theme in which Absalom, the son of Israel's King David, is tempted by a manipulative political counsellor (Achitophel) to rebel against royal authority. Both narratives note the popular nature of the uprising as well as King David's sadness at his son's betrayal.

As had been the case since Henry VIII's Reformation, political loyalties in late seventeenth-century England still had strong religious undertones. Both Charles's childless wife, Catherine, and his brother James, Duke of York, openly professed their faith at a time when long-standing prejudices against Catholicism (and fears concerning its reinstatement as the national religion) ran high. In 1678 these fears reached boiling point when a Catholic convert named Titus Oates (whose extremely dubious reputation should have alerted suspicion) offered a sworn testimony confirming the existence of a secret Jesuit plot to assassinate the King.

The aftermath of Oates's fabrications witnessed the execution of numerous innocent men and widespread political turmoil between 1679 and 1681. The Earl of Shaftesbury (represented by Achitophel in the poem) persuaded the King's illegitimate son the Duke of Monmouth (Absalom) to lead a popular campaign for a Protestant royal successor (thus excluding James). The attempt only narrowly failed; Shaftesbury was still being held in the Tower of London on charges of high treason when Dryden's *Absalom and Achitophel* was published. The poetic narrative allegorises authentic historical events up to this moment, foregrounding the rebellious plot against a backdrop of other important figures including King David (Charles II) and Corah (Titus Oates).

Charles II himself may have commissioned this indisputably Royalist poem.[6] What is clear, however, is that Dryden contemplated a literary remit far beyond the royal directive. Alan Roper observes that '*Absalom and Achitophel*, more obviously than most poems, requires an audience to complete its meanings. Absalom does not equal Monmouth, nor Achitophel Shaftesbury, until a reader says so, and saying so enlarges the poem's meanings by an act of interpretation.'[7] Roper's detailed exploration of diverse contemporary interpretations makes apparent that, even for readers who remembered first-hand the political events which inspired it, the poem's use of Biblical allegory is not necessarily straightforward.[8]

For readers now distant from the 'historical' events of the 1680s, Dryden's narrative is read differently again. Dryden's selective inclusion from the Biblical narrative, however, itself makes a point concerning the 'political' nature of allegorical interpretation. Since the Restoration, the use of scriptural allegory had commonly been associated with Puritan literature.* Since the Restoration, Puritans were widely derided as the seditious faction responsible for the Civil War's bloodshed. Here, Dryden contrasts the dark memories of that period's sinful plotting and king-killing with the moderate peace in Israel (England) now enjoyed under 'David' (Charles II):

> The sober part of Israel, free from stain,
> Well knew the value of a peaceful reign;
> And, looking backward with a wise affright,
> Saw seams of wounds, dishonest to the sight:
> In contemplation of whose ugly scars
> They cursed the memory of civil wars.
> The moderate sort of men, thus qualified,
> Inclined the balance to the better side;
> And David's mildness managed it so well,
> The bad found no occasion to rebel.
> But when to sin our biased nature leans,
> The careful Devil is still at hand with means;
> And providently pimps for ill desires:
> The Good Old Cause revived, a plot requires.
> Plots, true or false, are necessary things,
> To raise up commonwealths and ruin kings.[9]

The references to 'civil wars', 'Good Old Cause' and commonwealths are clearly intended to evoke the 'ugly scars' of the English Civil War. In employing a literary device which for so long was associated with its perpetrators, Dryden reclaims sacred history for the Royalist cause.[10] Properly interpreted, the Bible should (in Dryden's argument) uphold the peaceful authority of the rightful king. Elsewhere, the wrongful interpretation of God's word is associated with the dangerous illusory visions of the false prophet Corah (Titus Oates):

---

*   Particularly notable allegorical works after 1660 are *Paradise Lost* (1667) by John Milton (1608–74) and *The Pilgrim's Progress* (1678–84) by John Bunyan (1628–88).

To speak the rest, who better are forgot,
Would tire a well-breathed witness of the Plot.
Yet, Corah, thou shalt from oblivion pass:
Erect thyself, thou monumental brass,
High as the serpent of thy metal made,
While nations stand secure beneath thy shade.
What though his birth were base, yet comets rise
From earthly vapours, ere they shine in skies.
Prodigious actions may as well be done
By weaver's issue, as by prince's son.
This arch-attestor for the public good
By that one deed ennobles all his blood.
Who ever asked the witnesses' high race
Whose oath with martyrdom did Stephen grace? (ll. 630–43)

Dryden's richly allusive verse evokes the sheer volume of false evidence that the 'well-breathed' witness Corah brought to 'the Plot'. His obscure birth (Oates's ancestors engaged in the ribbon-weaving trade) suggests a self-propelled rise to fame ('Erect thyself, thou monumental brass'), further reinforced through Biblical references as in the allusion to the 'serpent of brass' erected by Moses in Numbers 21, and the final rhetorical question concerning Stephen, the first Christian martyr, whose death by stoning was occasioned by the testimony of false witnesses.[11] Dryden's deft coordination of scriptural allusions and contemporary references implicitly strengthens the bonds between royal power and divine authority. Also effective is the linguistic economy of Dryden's double meanings, in lines 633–4, of both 'brass' (as both the metallic substance of the serpent statue, or shamelessness as in 'bold as brass') and 'metal' (or 'mettle', as in the audacious character or spirit displayed by Oates's perjury).

Dryden's imagery conveys the partisan loyalties of the narrative's characters.[12] The poem's 'villains' (involved in the subversive plot) are associated with ugly or deformed corporeal imagery as well as the imagery of food and drink. Achitophel's decaying 'Pigmy Body' (ll. 156–8) and Corah's ugly face (ll. 646–9) are external signs of their corruption; the Jebusites' (or Londoners') former taste for 'Egyptian' (or French, thus Roman Catholic) rituals alludes to the practice of transubstantiation as a means of 'eating' as well as worshipping gods (ll. 118–21).* Ultimately, these images conflate to form David's terrifying vision of cannibalistic destruction which subversive factions bring upon themselves:

> By their own arts, 'tis righteously decreed,
> Those dire artificers of death shall bleed.
> Against themselves their witnesses will swear,
> Till viper-like their mother Plot they tear:
> And suck for nutriment that bloody gore,
> Which was their principle of life before. (ll. 1010–15)

Spoken near the poem's end by the 'godlike king' himself, these lines even find approval from God who 'nodding, gave consent' to the speech with 'peals of thunder'. Corporeal imagery associated with the seditious contrasts with the depiction of kingly and divine qualities in both David and his faithful supporters. Kingly qualities are also associated with the verbal authority of poetry itself. This is evident in the commemorative 'roll of honour' where Dryden lists the names and glories of those loyal to David, and the self-conscious way in which this list is presented: 'Some let me name, and naming is to praise./ In this short file Barzillai first appears' (ll. 816–17).

The 'naming and praising' of Barzillai (representing James Butler, Duke of Ormond, a staunch Stuart supporter) is quickly followed with a eulogy for his eldest son (the Earl of Ossory, who died, aged 46, the year before the poem was published). 'As opposed to the striking corporeality of the rebels,' Maresca observes:

> Dryden employs no physical description whatever in his
> catalogue of the royalists, and his opening encomium of

---

* Transubstantiation refers to the Roman Catholic Communion ritual in which it is believed that the Communion wafer and wine are transformed into the body and blood of Christ through their consumption.

Barzillai's sainted and angelic son casts a protective cloak of spirituality and immateriality over all the members of the group. Indeed, Dryden does not even have the royalists do very much; in contrast to the rebels who slide, rush, ebb, flow, etc., the royalists merely stand and speak – thereby making a minor but effective imagistic point about stability and motion that David will capitalize upon in the very final lines of his speech.[13]

Dryden thus aligns poetic speech, and rightful Scriptural interpretation, with a royalist manifestation of the political ideal of peaceful stability. The timely observance that 'never rebel was to arts a friend' also serves to remind readers that this poem itself is the product of royal patronage.

The obligations of patronage, royal or otherwise, complicate any poet's task. This is apparent in the fact that Absalom represents the (rebellious and misguided, but) still much-loved illegitimate son of his royal patron. Dryden's laureateship, however, did not exempt him from the obligation of seeking approbation from the wider reading public (many of whom would have sympathised with Shaftesbury's politics). His depictions of Absalom and Achitophel are therefore *necessarily* more nuanced than the poem's minor characters.

Michael Seidel has noted how Dryden 'pauses in his satirical attack and praises Shaftesbury for his role years before as a judge in Israel's (read England's) courts'; that Achitophel is 'sagacious, bold and turbulent of wit' makes him even more dangerous when his ambitions drive him to plot against the King.[14] In praising the narrative's villain, Dryden further strengthens the plausibility of his discourse.

Absalom is depicted as a tragic hero ('Tis juster to lament him than accuse') or a victim of destiny and mortal ambition (for Absalom's depiction, see ll. 305–12, 477–86). His character exemplifies Dryden's ambiguous treatment of the related themes of nature and paternity/ conception. Absalom is presented early on as the most beautiful and brave of the King's 'numerous progeny' whose paternal resemblance is discerned with 'secret joy' by his 'indulgent' father (see, in particular, ll. 17–34). The lustful pleasure implicated in the case of Absalom's conception ('his father got him with a greater gust'), and his correspondent beauty and strength, contrast with the 'unnatural' deformities and miscarriages that characterise the progeny of David's enemies.[15] 'Nature' too, however, is at the root of Absalom's betrayal of his father since Achitophel persuades him that, if he does nothing, 'the next heir' (his uncle) will be driven to kill him through jealousy – as Absalom is the people's favourite – unless 'nature's eldest law' (self-defence) asserts itself first (ll. 441–58). Nature, therefore, is a force for both good and evil as manifest in the King's 'natural' son.

It is not an overstatement to observe that royal paternity lies at the very heart of the English political crisis.[16] Howard Weinbrot's examination of the poem's many paternal relationships discovers, for example, implicit criticism in the praise for Barzillai's eight legitimate sons (which offers 'a silent rebuke to Charles's eight illegitimate sons').[17] Dryden garners all of his poetic brilliance to surmount the moral and political dilemma begotten by the 'vigorous warmth' of Charles's promiscuity; his use of Biblical allegory repositions kingly sexual conduct into a distant and indeterminate – but still sacred – historical moment in which the authority of God, and godlike kings, are more closely aligned.

The moral complexity of the poem's two eponymous characters reflects Dryden's prefatory observation that 'the true end of Satyr is the amendment of Vices by correction'.[18] Discerning vice in the King's conduct is necessarily problematic, but Dryden's portrait of Israel's Jews (the English) as a 'headstrong, moody, murmuring race' is more straightforward. The general populace is easily swayed by political rhetoric, specious factions and the handsome face of a new 'young Messiah':

> Youth, beauty, graceful action seldom fail;
> But common interest always will prevail;
> And pity never ceases to be shown
> To him that makes the people's wrongs his own. (ll. 723–6)

Dryden's image of the 'admiring crowd' harks back to Juvenal's Satire X in which the fickle mob 'follows Fortuna and cares for nothing but bread and circuses'.[19] The timeless universality of this image tacitly implies that history provides valuable lessons for future generations; here, it reinforces Dryden's underlying message that the peaceful stability of kingly authority is preferable to the political turbulence of popular rule (or democracy). History, Dryden argues, demonstrates that the general populace are poor judges of leadership; this is evident in the Biblical example of Absalom and Achitophel and in the cycles of rebellion that moved the 'giddy Jews' to 'change their lord' every twenty years – echoed also in the twenty-year cycles of civil unrest in England between 1640 and 1680 (ll. 216–19).

The Mob in English Politics: Dryden to Johnson

Thirteen years after *Absalom and Achitophel*, Dryden produced his own translations of Juvenal. His reworking of Satire X closely echoes the cynicism which shaped Juvenal's original work but also articulates, in the image of 'the Mob', the profound sea-change in English politics after the Glorious Revolution:

> How goes the Mob? (for that's a Mighty thing.)
> When the King's Trump, the Mob are for the King:
> They follow Fortune, and the Common Cry
> Is still against the Rogue Condemn'd to Dye …
> But long, long since, the Times have chang'd their Face,
> The People grown Degenerate and base;
> Not suffer'd now the Freedom of their Choice,
> To make their Magistrats, and sell their Voice.
> Our Wise Fore-Fathers, Great by Sea and Land,
> Had once the Pow'r and absolute Command;
> All Offices of Trust, themselves dispos'd;
> Rais'd whom they pleas'd, and whom they pleas'd, Depos'd.
> But we, who give our Native Rights away,
> And our inslav'd Posterity betray,

Are now reduc'd to beg an Alms, and go
On Holidays to see a Puppet show.[20]

The bitter nostalgia of these lines powerfully reflects the Jacobite sympathies of its author. (See Part Two: 'A Cultural Overview' for an overview of terms such as 'Glorious Revolution', 'Jacobite', 'Whig' and 'Tory'.) Under the guise of translation, Dryden could afford to express such sentiments. Steven Zwicker has observed:

> Profound structural changes in English politics were underway: a European war would determine the course of its politics, economy, and foreign policy for the next century and more. The 1690s proved to be years not so much for literary invention as for fabling, paraphrase, and translation ... Whether you are intent on hiding dangerous opinions or simply uncertain of what to say, fable and translation offer shelter, a space in which to negotiate a voice.[21]

On a wider cultural scale, Dryden's translations also reflect the increasing aptness of the Roman model to depict the English political climate after 1688.[22] The Biblical model of *Absalom and Achitophel*, uniting the spheres of divine and kingly authority, comprehensively gave way to visions of the Roman 'Mob'.

Although Johnson's *Vanity of Human Wishes* shares with Dryden's version of Juvenal its deeply cynical depiction of 'the Mob' within contemporary English culture, this poem is written nearly seventy years later, from within a very different political context. Johnson's poem takes its inspiration, in virtually equal measures, from its Classical source (it is not a direct translation of Juvenal) and its author's cynical but largely detached views on contemporary British politics. Here, the British populace are no longer moved by zeal for democratic rights or liberty, but by the bribes of an election campaign:

> But will not Britain hear the last appeal,
> Sign her foes' doom, or guard her favorites' zeal?

41

Through Freedom's sons no more remonstrance rings,
Degrading nobles and controlling kings;
Our supple tribes repress their patriot throats,
And ask no questions but the price of votes;
With weekly libels and septennial ale,
Their wish is full to riot and to rail.* 23

Bread and circuses have now been replaced by beer and slander in the political machinations of George II's England. The earliest lines of Johnson's poem are overwhelmingly cynical in nature and present a political landscape completely devoid of either integrity or even the dignity of statesmanship. In *Absalom and Achitophel* humanity's ambition for fame is portrayed as sinful only when it impinges on royal authority, for example when Achitophel 'disdained the golden fruit [of 'lawful fame'] to gather free,/ And lent the crowd his arm to shake the tree' (ll. 201–3). Yet 'fame deserved, no enemy can grudge' and is the rightful portion of virtuous nobility. In Johnson's poem, *all* ambition is ultimately pointless as fame 'on every stage' (noble, deserved or otherwise), dissipates into thin air:

Unnumbered suppliants crowd Preferment's gate,
Athirst for wealth, and burning to be great;
Delusive Fortune hears the incessant call,
They mount, they shine, evaporate, and fall.
On every stage the foes of peace attend,
Hate dogs their flight, and Insult mocks their end. (ll. 73–8)

Johnson's general survey of mankind's folly is non-partisan and apolitical.24 This is demonstrated by his provision of a diverse catalogue of ambitious men who suffer a similar fate, from ancient history (such as Xerxes) and from the not-so-distant past (such as Cardinal Wolsey), right through to the recent past of living memory (such as Robert

* 'Weekly libel' refers to the political slander of opposition parties and 'septennial ale' to the free beer given away by parliamentary candidates (from the time of William III, parliamentary elections were held every seven years).

Harley, Earl of Oxford).* Comprising approximately two-thirds of the poem, Johnson's catalogue poetically reduces the once-glorious legacy of famous men to little more than cameo roles in the great sweep of history.

Even more relevant in this respect is the extended portrait of Charles XII of Sweden, replacing Hannibal in Juvenal's original (Johnson, *Vanity*, ll. 199–222).† This selection reflects both the high level of popular interest in this dramatic figure from contemporary European history and the influential 1732 English translation of Voltaire's popular biography which (Weinbrot observes) Johnson's poem partially 'epitomizes'.[25] Weinbrot goes on to assert that, significantly, the sympathetic elements of Johnson's portrait of the defeated Charles (as a 'vanquished hero' and a 'needy supplicant') demonstrate a clear difference in authorial intention between Juvenal and Johnson:

> Juvenal chose Hannibal for obvious patriotic reasons: he was the alien general from an alien continent who invaded the mother country. Roman virtue and arms finally drove the madman … into suicide, and into perpetually punitive declamations by Roman schoolboys. Imitators are free to vary their adaptations, as Johnson does in the *Vanity* – but not with Charles XII as an analogue to Hannibal the foreign invader deservedly defeated, killed and mocked.[26]

The depiction of Charles's death by a 'dubious hand' (possibly one of his own subordinates) invites the reader to contemplate the true meaning of military heroism, as does the reduction of his final legacy to

---

* King Xerxes of Persia (modern-day Iran) led an unsuccessful invasion against Greece in 480 BC. Thomas Cardinal Wolsey (*c.* 1470/1–1530) was the favourite statesman of Henry VIII until his fall from grace in 1527. Robert Harley, Earl of Oxford (1661–1724) was an eminent Tory statesman under Queen Anne who was later impeached and imprisoned by the Whig government in 1715.

† Charles XII of Sweden (1682–1718) led a series of resounding military successes in northern Europe, conquering Poland and Russia by 1700, before his decisive defeat in 1709. He died in mysterious circumstances during a later campaign in Norway.

a concluding couplet: 'He left a name at which the world grows pale,/ To point a moral, or adorn a tale.' With this, the reader is returned to the poem's longer historical perspective. Military victory is glorious only in partisan versions of history. 'Reason' recognises it as always expensive and wasteful, and all of history's examples express the universal folly of war:

> The festal blazes, the triumphal show,
> The ravished standard, and the captive foe,
> The senate's thanks, the gazette's pompous tale,
> With force resistless o'er the brave prevail.
> Such bribes the rapid Greek o'er Asia whirled,
> For such the steady Romans shook the world;
> For such in distant lands the Britons shine,
> And stain with blood the Danube or the Rhine;
> This power has praise that virtue scarce can warm,
> Till fame supplies the universal charm.
> Yet Reason frowns on War's unequal game,
> Where wasted nations raise a single name,
> And mortgaged states their grandsires' wreaths regret
> From age to age in everlasting debt;
> Wreaths which at last the dear-bought right convey
> To rust on medals, or on stones decay. (ll. 175–90)*

Once again spanning history from the 'rapid Greek' (Alexander the Great) to contemporary British campaigns in Europe, these examples directly precede the portrait of Charles XII and invite readers to reconsider his – and all other – martial careers in this light. Johnson's *Vanity* therefore rejects the concept of martial glory, although there is more to be said concerning Weinbrot's observation that Johnson

---

* Johnson's references to the financial costs of war would have resonated strongly with his early readers: by 1749 England had been continually engaged in war for most of a century.

similarly reduces the heroic Duke of Marlborough* as it 'only shows him in his dotage, and forces him to share a couplet with his tormentor Swift (ll. 317–18)'.[27] The same couplet also reduces Swift to *his* dotage; the lesson of history provides the same salutary warning for poets and scholars, also:

> Yet hope not life from grief or danger free,
> Nor think the doom of man reversed for thee:
> Deign on the passing world to turn thine eyes,
> And pause a while from letters, to be wise;
> There mark what ills the scholar's life assail,
> Toil, envy, want, the patron, and the jail. (ll. 155–60)

Johnson's *Vanity* expresses the very personal concerns of an author who knew first-hand the 'ills' of a scholar's life.† [28] In asserting the need to 'pause a while from letters, to be wise', Johnson expresses the point at which his own belief in the relative power and virtues of rational thought and scholarly knowledge must give way to greater – Christian – hope and understanding. God alone can resolve the endless problems and vanities of human existence:

> Inquirer, cease; petitions yet remain,
> Which Heaven may hear, nor deem religion vain.
> Still raise for good the supplicating voice,
> But leave to Heaven the measure and the choice.
> Safe in his power, whose eyes discern afar
> The secret ambush of a specious prayer.

---

* John Churchill, first Duke of Marlborough (1650–1722) led a decisive military victory at the Battle of Blenheim in 1704 and was widely regarded as an English military hero. He was viciously lampooned by Jonathan Swift (1667–1745), writer and Dean of Dublin's St Patrick's Cathedral.

† Johnson's compendious *Dictionary* (1755) was being compiled when *Vanity* – the first work Johnson published under his own name – appeared; the *Dictionary* took nine years to complete (he had anticipated three). The first edition of *Vanity* had 'garret' in place of 'patron' in line 160, reflecting the famous dispute between Johnson and the *Dictionary*'s *Preface*'s patron, the fourth Earl of Chesterfield (1694–1773).

Implore his aid, in his decisions rest,
Secure, whate'er he gives, he gives the best. (ll. 349–56)

Ultimately, the poem advises Christian resignation to God's greater will combined with the powers of sincere prayer. Johnson's Christian Stoicism endorses the united powers of human reason with Christian faith and prayer as the only true means of attaining happiness.* The concept of 'celestial Wisdom', presented in Johnson's concluding couplet, seems to imply that Christian faith *united* with reason presented no inherent conflict for the author. In reality, profound cultural changes wrought by the intellectual advances of the European Enlightenment and the seventeenth century presented many challenges to deeply rational minds like Johnson's. John Wain argues:

> Johnson clung to reason as to a handrail in an unlighted passage. But to safeguard his religious faith it was necessary for him, now and then, to let go of this handrail of reason. The effort this cost, the agony it caused, are there in the records of his life ... Samuel Johnson's own difficult equilibrium, achieved at huge psychic expense, could not last. With one powerful hand he reached back to the Ages of Faith. With the other, he grasped the empirical spirit of the nineteenth-century sciences.[29]

The vast spectrum of time and space encompassed by the poem's perspective, as well as its characteristically declamatory tone, tacitly implies that faith provides the *only* means by which mankind might gain true solace. This is either the poem's greatest strength or greatest weakness. Its language lapses – inevitably – into abstraction and

---

* Stoicism is a profoundly influential system of thought 'which originated in Athens in the 3rd century BC, flourished in Rome, c.100 BC–c. AD 200 ... and enjoyed a vigorous revival at the time of the Renaissance': see Margaret Drabble (ed.), *The Oxford Companion to English Literature* (Oxford: Oxford University Press, 1985), p. 939. Stoicism, broadly, recognises the fundamentally material reality of experience along with the need for humans to exercise their capacity for rational thought (reason) over the concerns or desires of the physical body.

imprecision precisely when it tries to explain the accommodation of faith with reason:

> Yet when the sense of sacred presence fires,
> And strong devotion to the skies aspires,
> Pour forth thy fervors for a healthful mind,
> Obedient passions, and a will resigned ... (ll. 357–60)

The circular logic of these lines suggests that faith, or 'the sense of sacred presence', inspires prayer (yet surely prayer is unnecessary for those without faith). Moreover, such prayer seeks paradoxical forms of behaviour in which desires become self-regulating ('obedient' and 'resigned').

Johnson's version of reason appears to *control* desire. If so, it is precisely the kind of reason that, in his *Satire Against Reason and Mankind* (1679), Rochester 'despises':[30]

> Our sphere of action is life's happiness,
> And he who thinks beyond, thinks like an ass.
> Thus, whilst against false reasoning I inveigh,
> I own right reason, which I would obey:
> That reason which distinguishes by sense,
> And gives us rules of good and ill from thence;
> That bounds desires with a reforming will,
> To keep them more in vigor, not to kill.
> Your reason hinders, mine helps to enjoy,
> Renewing appetites yours would destroy.
> My reason is a friend, yours is a cheat,
> Hunger calls out, my reason bids me eat ... (ll. 96–107)

It is important to note that Rochester wrote these lines nearly a century before Johnson's poem was published. What makes them relevant here is that Rochester's perception of 'right reason' – which helps rather than hinders enjoyment, and renews 'appetites' – contrasts with Johnson's notion of a (Christian) reason which makes appetite seek to curb its own desires. It might be argued that Dryden too, like his contemporary Rochester, sees no conflict between the energies of sexual desire and Christian faith since his poem depicts a sexually libidinous King David who exercises rational control over his subjects.

Rochester's 'right reason' is aligned with sensory experience; its reforming powers curb desire only to make experience *more* pleasurable (in the sense that there is greater pleasure in eating a single slice than in eating an entire chocolate cake). Rochester and Johnson both derive valuable inspiration from their Classical predecessors, but their writing evinces profoundly different views on how humanity's capacity for rational thought impinges upon the realm of sensory experience and faith.

Extended Commentary: Rochester, *The Imperfect Enjoyment* (1680)

Rochester's popular image as a swaggering, obscene and sometimes violent Court Wit is probably not inaccurate but it is, however, incomplete if it neglects the intellectual context of his writing. His vigorous rhetoric echoes the Roman Stoicism of Seneca while his focus on sensory experience as the source of all knowledge aligns him with seventeenth-century models of Epicurean philosophy as well as his contemporary Thomas Hobbes.* Rochester's fragmentary translation from Seneca's *Troades* asserts what he shared with all of these thinkers concerning the utter impossibility of mankind truly understanding divine power; as such, understanding any form of existence beyond mortal life – death – is also 'unknowable':

---

* Roman Stoic poet and dramatist Seneca (*c.* 4 BC–AD 65) profoundly influenced seventeenth- and eighteenth-century literature; the original concepts of Epicurus (341–270 BC) concerning free will and the ethical importance of peace of mind were modified by seventeenth-century Epicureans to reflect the utmost importance of physical pleasure and sensory experience. Thomas Hobbes (1588–1679) was mathematics tutor to the young Charles II while in exile (prior to 1660); his writings heavily influenced those of Rochester and the Court Wits.

Dead we become the lumber of the world,
And to that mass of matter shall be swept
Where things destroyed with things unborn are kept.
Devouring time swallows us whole;
Impartial death confounds body and soul.[31]

These lines do not assert that 'the soul' (or God) do not exist, only that the end of life 'confounds' every conceivable concept of existence.[*] [32] His views lead logically to a conscious rejection of Christian mythology (as 'senseless stories, idle tales') and (Christian) systems of morality which place reason in conflict with the senses.[33]

The beginning of *The Imperfect Enjoyment* celebrates, in erotic terms, the notion of 'right reason' that Rochester espouses in *A Satire Against Reason and Mankind*. It also reflects the contemporary vogue for poems on the theme of male impotence (also exemplified by Aphra Behn's contemporary poem *The Disappointment*, published in 1680), a genre whose Classical origins derive from the works of Ovid and Petronius.[†] [34] The reader is immediately faced with the sensory pleasure of the present moment in which the speaker and his beloved Corinna engage in a mutually passionate embrace: 'Naked she lay, clasped in my longing arms … Both equally inspired, with eager fire'.[35] That the speaker's reason is working in tandem with his senses is suggested by the formal, courtly language:

Her nimble tongue, Love's lesser lightning, played
Within my mouth, and to my thoughts conveyed
Swift orders that I should prepare to throw
The all-dissolving thunderbolt below.
My fluttering soul, sprung with the pointed kiss,
Hangs hovering o'er her balmy brinks of bliss. (ll. 7–12)

---

[*]   Rochester – and Hobbes – were frequently accused of atheism both during and after their lifetime though no real evidence exists for these claims. Both, more accurately, were probably anti-Trinitarians (denying the divinity of Jesus Christ, but not God).

[†]   *Amores*, the love elegies of Ovid (43 BC–AD 18), heavily influenced Renaissance courtly love poetry; Petronius is best known for his Latin prose work, *Satyricon*, which gives a frank portrait of sex and scandal in the Roman Republic.

With coy humour, Rochester's language combines the conscious evocation of the courtly tradition of heroic poetry with explicitly sexual imagery. The 'all-dissolving thunderbolt below' and 'balmy brinks of bliss' may *equally* connote the heroic realm of gods in a Golden Age or the erotic zones of lovers' bodies. Captured within these lines' idealised present moment of erotic arousal, the reference to the speaker's 'fluttering soul' suggests a wholly united mental, physical and emotional state.

Soon after, however, the poem's pace and language change. The amorous fluidity of the previous lines, conveyed as much through sound as imagery (consider the rhymes of arms/charms, fire/desire, kiss/bliss), shifts to reflect first the dissolving 'liquid raptures' of ejaculation, and then a second abrupt linguistic shift:

> In liquid raptures I dissolve all o'er,
> Melt into sperm, and spend at every pore.
> A touch from any part of her had done 't:
> Her hand, her foot, her very look's a cunt. (ll. 15–18)

The first eighteen lines of this poem, through linguistic shifts and the correspondent depiction of bodily imagery, convey a realm uniting physical sensation (sexual desire, for example) and reason (as expressed through language, and the specific choice of words to convey images). Represented in the poem as male sexual arousal approaching orgasm, and poetically confined to an idealised present moment in which neither the past nor future interfere, such a union *is* possible, although it cannot last long.

Beyond its preliminary, erotic, celebration of 'right reason', the poem progresses to question the relationship between reason and sensory experience. It does so by restoring to the perception of the speaker the inescapable memory of the past (history) and anticipation of the future. The remainder of the poem articulates the speaker's frustration at his inability to perform for a second time:

Eager desires confound my first intent,
Succeeding shame does more success prevent,
And Rage at last confirms me impotent. (ll. 28–30)

It is precisely the speaker's memory of past shame that prevents his
future success. Ironically, his sexual impotence represents a kind of
linguistic triumph. Jonathan Brody Kramnick notes how 'Rochester
describes the moment of spectacular failure, strangely, as a victory of the
emotions ... The triplet makes impotence of philosophical interest by
showing how it troubles our expected sense of causation.' This moment
subverts the usual Hobbesian order (uniting the senses with reason)
since 'it would be logically impossible for desire to confound "intent"
because the two are the same thing'.[36] The poem's paradox is that it is
precisely the speaker's mental and emotional commitment to Corinna
which prevents him from fulfilling his erotic desires.

The moment of orgasm (depicted in ll. 15–16) reintroduces the
speaker's perception of past experience (history) and also dramatically
shifts the linguistic register of the poem. Reba Wilcoxon contrasts the
emotional involvement and passion of the speaker's language towards
Corinna (whether formal and courtly or, in ll. 17–18, erotic in nature)
with the explicit and brutal language associated with his sexual past:

> The narrator conveys affection and tenderness toward the
> disappointed mistress ... she has a fair hand, she is his 'great
> Love,' and she is the 'wronged Corinna'. That he wishes to show
> his 'wished obedience' implies a concern beyond the satisfaction
> of his lust.

> In the account of past triumphs, debased sexual objects are
> dominant ... [a]nd the insufficiency of sexual power alone is
> poetically reinforced by the insistence on unrefined language of
> sex-tingling cunt, oyster-cinder-beggar-common whore, fucking
> post ... and the like. By contrast, when the fair mistress is present,
> the language of sex, though ... unrefined ... is not conjoined with
> images that debase her.[37]

Wilcoxon's linguistic analysis addresses the charges of pornography and obscenity to which Rochester's writings have been subject for many centuries.[38] She distinguishes between the lustful (but not degrading) description of Corinna in line 18 and the far more brutal linguistic constructions of the poem's later stages when the speaker expresses his disgust in not achieving with Corinna what he has many times managed with an 'oyster-cinder-beggar-common whore'. All of the speaker's anger is directed to his *past* experiences or projected forward into curses on the *future* experiences of his phallus:

> Thou treacherous, base deserter of my flame,
> False to my passion, fatal to my fame, …
> May'st thou to ravenous chancres be a prey,
> Or in consuming weepings waste away;
> May strangury and stone thy days attend;
> May'st thou ne'er piss, who didst refuse to spend
> When all my joys did on false thee depend. (ll. 46–7, 66–70)*

Rebuke of the phallus is not unique to Rochester's contribution to the 'imperfect enjoyment' genre.[39] More unusual, however, is the extended use of metaphor by which the sexual history of his phallus is reconfigured to the acts of a roaring bully or a soldier who betrays his country:

> Like a rude, roaring hector in the streets
> Who scuffles, cuffs, and justles all he meets,
> But if his King or country claim his aid,
> The rakehell villain shrinks and hides his head …
> Base recreant to thy prince, thou dar'st not stand.
> Worst part of me, and henceforth hated most,
> Through all the town a common fucking post. (ll. 54–7, 61–4)

The originally playful tone of this extended metaphor progressively gives way to a form of self-centred loathing which extends far beyond

---

* *The Norton Anthology* notes that 'strangury' and 'stone' caused painful urination while 'chancres' and 'weepings' are symptoms of venereal disease.

the speaker's immediate sexual failure. The image of the phallus as a 'rakehell villain' who abandons King and country presents a disturbingly 'genital-centred' social order in which sexual promiscuity reigns (following the monarch's own example) such that the phallus must 'stand up' for his King. In this reading, the 'great Love' of public or civic duty is debased into the form of nationalism, cited earlier in this chapter, in which the 'Isle of Britain' might take pride in breeding 'the best cunts in all Christendom'. It is, arguably, only under the cultural conditions in which a king openly engages in sexual promiscuity that such a metaphor of nationalism could resonate so powerfully. Under such conditions, his angry rebuke of his '[w]orst part ... henceforth hated most', moving towards the wish for self-castration expressed in line 66 onwards, articulates the speaker's profoundly divided loyalties towards his/his phallus's King and country.

Failed performance (in both sexual and military terms) and civic disorder are key themes in both *The Imperfect Enjoyment* and *The Disabled Debauchee*. In the latter, the speaker comforts himself against his fast-approaching 'days of impotence' by comparing his past with that of a battle-scarred retired admiral. In both poems, the speakers' past actions ('whores attacked ... Windows demolished') comprise a combined history of military 'glory' and violent civil disorder.[40] In both poems, also, the speakers' present experience ('safe from action' and 'sheltered in impotence') is centred in linguistic acts which incite future disorder (or future sexual promiscuity, in Corinna's case) by 'firing the blood' of the next generation:

> With tales like these I will such thoughts inspire
> As to important mischief shall incline:
> I'll make him long some ancient church to fire,
> And fear no lewdness he's called to by wine. (*The Disabled Debauchee*, ll. 41–4)

An ancient and revered institution, such as a church or even the monarchy itself, can come under attack in the general riot of libidinous energy inspired by the disabled debauchee's tales of the past.

Johnson's *Vanity* suggests that history can provide morally valuable lessons to future generations; here, Rochester implies that a certain kind of history can inspire 'important mischief' – and widespread civic disorder – as well. It would take no great imaginative leap, for either contemporary or later readers, to associate these combined images of past military glory, civil disorder and sexual licence with Restoration courtiers such as Rochester himself.* This observation is *not* intended to suggest that Rochester's verse is autobiographical *per se*. More accurately, poems such as *The Imperfect Enjoyment* and *The Disabled Debauchee* demonstrate profound awareness of the negative future implications of such conduct as practised by the King and his inner circle of noble 'Court Wits':† 41

> [T]he court of Charles II made a farce of the chivalric and classical icons of aristocratic and regal identity … [and] seemed to betoken a crisis of nobility after the civil wars despite the control and political influence which it had maintained.

> … The Restoration Court projected a collective image of living in ironic and even defiant incompatibility with its inherited forms of public representation. It was carelessly demonic, nonchalantly outrageous, cynical in the way that only a class which despises its compromises can be cynical.42

As articulated from within that Court, Rochester's has emerged as one of the most memorable voices to represent the aristocratic nonchalance – as well as the political crisis – to emerge from the English Restoration. Even more compelling is the manner in which Rochester's poetry breathes new life and urgency into the Restoration

---

* Rochester had followed his father's example of extreme loyalty to the Stuart cause in valorous military exploits during the Second Anglo-Dutch War (1665–6); back at Court, heroic military valour was largely replaced by sexual adventures, violence and riotous behaviour in which the King also engaged.

† Notable Restoration Court Wits include the fifth and sixth Earls of Dorset, Richard (Lord Buckhurst) and Charles Sackville; Sir Charles Sedley (1639–1701); and Alexander Radcliffe (*c.* 1653–*c.* 1696).

concept of the body politic. The next chapter argues that the Restoration's cultural impact on the English stage extended further still, for more than a century beyond the reign of Charles II, to address fundamental questions about the nature of dramatic representation itself.

Notes

1   This complex political notion has a long history. See, for example, P. Archambault, 'The Analogy of the "Body" in Renaissance Political Literature', *Bibliotèque d'humanisme et renaissance*, 29 (1967), pp. 21–53; and Norman O. Brown, *Love's Body* (New York: Random House, 1966). See also Part Four: 'Man, Nature and Liberty' in this volume.

2   Jonathan Brody Kramnick, 'Rochester and the History of Sexuality', *English Literary History*, 69:2 (Summer 2002), pp. 277–301.

3   John Wilmot, *Verses for Which He Was Banished*, ll. 1–4, 8–11, in Paddy Lyons (ed.), *Lord Rochester* (London: J. M. Dent, 1996), pp. 88–9. See Kramnick, 'Rochester and the History of Sexuality', pp. 278–9.

4   John Wilmot, *On the King*, in Lyons, *Lord Rochester*, p. 96.

5   Frank H. Ellis, 'Wilmot, John, Second Earl of Rochester (1647–1680)', *Oxford Dictionary of National Biography* (Oxford: Oxford University Press, 2004–9). See also the *ODNB* entries for Charles Sackville, sixth Earl of Dorset (1643–1706), and his father, Richard Sackville, Lord Buckhurst, fifth Earl of Dorset (1622–77).

6   See Steven Zwicker, 'John Dryden', in Steven N. Zwicker (ed.), *The Cambridge Companion to English Literature 1650–1740* (Cambridge: Cambridge University Press, 1998), p. 192.

7   Alan Roper, 'Who's Who in *Absalom and Achitophel*?', *Huntington Library Quarterly*, 63:1/2 (2000), p. 101.

8   Ibid., pp. 99–138. Roper's findings are based on a detailed examination of 149 versions of the poem from the 1680 and 1681 editions, including marginalia from annotated copies plus manuscript 'keys'.

9   John Dryden, *Absalom and Achitophel*, in Lawrence Lipking and James Noggle (eds), *The Norton Anthology of English Literature*, Volume C: *The Restoration and the Eighteenth Century* (New York and London: W. W. Norton, 2006), pp. 2089–111, ll. 69–84.

10   Zwicker, 'John Dryden', pp. 192–3.

11   Stephen's martyrdom is depicted in Acts 6–7.

12   See Thomas A. Maresca, 'The Context of Dryden's *Absalom and Achitophel*', *English Literary History*, 41:3 (Autumn 1974), pp. 340–58.

13   Ibid., p. 352.

14   Michael Seidel, 'Satire, Lampoon, Libel, Slander', in Zwicker (ed.), *Cambridge Companion to English Literature*, p. 34.

15   Howard D. Weinbrot, '"Nature's Holy Bands" in *Absalom and Achitophel*: Fathers and Sons, Satire and Change', *Modern Philology*, 85:4 (May 1988), pp. 373–92.

16   In addition to Weinbrot, see also Larry Carver, '*Absalom and Achitophel* and the Father Hero', in Robert Folkenflik (ed.), *The Father Hero, 1660–1800* (Newark: University of Delaware Press, 1982), pp. 35–45; and Gayle Edward Wilson, '"Weavers Issue", "Princes Son", "Godheads Images": Dryden and the Topos of Descent in *Absalom and Achitophel*', *Papers on Language and Literature*, 28 (1992), pp. 267–82.

17   Weinbrot, '"Nature's Holy Bands" in *Absalom and Achitophel*', p. 386.

18   From Dryden's address 'To the Reader', in *The Works of John Dryden* (Ware: Wordsworth Editions, 1995), p. 49.

19   Juvenal, *Satires*, IV.10.56–89.

20   John Dryden, *Translation of Juvenal's Tenth Satire* (1693), in *Works of John Dryden*, p. 564, ll. 112–31.

21   Zwicker, 'John Dryden', p. 197.

22   Zwicker makes a similar point in relation to Dryden and the poetry of Virgil: ibid., pp. 199 ff.

23   Samuel Johnson, *The Vanity of Human Wishes*, in Lipking and Noggle (eds), *Norton Anthology of English Literature*, Volume C, pp. 2666–74, ll. 91–8.

24   Johnson's use of metaphor further extends the broad rhetorical survey he conducts in this poem. See Paul D. McGlynn, 'Rhetoric as Metaphor in *The Vanity of Human Wishes*', *Studies in English Literature, 1500–1900*, 15:3 (Summer 1975), pp. 473–82.

25   Howard D. Weinbrot, 'Johnson, Jacobitism, and Swedish Charles: *The Vanity of Human Wishes* and Scholarly Method', *English Literary History*, 64:4 (Winter 1997), pp. 945–81, at p. 960.

26   Ibid., p. 963.

27   Ibid., p. 960.

28   On Johnson's life during and after the compilation of the *Dictionary*, see Margaret Lane, *Samuel Johnson and His World* (New York: Harper & Row, 1975); and Robert Demaria, Jr, *The Life of Samuel Johnson* (Oxford: Blackwell, 1993).

29   John Wain, 'Reason, Bias and Faith in the Mind of Johnson', *Samuel Johnson 1709–84: A Bicentenary Exhibition* (London: The Arts Council of Great Britain, 1984), p. 23.

30   John Wilmot, *A Satire Against Reason and Mankind*, in Lipking and Noggle (eds), *Norton Anthology of English Literature*, Volume C, pp. 2173–7, l. 75.

31   John Wilmot, *Translation: From Seneca's 'Troades'*, in Lyons (ed.) *Lord Rochester*, pp. 33–4, ll. 8–12.

32   See Benjamin Miller, 'Hobbes: On Religion', *Political Theory*, 16:3 (August 1988), pp. 400–25; and Sarah Ettenzweig, 'The Faith of Unbelief: Rochester's *Satyre*, Deism, and Religious Freethinking in Seventeenth-century England', *Journal of British Studies*, 44:1 (January 2005), pp. 27–45.

33   See Edward Burns (ed.), *Reading Rochester* (Liverpool: Liverpool University Press, 1995); and David M. Vieth and Dustin Griffin, *Rochester and Court Poetry: Papers Presented at a Clark Library Seminar* (Los Angeles: Williams Andrews Clark Memorial Library, University of California, 1988).

34   Aphra Behn's *The Disappointment* was first published anonymously in 1680 in a collection of Rochester's verse; it is a translation (and significantly altered version) of a contemporary French poem on the same subject; it appears in Lipking and Noggle (eds), *Norton Anthology of English Literature*, Volume C, along with Rochester's *Imperfect Enjoyment*, pp. 2180–1. See Reba Wilcoxon, 'Pornography, Obscenity, and Rochester's *The Imperfect Enjoyment*', *Studies in English Literature, 1500–1900*, 15:3 (Summer 1975), pp. 375–90; and Ian Donaldson, 'The Argument of *The Disabled Debauchee*', *Modern Language Review*, 82 (1987), pp. 30–4.

35   John Wilmot, *An Imperfect Enjoyment*, in Lipking and Noggle (eds), *Norton Anthology of English Literature*, Volume C, p. 2169, ll. 1–4.

36   Kramnick observes that, here, Rochester departs from his (traditional) concurrence with Hobbes's views. See Kramnick, 'Rochester and the History of Sexuality', p. 288.

37   Wilcoxon, 'Pornography, Obscenity, and Rochester's *The Imperfect Enjoyment*', p. 389.

38   *An Imperfect Enjoyment* was excluded from collected editions of Rochester's verse in Great Britain as late as 1961. See Wilcoxon, 'Pornography, Obscenity, and Rochester's *The Imperfect Enjoyment*', pp. 375–6.

39   This is also a feature of the work of Ovid and Petronius. See Wilcoxon, 'Pornography, Obscenity, and Rochester's *The Imperfect Enjoyment*', pp. 382–3.

40   John Wilmot, *The Disabled Debauchee*, in Lipking and Noggle (eds), *Norton Anthology of English Literature*, Volume C, pp. 2168–9, ll. 33–6.

41 See the first section of Harold D. Love (ed.), *The Penguin Book of Restoration Verse* (London: Penguin Books, 1997), pp. 3–32.

42 Peter Stallybrass and Allon White, *The Politics and Poetics of Transgression* (London: Methuen, 1986), pp. 100–1. The inappropriately bawdy conduct of the King and his Court was remarked upon by Samuel Pepys as early as January 1663; see Clare Tomalin, *Samuel Pepys: The Unequalled Self* (London: Penguin Books, 2003), pp. 206–7.

The English Comedy of Manners: Behn, Congreve and Sheridan

Nowhere are the profound changes in literary notions of propriety and moral decency during this period more evident than in the English 'comedy of manners'.[1] These five-act plays possess complex plots centred around sexual intrigue and marital conduct; virtually all feature witty, often wryly cynical, dialogue and the liberal employment of recognisable character 'types'. Though strikingly consistent in these terms, the *treatment* of these elements – the changing moral judgement meted out to varying modes of sexual conduct, in particular – tells the story of English drama during the long eighteenth century.

Earlier comedies from the period such as Behn's *The Rover* (1677), discussed in this chapter's Extended Commentary, tend to display a more ambiguous moral attitude towards the sexual intrigues of the individuals portrayed; infidelity, male promiscuity and seduction (sometimes conducted with a level of sexual aggression that can now appear unseemly) are commonplace. The longevity of such themes implies their popular appeal although after 1700 they are treated with increasing moral conservatism. Marriage and female virtue are particularly subject to this moralising tendency (as in other literary genres); as the period progresses, increasing social value is also afforded to the realm in which marital relationships are conducted – the family home – as a private and domestic space.

The Patronage System and the Box Office

Plays necessitate that popular taste and financial practicalities go hand in hand. Dramatic productions entail upfront investment – either from a wealthy patron or a theatre owner who seeks their own profits – and necessitate income via the box office (at this time many popular plays also sustained a secondary income as printed publications). The standard arrangement during this period was for playwrights to receive the takings from the third night of their play's performance. Ultimately, the box office dictated the playwright's personal income and improved their chances of staging further productions.

Previously, noble patronage had been a key feature of Elizabethan drama's prolific creativity but so too was its popular appeal to a wide social spectrum of theatregoers.[2] In contrast, the first audiences of London's Restoration theatres were smaller but more affluent, mostly the courtly elite, whose interests *and* patronage dictated the content of new dramatic material. The Interregnum's official closure of all London theatres had largely reduced dramatic performance to unofficial productions and sporadic Parliament-endorsed masques for state occasions; only its last years saw faint signs of the theatre's recovery. Jessica Munns explains that, in 1660, Charles II and his Court envisaged an important but strictly controlled cultural remit for English drama, limited to royal patents for two theatre companies:

> [T]he 'restoration' of theatre was a significant part of the Stuart resumption of control in the capital. The new patentees went rapidly into action, quashing all rivals, dividing up the existing stock of plays, recruiting actors, and staging dramas. During the reign of Charles II the relationship between court and theatre was very close: legally in terms of the status and privileges of the actors as royal servants; financially, in terms of gifts of cash and clothing; politically, in terms of censorship; and more generally, in terms of the need for noble patrons.[3]

The close – sometimes intimate – relationship between the Court and the Restoration stage is usually associated with Nell Gwyn* but its roots are earlier: Charles's granting of the joint monopoly on all London drama after 1660 to Thomas Killigrew (1612–83) and Sir William D'Avenant (1606–68) was in recognition of loyalty and services they had rendered to Charles I both before and during the Civil War.[4] As *The Rover* demonstrates (see Extended Commentary below), recollections of Charles's exile and the pre-Restoration period form an important element of English drama, particularly the plays written and performed during Charles's lifetime.[5]

The Legacy of Restoration Theatre

As well as its courtly associations, the plays of the English Restoration period are popularly associated with two important dramatic innovations. Movable – sometimes highly elaborate – stage scenery added a visual dimension while the introduction of female actors to the London stage was actually enforced through legislation. For a long time before and after the Restoration, commonly-held associations between stage acting and prostitution would have deterred all but the most determined females from pursuing acting careers, but their immense popularity on the Restoration stage proved highly rewarding for individuals such as Elizabeth Barry.[6] The cultural impact of such a profoundly public display of the female body (often heightened through cross-dressing or 'breeches roles' for women) – as well as the central metaphor which connects the professions of acting and prostitution (that is, the commercial exchange of money for pleasurable diversion) – was widely explored by Aphra Behn and other early playwrights.

Idealised notions of passive and silent female virtue proliferate in English literature as the eighteenth century progresses, but the early Restoration stage presents a more diverse representation of (virtuous) female conduct. Behn's Hellena and Florinda and Congreve's Millamant

* The stage actress Nell Gwyn (1650–87) bore Charles a son; after Charles's death, his brother James II provided her with a pension.

are not isolated examples, but their representation must be reconciled with the simultaneous representation of more predictable sexual stereotypes. Moreover, even the most outspoken heroine (such as Behn's Hellena) is transformed into a wife by the end of the fifth act. Assertive female virtue in early Restoration comedy needs to be understood within its own dramatic context, just about chronologically equidistant between Shakespeare's *The Taming of the Shrew* (c. 1623) and Sheridan's *The School for Scandal* (first produced in 1777). In the latter play, female reputations are so vulnerable to public scandal that silent passive virtue becomes the only effective remedy to the dangers of gossip and slander.

Character 'Types' and the Urban Milieu

Restoration comedies such as Congreve's *Way of the World* (first produced in 1700) reflect the interests of their aristocratic audience through recognisable character 'types'. Numerous libidinous wives (younger with much older – presumably impotent – husbands, or older widows) abound. Although this dramatic type was apparent in English literature long before the Restoration – seen, for example, in Chaucer's *Canterbury Tales** – courtly audiences – for whom marriage transactions were often motivated by economic or social advantage – evidently took particular interest in their depiction. The sexual jealousy of older (but wealthier) females – as in Congreve's Lady Wishfort and Sheridan's Lady Sneerwell – is underscored by a very real economic aspect of eighteenth-century upper-class marriage; Lawrence Stone has suggested that the relative lack of eligible males in the late seventeenth and early eighteenth century left perhaps a quarter of the female upper-class population unmarried.[7]

The upper-class social milieu of eighteenth-century London provides the setting for the vast majority of comedies. Fashionable pursuits of London's leisured elite – gambling, gossip and socialising, frequenting coffee and chocolate houses, seeing and being seen in St James's Park or

---

* Geoffrey Chaucer's *Canterbury Tales* dates back as far as the late fourteenth century and contains character 'types' such as those described here.

the theatre – form a common backdrop for dramatic action while the cultural divide between town and country provides one of the richest sources of the genre's comedy. Fashions and manners associated with a sense of urban refinement and sophistication (but also with looser morals) are generally favoured while the countryside is often the source of boorish squires (like Congreve's Sir Wilfull Witwoud) or naive young women.* [8] The genre's many fops (ineffectual or incompetent males characterised by inferior social or sexual ability but greatly interested in fashion) are also a strikingly urban phenomenon.†

The most recognisable character type associated with Restoration comedy is the rake. A complex cultural entity, reinvented in the popular imagination of virtually every generation, the rake combines libidinal and transgressive energy with masterful linguistic command.[9] In earlier Restoration drama, the rake's depiction is closely associated with the sexual licence of Charles's Court in general and the exploits of John Wilmot, second earl of Rochester, in particular. The specific parallels between Rochester and *The Rover*'s Willmore were underlined by his personal friendship with Behn, and the fact that Hellena was played by Rochester's real-life mistress, the actress Elizabeth Barry, in its first production.[10]

The rake long outlives Rochester and Charles II, but only by reforming his ways. Stricter standards of sexual conduct are asserted in popular culture and in the English Court from around the time of William III's ascension to the throne. As the eighteenth century progresses, playwrights actively seek to extend their popular appeal beyond the fickle tastes – and unreliable profits – presented by the elite coterie of courtly audiences. As demonstrated by Congreve's *The Way of the World* the eighteenth-century English comedy of manners was demonstrably changing to accommodate the very different tastes and moral standards of a new, more socially diverse, popular audience.

---

* Sheridan's Lady Teazle adopts 'London ways' (as a gossip and spendthrift) after she marries. William Wycherley's Margery Pinchwife in *The Country Wife* (1675) provides the most representative example of this type.

† For example, Congreve's Sir Wilfull, visiting from Wiltshire, accuses his brother Anthony Witwoud of acquiring foppish affectations along with his London education.

Moral Reformation and Marriage: *The Way of the World*

The Way of the World's complex plot follows the interrelationships of several couples and single people. Having married off his former mistress to his friend Fainall, the male lead character Mirabell wishes to marry the beautiful and virtuous (if somewhat capricious) Millamant. Meanwhile, Fainall squanders his wife's money on his mistress (Mrs Marwood). In order to gain access to Millamant, Mirabell has previously pretended to pay court to the elderly and amorous Lady Wishfort (Millamant's guardian and Mrs Fainall's mother) but his strategy is foiled by Mrs Marwood (who still jealously loves Mirabell, despite her affair with Fainall). In order to ruin Mirabell's chances of obtaining Lady Wishfort's permission to marry Millamant (Wishfort, as her guardian, controls half of Millamant's fortune), Mrs Marwood has told Lady Wishfort of Mirabell's duplicity.

The 'villains' (Mrs Marwood and Fainall) are driven by mercenary instincts, marital infidelity and selfish spite while the play's hero and heroine (Mirabell and Millamant) are motivated by their mutual love.[11] Mirabell possesses a moral dimension and dynamism lacking in other characters; it is he who successfully orchestrates all of the play's sub-plots.[12] As is often the case, characters' names reveal their natures; Fainall, Mrs Marwood and Lady Wishfort reflect a moral code (or lack thereof) associated with much earlier Restoration comedies.[*]

As the hero of the piece, Mirabell is an elegant but reformed rake who seeks a loving and faithful marriage; the play's more explicit sexual references are confined to the drunken ranting of the country squire while immoral acts are punished. *The Way of the World* marks a cultural turning-point between the sexual energy and self-conscious dramatic display which characterise earlier Restoration comedies and the refined

---

[*] Fainall's greedy conduct (he seeks to 'rob [his wife] for all she's worth' to fund his affair with Mrs Marwood) is such that he would, in eighteenth-century parlance, *'fain* – gladly or greedily – have *all'*. As her name suggests, Mrs Marwood would mar (or damage) Millamant's and Mirabell's chance for happiness together through jealousy. Lady Wishfort's name is clearly a take on 'wish for it', indicating her sexual voracity.

comedy of manners which evolves after 1700. It is a play which consciously displays this transitional cultural moment. Early in Act III, the ageing but still amorous Lady Wishfort recommends that her friend Mrs Marwood might like to peruse certain 'books over [the mantelpiece of] the chimney': 'Quarles and Prynne, and the *Short View of the Stage* [by Jeremy Collier, published in 1698], with Bunyan's works to entertain you.'[13] Their reference is ironic on several fronts: two are Puritan works of devotion while the others are vicious attacks on the stage's immorality (Prynne and Collier).

Given their previous conduct as hypocrites and sexual predators, neither Mrs Marwood nor Lady Wishfort is likely to read any of them; moreover, Collier – a High Church Anglican minister – would have been horrified to find his name and the highly influential *Short View of the Prophaneness and Immorality of the English Stage* evoked in the same breath as William Prynne.* In doing so, Congreve draws a parallel between Collier's vicious attack (which singled out in particular the plays of Congreve, Dryden and John Vanbrugh) and Puritan moralism. By 1700, Puritans were largely derided as seditious religious dissenters and troublemakers; here, Congreve amalgamates these inferences with the implication that Collier's work might be read – or owned, at least – by hypocrites with inferior moral standards. Despite Congreve's contempt for the impact made by Collier's pamphlet, his play reveals a distinct moral agenda which upholds certain forms of marriage conduct and family relations while it clearly rejects others. Read this way, *The Way of the World* is Congreve's response to Collier's attacks enacted through the 'reformed' comedy of manners.

Act IV's dramatisation of three 'courtship' scenes – one sincere and two farcical – clearly demonstrates the play's moral agenda concerning marriage. Here, pairs engage in dialogue preliminary to potential nuptial arrangements; contrasting language emphasises the distance between the sincere love of Mirabell and Millamant – and their earnest desire to engage in a mutually happy marriage – and the comic parodies of courtship (based on anything but love) that occur, first between the

---

* William Prynne (1600–69) was a prolific and fiery Puritan pamphleteer whose lengthy work *Histriomastix* (1632) attacked the English stage during the reign of Charles I.

ageing Lady Wishfort and 'Sir Rowland', and subsequently between a bewildered Millamant and a drunken 'country cousin' named Sir Wilfull Witwoud.

Allegedly Mirabell's wealthy uncle, Sir Rowland, is in fact Mirabell's servant Waitwell in disguise; his attentions to Lady Wishfort are highly comic orchestrations which reveal her woefully deluded sense of personal attractiveness to great comic effect. Lady Wishfort wishes to marry Sir Rowland in order to have him disinherit his nephew. Her spite – and desperation – leads her to agree to marriage within minutes of first meeting Sir Rowland:

Lady Wishfort Dear Sir Rowland, I am confounded with confusion at the retrospection of my rudeness … But I hope where there is likely to be so near an alliance – we may unbend the severity of decorum – and dispense with a little ceremony.

Waitwell My impatience, madam, is the effect of my transport – and till I have the possession of your adorable person, I am tantalized on the rack; and do but hang, madam, on the tenter of expectation.

Lady Wishfort You have excess of gallantry, Sir Rowland; and press things to a conclusion, with a most prevailing vehemence … as I am a person, Sir Rowland, you must not attribute my yielding [to early marriage] to any sinister appetite, or indigestion of widowhood; nor impute my complacency to any lethargy of continence …

| Waitwell | Dear madam, no. You are all camphire and frankincense, all chastity and odor. (Act IV, pp. 2270–1)* |

The scene anticipates a state of marriage as deplorable as it is impossible.† Equally deplorable is the second potential marriage of Millamant to Sir Wilfull. His coarse language – made more offensive by his drunken failure to remember Millamant's name – contrasts markedly with the ludicrous formality of his aunt's courtship scene:

| Sir Wilfull | A match or no match, cousin with the hard name? … If she has her maidenhead, let her look to't; if she has not, let her keep her own counsel in the meantime, and cry out at the nine months' end. (Act IV, p. 2268) |

Act IV's third courtship scene – the highly memorable 'proviso scene', in which Millamant and Mirabell discuss their future married life together – is a traditional element of the English comedy of manners.[14] The scene's resonance derives from the fact that both lovers have stipulations to bring to the negotiation table which imply their mutual desire for a happy marriage. Millamant makes an unusual proviso regarding public displays of affection:

| Millamant | I won't be called names after I'm married … Aye, as wife, spouse, my dear, joy, jewel, love, sweetheart, and the rest of that nauseous cant, in which men and their wives are so fulsomely familiar … Good Mirabell, don't let us be familiar or fond, nor kiss before folks … nor go |

---

*   In contrast to these lines, Millamant's contempt for elaborate language in courtship, as opposed to sincere feelings, is suggested by her use of her many admirers' verses to pin up her hair in Act II, p. 2245.

†   Mirabell ensures that Waitwell is already married, to Lady Wishfort's maid Foible, prior to his assuming the disguise of Sir Rowland. This is also the case with Millamant and Sir Wilfull Witwoud, as she has previously accepted Mirabell's proposal.

to Hyde Park together the first Sunday in a new
chariot, to provoke eyes and whispers; and then
never be seen there together again ... let us be
as strange as if we had been married a great
while; and as well bred as if we were not
married at all. (Act IV, pp. 2264–5)

Millamant's point is that she desires private and sincere love with her
future husband (not public affectation). In Act II, Fainall demonstrates
precisely this sort of hypocritical marital conduct only moments before
he confides to his mistress that he wishes his wife was dead (Act II, pp.
2240–1).

Also notable in this scene is Mirabell's humorous use of Latinate
terms: these serve to underscore the legal dimension of the marriage
contract (and therefore the respect with which marriage should be
treated). Of particular interest is Mirabell's reference to when, 'with a
blessing on our endeavours', they should have children. Though
marriage is the central concern of all eighteenth-century dramatic
comedies, procreation is rarely ever mentioned. Susan McCloskey has
suggested that Congreve's play provides a glimpse of much wider
cultural changes wrought on the English family as it drew away from
the bonds of kinship and community to embrace the domestic and
private realm of the nuclear family:

> What the family in history took two centuries to accomplish,
> Congreve compresses into five carefully structured acts. Through
> the first three acts, he describes Lady Wishfort's chaotic family, an
> extended kin group with all the stability of a house of cards ... All
> the children (save Arabella Fainall) are orphans, and feel bound to
> one another less by blood and affection than by ties of self-
> interest ... The last two acts involve Mirabell's attempts to defend
> the family against Fainall's assault. He assumes the central role
> abdicated under pressure of circumstance and incapacity by Lady
> Wishfort ... Through his efforts, a new kind of family emerges
> from the old.[15]

Older versions of marriage and family life are rejected in Congreve's play as corrupt and – like the paint on Lady Wishfort's face in Act III – showing its cracks (Act III, p. 2251). Through the union of Mirabell and Millamant, Congreve embodies the new moral ideal of companionate marriage and the private domestic sphere; his reinterpretation of the traditional proviso scene accommodates the possibility of procreation into the marital realm and thereby anticipates a 'new kind of family'.

Gossip, Intrigue and *The School for Scandal*

Mirabell agrees to another of Millamant's demands in Act IV's proviso scene, that she be allowed to remain 'the sole empress of [her] tea table', although he stipulates that conversation is limited to 'genuine and authorized tea-table talk – such as mending of fashions, spoiling reputations, railing at absent friends, and so forth' (Act IV, pp. 2265–6). His raillery here implies that such talk constitutes little more than harmless female gossip. In this same scene, however, he requests that she keep her 'acquaintance general; that you admit no sworn confidante or intimate of your own sex; no she-friend to screen her affairs under your countenance and tempt you to make trial of mutual secrecy'. Such a request suggests that Mirabell is equally aware of potentially more sinister and corrupting by-products of females' 'mutual secrecy': plots and intrigue, deceit, even marital infidelity.

'Mutual secrecy', then, can foment all of the negative elements of marital discord and disjointed, non-procreative, families that feature in the Fainall/Marwood/Wishfort clan. Plots, intrigues and gossip engender further plots, intrigues and gossip; it is a powerful but circular destructive energy that fails to create the 'new kind of family' that Mirabell envisages for himself and Millamant. Subtly, the proviso scene reveals that, as early as 1700, morally upright wives (as Millamant will be) are being directed away from the potentially dangerous 'mutual secrecy' of females and towards the very different realm of maternity and benign (or 'genuine and authorized') 'tea-table talk'. A number of social and literary historians have explored the idea that female gossip begins, in the late seventeenth or early eighteenth century, to acquire its reputation as a powerfully destructive force. For example, Patricia Spacks argues:

> Alliance, secrecy, shared values never proclaimed aloud: these foster collective as well as individual force. Social condemnation of the female activity of lengthy, trivial conversation may reflect anxiety about the dimensions of this power … Women tend to associate gossip first with pleasure (although sometimes also with prohibition); men, more often with danger, catty destructive women, schools for scandal. The sense of danger acknowledges the power – power never claimed out loud, never charted.[16]

Though gossip does appear to be gendered in this way in earlier eighteenth-century comedies, its destructive power is relatively limited. Only females and fops engage in gossip in the earlier play; the moral prerogative of the male protagonist Mirabell overrides any real sense of gossip's destructive power.*

The moral reformation of the family depicted in Congreve's *Way of the World* becomes, as the eighteenth century progresses, drama's central concern. Despite the prophetic nature of Congreve's dramatic vision in this play, it was not initially a success at the box office. Its relative failure in these terms is often implicated in Congreve's decision to cease writing comedies, despite his extensive previous success, at the age of 31. English audiences were changing to accommodate an increasing number of middle-class theatregoers, broadly the result of the eighteenth's century expanding economic climate. As such, eighteenth-century English drama becomes increasingly interested in the depiction of a social realm which reflects a wider class spectrum; *The London Merchant* (1731) was the most successful prose domestic tragedy of George Lillo (1693–1739) whose drama often depicted the lives of middle-class characters. In turn, the growing possibility of shifting social identity –

---

* The fops Witwoud and Petulant are part of Lady Wishfort's 'cabal' as discussed by Mirabell and Fainall in the first scene of Act I.

problematising any stable relationship between class and moral character – increasingly witnesses the foregrounding of sincerity and honesty as idealised forms of moral virtue.

Some of the central themes of the eighteenth-century comedy of manners – such as seduction, family inheritance and disguise – remain in place in the third quarter of the eighteenth century even as profound changes to the genre are underway. Increasingly sentimental and morally didactic plays such as Joseph Addison's *Cato* (1713) gained in popular appeal; the highly successful moral tragedies of Nicholas Rowe (1674–1718), such as *Jane Shore* (1714), often focused on the pathos aroused by the depiction of female penitential suffering. The kind of sexual transgressions which had once served comic ends in earlier comedies are increasingly depicted, as the century progresses, in terms of their destructive or tragic consequences.* Authors now more readily associated with other genres wrote plays which demonstrate these concerns; Samuel Johnson's blank verse tragedy *Irene* (performed in 1749, the year he also wrote and published the much more successful poem *The Vanity of Human Wishes*) also depicts a tragic female figure destroyed by her own weakness.

Sheridan's central character in *The School for Scandal*, Joseph Surface, conceals a character largely consisting of selfishness and hypocrisy behind a veneer of moral virtue and sentimentality. This play, like Goldsmith's highly popular *She Stoops to Conquer* (1773), reflects its author's dismissal of a trend towards 'sentimental' literature that was popular in both contemporary fiction and drama. Joseph constantly professes higher moral aims but his real intentions are to seduce one married woman (Lady Teazle), marry the virtuous Maria for her fortune (although he is indifferent to her), and to defraud his own brother Charles (Maria's true love) out of his inheritance. Sir Oliver, the wealthy uncle of Charles and Joseph, returns from abroad and adopts a series of

---

* Joseph Addison (1672–1719) was highly influential in developing the increasingly moral and middle-class values of eighteenth-century readers; Sir Richard Steele (1672–1729) penned a number of modestly successful comedies and other dramas but is more often remembered for his attacks on stage immorality in periodical essays such as *The Spectator* and *The Theatre* (1718–20). For more on these authors, see Part Four: 'A Culture of Print'.

disguises in order to test his nephews' moral integrity. His efforts discover Joseph's hypocrisy and Charles's true virtues (and allow for the happy union of Charles and Maria) but also help to reiterate the importance of an underlying social system in which inheritance and financial dependence underpin moral conduct.

In another series of related sub-plots in *The School for Scandal*, the fragility of social reputation, particularly in terms of how female moral virtue is perceived by others, is underlined by the efforts of the members of the 'school for scandal' (a series of characters who, for various self-serving and cynical reasons, endeavour to destroy the social reputation of others). By 1777, however, as Sheridan's play demonstrates, the manufacture of malicious scandal goes far beyond harmless drawing-room gossip in terms of its scope and its harmful effects. This 'raising of the stakes' reflects not only the increased social value afforded to the notion of female virtue in this latter period, but also the increased attention afforded to the cultural medium in which that virtue was debated.

Always a highly self-conscious medium, the English comedy of manners becomes, by the latter half of the eighteenth century, an integral element of the wider milieu of contemporary debate and popular literary culture which also includes periodical essays and newspaper 'gossip' columns. In contrast to the more domestic and 'feminised' model of drawing-room gossip presented in Congreve's *Way of the World*, Sheridan's *School for Scandal* depicts a male character (Snake) inserting scandalous paragraphs into a newspaper. This is an important transition because it suggests that the corrupting influence of 'mutual secrecy' that worried Mirabell has finally come of age, by 1777, to resemble the media-fuelled intrigues of our own time. In the opening scene, the conversation between the aptly named servant Snake and the stereotypically bitter and middle-aged Lady Sneerwell demonstrates that the practice of malicious slander has now been honed to a fine art:

> *Snake*   … To my knowledge, she has been the cause of six matches being broken off, and three sons being disinherited; of four forced elopements,

and as many close confinements; nine separate maintenances, and two divorces. Nay, I have more than once traced her causing a *tête-à-tête* in the 'Town and County Magazine', when the parties, perhaps, had never seen each other's face before in the course of their lives.

Lady Sneerwell   She certainly has talents, but her manner is gross.

Snake   'Tis very true. She generally designs well, has a free tongue and a bold invention; but her colouring is too dark, and her outlines often extravagant. She wants that delicacy of tint, and mellowness of sneer, which distinguish your ladyship's scandal.[17]

Lady Sneerwell's zest for scandal is motivated by personal malice but Snake is a true professional with a reputation to uphold, as he explains in the play's closing scene: 'I live by the badness of my character; and, if it were once known that I had been betrayed into an honest action, I should lose every friend I have in the world.' The play reflects a culture acutely aware of the power of the press to destroy reputations; it associates that power with amateur scandalmongers *and* the press.[18] While, in *The Way of the World*, Fainall's and Mrs Marwood's marital infidelity and financial deceptions constitute actual acts of immoral conduct, in Sheridan's play the School can manufacture evidence of immorality regardless of whether or not such acts have taken place.[19] That printed scandal is at least as dangerous as verbal forms reflects the powerful contemporary influence wielded by moral and didactic writing (a point considered in Part Three: 'Fact and Fiction', regarding the development of the novel). As Richard Shoemaker demonstrates, contemporary newspapers and scandal sheets must be included in this consideration:

The newspaper and periodical press which developed in the late seventeenth century treated morality as one of its central concerns, but the new publications sought to censure actions, not individuals ... Eighteenth-century newspapers also avoided naming those they accused of bad behaviour, particularly when the accused was not a public figure, using instead vague references, such as 'a certain nobleman', 'a tradesman', or giving only initials.[20]

Newspapers, then as now, are only ever as reliable as their sources: 'insertion of [false] paragraphs' incapacitates their ability to pass moral judgement.

Sheridan's 'villains' in *The School for Scandal* – Lady Sneerwell's 'School' and Joseph Surface – all operate under the guise of moral judgement. When Lady Teazle informs Lady Sneerwell that she wishes 'to return the diploma [the School] granted her, as she leaves off practice, and kills characters no longer', she is rejecting outright both the practice of malicious gossip and the (related) practice of passing moral judgement on others. Her renewed marital concord with Sir Peter constitutes the sort of wifely moral reformation favoured over the Restoration model of marital infidelity.*

The subject of family relations is further explored in *The School for Scandal* through the plot concerning Joseph and Charles Surface and their rich uncle. Sir Oliver's disguises and 'tests' reveal – contrary to popular opinion – that Charles is generous and honest (though perpetually in debt) while Joseph is a sanctimonious fraud in league with the 'School' of scandalmongers led by Lady Sneerwell. This is seen early in Act IV when Charles sells all but one of the family portraits he still owns (all other possessions have already gone to pay debts) to a moneylender (unknown to him, his uncle Oliver in disguise); Charles's steadfast refusal to part with the last portrait – portraying a younger Uncle Oliver – wins him his uncle's affections.

---

* Although a much earlier example of 'wifely reformation' is found in Mrs Sago in Susannah Centlivre's *The Basset Table* (1705).

Charles's willingness here to sell off his relations' portraits – in the form of a mock-auction in which a rolled-up copy of the family tree is used as an auction hammer – implies a symbolic rejection of older versions of family relationships based on kinship in favour of sincere bonds of mutual affection. Affection, however, is not the same as sentimentality; the play makes clear its rejection of false moral piety and the 'sentiments' repeatedly expressed by Joseph in favour of the 'plain speaking' Charles.[21]

'The End' of the English Comedy of Manners

One of the most pivotal episodes in *The School for Scandal* occurs in the first scene of Act V. The scene begins with Joseph's attempt to seduce Lady Teazle before a series of interruptions and unexpected visits leads, instead, to a series of surprising discoveries and revelations. Stagecraft is consciously foregrounded through the employment of both a screen and a cupboard to hide and then reveal characters to powerful dramatic effect.[22] The scene's action also neatly brings together several of the play's many sub-narratives; its intense complexity and dramatic excitement, however, bear little relation to the myriad of increasingly fantastical versions of 'what happened' as speculated on by Lady Sneerwell and her friends in the following scene. One particularly intriguing story tells of a duel between Sir Peter and Charles:

| Crabtree | Sir Peter forced Charles to take one, and they fired, it seems, pretty nearly together. Charles' shot took effect, as I tell you, and Sir Peter's missed; but, what is very extraordinary, the ball struck against a little bronze Shakespeare that stood over the fire place, grazed out of the window at a right angle, and wounded the postman, who was just coming to the door with a double letter from Northamptonshire. (V.ii) |

The account of the pistol shot's trajectory is remarkable not only for its symbolic resonance – in passing from Shakespeare to wounding the postman – but also for the detail with which it fabricates an event that never occurred. Left to the idle speculation of the scandalmongers, any resemblance to truth is entirely accidental. It also demonstrates Sheridan's characteristically 'pervasive focus upon a wide range of linguistic and pictorial objects ... a vast plethora of signs and symbols' as evident throughout the play.[23] The episode concludes with Sir Peter's exasperated ejection of the School from his house ('Fiends! vipers! furies! ... Leave my house!'), thereby severing forever the links between public scandal and gossip and the private realm of his domestic and marital concord with Lady Teazle.

Unlike the women in *The Way of the World* and *The Rover*, Maria makes no stipulations concerning her impending marriage and, indeed, speaks only six lines during the entire play. Her last utterance is interrupted when Sir Oliver's and Charles's mutual agreement for the date of the wedding leads Sir Peter to ask Charles if he intends to 'ask the girl's consent first?':

Charles	Oh, I have done that a long time – a minute ago – and she has looked yes.
Maria	For shame, Charles! – I protest, Sir Peter, there has not been a word –
Sir Oliver	Well, then, the fewer the better; may your love for each other never know abatement.

The marriage of Charles and Maria shall be conducted through the communication of 'looking' (rather than saying) and a moral code based on 'the fewer [words] the better'. Words may mask false morality or false promises, and in the final lines of the play Charles, too, asserts that silence and making no promises are a safer bet than any verbal promise of moral reformation:

Charles	Why, as to reforming, Sir Peter, I'll make no promises, and that I take to be a proof that I intend to set about it. But here shall be my monitor – my gentle guide. – Ah! can I leave the virtuous path those eyes illumine? ... [*To the Audience.* You can, indeed, each anxious fear remove, For even Scandal dies, if you approve. (V.iii)

The lovers' complicit silence implies a mode of marital conduct wholly accommodated to the private sphere of domestic harmony; following the 'virtuous path', Charles and Maria abandon for good the public realm of verbal exchange, scandal, intrigue and plots. Seen in this way – as a play which concludes with a tacit rejection of many of the key dramatic components of the English comedy of manners, even as it deploys them – its ending serves as a fitting testament to an author who professed a lifelong dislike of the theatre. Although, unlike Congreve's *Way of the World*, Sheridan's *School for Scandal* was enormously popular from the outset, its conclusion also attests to the decline of its own dramatic medium – the eighteenth-century comedy of manners – even as it heralds the enormous success to be enjoyed by its closest literary successor, the popular courtship novel of the latter eighteenth and early nineteenth century.

Extended Commentary: Behn, *The Rover* (1677–81)

This play brings together a large cast of exclusively young, unmarried characters whose interactions are staged against the backdrop of the (symbolically significant) carnival season. The English 'banished cavaliers' of the play's extended title (*The Rover,* or *The Banished Cavaliers*) comprise Willmore, the chivalrous Colonel Belvile (in love with Florinda), Frederick and Blunt (as his name suggests, an oafish 'country bumpkin' fully exploited for comic diversion). The play opens with a young Spanish nobleman, Don Pedro, determined to dispose of his two unmarried sisters (Florinda and Hellena) in ways most advantageous to himself. Contrary to his absent father's wish to see Florinda married to the elderly Don Vincentio – and Florinda's own choice of impoverished Belvile – Don Pedro intends her to marry Antonio, a young nobleman. Pedro also wants Hellena to become a nun, thereby keeping her dowry for himself.

The differences in the courtship of the sisters provides much of the play's dramatic interest. Between Florinda and Belvile, courtship largely consists of repeated episodes in which male chivalry comes to the rescue of maidenly virtue; in contrast, Hellena and Willmore conduct their courtship through a series of witty and sexually-charged verbal sparring matches. Through a series of adventures and twists of fate, and the help of their kinswoman Valeria (who marries Frederick), Pedro is obliged to give his consent to Florinda's marriage to Belvile, and Hellena's to Willmore.

The Rover's opening scene clearly demonstrates the strong contrast between Sheridan's silent Maria and the dynamic stage presence of Behn's 'wildcat' Hellena. In it, Hellena speculates about what bedtime might be like for a young woman married to a much older man:

Hellena	… the giant stretches himself, yawns and sighs a belch or two, loud as a musket, throws himself into bed, and expects you in his foul sheets; and ere you can get yourself undressed, calls you with a snore or two … And this you must submit to for threescore years, and all for a jointure … Hang me, such a wedlock would be worse than adultery with another man …[24]

Hellena's outspokenness is one of Behn's principal contributions to a play otherwise closely modelled on Sir Thomas Killigrew's earlier two-part play *Thomaso, or The Wanderer* (printed in 1664).[25] Despite her audacity, Hellena's desires for 'innocent freedoms' to be enjoyed while attending the Neapolitan carnival are just that; she wishes to escape from Don Pedro's oppression and, in carnival disguise, acquire a lover ('a handsome proper fellow of my humour'). Still sexually innocent, however, Hellena's language and occasional appearances in male costume are the full extent of her rakishness while Willmore's authentic libertine conduct includes casual promiscuity, brawling and episodes of drunken sexual predation approaching rape.[26]

Willmore's consistent depiction as being 'stark mad for a wench' sits incongruously with his subsequent marriage to feisty Hellena, but this provides a resonant example of the highly artificial and performative mode of character depiction that prevailed in Behn's drama. Also of note is the lack of plot manipulation on the part of Behn's characters: beyond the use of carnival disguises, the play's action depends entirely on twists of fate and coincidence, thus contrasting with the strong element of dramatic intervention exercised by Congreve's Mirabell or Sheridan's Sir Oliver.

Also notable within the dramatic action of *The Rover* is the predatory and potentially violent treatment meted out to Hellena's sister Florinda. Anita Pacheco has noted that Florinda's desire to reject patriarchal authority (in the form of her brother's commands) leads her to enter a 'world where the word "rape" has no meaning';[27] she is caught out by rejecting the social order which gave her the exalted self-image which justified her rebellion in the first place ('I shall let him see I understand better what's due to my beauty, birth and fortune, and more to my soul, than to obey those unjust commands').* Florinda's experiences dramatise the contradictions inherent within a patriarchal society which values beautiful, upper-class virgins (both as commodities which enhance wealth through their ability to breed, and as beings with souls 'worthy' of courtly worship).†

Florinda's attempts to escape from her brother's oppression result in a series of near-rapes which demonstrates the vulnerability of her position 'outside' of patriarchal protection. On each occasion she

---

* Florinda makes this speech early in the opening scene of Act I.

† The class distinction is particularly evident in the depiction of lower-class Moretta (Angellica's maid) who has no difficulty in sustaining the straightforward equation of sexual and financial exchange.

narrowly escapes, but the first episode ably demonstrates the extent of Willmore's sexual opportunism if left unbridled. Encountering the scantily dressed Florinda in the dark, drunken Willmore's efforts at what he calls 'seduction' (and Florinda calls rape) present a scene whose original comic intent is lost on most twenty-first-century audiences (III.v.1–90).

In the fifth scene of Act IV, Florinda is again misconstrued as a lower-class prostitute (and therefore, according to her potential attackers Blunt and Frederick, one whose social status justifies their treatment). Blunt's resentment is directed neither towards Florinda nor any particular female, but towards 'all womankind … Any mortal thing in petticoats', the result of an earlier misadventure in which – what he thinks will be an amorous liaison with a married woman ends instead when – he is robbed, stripped and dumped into a sewer. On one level, this scene offers a consummate example of the intensely complex and elaborate use of stagecraft that Behn sometimes employs (at one point Blunt, on a bed, must be dropped through a trapdoor in the floor).[28] On another, the scene's ending makes clear what foolish Blunt himself should also realise; he was not tricked by a female thief (Lucetta) acting alone but by a group of thieves acting in concert with Lucetta as 'bait'. Blunt's aggressive response to his experience of theft (in attempting to rape Florinda) is made all the more foolish by the closing lines of the third scene of Act III; here, Lucetta expresses pity for Blunt's plight while her lover, the true thief Philippo, calls her to his bed.

The play's conventional ending of a multiple marriage attempts to efface – arguably unconvincingly – the dramatic incongruities of previous scenes such as the near-rapes of Florinda. It also demonstrates an instance in which Behn contrives to meet the popular demand for the dramatic convention of a (financially advantageous) marriage rather than remain true to any libertine ideal of unregulated sexual pleasure. In the final scene, Hellena is discovered to be the independent heir of her uncle's vast fortune and therefore unrestricted by her brother's control. In the second part of *The Rover* (1681), however, Hellena's death through childbirth has already occurred and the play concludes with Willmore once again in love but choosing not to marry. Though it never matched the success of the first part, the second part of *The Rover* is one of several plays in which Behn consciously rejects the dramatic convention of concluding Act V with a marriage.*

There is a third principal female in Part One of *The Rover* whose social status excludes her from the patriarchal order of marriage already discussed. Angellica Bianca is a famous courtesan and the former mistress to Don Pedro's recently deceased uncle. Much of the critical discussion of this play has rightly centred on the depiction of Angellica and her profession; prostitution makes explicit the exchange of pleasure for cash implicit in so many elements of cultural practice, including arranged marriage and theatrical performance itself.[29]

Angellica's depiction compellingly combines pride with vulnerability. She observes that poorer men (who cannot afford her high price but merely admire her beauty from afar) feed her proud vanity – a form of pleasure – far better than paying customers. This preference makes clear her desire to retain the power of sexual fascination in her exchanges with men; love is not an option since 'inconstancy's the sin of all mankind, therefore I'm resolved that nothing but gold shall charm my heart'. If, as her servant Moretta asserts, it is best for a courtesan to avoid 'the general disease of our sex' (falling in love), Angellica's ambivalent confirmation – that her inability to love is the result of a 'kind, but sullen star under which I had the happiness to be born' – equally implies the emotional bleakness and social exclusion of her situation (II.i.120–46).

Angellica is ultimately returned to this position by the play's conclusion. In Act II, however, the complex dialogue between Angellica and Willmore further interrogates the contradictions inherent in a patriarchal system which ultimately equates notions of value between money and *all* females. Early in the scene, Willmore steals one of the smaller portraits which advertise Angellica's availability for business and the exorbitant cost of purchasing her sexual favours, thereby substituting

---

* See 'Further Reading' in this volume for references to the comprehensive body of critical writing on Behn.

for the unattainable original sexual object an object-substitute – pornography, in other words – with which to 'beget a warm desire'. With libertine audacity, he later justifies its theft to Angellica herself by accusing her of provocation:

> Willmore   Is all this heaven of beauty shown to move
> despair in those that cannot buy? …
> I came to rail at you,
> And rail at such truths too, as shall let you see
> The vanity of that pride, which taught you how
> To set such price on sin:
> For such it is whilst that which is love's due
> Is meanly bartered for. (II.ii.4–16)

Willmore repeatedly rejects the baseness of equating any price with Angellica's beauty, and Angellica counters his arguments, through an elaborately complex dialogue incorporating both prose and formal courtly verse. As a whole, the scene demonstrates the verbal and *performative* dimension of mutual sexual attraction with consummate skill. Angellica notes in an aside that 'His words go through me to my very soul' but is equally aware – and ensures that Willmore knows – that she is willingly seduced by words when she asks him to 'flatter me a little, 'twill please me from thy mouth'. Nevertheless, as Willmore himself notes in an aside, his contempt at the cost of her sexual favours is 'feigned' because he cannot afford to pay it, not because he actually rejects the principle itself. Willmore (as well as Blunt and Frederick) relies on patriarchal notions in which raping a 'maid of quality' is a far worse crime than 'ruffling a harlot' (IV.v.121–3). Though complicit, rather than 'ruffled' (or coerced) into bed by Willmore, Angellica questions how far Willmore can truly reject the equation of price with sex when he seeks access to her bed. As well as anticipating her own fate, Angellica points out that he, too, is subject to the same patriarchal order in which mercenary concerns outweigh emotional ones:

Angellica	… Pray tell me, sir, are not you guilty of the same mercenary crime? When a lady is proposed to you for a wife, you never ask how fair, discreet, or virtuous she is; but what's her fortune: which if but small, you cry 'she will not do my business', and basely leave her, though she languish for you. Say, is this not poor?
Willmore	It is a barbarous custom, which I will scorn to defend in our sex, and do despise in yours.
Angellica	Thou'rt a brave fellow! Put up thy gold, and know That were thy fortune large as is thy soul, Thou shouldst not buy my love … Canst thou believe [my consent and sexual pleasure will] be entirely thine, Without considering they were mercenary?
Willmore	I cannot tell, I must bethink me first. (*Aside*) Ha, death, I'm going to believe her. (II.ii.89–106)

When he later betrays Angellica for virginal Hellena, patriarchal order is reasserted by Willmore's willing acceptance of the shackles of marriage (and Hellena's independent fortune of 300,000 crowns).* In this particular transaction involving sex, love and money – as well as in Behn's conventional ending for this play – Angellica loses a great deal more than she gains. Through the character of Angellica Bianca, Behn's play interrogates the possibility of a social existence in which males and

---

* In Act V this is reinforced by Willmore's offering a purse of gold to Angellica, thereby reasserting the equation of pleasure and money embodied by her profession. Willmore's gold, however, is either a repayment of Angellica's original gift to him or an advance from his wife-to-be; either way, it derives from the same place (the deceased general who was both Angellica's lover and Hellena's uncle).

females may be freed from the restrictions of the exchange economy, and finds such a proposition impossible.[30]

What is ultimately shared by all of the plays considered in this chapter is their affirmation of a social and economic order based on family inheritance and marriage. Even a quintessential Restoration rake such as Willmore, near the very beginning of this cultural period, can be seen to submit to the same marital 'yoke' that Mirabell and Charles Surface later accept much more readily. In all three cases, however, their marital partners represent suitably virginal and therefore virtuous sources of fortune (despite other variations in their characterisation) through which social values such as fidelity and domestic harmony may be perpetuated. As the period progresses, both the social value afforded to these marital assets, as well as the threat of accompanying dangers to female virtue which ultimately help to safeguard them, will come to dominate – if not subsume – the very dramatic genre which created them.

Notes

1   For definitions of theatrical terms, see Susan J. Owen (ed.), *A Companion to Restoration Drama* (Oxford: Blackwell, 2008).

2   A. R. Braunmuller and Michael Hattaway (eds), *The Cambridge Companion to English Renaissance Drama* (Cambridge: Cambridge University Press, 2007).

3   Jessica Munns, 'Theatrical Culture I: Politics and Theatre', in Steven N. Zwicker (ed.), *The Cambridge Companion to English Literature 1650–1740* (Cambridge: Cambridge University Press, 1998), p. 83; see also Owen (ed.), *Companion to Restoration Drama*.

4   On Killigrew and D'Avenant, see Munns, 'Theatrical Culture I: Politics and Theatre'.

5   On Behn's setting in *The Rover*, see Laura Brown, *English Dramatic Form, 1660–1760: An Essay in Generic History* (New Haven: Yale University Press, 1981); and Stephen Szilyagi, 'The Sexual Politics of Behn's *Rover*: After Patriarchy', *Studies in Philology*, 95:4 (Autumn 1998), pp. 435–55.

6   See Mary Anne Schofield and Cecilia Macheski (eds), *Curtain Calls: British and American Women and the Theatre, 1660–1820* (Athens: Ohio University

Press, 1991); and Elizabeth Howe, *The First English Actresses* (Cambridge: Cambridge University Press, 1992).

7   Lawrence Stone, *The Family, Sex and Marriage in England 1500–1800*, abr. edn (London: Penguin Books, 1979), pp. 41, 241.

8   See Leonard J. Leff, 'The Disguise Motif in Sheridan's *The School for Scandal*', *Educational Theatre Journal*, 22:4 (December 1970), p. 355.

9   See Richard Braverman, 'The Rake's Progress Revisited: Politics and Comedy in the Restoration', in J. Douglas Canfield and Deborah C. Payne (eds), *Cultural Readings of Restoration and Eighteenth-century Theater* (Athens and London: University of Georgia Press, 1995), and *Plots and Counterplots: Sexual Politics and the Body Politic in English Literature, 1660–1730* (Cambridge: Cambridge University Press, 1987).

10   Elin Diamond, 'Gestus and Signature in Aphra Behn's *The Rover*', *English Literary History*, 56:3 (Autumn 1989), p. 528.

11   A number of critics have (rightly) pointed out that Mirabell is also partly motivated by money since he plots to obtain Lady Wishfort's consent – and thus Millamant's entire inheritance – rather than simply eloping with Millamant. See, for example, Kevin J. Gardner's discussion of this point in 'Patrician Authority and Instability in *The Way of the World*', *South Central Review*, 19:1 (Spring 2002), pp. 53–75.

12   See Jean Gagen's defence of Mirabell in 'Congreve's Mirabell and the Ideal of the Gentleman', *Papers of the Modern Language Association*, 79:4 (September 1964), pp. 422–7.

13   William Congreve, *The Way of the World*, in Lawrence Lipking and James Noggle (eds), *The Norton Anthology of English Literature*, Volume C: *The Restoration and the Eighteenth Century* (New York and London: W. W. Norton, 2006), pp. 2228–84, at p. 2249, Act III.

14   See Susan J. Rosowski, 'Thematic Development in the Comedies of William Congreve: The Individual in Society', *Studies in English Literature, 1500–1900*, 16:3 (Summer 1976), p. 403; and Richard W. F. Kroll, 'Discourse and Power in *The Way of the World*', *English Literary History*, 53:4 (Winter 1986), p. 748.

15   Susan McCloskey, 'Knowing One's Relations in Congreve's *The Way of the World*', *Theatre Journal*, 33:1 (March 1981), p. 72.

16   Patricia Meyer Spacks, 'In Praise of Gossip', *The Hudson Review*, 35:1 (Spring 1982), pp. 30–1, and *Gossip* (Chicago: University of Chicago Press, 1986). See also Nicola Parsons, *Reading Gossip in Early Eighteenth-century England* (London: Palgrave Macmillan, 2009) which focuses on literature in the reign of Queen Anne (1702–14).

17   Richard Brinsley Sheridan, *The School for Scandal*, I.i in *The Harvard Classics*, Volume 18, Part 2 (New York: P. F. Collier & Son, 1909–14); Bartleby.com, 2001, www.bartleby.com/18/2/ (all further references to the text derive from this source). See also Christine S. Wiesenthal, 'Representation and Experimentation in the Major Comedies of Richard Brinsley Sheridan', *Eighteenth-century Studies*, 25:3 (Spring 1992), pp. 309–30.

18   On this point, see John M. Picker, 'Disturbing Surface Representations of the Fragment in *The School for Scandal*', *English Literary History*, 65:3 (Fall 1998), pp. 641–2.

19   See also Peter Davison (ed.), *Sheridan's Comedies* (London: Macmillan Education, 1986); and Mark S. Auburn, *Sheridan's Comedies* (Lincoln: University of Nebraska Press, 1977).

20   Robert Shoemaker, *The London Mob: Violence and Disorder in Eighteenth-century England* (London: Hambledon, 2004), p. 269.

21   See Jack Durant, 'Sheridan's Picture-auction Scene', *Eighteenth-century Life*, 11 (1987), pp. 34–47.

22   Sheridan, *The School for Scandal*, IV.iii.

23   See Wiesenthal, 'Representation and Experimentation in the Major Comedies of Richard Brinsley Sheridan'.

24   Aphra Behn, *The Rover*, in Jane Spencer (ed.) *The Rover and Other Plays* (Oxford: Oxford University Press, 2008), pp. 1–88, at pp. 7–8, I.i.115–26. Spencer notes that during the eighteenth century, 'Hellena's outspokenness throughout this scene had to be toned down ... this entire speech, and several of her phrases elsewhere, were cut in some performances': p. 338, n.126.

25   For a discussion of Behn's revision of *Thomaso*, see Jones DeRitter, 'The Gypsy, *The Rover*, and The Wanderer: Aphra Behn's Revision of Thomas Killigrew', *Restoration*, 10 (1986), pp. 82–92. Behn frequently adapted the work of other English and Continental writers to suit Restoration audiences' tastes: see Sara Mendelson, *The Mental World of Stuart Women* (Brighton: Harvester Press, 1987), pp. 138–46.

26   Anita Pacheco, 'Rape and the Female Subject in Aphra Behn's *The Rover*', *English Literary History*, 65:2 (Summer 1998), pp. 323–45. See also Kevin J. Gardner, 'Patrician Authority and Instability in *The Way of the World*', *South Central Review*, 19:1 (Spring 2002), pp. 55–6.

27   Pacheco, 'Rape and the Female Subject in Aphra Behn's *The Rover*', p. 323.

28   On Behn's use of stagecraft, see Spencer (ed.) *The Rover and Other Plays*, p. xii; and Diamond, 'Gestus and Signature in Aphra Behn's *The Rover*', pp. 521–4.

86

29   On this point, see Catherine Gallagher, *Nobody's Story: The Vanishing Acts of Women Writers in the Marketplace, 1670–1820* (Berkeley: University of California Press, 1994).

30   On this point, see Diamond, 'Gestus and Signature in Aphra Behn's *The Rover*', pp. 534–5.

Political and Social Satire: Pope, Swift and Montagu

What is satire, and how does it work? The enduring popularity of any form of literature is due in part to its recognition of the universal and timeless qualities of human nature. In the case of satire, those qualities are negative ones (such as selfishness, hypocrisy or cruelty) usually treated with a degree of humour or irony. Satirical writing may take for its subject a specific person or contemporary issue, and thus depend for its effectiveness on the reader's ability to recognise this subject. The best satire can also outlive its contemporary relevance and resonate with each new generation of readers.[1]

English satire of the long eighteenth century is built on Classical foundations, in particular, the Roman authors Horace and Juvenal. For most readers and writers of the time, the concept of literary creativity depended on an education comprising extensive reading and imitation of the Classics; it would be unimaginable to any of the authors considered here that their work is now far more widely read than their Classical predecessors. Indeed, imitation as a means of producing new literature was practised by Horace (65–8 BC) himself, since his *Satires and Epistles* drew inspiration from ancient Greek lyric poetry.

Features of Horatian satire most readily adopted by English authors included an ironic, urbane tone and elements of self-mockery (that is, criticism of the satirist as well as the subject). The sixteen satires of Juvenal (*c.* AD 60–*c.* 136) are characterised by a more indignant tone than that of Horace; his influence on English satire is apparent in writing which depicts individuals or scenes intended to arouse similar feelings in the reader.

Of course, English satire existed before the long eighteenth century. Chaucer and Jonson, for example, ridiculed both the general vices and follies of mankind and their contemporary society. During the long eighteenth century, however, English satire gained a cultural resonance which it had never before – and never since – attained. Ironically, this success is due in part to the obstacles that English satire encountered in the period during this turbulent historical period.

Politics and Censorship

English political satire faced varying forms and degrees of state censorship over the centuries.[2] Royal proclamations forbidding 'seditious' writing were issued by Henry VIII and Queen Mary; under the latter's reign the incorporation of the Stationers' Company in 1557 imposed state-regulated control of all printed matter. Regulation continued until the Interregnum; during that period, the Star Chamber controlled the press through a series of decrees. After the Restoration, a series of Licensing Acts actively and effectively continued to restrain the nature of political expression in printed matter.

By this period, however, English writers were employing increasingly sophisticated strategies to evade state censorship. Works were sometimes printed abroad, or without a licence. A key strategy was the refinement of literary genres such as satire, which rely on the interpretation of underlying (rather than explicit) meaning. In works such as Samuel Butler's *Hudibras* for example, published in parts between 1663 and 1680, the outward form of the work (a mock romance based on Cervantes's *Don Quixote* (1605–15)) loosely conceals the true subjects of Butler's poem: political skirmishes during the Civil War period and associated disputes between English Protestant sects. Butler's work also features satirical portraits of contemporary politicians, such as the first Earl of Shaftesbury (leader of the Parliamentary opposition to Cromwell during the Interregnum, and widely satirised in contemporary literature).

The period immediately before and after the English Civil War was unprecedented in its production of literary works which responded keenly – though rarely explicitly – to contemporary politics. In the last quarter of the seventeenth century, John Dryden produced a number of masterful verse satires which deployed the elegance and control of the heroic couplet while also depicting the troubled state of the nation. These were the final years of Charles II's reign, marked by bitter divisions within a government facing the imminent prospect of a Roman Catholic monarch succeeding to the throne. Dryden's *Absalom and Achitophel* (1681), considered in Part Three: 'Poetry and History', offers a thinly veiled political satire in the form of 'coded' Biblical allegory. In this poem, the story of Absalom's revolt against his father King David (from Samuel 14–18) conceals a vivid depiction of the people and events which led up to the Exclusion Crisis and the subsequent abdication of James in 1688.

The Development of the Genre

As the long eighteenth century progressed, English satire extended beyond poetry into other genres. While the political agenda remained intact, the topical subject was extended to encompass a significantly wider social and cultural remit. This chapter considers a lengthy work of prose fiction, an epic poem and another shorter poem. In the case of *The Rape of the Lock* (1712–14), discussed in the Extended Commentary to this chapter, Pope's use of poetic metre and form are intricately related to the satirical intentions of his work. This is an epic poem about a trivial incident (a 'mock epic') which in turn reflects on universal follies and paradoxes within human nature. Pope's stylistic mastery ensures that his satire always seems light in tone and intent. Swift's satire is considerably more explicit and sometimes unsavoury but continues to present its own problems of interpretation. On one level, *Gulliver's Travels* (1726) offers a satirical portrait of humanity depicted within a fantastical prose narrative (itself a send-up of popular travel narratives such as Daniel Defoe's *Robinson Crusoe*, published in 1719) about strange and exotic beings in unknown landscapes.

First impressions of Mary Wortley Montagu's *The Reasons that Induced Dr. Swift to Write a Poem Called 'The Lady's Dressing Room'* (1734) suggest it is a direct satirical response to the misogyny implicit in Jonathan Swift's poem *The Lady's Dressing Room* (1732). What makes Montagu's work particularly significant here is that it also demonstrates a female author skilfully employing the satirical weapons usually associated with the writing of men in order to mock its subject. Its content also highlights an important aspect of eighteenth-century satire as a form of public dialogue between authors. Montagu's poem therefore helps to foreground important questions about the complex relationship between social satire and print, gender and public identity in eighteenth-century English literary culture.

Sharp satirical literature abounded in the late 1720s. As well as *Gulliver's Travels*, this period witnessed the publication in 1728 of the first edition of Alexander Pope's *Dunciad,* and John Gay's highly successful theatrical comedy *The Beggar's Opera*, principally set in Newgate prison, and combining popular burlesque elements (reminiscent of Italian comic opera) with biting political satire. Swift's *Modest Proposal (for Preventing the Children of Poor People in Ireland from being a Burden to their Parents or Country, and for Making Them Beneficial to the Public)*, the best-known of his anonymous ironic pamphlets which addressed the plight of the Irish poor, appeared in 1729; his most notorious 'excremental' verse, including *The Lady's Dressing Room*, *A Beautiful Young Nymph Going to Bed* and *Strephon and Chloe* all appeared in the early 1730s.

From the mid-1730s, the writing of Swift's friend Alexander Pope consciously begins to move away from satire towards philosophical and moral treatises such as his *Essay on Man* (1733–4). The longevity of Swift's satirical mode, in contrast, is evident in an ironic self-reference he makes in *Verses on the Death of Dr. Swift* (1739). Here, an imaginary speaker of Swift's epitaph remarks that 'Perhaps … the Dean/ Had too much satire in his vein', the expression of which is merited since 'no age could more deserve it'. As Swift himself had remarked in the preface to

A Tale of a Tub (1704), his sustained satirical vision provided this cultural age and posterity with a mirror, albeit not a very flattering one, in which to contemplate itself.

How we interpret the meaning of satire can provoke diverse critical debate concerning the seriousness, or bitterness, of its 'attack'. At one end of the critical spectrum, *Gulliver's Travels* is depicted as a gently humorous and entertaining portrait of human foibles, suitable for readers of all ages. At the opposite end of the spectrum, and aligned with his other more explicit satire, Swift's best-known work is seen as a vicious diatribe against all of the cruelty, perversion and inhumanity which the misanthropic author despised in contemporary society. For all of the satirical works under discussion in this chapter, the intention is to offer the reader a range of the interpretative possibilities of the texts rather than foregrounding any single critical approach.

Gulliver's Travels: Allusions and Interpretation

The allegorical mode of satire employed in *Gulliver's Travels* offers much interpretative possibility. Beyond the question of where readers locate this work along the critical spectrum mentioned above, *Gulliver's Travels* is a work of political satire which recalls the turbulent and sometimes absurd nature of Stuart and Georgian Court politics. It also reflects Swift's keen sense of exclusion from this arena. In addition, the depiction of Gulliver's bewilderment when encountering the (relatively bizarre) social behaviour and moral conduct of Lilliputians, Brobdingnagians, Laputans, Houyhnhnms and Yahoos allows Swift to comment satirically on a wide array of current thinking in philosophical and intellectual circles.

Each of the book's four parts depicts a lengthy sea voyage undertaken by Doctor Lemuel Gulliver and concludes with his return to England. In Part I, Gulliver gives a brief autobiographical account of himself – this writing is clearly intended to remind readers of the contemporary 'bestseller' *Robinson Crusoe*. Like Crusoe, Gulliver soon finds himself shipwrecked in a strange land. Satirical references to *Robinson Crusoe* continue throughout the narrative; these are particularly evident in Gulliver's laborious depictions of the material detail of his island experiences and his equally laborious maritime references to latitudes, longitudes and prevailing weather conditions.

Gulliver is washed ashore in Lilliput, a country populated by 'human creature[s] not six inches high', and soon manages to gain the favour of the Lilliputian Emperor and court.[3] Lilliputian political life is mired by corruption, intrigue and absurd levels of bureaucracy which are clearly intended to echo aspects of their English counterparts. There are, for example, endless Lilliputian disputes with the neighbouring nation of Blefuscu, originating from a heated dispute concerning the correct method of breaking the shell of a boiled egg. These circumstances broadly reflect the contemporary relationship between England and France and differences between Protestants and Roman Catholics derived from arguably minor variations in religious observance. Gulliver progressively discovers that the Lilliputians are a pompous and arrogant nation; in one episode he causes great offence to the Lilliputian Empress – despite his saving many lives – when he puts out a fire at the palace by urinating on it. This episode is intended to reflect Swift's contempt for 'prudish' Queen Anne's strong objections to his 'coarse' work, *A Tale of a Tub*.

When a Lilliputian friend at court warns Gulliver of a secret plot to accuse him of high treason, he flees to Blefuscu for temporary refuge before returning to his family in England. In Part II, Gulliver resumes his sea travels but soon finds himself once again stranded in a strange country. Gulliver notes that Brobdingnag is inhabited by people 'as tall as an ordinary [church] spire-steeple'; his experiences in their midst give him a keen relative sense of how his stature would have appeared to the Lilliputians although he remains, throughout the text, broadly intolerant of cultural difference (II.i, p. 69).

The moral characters of the Lilliputians and Brobdingnagians are in direct inverse proportion to their physical size. The former are minute in stature but warlike in conduct; in contrast, the Brobdingnagian Court is singularly benign and frank in all of its dealings. This is evidenced by the King's horrorstruck response to Gulliver's proud description of gunpowder as an innovation of warfare and bloodshed. The arrogance with which Gulliver explains English courtly customs and politics (not so very different from that of the Lilliputians) is set ironically against his pity for the Brobdingnagian lack of cultural 'sophistication'. Gulliver considers Brobdingnagian learning as defective (since its purposes are merely of practical and material benefit) and in an extended conversation about politics and government with the King of Brobdingnag differs with him about the desirability of 'mystery, refinement and intrigue, either in a prince or a minister' (II.vi, pp. 102–7). There seems little doubt that we are meant to view Brobdingnag's governmental policies in a favourable light, and to question English Gulliver's smug sense of cultural superiority.

Gulliver returns home with a strangely altered sense of perspective such that fellow humans and family members now appear to him as 'pygmies'. Despite his wife's protestations, Gulliver soon embarks on a third sea voyage. He first arrives in Laputa, a nation whose court and social elite inhabit an airborne island that floats above the mainland of Balnibarbi. Laputans are deeply studious beings whose 'intense speculations' in music, astronomy and mathematics leave them too distracted to accomplish much else. So preoccupied are the Laputans with their deliberations that they 'neither can speak, nor attend to the discourses of others, without being roused by some external taction upon the organs of speech and hearing' (III.ii, p. 128). In other words, Laputans employ servants or 'flappers' to strike them gently on the ear or mouth with an implement (also called a flapper) when a conversation is imminent.

The ironic humour of the depiction of the Laputans is derived from the discrepancy between their deep and gravely earnest absorption in matters intellectual and, in contrast, the woeful inadequacy of their practical skills. Gulliver notes in passing that 'their houses are very ill built, the walls bevil, without one right angle in any apartment'. He also remarks on the frequent errors made by Laputan tailors, one of whom calculates Gulliver's measurements via a set of geometrical instruments and produces 'clothes very ill made, and quite out of shape, by happening to mistake a figure in the calculation' (pp. 130–1).

If the habits of the male inhabitants of Laputa depict, therefore, the absurd implications of a life devoted to useless and abstract speculation, Gulliver's observations concerning the females imply its darker consequences. Their husbands' scholarly pursuits leave Laputan women bored and sexually frustrated to the extent that infidelity has become a favourite national pastime. Gulliver observes that 'the mistress and lover may proceed to the greatest familiarities before [the husband's] face, if he be but provided with paper and implements, and without his flapper at his side' (p. 133). Gulliver reveals here his implicit contempt for females of any nationality when he concludes that 'the caprices of womankind are not limited by any climate or nation, and that they are much more uniform than can be easily imagined' (ibid.).

As suggested previously, however, it is important to distinguish between the views of Swift's male protagonist and views that Swift may or may not have possessed himself. The increasingly questionable nature of Gulliver's judgement has already been revealed to readers during his travels to the Brobdingnagian court. It could even be argued that Laputan women's boredom with their husbands is in fact borne out by Gulliver's own experiences, since he himself becomes 'heartily weary of those people' after two months' residence on their floating island.

The unreliable and unstable nature of Gulliver's judgement is progressively apparent during his sojourn in Laputa. This is particularly evident in his deeply negative response to the nobler ambitions of the school of political studies at the Grand Academy of Lagado. Here, Gulliver dismisses out of hand schemes designed to promote 'wisdom, capacity and virtue' and those which propose to reward 'merit, great abilities and eminent services' (III.vi, pp. 152–6). Elsewhere, he heartily endorses other, clearly absurd, political projects (such as the proposed scheme to discover assassination plots through the careful examination of the faeces of suspected traitors).

Critical investigation of *Gulliver's Travels* often reflects on what Norman O. Brown famously described as Swift's 'excremental vision'.[4] There is little doubt that dirt, disease and bodily ordure feature prominently both throughout this narrative and, arguably, Swift's canon as a whole. This is strongly evident in Swift's depiction of the Yahoos in

Part IV of *Gulliver's Travels*. The combined sense of fear and fascination that Gulliver has exhibited towards bodily waste and disease throughout *Gulliver's Travels* now comes to the fore; in this sense the Yahoos serve as corporeal symbols of moral and sexual corruption. It is tragically ironic that, in Part IV, Gulliver comes to identify the filthiest and most corrupt aspects of Yahoo behaviour as evidence of his own identity as a human Yahoo.

Part IV of *Gulliver's Travels* comprises the longest section of the text. Following a dispute with the men on his ship, Gulliver is set down in a strange new land and almost immediately encounters two very different sorts of creatures. Yahoos are hairy, filthy and hideous savages whose behaviour is made all the more disturbing by their close resemblance to human beings. In contrast, Gulliver finds the conduct of the second group of creatures, the Houyhnhnms, 'so orderly and rational, so acute and judicious' that he surmises their outward appearance (identical to that of a horse) must be the result of some act of clever sorcery (IV.i, p. 183). Gulliver's subsequent understanding reveals the consummate irony of his own position in this new social order. Houyhnhnms, the intellectual and moral elite of this society, identify Gulliver as a Yahoo, one of the savage creatures whose violent and irrational behaviour Gulliver himself has come to detest and fear in equal measure.

During the course of Part IV, Gulliver engages in a series of extended dialogues with his Houyhnhnm 'master' and explains some of the principal features of his background and English culture in general. In doing so, he finds the superior reasoning and moral integrity of the Houyhnhnms contrasts markedly with what he progressively comes to despise as the tendency of his own species towards vice, malice and hypocrisy. He becomes ashamed of his Yahoo-like physical appearance and, like the Yahoos themselves, comes to despise their presence near him.

The enforced subordination of the Yahoos as an inferior race of beings, however, must also be interpreted within the wider context of English prejudice and colonial supremacy during the long eighteenth century. As his ironic 'Irish pamphlets' will express even more openly in the next decade, Swift's satire here reflects the appalling maltreatment of the Irish colonial population at the hands of an indifferent English ruling class. The Houyhnhnms' treatment of the Yahoo population also recalls the contemporary role of the English in the traffic and subjection of African slaves. In either reading, the primary target for Swift's satirical attack is an English public that smugly regarded its own moral and social superiority as sufficiently evident not to warrant scrutiny of its practices towards other cultures.

After several years' contented residence, Gulliver is exiled from the Houyhnhnm community and, after a brief series of adventures, returns home once more. He finds his wife and family so reminiscent of the odious Yahoos that he now deplores and fears their physical presence. Five years after Gulliver's return home, his happiest moments are spent in the stable when, for four hours every day, he converses 'tolerably well' with his horses.

There is a tragic paradox implicit in the final state of Gulliver's mind. Gulliver's self-identification and self-loathing as a Yahoo is an appalled recognition of his own physical mortality (in terms of his vulnerability to Yahoo-like disease and corruption) and his capacity for mental weakness. Even more tragic, however, is Gulliver's inability to recognise that his madness constitutes his rejection of the very qualities that make him human. This profound and highly irrational state of misanthropy is hardly celebrated as the ideal position for a satirist to occupy in relation to his fellow man; Gulliver's plight at the end of this narrative represents that of the satirist who fails to see his own reflection in the mirror.

Swift's writing has occasioned much biographical speculation concerning possible reasons for the author's misanthropy (and misogyny); this is also apparent in contemporary responses to his writing, as demonstrated by Montagu's poem (see below). Similarly, contemporary responses to Pope's poem included a series of anti-*Rape* treatises, often in the form of sexual lampoons, directed at Pope himself. The facts that both men suffered chronic ill health and neither married have proved particularly popular topics in this context. Arguably, such responses tell us as much or more about the cultural context and assumptions of the reader than about the satirical text itself. It is difficult, if not impossible, to identify misanthropy in an author without making implicit assumptions about that author's own psychological condition (hence the critical usefulness of psychoanalytic readings of Swift's and Pope's writing). The temptingly rich scope for such readings needs, therefore, to be approached with a clear sense of the critical assumptions employed in such practice.

These observations are not made to suggest that misogyny (in particular) does not feature in Swift's and Pope's writing. It is clear, however, that the vast majority of literature written during the long eighteenth century reflects the hierarchical and deferential social structure that was considered at the beginning of Part Two of this volume; as such, it is important that we continue to clarify our understanding of what 'misogyny', versus social and sexual bias, actually constitutes in these texts.

Satire, Science and the Royal Society

With the possible exception of Samuel Johnson, the scope of the most effective Augustan satire is rarely confined to universal or timeless portraits of human nature. The writings of Pope and Swift, in particular, are abundant sources of contemporary allusions and current issues, ranging from politics and economics to ongoing debates concerning matters of taste and cultural refinement. The very multiplicity of subjects held up for satirical treatment within texts such as *Gulliver's Travels*, or Pope's *Dunciad*, demands an open-minded approach to the interpretation of their satire.

One particular aspect of contemporary popular culture, a fascination with the microscope, is evident in both *The Rape of the Lock* and *Gulliver's Travels*. Pope's depiction of the minute 'machinery' of sylphs and Swift's repeated references to exaggerated contrasts of scale (between, for example, the Lilliputian and Brobdingnagian populations) both allude to the powers of an instrument which revealed previously unseen details of the physical world. Though not a new invention, small and portable microscopes became more readily available during this period and inspired many contemporary authors.[5] Its cultural prevalence is mockingly recalled in Gulliver's depiction of a crowd of Brobdingnagian beggars with giant 'lice crawling on their clothes' and 'a woman with a cancer in her breast, swelled to a monstrous size, full of holes, in two or three of which I could have easily crept' (II.iv, p. 90).

The image of giant lice will recall, for many readers, the famous illustration of a magnified flea from Robert Hooke's *Micrographia*, first published by the Royal Society of London in 1665. Here and elsewhere in *Gulliver's Travels*, Swift's satire is specifically directed at the scientific innovations associated with the Royal Society, England's foremost centre for the advancement of scientific learning from the late seventeenth century onwards. Here, the Society is satirised as the Grand Academy of Lagado, an institution devoted to quasi-scientific experimentation and the promotion of 'projects'.

Then and now, the highly distinguished public reputation of the Royal Society is due in no small part to the great achievements of its most brilliant Fellows (including Robert Boyle and Isaac Newton). These associations often outshine the memory of some of its more questionable 'projects'. Swift's depiction of the bizarre experiments conducted by the professors of the Grand Academy of Lagado reveals the comic potential of projects at the 'cutting edge' of scientific discovery. These include the extraction of sunbeams from cucumbers, the propagation of naked sheep, and coloured spider's webs (III.v–vi, pp. 45–56).

The Society and its ambitious intention (the improvement of all forms of human knowledge) had been the frequent subject of public criticism and satire since it first received its royal charter in 1662. These attacks ranged from humorous lampoons through to grave indictments of the atheistic implications of searching 'too far' into the origins and mysteries of God's creation. By 1726, Swift's evocation of this well-established satirical subject in *Gulliver's Travels* would have amused, but hardly surprised, his contemporary readers.[6] Swift's allusions suggest that the Royal Society remained a subject of popular currency, though one now marked by humour rather than invective.

Certain aspects of Gulliver's visit to the Grand Academy closely resemble authentic projects endorsed by the Royal Society. On his visit to the school of languages, Gulliver learns of a language reform project intended to remove corruptions and inaccuracies in the native language. Bishop John Wilkins, a founding member and one of the first secretaries of the Royal Society, proposed just such a project in his *Essay Towards a Real Character and a Philosophical Language* (1668) which suggests that English be wholly replaced by a system of Hebrew-based signs solely representing material objects (nouns). The Grand Academy project also intends to 'shorten discourse by cutting polysyllables into one, and leaving out verbs and participles, because in reality all things imaginable are but nouns' (III, p. 150).

The absurdity of the Academy's language projects evokes, ironically, one of the most influential philosophical treatises of the period. Locke's *Essay Concerning Human Understanding* (1690) argues that human language originated in the first instance from the sensory perception of 'things', that is, material objects rather than abstract ideas. Locke's *Essay* exerts a profound and diverse influence on many authors in this period, from Defoe to Mary Astell. Swift's allusions to Lockean philosophy would have been recognised and enjoyed by many of his first readers, and served to exploit the comic potential of some of Locke's more questionable premises concerning the derivation of human language.[7]

Empire, Trade and Gender Politics

Gulliver's Travels and *The Rape of the Lock* both reflect the eighteenth century's fascination with the theme of global exploration. While Swift's work clearly parodies elements of popular travel narratives, Pope's poem specifically reflects the burgeoning power and influence of the British empire during this period. Global exploration, for trade or colonial settlement, offered the English public not only a wider knowledge of foreign landscapes but also the 'Off'rings of the World' in the form of luxury imported goods such as those which occupy Belinda's dressing table:

This casket India's glowing gems unlocks,
And all Arabia breathes from yonder box.

The tortoise here and elephant unite,
Transformed to combs, the speckled and the white.[8]

These objects possess great aesthetic and financial value; their presence in *The Rape of the Lock* recalls not only the realms of British empire beyond the landscape of the poem but also the economic power and influence of the affluent social classes who, like Belinda, may claim the 'glittering spoil' for their own.

If Belinda is representative of the vast realm of British economic and imperial power which has appropriated these luxury objects, she is also 'merely' a female. Her depiction throughout *The Rape of the Lock* renders her as little more than a luxury object herself – decorative, expensive, but lacking any intrinsic value beyond the aesthetic. Pope, like Swift, contributed actively to a series of ongoing contemporary debates concerning the social and intellectual status of women. He also engaged in direct correspondence with several contemporary female authors including Lady Mary Wortley Montagu and Anne Finch, Countess of Winchilsea.* [9]

In the first paragraph of his dedication of *The Rape of the Lock* (to Arabella Fermor), Pope suggests that his work was originally intended 'only to divert a few young Ladies, who have good Sense and good Humour enough, to laugh not only at their Sex's little unguarded Follies, but at their own' (p. 2514). Such an observation cleverly implies that any (female) reader who fails to be amused by the poet's mockery of female folly condemns herself as a reader who lacks the sufficient intelligence or generosity of spirit to understand his work.

Many critical responses to the poem have discerned in Pope's delicate gallantry an underlying misogyny; his rather glib and condescending dedication seems to endorse such views.[10] In the 1717 version of the poem, an important episode is added which has provoked further critical discussion in this context. In the final canto, Clarissa (who had loaned her scissors to the Baron in Canto III) makes a speech. Her subject is the ephemeral nature of feminine beauty compared to the timeless

---

* A warm early friendship between Montagu and Pope descended into bitter arguments and mutual attack sometime after 1720.

qualities of sense, good humour and virtue. The wholly reasonable aspects of Clarissa's argument – 'Charms strike the sight, but Merit wins the Soul' – need to be balanced against others, for example that 'she who scorns a Man, must die a Maid' (V.9–34, p. 2529). Taken to its logical extreme, this implies that women should resign themselves to virtually anything in order to avoid spinsterhood. This position is further reinforced by the poem's explicit division of women into prudes and coquettes, a distinction which provides precious little scope for female experience outside the realm of marriage.[11]

On one level, *The Rape of the Lock* mocks females whose vanity and shallowness allow them to lose all sense of proportion and engage in absurd 'battles' with the opposite sex. Notwithstanding its dedication, the satirical subject of this poem as a whole clearly encompasses both genders (as seen in the depiction of the Baron and his foppish companions in Canto V). Pope's real target in this poem is those leisured members of the social elite who fail to conduct themselves with sufficient generosity of spirit and good sense.

Swift's satire poses an equally complex but different series of questions concerning the misogynistic representation of women. The frequency with which he depicts repugnant and sometimes frightening images of female bodies has prompted a great deal of critical attention.[12] In *Gulliver's Travels*, this is borne out by Gulliver's observations of a Brobdingnagian mother breastfeeding her child with a 'dug so verified with spots, pimples and freckles, that nothing could appear more nauseous', a sight which leads him to reflect that the beauty of 'our English ladies' is 'only because they are of our own size, and their defects not to be seen with a magnifying glass' (II.i, p. 74). Gulliver later describes one Brobdingnagian female as a 'pleasant frolicsome girl of sixteen, [who] would sometimes set me astride upon one of her nipples, with many other tricks'; and he later only just manages to escape a near-rape at the hands of an amorous female Yahoo. Such scenes make clear that darker emotions and anxieties underlie the sense of absurdity produced by Swift's satire.

Elsewhere in Swift's canon, particularly his poetry of the early 1730s, the intensity of invective against women can still be shocking for twenty-first-century readers. *The Lady's Dressing Room* (1732) is no exception. Swift's narrative relates the experiences of the hapless Strephon, who is intensely curious to see the mysterious inner sanctum from which 'haughty Celia' – a vision of female loveliness – has recently departed. The remainder of the poem provides, in short, a brutally frank 'inventory' of Celia's dressing room. From its very first image of a filthy smock with 'armpits well besmeared', Swift's depiction of Celia's private chamber is far removed from the 'sweet and cleanly' image which had been conjured up by Strephon's naive and besotted imagination.[13]

The poem constructs a landscape consisting wholly of soiled and corrupted material objects 'left behind' by Celia. These objects signify, for Strephon, both the various and abundant bodily wastes that Celia must therefore possess and the hypocrisy of feminine cosmetic application which he now feels acts as a mask for her 'true' corrupted condition. It is clear that Strephon is disgusted with the material reality of Celia's dressing room and its discrepancy with his former preconceptions of female 'purity'. The poet, however (depending on how we interpret his tone), seems to pity Strephon's plight. Strephon has made the fatal error of lumping together 'All women' ('By vicious fancy coupled fast,/ And still appearing in contrast') (pp. 2591–2, ll. 27–8). In the famous concluding couplet of the poem, the poet observes that Strephon would do well to see instead, in Celia's person, the notion of 'order from confusion sprung' and 'gaudy tulips raised from dung' (p. 1593, ll. 143–4). The latter reference alludes to both the artificially cultivated nature of Celia's beauty and to the artificially inflated prices which such luxury imported goods commanded during this period.* [14]

The dressing room embodies a private space in which the female (or gathered females) may retreat from the realm of public and social scrutiny and engage in activities which are, necessarily, shielded from

---

* Pope's *Epistle to a Lady* (1735) also compares females to artificially cultivated 'variegated tulips'. Pigeon dung was one of many ineffective substances that early cultivators employed in order to promote colour variegation (or 'breaking') in tulips. Eighteenth-century 'tulipmania' is widely regarded as one of the earliest speculative 'bubbles' where prices were artificially inflated by demand until the 'bubble' burst.

the male gaze. The incipient mystery of this private space, akin to both the internal recesses of the female body and her (unknowable) mind, provoke both male desire and anxiety in equal measure. If Pope's depiction of Belinda at her toilette could encompass whole realms of colonial and economic power (seen in the exotic commodities which clutter her dressing table), the clear details of Belinda's process of beautification (or 'sacred Rites of Pride'), conducted in that same space, remained well beyond the poet's imagination.

Swift's *Dressing Table* shatters that illusion of sacred mystery and, with it, the mystical powers of cosmetics. If, however, such cosmetics serve merely to endorse the validity of idealised – and thus false – notions of feminine beauty, then such treatment is surely merited. Some readers of Swift's poem have even discerned, in his frank 'inventory' of the physical realities of female hygiene (or lack thereof), certain liberating qualities. For these readers, the depiction of dirt in poetry can work reflexively, either expanding to encompass wider meanings implying moral or sexual corruption or – as in the case of Celia's dressing room – merely to supply a more neutral observation about everyday dirt and detritus.

Lady Mary Wortley Montagu's response to his *Dressing Room* poem appears to suggest that Swift's misogyny is derived from his own sexual impotence and subsequent frustration. However, as a public response (and thus presented consciously as a poem), *The Reasons that Induced Dr. Swift to Write a Poem Called 'The Lady's Dressing Room'* (1734) also implicitly questions the notion of 'authentic' feelings on the part of the author. The ambivalence afforded to this text, by virtue of its publication, remains an important component of how we interpret its satire.

What Montagu's poem clearly *does* offer to readers of eighteenth-century social satire is a vivid sense of how one contemporary female author responded to the virulent attacks on her gender from within the same literary arena. Montagu was not alone; the prevailing image of the dressing room in satirical writing (it is of course also present in Canto I of Swift's *Rape of the Lock*) spawned a series of responses from female authors, some penned anonymously.* Montagu's poem not only

---

* Mary Chudleigh (1656–1710) and Elizabeth Thomas (1675–1731), authors contemporary with Montagu (1689–1762), also responded to Swift's *Dressing Room* poem.

104

provides readers with a useful example of a fascinating sub-genre of eighteenth-century satire, but also gives a strong sense of the responsive and controversial literary culture which inspired such writing.[15]

Lady Mary Wortley Montagu versus Dr Swift

In her 1734 poem, lengthily entitled *The Reasons that Induced Dr. Swift to Write a Poem Called 'The Lady's Dressing Room'* (and originally published anonymously as *The Dean's Provocation for Writing 'The Lady's Dressing Room'*), Lady Mary Wortley Montagu does not echo the satirical evocation of pastoral conventions as seen in Swift's *Dressing Room* although her verse, like Swift's, is composed entirely of four-foot couplets. She describes a meeting between 'the Doctor in a clean starched band' (alluding to Swift's position as Dean of St Patrick's Cathedral, Dublin) and Betty, a prostitute whom he has long tried to seduce with 'gallantry and wit' and tales of his former victories as a political mover and shaker ('in [the earl of] Oxford's schemes in days of yore').[16] The personal nature of her attack is also discernible in Montagu's reference to the showy arrogance of his personal ornamentation with a 'golden snuff box' and the 'artful' display of his diamond ring.

Betty's maid Jenny, sensing the Doctor's ignorance of what is required to 'move' her mistress (namely, four pounds sterling), enlightens him; Betty then locks his payment in a trunk for safekeeping. At this point in the poem, the anonymous speaker makes 'a small digression' which offers the reader an extended display of Montagu's wide-ranging satirical wit. This interlude provides both a diatribe against the follies and vices of humanity in general ('Alas for wretched humankind,/ With learning mad, with wisdom blind! ... None strive to know their proper merit ...') as well as specific satirical references to, for example, Pope's recently published *Essay on Man* (pp. 2594–5, ll. 35–62).

Here, Montagu demonstrates her capacity to engage in the same literary arena as her male peers but, perhaps more importantly, her careful positioning of this satirical 'digression' further delays the moment in her poem's narrative when 'the Doctor' will consummate his liaison with Betty. This delay serves to heighten the reader's anticipation while implicitly foregrounding the way in which authors manipulate, or wield power over, their readers. Such authorial power arguably transcends the gender-based conflicts that this poem (and the wider contemporary debate) ostensibly considers.

The final section of Montagu's poem depicts the 'reverend lover' attempting, in vain, to consummate his ludicrous seduction of Betty. Kissing both her breasts and her eyes, he 'tries – and tries' in a 'hellish play' of impotence that he angrily attributes to the disgusting smells in her dressing room (p. 2595, ll. 65–71). When Betty refuses to refund his four pounds, the 'disappointed Dean' threatens revenge; he will write a poem depicting her dressing room in such a disgusting state that the 'very Irish shall not come' (p. 2595, l. 87). This last reference cleverly invokes both the extremely low social status of the Irish populace in contemporary England and Swift's own nationality (as well as, more obviously but equally intentionally, the double meaning of 'come').

The concluding couplet of Montagu's poem provides Betty's response to the Doctor's threat: 'She answered short, 'I'm glad you'll write,/ You'll furnish paper when I shite.' Here and throughout the poem, Montagu's central satirical object is the contrast between words (particularly in the form of satirical writing) and material action (in the form of the sexual act or, alternatively, the money which pays both for publications and prostitutes). In absence of payment, the Doctor's wit clearly fails to seduce Betty and, in light of his failed sexual performance, she is equally unmoved by the threat of his satire. This is not to suggest, however, that satire is powerless; beyond the personal nature of the attack on Swift, Montagu's indication of his failed 'performance' underlines the different potencies of action versus language. That Montagu consciously chooses to retaliate by using the same literary vehicle as Swift, a satirical poem, must indicate her conviction that satire remains a very potent method of attack.

Betty's response to the Doctor's threats also posits the idea of (male) authorial impotence in satirical writing from a different economic perspective. Betty's dismissal of the Doctor's power to mock her social status is entirely correct; as a prostitute, her public reputation is the least of her concerns. Betty is simply angry because she is being cheated out of her four pounds; the sexual (or rhetorical) performance of her customers is entirely irrelevant, as is emphasised by the explicit language of Montagu's closing couplet. While the Doctor's verse may be, quite literally for Betty, worth only the paper it is printed on, for Montagu and her literary adversaries, ink and paper proved to be highly refined but deadly instruments of war.

Extended Commentary: Pope, *The Rape of the Lock* (1712–14)

Composed entirely of verse couplets (pairs of rhyming lines), the poem's subject and human characters were inspired by an actual event, albeit a seemingly trivial one.* A young nobleman named Lord Petre snipped some hair from the head of an unmarried young lady, Arabella Fermor, without her permission. The act caused sufficient offence to raise an argument between the families and John Caryll, tutor and cousin to Lord Petre, suggested to his friend Pope that the episode might be a worthwhile subject for a comic poem and a means to 'make a jest of it, and laugh [the two families] together again'.

Pope took up Caryll's suggestion, perhaps because he felt charitably towards the families (who shared his Roman Catholic faith, as did Caryll) or perhaps because the subject ideally suited his existing intention to write a mock-epic poem. The mock-epic genre implies the use of humorous irony and inversion. Here it parodies the scale and grandeur of Classical tales of warfare and heroism with elaborate depictions of miniaturised scenes of 'battle' centred around the lady's dressing table, the card game or the coffee pot.

---

*   The 'rape' of the work's title needs to be understood in terms of the Latin verb *rapere* ('to carry away') rather than as a term connoting sexual violence.

For Pope's readers, heroic narratives such as Milton's *Paradise Lost* and Homer's *Iliad* were highly familiar and popular works.* Indeed, Pope's composition of *The Rape of the Lock* coincides with his translation of *The Iliad*, whose first volume appeared in the press in June 1715. Pope also drew inspiration from other popular mock-epics such as Boileau's *Le Lutrin* (1674) and Samuel Garth's *The Dispensary* (1699). The 'machinery' of sylphs and gnomes featured in the two latter versions of the poem were adapted from a French erotic romance, *Le Comte de Gabalis* (1680), as well as writings associated with the Rosicrucians.† Their depiction also inverts the representation of Classical deities who reigned over the world of earthly mortals and serves to emphasise further the contrast of scale between the epic and the petty social milieu foregrounded here.

Canto I

The main narrative of the poem commences with a depiction of the beautiful Belinda half-dozing while her slumbers are carefully watched over by Ariel (her 'Guardian Sylph'). Ariel then provides a description of the origins of sylphs as the departed spirits of airy and shallow coquettes (fashionable females who manipulate men's affections), now fashioned into ethereal creatures whose task is to guard the chastity of beautiful young maidens. More sober females, or 'Prudes', are translated after death into earthbound spirits called Gnomes. Ariel informs Belinda that he can foresee a portent of some disastrous event that is about to occur, although 'Heav'n reveals not what, or how, or where'; his parting words warn Belinda to 'beware of Man!' (p. 2517, I.114).

---

* John Milton's epic poem *Paradise Lost* (1667) is arguably one of the most influential texts in the English language. Its narrative is that of the Creation story, but within this framework Milton provides a powerfully complex portrait of humanity's nature, good and evil, and political ambition as it relates to the events in contemporary English history (particularly the Civil War and Cromwell's rule). Homer's *Iliad* is an epic poem which tells the story of the Trojan Wars.

† A mysterious secret society supposedly founded in the late fifteenth century whose members allegedly possessed mystical powers. It is unlikely that they ever actually existed and Pope's evocation of them is another indication of his satirical intent.

Belinda awakes and begins her morning beauty routine. The scene is powerfully described with imagery that purposely recalls both the sacred rites of religious ritual and the spoils of a victorious military campaign:

> And now, unveiled, the toilet stands displayed,
> Each silver vase in mystic order laid.
> First, robed in white, the nymph intent adores,
> With head uncovered, the cosmetic powers ...
> The inferior priestess, at her altar's side,
> Trembling, begins the sacred rites of Pride.
> Unnumbered treasures ope at once, and here
> The various offerings of the world appear;
> From each she nicely culls with curious toil,
> And decks the goddess with the glitt'ring spoil. (pp. 2517–18,
> I.121–32)

Through the imagery and rituals associated with Belinda's dressing table, Pope evokes a series of parallel worlds (including the 'battle of the sexes' within the context of fashionable society, military conflict and the realm of English economic and cultural imperialism) seemingly united in their rules of engagement.

Other literary features may be discerned through the depiction of Belinda's dressing table in Canto I. There is paradox, for example, in the beauty routine's description as 'sacred Rites of Pride'; similarly, Belinda's layered application of cosmetics sees 'by Degrees a purer Blush arise' from her face. Perhaps more pointed is the poet's listing of the jumble of items which clutter the table as 'Puffs, Powders, Patches, Bibles, Billet-doux'; their juxtaposition tacitly implies that Belinda's Bibles are, like her cosmetics, mere accessories to enhance her appearance (p. 2518, I.137–8). This implication is strengthened early in Canto II with the depiction of Belinda wearing a 'sparkling Cross ... Which Jews might kiss, and Infidels adore' (p. 2518, II.7–8). The material objects which signify Belinda's faith are showy and expensive decorations rather than symbolic representations of religious devotion.

Canto II

In the opening of this canto, Belinda and the 'well-drest Youths' who serve as her companions glide towards Hampton Court in a Thames pleasure-boat. Belinda's destination provides further evidence of her superior social position and the real satirical target of Pope's poem; a day's visit to the Royal Court for coffee and cards would have been available only to the wealthy leisured classes of the English social elite during this period.

Pope moves from this large-scale depiction of social privilege to the central image of the poem. The two long ringlets which adorn Belinda's neck signify, in visual terms, the perfection of her beauty; these shining locks then inspire the poet to draw a series of analogies contrasting the delicate fineness of hair with the power it wields over mankind. Hairs, he observes, are the 'slender Chains' which hold captive 'mighty Hearts' in love or sexual fascination; fine hairs or filaments are also used to trap birds or fish (pp. 2518–19, II.20–8).

The poem's principal narrative then resumes with the depiction of the male protagonist, the Baron. Any consideration of the misogynistic elements in this poem needs to acknowledge that the Baron's early morning ritual before his own 'Altar to Love' provides a compelling parallel for the previously described image of Belinda's dressing table. The Baron's altar is piled with items collected from previous amatory conquests (including love letters and French romances). As with the 'sacred rites of Pride' enacted by Belinda in the previous canto, the Baron's pseudo-religious rituals on a cluttered altar of social detritus heighten the contrast between the many different realms of power and meaning evoked by Pope's imagery (p. 2519, II.37–44).

After this brief interlude, the narrative returns to the Thames boat trip. Ariel addresses the assembled ranks of sylphs, and delegates them to the protection of specific parts of Belinda's ensemble (including her fan, her diamond earrings, her favourite lock of hair and her lapdog). He also describes further aspects of these mysterious 'Transparent Forms, too fine for mortal sight' who populate both the mortal and celestial realms, with correspondent duties ranging from the rolling of planets through the sky to the creation of rainshowers. A hierarchy of sylphs protects the human race (including a special sylph whose charge is the British monarch). While Ariel's 'humbler Province' is to protect the virtue of beautiful young maidens like Belinda, the poet's references to other sylphs and other realms serve once again to remind the reader of a wider context outside the glittering social milieu inhabited by Belinda and the Baron. At the close of this canto, the assembled sylphs wait, trembling, for the disaster that awaits them.

Canto III

This canto opens with a description of Hampton Court whose 'Majestick Frame' represents both the centre of political power and, in contrast, the leisurely pastimes of the nation's idle rich. The imagery moves fluidly between these parallel realms; matters of state and matters of gossip and flirtation assume the same level of significance. Politicians discuss the fall of 'Foreign Tyrants' and the reputations of 'Nymphs at home' in the same breath; courtiers admire the interior décor of Hampton Court in terms equal with the praise meted out for the Queen (p. 2521, III.1–18).

Queen Anne herself (who ruled 1702–14) is depicted taking both tea and the counsel of her political advisers in equal measure. The monarch's 'taking tea' cleverly juxtaposes two images, one signifying a leisurely moment of liquid refreshment, the other, an act of British economic imperialism. As with Canto I's image of the 'glitt'ring spoil' that clutters Belinda's dressing table, this reference to the 'Queen's tea' evokes the wider context of British military and economic might through the process of metonymic extension (in which the meaning of an object is extended to incorporate much wider significance). Pope's depiction of the Queen and Court is lightly nuanced and at no point does his satire move towards the realm of parody or, indeed, overt political comment. The interpretative possibilities remain, enticingly enough, in the hands of the reader at all times. This is also evident in Pope's brief vignette of English life beyond Hampton Court, in which parallel realms of power and privilege (the City and the law courts) are observed. The scene's moral ambiguity is kept firmly in balance as seen when merchants at the Exchange finish trading, and the judicial process is impatiently curtailed by 'hungry Judges' more eager for their lunch than for social justice to be served ('Wretches hang that Jury-Men may Dine') (p. 2521, III.20–5).

The Court scene, too, witnesses the use of material objects to recall the imperial power of Britain through metonymic extension (lacquered coffee tables are 'altars of Japan' and cups are 'China's earth'). It is perhaps significant that, from within this centre of political, social and economic power, it is coffee itself (that luxury commodity so representative of British eighteenth-century imperialism) which acts as a catalyst in the poem's narrative since its heady Vapours induce the Baron to commit the act of appropriation which gives the poem its name.[17]

The moment of the 'rape' itself provides a consummate example of Pope's mock-heroic language and form. The narrative's emotional rhythm alternates throughout between heroic drama and its inversion through gentle mockery. The Baron's scissors, described as a 'glitt'ring Forfex', assume the cruel power of a military instrument (p. 2524, III.147 ff.).* With them, he severs not only Belinda's lock of hair, but also an unfortunate sylph; the seeming violence of the act is quickly mitigated by the poet's assurance that 'Airy Substance soon unites again'. The comparison of Belinda's 'Screams of Horror' at her shorn state with women's shrieks when 'Husbands or when Lap-dogs breathe their last' provides another humorous counterpoint to this moment of dramatic intensity.

Canto IV

A dismal scene opens which finds Belinda in the 'Cave of Spleen', a physical manifestation of her now-anxious and resentful mood. Bereft of her sylphs, she is attended by Umbriel, a 'dusky melancholy Spright'

---

* Pope's use of 'forfex' here is an example of periphrasis, an unnecessarily elaborate or archaic use of language for poetic/literary purposes (in this case, reflecting the Latin term for 'shears').

(or gnome), whose gifts from the goddess Hysteria serve as powerful weapons in the imminent battle of the sexes (pp. 2525–6, IV.15 ff.). These include 'a wondrous Bag' of all the energies of female fury ('the Force of Female Lungs,/ Sighs, Sobs, and Passions, and the War of Tongues') and a vial of 'Fainting Fears,/ Soft Sorrows, melting Griefs, and flowing Tears'. The bag, emptied over Belinda's head, changes her dejection into 'more than mortal Ire'; the vial sees Belinda's anger give way to melancholy. Belinda's marvellously ambiguous final wish in this canto, that the Baron had taken 'Hairs less in sight, or any Hairs but these!', implies that she values the public appearance of her maidenly beauty far more than its reality (p. 2528, IV.175–6).

Canto V

Clarissa's previously discussed speech, which opens this canto, is unanimously met by 'no Applause'. Battle then commences, punctuated by the clap of fans and cracking of whalebones (in ladies' corsets) (pp. 2529–30, V.37 ff.). Death on this courtly battlefield takes place through the literary metaphor of 'killing' with glances and frowns, humorously underlined by one warrior's accidental revival of her last victim (when she smiles at the death of her enemy).

In this canto, Pope's poetic virtuosity is demonstrated in the densely compressed brilliance of the single image of the bodkin (or hairpin) with which Belinda makes her final attack on the Baron. Over ten lines, the poet recounts the history of the bodkin in Belinda's family through a series of material incarnations:

> Now meet thy Fate, incens'd Belinda cry'd,
> And drew a deadly Bodkin from her Side.
> (The Same, his ancient Personage to deck,
> Her great great Grandsire wore about his Neck
> In three Seal-Rings; which after, melted down,
> Form'd a vast Buckle for his Widow's Gown:
> Her infant Grandame's Whistle next it grew,
> The Bells she gingled, and the Whistle blew;

Then in a Bodkin grac'd her Mother's Hairs,
Which long she wore, and now Belinda Wears.) (p. 2530, V.87–96)

Here, Pope combines many of the poem's central themes and moral concerns through the compressed history of this object which, in itself, recalls not only Belinda's distinguished ancestral pedigree but also the family loyalties implicated and endangered by the Fermor/Petre feud itself. The history witnesses the intrinsic value of an object that transcends gender (since male and female ancestors enjoy its use) and age. As an object that touched the lives of generations of women before her, Belinda's bodkin looks forward as well as back, demonstrating that a mere accessory for female adornment – like the female adorned by it – possesses a value deeper than its external form.

This episode restores at once the stability and scale of mortal life within the midst of a mock-heroic battle; it is directly followed by the battle's final moments and the mysterious disappearance of the lock of hair which rises up into the sky.[*] Its ascent is witnessed by many on earth who each, like critics reading a text, differently interprets the lock's meaning.

This is a meaningful image, too, for considering the role of satire in eighteenth-century literature. In conclusion, the poet urges Belinda to cease mourning her absent lock since, now immortalised in verse, it shall gain her even greater envy and fame. Like all great works of literary satire, Pope's poem imparts to its subject the ambiguity of immortal fame, a feature which neither includes, nor precludes, any intrinsic virtue or value.

---

[*] Some of the scene's participants assume that the lock has ascended to the 'Lunar Sphere'. The idea that paraphernalia from lovers' affairs ascends to the moon was first suggested in Ariosto's poem *Orlando Furioso* (1532); here, this is extended to incorporate a long list of pointless and moribund objects 'lost on Earth', ranging from 'broken Alms' and 'Sick Man's Pray'rs' to the 'Dry'd Butterflies' left over from failed scientific experiments.

Notes

1   A useful introductory guide to satire is Arthur Pollard, *Satire* (London: Methuen, 1970).
2   See F. S. Siebert, *Freedom of the Press in England 1476–1776* (Urbana: University of Illinois Press, 1965).
3   Jonathan Swift, *Gulliver's Travels*, in Louis A. Landa (ed.), *Gulliver's Travels and Other Writings* (Boston: Houghton Mifflin, 1960), pp. 1–239, at Part I, Ch. 1, p. 17.
4   See Norman O. Brown's highly influential essay on this subject in his *Life Against Death: The Psychoanalytic Meaning of History* (Middleton: Wesleyan, 1959).
5   On the early social history of the microscope, see Brian J. Ford, 'The Royal Society and the Microscope', *Notes and Records of the Royal Society of London*, 55:1 (January 2001), pp. 29–49.
6   For an overview of satirical attacks on the Royal Society, see Roslynn D. Haynes, *From Faust to Strangelove: Representations of the Scientist in Western Literature* (Baltimore and London: Johns Hopkins University Press, 1994), pp. 36–49; and R. H. Syfret, 'Some Early Reactions to the Royal Society', *Notes and Records of the Royal Society of London*, 7 (1950), pp. 207–58.
7   On Swift's parody of scientific language/the language of sensory perception, see his *A Tale of a Tub* and *The Mechanical Operation of the Spirit* (both 1704), as well as Donald Davie, *The Language of Science and the Language of Literature, 1700–1740* (London and New York, Sheed & Ward, 1963), pp. 21–40.
8   Alexander Pope, *The Rape of the Lock*, in Lawrence Lipking and James Noggle (eds), *The Norton Anthology of English Literature*, Volume C: *The Restoration and the Eighteenth Century* (New York and London: W. W. Norton, 2006), pp. 2513–32, I.133–6. On the colonial imports which clutter Belinda's dressing table, see Louis Landa, 'Pope's Belinda, The General Emporie of the World, and the Wondrous Worm', *South Atlantic Quarterly*, 70 (1971), pp. 215–35.
9   See, for example, Pope's *Epistle 2. To a Lady* (first published 1735) from his *Moral Essays*. Pope's unflattering reference to female authors in Canto IV of *The Rape of the Lock* occasioned his 'Impromptu to Lady Winchilsea' which exempted her from his castigation; Anne Finch responded with an ambiguous 'Answer' in verse in 1717.

10   The subject of misogyny in the writing of Swift and Pope writing is discussed in Ellen Pollak, *The Poetics of Sexual Myth: Gender and Ideology in the Verse of Swift and Pope* (Chicago: University of Chicago Press, 1985).

11   In her introduction to *The Rape of the Lock*, Cynthia Wall observes that Clarissa's poetic authority should also be considered with reference to Glaucus's speech to Sarpedon in *The Iliad*: see Alexander Pope, *The Rape of the Lock*, edited by Cynthia Wall (Basingstoke: Macmillan, 1998), p. 34. For wider discussion of this point, see Felicity Nussbaum, *The Brink of All We Hate: English Satires on Women 1660–1750* (Lexington: University of Kentucky Press, 1984).

12   On this subject, see for example Laura Brown, 'Reading Race and Gender: Jonathan Swift', *Eighteenth-century Studies*, 23:4 (Summer 1990), pp. 425–43.

13   Jonathan Swift, *The Lady's Dressing Room*, in Lipking and Noggle (eds), *Norton Anthology of English Literature*, Volume C, pp. 2590–3.

14   On the economic history of the tulip, see two articles by Peter M. Garber: 'Tulipmania', *Journal of Political Economy*, 97:3 (June 1989), pp. 535–60, and 'Famous First Bubbles', *Journal of Economic Perspectives*, 4:2 (Spring 1990), pp. 35–54.

15   On the cultural importance of the dressing room in eighteenth-century literature, see Tita Chico, *Designing Women: The Dressing Room in Eighteenth-century English Literature and Culture* (Bucknell: Eighteenth-century Literature and Culture Series, 2005).

16   Mary Wortley Montagu, *The Reasons that Induced Dr. Swift to Write a Poem Called 'The Lady's Dressing Room'*, in Lipking and Noggle (eds), *Norton Anthology of English Literature*, Volume C, pp. 2593–5, at p. 2593, ll. 1–12.

17   See, on this subject, Richard W. F. Kroll, 'Pope and Drugs: The Pharmacology of the *Rape of the Lock*', *English Literary History*, 67:1 (Summer 2000), pp. 99–141.

Pastoral and Anti-pastoral Poetry: Thomson, Goldsmith, Crabbe and Cowper

Some works of literature are difficult to describe in direct relation to a mainstream literary tradition. We might, for example, consider a poem as one that 'anticipates' elements of Romanticism, or 'recalls' aspects of Restoration verse. In doing so, it may at first appear that we consign that work to something of a cultural wasteland. Wastelands, however, can become very fertile spaces by virtue of the fact that they tend to lie neglected for long periods of time. Much of the poetry written between the last years of Pope's career (he died in 1744) and the publication of Wordsworth's and Coleridge's *Lyrical Ballads* in 1798 (the traditional 'beginning' point of Romanticism) occupies just such a liminal space.[1]

By no means confined to the pastoral genre, the poetry of this period deserves special attention because it addresses first-hand the cultural tensions between the prevailing literary traditions of the first half of the eighteenth century and the emerging Romantic aesthetic. Pastoral poetry, however, formed a substantial proportion of the popular verse written during the eighteenth century, and therefore commands our particular consideration in this chapter.

In this chapter, the term 'pastoral poetry' reflects the poems' subject matter and their shared sense of the intrinsic value, in imaginative terms, to be derived from contemplation of the natural environment. Many pastoral poems from this period reveal the extent to which England's eighteenth-century rural landscape increasingly becomes a site which inspires social and political debate. Depopulation of the countryside – due to poor agricultural yields, economic migration to urban centres or the British colonies and the wide-scale enclosure of common lands – were genuine concerns.[2] Also rife was widespread abuse of the electoral system in the desolate 'rotten boroughs' and 'pocket boroughs' of the rural constituencies.[*][3] The glaring discrepancies between the actual plight of the English rural poor and the idyllic pastoral existence depicted in Classical poetry (widely imitated in English literature from the Renaissance onwards) itself becomes the subject of pastoral (or anti-pastoral) poetry in the latter decades of the eighteenth century.

From Virgil to the Eighteenth Century: An Overview of Pastoral Literature

The pastoral verse of the Roman poet Virgil exercised a profound influence on English literature from the Renaissance through to the Romantic period and gave first expression to the idealised rural existence of song and romance amongst the shepherds and swains of a Golden Age.[†] His *Eclogues* incorporated contemporary social comment, serving to accentuate the simple pleasures of rural retreat, while his *Georgics* gave a more elaborate depiction of daily life both in terms of rural labour and traditional pastimes. These are particularly apparent in Thomson's *Seasons* (1726–30) and Goldsmith's *Deserted Village* (1770). Dryden's complete translation of Virgil, published in 1697, would have been known to all the authors considered here but pastoral poetry had been a familiar feature of the English classroom – in the translation and imitation of Latin texts – for several centuries. During the Renaissance,

---

* 'Pocket boroughs' were boroughs whose voting inhabitants were said to be 'in the pocket' of wealthy local landowners and gentry; despite the instigation of electoral reforms under the ministry of Lord Chatham (Pitt the elder), 'rotten boroughs' – generally rural areas with few or no inhabitants – continued to return members to Parliament until the passing of the 1832 Reform Act.
† The pastoral poetry of Virgil (70–19 BC) was inspired by Theocritus (c. 308–c. 240 BC), whose poetry first established the traditional pastoral setting and tone (Virgil's Roman model was more familiar to English authors than that of his Greek predecessor).

Virgil's pastoral model was widely imitated by the greatest European authors, including Petrarch, Wyatt, Spenser, Shakespeare and Milton.* One well-known passage from Book III of Cowper's *The Task* (1783–4) provides a very personal reinterpretation of pastoral poetry's conventional imagery (here, related to the hunting of deer, or hind) which is also highly evocative of the love sonnets of Sir Thomas Wyatt (1503–42).[4] In *Whoso List to Hunt, I Know Where is an Hind* (*c.* 1540), Wyatt's speaker takes the position of the weary hunter:

> The vain travail hath wearied me so sore,
> I am of them that farthest cometh behind.
> Yet may I by no means my wearied mind
> Draw from the deer, but as she fleeth afore
> Fainting I follow. (ll. 3–7)

In Cowper's verse, however, the speaker's position is that of the deer:

> I was a stricken deer that left the herd
> Long since; with many an arrow deep infixt
> My panting side was charged when I withdrew
> To seek a tranquil death in distant shades.
> There was I found by one who had himself
> Been hurt by th'archers. In his side he bore
> And in his hands and feet the cruel scars. (III.109–15)

The poems share an emotional register (evident through words such as 'stricken', 'panting', 'wearied' and 'Fainting') but Cowper's lines, through their use of crucifixion imagery, address very personal aspects of his faith. Wyatt's poem has been variously interpreted to represent his dangerous love for Anne Boleyn, his precarious position in Henry VIII's Court, or the religious predicament of an early English Protestant in the mid-sixteenth century. That Cowper should choose to employ such similar pastoral imagery in the last quarter of the eighteenth

---

* Wyatt is often accredited with bringing the Petrarchan sonnet form to England (following his travels in Italy while on diplomatic service on behalf of Henry VIII).

century suggests a literary convention still capable of yielding rich interpretative possibilities, albeit to very different ends.

Patriotic Topography in Thomson's *The Seasons*

Cowper's is a very personal vision of God, but, fifty years before, Thomson's God in *The Seasons* is a universal deity. The opening lines of the 'Hymn' which concludes the earlier poem asserts that the seasons themselves are 'but the varied God. The rolling year/ Is full of thee'. His broad survey of the English natural landscape and seasons celebrates God's mighty glory and national virtues as manifest *through* nature itself, thereby readily identifying *The Seasons* with the popular sub-genre of topographical poetry, in which particular attention is paid to landscape and scenery. John Denham's *Cooper's Hill* (1642) is often recognised as the first English topographical poem although Thomson probably also took inspiration from Pope's *Windsor Forest* (1713). Both Pope and Thomson wrote patriotic (and commercially successful) verse which paid homage to their patrons and political loyalties. Such works embrace the pastoral ideal of a natural landscape – often surveyed from above – grounded in a sense of the past, present and future events which shape it. Looking outward, the poet sees that nature provides the inspirational means to affirm this national portrait; the verse is therefore contemplative rather than introspective.

Thomson's compendious work surveys the English landscape as it changes through the seasons of the year. The poem incorporates, but is not confined to, the traditional elements of English pastoral poetry. The vast canvas of subjects and images includes references to both mainland Britain and the vast imperial realm; at the same time, the poem includes many passages which seem at first reading to contradict entirely its pastoral ethos. In *Autumn*, his vision of the growth of cities and commerce provides one such example:

> … Society grew numerous, high, polite,
> And happy. Nurse of art! The city rose …

In every street the sounding hammer ply'd
His massy task ...
Then COMMERCE brought into the public walk
The busy Merchant; the big ware-house built;
Rais'd the strong crane; choak'd up the loaded street
With foreign plenty ...[5]

This scene is in no way 'rural' in any sense, nor does it have anything to do with autumn. It does, however, usefully demonstrate how Thomson's verse characteristically advances through a series of images and ideas in order to consider the poem's true subject: the progress of humanity. In this particular passage, the analogy between autumn and industrial growth as depicted here is the impetus of human labour which, in both cases, transforms the scene into one of fruitful production (whether of the autumn harvest or 'foreign plenty' gleaned by urban commerce). While this might, now, seem a tenuous analogy, it points to the very different terms in which the (pre-industrial) English landscape of the 1730s was viewed by many of Thomson's first readers, as a seemingly limitless source of both agricultural produce and potential rural employment.

The poem's four-season version, with an accompanying 'Hymn', followed the previous successful publication of *Winter* (1726), two versions of *Summer* (1727) and *Spring* (1728). Thomson was an astute promoter of his verse, dedicating the previous (single-season) poems to prominent Whigs (including two successive Speakers of the House of Commons). The revised and extended work of 1730 was offered by subscription; its lengthy list of subscribers, headed by the Queen, includes virtually every powerful and influential member of contemporary British society and firmly established Thomson's reputation as a prominent member of the literary establishment.* [6]

---

*   James Sambrook notes in the *ODNB* that '[b]y the middle of 1730, five years after leaving Scotland, Thomson had achieved a measure of fame and fortune. He had received royal notice as playwright and poet, he enjoyed the friendship and respect of men of wit, and the support of some discriminating patrons.' These included Sir Robert Walpole (1676–1745), England's longest-serving Prime Minister, Arthur Onslow (1691–1768), who served as Speaker (1728–61), George Bubb Dodington, later Lord Melcombe (1691–1762) and Frances Thynne, later Countess of Hertford (1699–1754).

The poem celebrates the British landscape as a physical incarnation of the nation's beneficence and contented prosperity:

> Happy BRITANNIA! where the Queen of Arts,
> Inspiring vigour, LIBERTY abroad
> Walks thro' the land of Heroes, unconfin'd
> And scatters plenty with unsparing hand.
> RICH is thy soil, and merciful thy skies …
> … On every hand,
> Thy villas shine. Thy country teems with wealth …
> (*Summer*, pp. 116–17, ll. 549–56)

If seen only in these terms, *The Seasons* might be dismissed as a mere piece of government propaganda. Beyond its patriotic intent, however, Thomson's poem is consciously grounded in a much older literary tradition which values natural surroundings as the sublime source of poetic inspiration. This is seen in the wish of the speaker in *Summer* to retreat into the 'awful, silent gloom' of a shady bower:

> … the haunts of Meditation, these
> The scenes where antient Bards th'inspiring breath,
> Extatic felt; and, from this world retir'd,
> Convers'd with angels, and immortal forms,
> On heavenly errands bent … (pp. 110–11, ll. 445–9)

The word 'sublime' is used advisedly in the previous paragraph. The speaker's response here anticipates an important philosophical and aesthetic concept developed during the course of the eighteenth century.* [7] Summer inspires the speaker's desire for shady retreats, but

---

* The notion of 'the Sublime' originated from an ancient and anonymous Greek critical treatise, *On the Sublime* (later associated with the authorial name Longinus), which considered the profound and intense feelings inspired by poetic expression. The concept became prominent in eighteenth-century culture, partly through its influence on Dryden and the critical essays of (among others) Addison and Shaftesbury, before being more thoroughly developed in the second half of the eighteenth century by Edmund Burke and the Romantic poets.

autumn brings with its 'desolated prospect' the inspirational 'power of philosophic melancholy':

> He comes! he comes! in every breeze the POWER
> Of PHILOSOPHIC MELANCHOLY comes!
> His near approach the sudden-starting tear …
> O'er all the soul his sacred influence breathes;
> In all the bosom triumphs, all the nerves;
> Inflames imagination … (*Autumn*, pp. 227–8, ll. 945–53)

Beyond its interesting conjunction with the potentially 'sublime' powers of melancholy and solitude in these lines, the use of 'Philosophic' significantly and consciously relates to another set of productive intellectual processes – as seen in the concept of natural philosophy – which may also be employed for public benefit.[8] The profound importance of the new sciences, represented in England by the Royal Society, is equally embraced in Thomson's Whig vision of British social progress. (See Part Four: 'Man, Nature and Liberty' for an extended discussion of the Royal Society's important contribution to eighteenth-century English culture.) This is particularly evident in *Spring*, in which a rainbow is surveyed in very different terms by the 'mighty Newton' and a 'wondering' swain:

> Mean time refracted from yon eastern cloud,
> Bestriding earth, the grand aetherial bow
> Shoots up immense! and every hue unfolds
> In fair proportion, running from the red,
> To where the violet fades into the sky.
> Here, mighty Newton, the dissolving clouds
> Are, as they scatter'd round, thy numerous prism,
> Untwisting to the philosophic eye
> The various twine of light … Not so the swain,
> He wondering views the bright enchantment bend,
> … and runs
> To catch the falling glory; but amaz'd

Beholds th'amusive arch before him fly,
Then vanish quite away. (*Spring*, pp. 18–19, ll. 228–42)

Three separate visions of the rainbow are presented here; the passage implies that poetic contemplation of nature accords with Newtonian principles (and does not vanish, as does the swain's vision). Elsewhere in *Spring*, the speaker's contemplation of 'amazing scenes/ Of lessening life' revealed by the 'inspective glass' of the microscope further commands his admiration. It also inspires, in strikingly progressive terms, his respect for the delicate balance of eco-systems in the natural world:

Each liquid too, whether of acid taste,
Potent, or mild, with various forms abounds...
... Even animals subsist
On animals, in infinite descent;
And all so fine adjusted, that the loss
Of the least species would disturb the whole. (pp. 13–14, ll. 151–8)

The microscopic scale of natural life prompts protective feelings in the speaker, but the opposite end of the scale usually progresses (sometimes rather tenuously) towards patriotic visions of Britain's imperial expansion:

Let Autumn spread his treasures to the sun,
Luxuriant, and unbounded. As the sea,
Far thro' his azure, turbulent extent,
Your empire owns, and from a thousand shores
Wafts all the pomp of life into your ports;
So with superior boon may your rich soil,
Exuberant, nature's better blessings pour
O'er every land, the naked nations cloath,
And be th'exhaustless granary of the world. (pp. 7–8, ll. 67–75)

This poetic progression relies on a shift in meaning whereby the reference to the nation's 'rich soil' tacitly includes the soil of its colonies. The association of ideas runs as follows: autumn harvest – abundance – the sea – the British empire – abundance – 'rich soil'. Since Britain's small land mass could never clothe or feed the world on its own, the passage makes sense only if this shift in meaning occurs. In turn, the passage 'naturalises' and makes inevitable the process of British colonial expansion by aligning it with the seasonal cycle.

A Poetic Conversation

The association of ideas, as Tristram Shandy discovers to his cost, can lead in many strange and unexpected directions. (See the discussion of Sterne's *Tristram Shandy* in Part Three: 'The Novel and the Individual', and the discussion of Locke's concept of the association of ideas in Part Four: 'Man, Nature and Liberty'.) At its best in *The Seasons*, the progressive and associative poetic technique allows Thomson to unite his patriotic project almost seamlessly with the poem's other principal concerns (specifically, the profound poetic inspiration to be derived from nature, or the poem's place in literary tradition). In a sustained passage midway through *Winter* (the work's concluding season), approximately lines 425–533, a particularly fluent poetic progression moves through a series of images and ideas all connected with the notion of conversation. What makes this passage so successful is that the first half is devoted to the 'conversations' sustained between solitary readers and their books – the act of reading itself – which 'blest mankind/ With arts, and arms, and humaniz'd a world'. The speaker first celebrates a long list of Classical authors, beginning with Socrates, before progressing to Pope, whose translations of Homer distinguishes him as 'equal by [Homer's] side ... the British muse'. (Pope's translations of *The Iliad* in 1720 and *The Odyssey* in 1725–6 had been literary and commercial triumphs.) Greater still than Pope's literary masterpieces, however, is the company of Pope himself:

To raise the sacred hour, to make it smile,
And with a social spirit warm the heart:
For tho' not sweeter than his own HOMER sings,
Yet is his life the more endearing song. (*Winter*, p. 282, ll. 470–4)

The passage progresses from extolling the rural pleasures of solitary reading of the Classics on a winter's evening, to reading Pope, to the company of Pope himself, to the company of various friends engaged in far-ranging conversations to 'put the world to rights':

... larger prospects of the beauteous whole
Would gradual open on our opening minds;
And each diffusive harmony unite,
In full perfection ...
Thence would we plunge into the moral world;
Which, tho' more seemingly perplex'd, moves on
In higher order; fitted, and impell'd,
By Wisdom's finest hand, and issuing all
In universal good. (pp. 282–3, ll. 482–9)

Conversation brings with it 'universal good' and true human progress.* If Thomson's implication that conversation can reap such rich benefits seems idealistic to modern-day readers, it is worth remembering that such sentiments embrace in spirit at least the democratic ideals of a society in which persuasion is valued over coercion (as when, for example, the United Nations policy of negotiation is valued over warfare). Forty years ago, Earl Miner observed in this context:

Conversation has replaced warfare as the means of gaining one's ends ... Eighteenth-century poetry is imbued with faith in social values that work through conversation and persuasion to arrive at

---

* A similar observation regarding the pleasures of conversation, also arrived at through an initial discussion of the delights of reading on a winter's evening, occurs in the opening of Book IV of Cowper's poem *The Task*.

sound judgements; or conversely its sound judgement informs conversation and persuades.[9]

It is hard to find fault with the poem's evaluation of conversation and friendship as true sources of human social progress. The pomp and circumstance of Thomson's patriotism, however, and his celebration of British imperialism, sit awkwardly with the modern reader's expectations of what poetry – and pastoral poetry in particular – should do. In a very real sense, *The Seasons* still serves to interrogate the reader's cultural conceptions of what poetry, conversation and friendship are capable of achieving.

The Task: Introspection and Social Conscience

Like Thomson, William Cowper seeks poetic inspiration from the English natural landscape, but is often deeply introspective. The sympathy with which Cowper views his natural surroundings, and the solace such scenes afford him, also reflect the poet's acute emotional vulnerability; Cowper suffered from bouts of severe depression and melancholia throughout his adult life. Both poets progress, through the association of ideas and images, towards a higher form of vision. Cowper's perspective remains on the human scale, but also demonstrates a far more acute sense of social conscience than Thomson's. His subject matter ranges far and wide – from contemplation of the sofa to the oppression of slaves – but equally acknowledges the limitations of any individual's power to change social injustice. His stance in *The Task* is that of a fragile soul whose retreat is a psychological necessity, but one that remains keenly aware of (and sympathetic towards) humanity's condition from the safe distance of rural retirement. As we shall see, he shares with Goldsmith – and, to a lesser extent, Thomson – a sense of disillusion with contemporary urban culture's frenetic and corrupt state. More than anything else, it is this preference for a simpler, plainer, more 'authentic' experience of rural life that aligns their poetry with Romanticism.

For a literary work of such profound emotional resonance, the opening of *The Task* is misleadingly light – almost frivolous – in tone. The first 103 lines of Book I (subtitled *The Sofa*) take the form of a mock-heroic poem, describing the history of seated furniture from ancient times (when half-naked ancestors sat on rocks) through its development into a three-legged joint-stool, a chair, a 'soft settee; one elbow at each end', and so on (pp. 1 ff., I.1–103). Book I's preliminary section then progresses, through the speaker's musings, to observations of his rural surroundings. The journey undertaken by the speaker is very much on the human scale; moreover, the first book's ostensibly unrelated ideas – the sofa, journeys through the natural environment, the solace and joys of its observation – are powerfully and subtly linked together by the speaker's nostalgic memory:

> E'er since a truant boy I pass'd my bounds
> T'enjoy a ramble on the banks of Thames …
> How oft, my slice of pocket store consumed,
> Still hung'ring penniless and far from home,
> I fed on scarlet hips and stoney haws,
> Or blushing crab[apple]s, or berries that imboss [sic]
> The bramble …
> Hard fare! But such as boyish appetite
> Disdains not, nor the palate undepraved
> By culinary arts, unsav'ry deems.
> No SOFA then awaited my return,
> Nor SOFA then I needed … (p. 7, I.114–27)

In the 'Golden Age' of youth – before sofas were needed – the speaker fed on simple pastoral fare in the manner of a rustic shepherd from Virgil's poems. It is an evocative image, combining the personal and introspective tone of the entire six-book poem with a self-conscious nod towards the poetic tradition. Cowper's poetic progression is subtle and nuanced, thus engaging the reader in a complex dialogue between the proper appreciation and observation of the (genuine) pastoral landscape he evokes and other realities – the need for sofas as one gets older, for example – which in turn allow him to adjust his understanding of the natural environment he occupies.

The speaker is intensely aware of the importance of his own emotional engagement with his environment: 'Scenes must be beautiful which daily view'd/ Please daily, and whose novelty survives/ Long knowledge and the scrutiny of years'; even 'Sounds inharmonious in themselves and harsh' ('cawing rooks, and kites ... screaming loud') when 'heard in scenes where peace for ever reigns' can bring pleasure (pp. 10–11, I.203–9). At the same time, the speaker's appreciation of nature is never cloyingly idealistic; his reasoned contemplation of a hermit's cottage (which first evokes the pastoral realm in which a peasant's isolated life is deemed idyllic), for example, leads him to conclude that such a dwelling offers a hard life of hungry, laborious tedium – 'So farewell envy of the *peasant's nest.*/ If solitude make scant the means of life,/ Society for me!' (pp. 12–14, I.227–51).

Notwithstanding the countryside's superior charms, the speaker is equally aware of London's glittering – though morally questionable – attractions, 'in whom I see/ Much that I love, and more that I admire,/ And all that I abhor' (p. 134, III.838–40). He clearly recognises that his rural existence is a necessary retreat from the larger and more corrupt realities of modern urban life:

> ... We can spare
> The splendour of your lamps, they but eclipse
> Our softer satellite. Your songs confound
> Our more harmonious notes ...
> There is a public mischief in your mirth,
> It plagues your country. (pp. 40–1, I.764–70)

If the theme of urban corruption is common enough in eighteenth-century literature, here the distinct sense of unease in these lines also reflects a discernible emotional fragility on the part of the speaker. Throughout *The Task*, the individual personality of the speaker (the moral barometer of his views concerning contemporary social issues, his devout Christian faith, his idiosyncratic tastes and opinions) is carefully developed. His physical proximity to his rural retreat remains constant, but so, too, does a sense that he is engaging in a subjective dialogue with – rather than an objective description of – both his immediate surroundings and the wider world he encounters through newspapers and correspondence.

Early in Book II (subtitled *The Timepiece*), the speaker describes a series of recent global occurrences as 'portents' (natural events, such as the sighting of meteors and heavy fogs, to which is ascribed particular moral significance) which 'preach the gen'ral doom' of an immoral world engaged in the inhumane practice of slavery. His lengthy diatribe against slavery in the opening pages of Book II is echoed in other aspects of social injustice considered in *The Task*, but slavery (which is also briefly referred to in Goldsmith's and Crabbe's poems) remains the first and most prevalent element of Cowper's humanitarian concerns (pp. 45 ff., II.1 ff.).

The 'Train of Ideas'

The social concerns of *The Task*'s speaker therefore extend far beyond the narrow compass of his rural domain, and his sofa, from which – he notes early in Book III – he has 'rambled wide' (pp. 91–2, III.11–14). The speaker shares with humanity the strong fellow-feelings that should make slavery so abhorrent. His Christian devotion, however, is divided between an admiration of humanity's pursuit of greater knowledge (as evident in scientific investigation) while at the same time it dismisses as naught those scientific principles which ignore the discernible presence of the hand of God. This view contrasts significantly with Thomson's (much earlier) celebration of the new sciences in terms which clearly saw no conflict between natural philosophy and Christian faith. Cowper's Christian convictions also temper his more general views concerning all human intellectual ambition. Reminiscent of Samuel Johnson's *The Vanity of Human Wishes* (1749), the speaker of *The Task* seeks a human scale for human endeavour when he expresses profound ambivalence concerning the 'sober dreams, grave and wise' – of historians, biographers and natural philosophers – who

> ... spend
> The little wick of life's poor shallow lamp
> In playing tricks with nature, giving laws
> To distant worlds and trifling in their own. (p. 118, III.138 ff.)

It is not the 'sober dreams' themselves with which the speaker finds fault, but the dreamers' tendency to ignore the 'truth' found in their immediate surroundings in pursuit of other, better, 'truths'. As suggested by its subtitle, *Gardening*, Book III is focused on the speaker's cultivation of his immediate and very personal spiritual 'landscape'. Taken as a whole, as T. E. Blom has suggested:

> *The Task* is a spiritual autobiography which begins where *Paradise Lost* ends, with fallen man seeking that 'paradise within' which Michael promises Adam; and Cowper's intention is to show his spiritual progress to that inner paradise by recording the train of ideas passing momentarily through his mind.[10]

The 'train of ideas' considers objects both in terms of their immediate presence and their wider spiritual or social significance. Each of the books' titles – as already discussed in relation to *The Sofa* – considers a deceptively simple and personal element of the speaker's rural retreat. As sofas are contemplated in Book I, the recreational and pleasurable aspects of gardening itself, in very literal terms, are considered in Book III; Cowper's subtle poetic progression allows him to move fluidly between the realms of literal and symbolic 'gardens'. This fluid progression in turn 'gives the impression of literature as process, as created on the spot out of the events it describes' and implies that spiritual progress may be just as easily – perhaps more easily – achieved through the peaceful contemplation of a rural retreat than by travelling further afield.[11]

    The Task is not confined to the speaker's solitary consideration of his rural surroundings or his isolated response to his larger world. This is particularly evident in Book IV (*The Winter Evening*) in which the speaker progresses through a series of ideas similar to those previously considered in Thomson's *Winter*. The solitary pleasures of reading on a winter's evening are once again extolled before the speaker moves on to consider how this particular season lends itself to the quintessential English delights of a cup of tea (the drink that 'refreshes without inebriation'), company and conversation (pp. 140–6, IV.88–100, 133–43). Cowper makes no effort to outline, in explicit terms, the kind of grand project of human progress that Thomson envisions may be achieved through teatime chat. What these poets share, however, is a sense of the intrinsic value to be gained – through conversation or shared contemplation – from the peaceful rural retreat as a social, rather than an isolated, environment.

Goldsmith's Lost Worlds

Oliver Goldsmith, too, yearns for rustic retreat and social engagement as represented by the vision of now-departed Auburn, 'the loveliest village in the plain'. Inspired by Virgil's *Georgics*, *The Deserted Village* (1770) depicts a nostalgic and melancholy portrait of English village life now gone forever. In doing so, it recalls the cynicism of eighteenth-century satirists working in the Classical tradition (such as Pope and Swift, and also seen in the 1749 poem *The Vanity of Human Wishes* by Goldsmith's friend Samuel Johnson). What *The Deserted Village* shares with *The Task* is a contemporary revelation of wider social misery, in particular that of displaced populations. In Cowper's and Goldsmith's poetry, this is reflected in the shared experience of both the English rural poor and oppressed colonial subjects (including slaves). Goldsmith's poem considers the plight of the English rural poor removed to the filth and corruption of London or, further, to the colonies. Both poets also directly address the moral conscience of that small but powerful proportion of English culture which had so rapidly acquired enormous material wealth – largely at the cost of labour to their rural and colonial subordinates – and which would also have constituted their early readers.

In political and aesthetic terms, *The Deserted Village* is diametrically opposed to Thomson's (much earlier) Whig celebration of human progress as realised through commercial enterprise and imperialism. Goldsmith's poem is unequivocal in its condemnation of avarice and luxury obtained at the expense of rural dwellers' livelihoods. The solemnity of the verse's content is emphasised by its halting pace:

> Ye friends to truth, ye statesmen, who survey
> The rich man's joys increase, the poor's decay ...
> Yet count our gains. This wealth is but a name
> That leaves our useful products still the same.
> Not so the loss. The man of wealth and pride
> Takes up a space that many poor supplied ...
> The robe that wraps his limbs in silken sloth
> Has robbed the neighboring fields of half their growth ...[12]

In structural terms, the poem makes its political message clear through the paralleling of opposites; the simple pleasures of rural life in the bygone days in Auburn are juxtaposed against the bleak decimation of the contemporary English countryside. Blom has suggested that Goldsmith and Cowper shared the conviction that

> only by means of disjunction may a poet express an epoch's sudden blossoming and all that such a blossoming implies: an irreversible break between past and present, between imitation and originality, between tradition and innovation, between education and inclination.[13]

This broad critical observation certainly goes some way towards addressing the poetic effects by which both poets' strong sense of social conscience is conveyed. In the latter case, the irreconcilable nature of the lost Auburn with Goldsmith's depiction of present-day rural England highlights the underlying political intent of the poem. The speaker's assertion, for example, that in former days, 'every rood of ground maintained its man' in Auburn* was deemed unrealistic even by those contemporaries sympathetic to the economic and political implications of Goldsmith's poem (p. 2878, ll. 57–8).[14] Alfred Lutz observes that '[r]ather than agree that the dependence of the poor on their betters is a positive result of economic reality, Goldsmith presents the rural population of the Auburn of old as independent owner-occupiers', thereby heightening the contrast with the social degradation suffered by the contemporary rural poor.[15]

Goldsmith seeks to counteract a prevailing view that justified channelling the labour of England's rural poor into 'productive' measures (trade, colonial expansion and so on) as an economic necessity since, left to their own devices, the rural population would remain idle and drain the country's resources.[16]

Changes wrought on the English countryside by eighteenth-century parliamentary enclosures still provoke debate among historians. Lutz demonstrates that public protest against enclosure (as a means of destroying ancient communal property rights, and privileging large-scale landowners over poorer labourers) was prevalent before and after *The Deserted Village* was published and that 'the poem could apparently be understood as shorthand for a particular economic view'. W. A. Speck has observed, however, that

> most enclosed land was used for arable in this period. Since traditional methods of arable farming, which were labour intensive, persisted until the coming of machinery, the demand for labour cannot have fallen in agricultural districts. On the contrary, there appears to have been an increase in the numbers of people employed on the land … there were even new villages settled.[17]

Conflicting interpretations concerning the impact of parliamentary enclosures on rural England reflects fundamental political distinctions between Whigs and Tories during Goldsmith's own lifetime. Broadly speaking, Whig interests sought (as in Thomson's poem) the promotion of relatively new economic opportunities represented by

---

* A 'rood' is a quarter of an acre (0.10 ha).

the 'City' (speculation in colonial expansion, for example) and encouraged the higher agricultural yields made possible by large-scale farming. In contrast, Goldsmith's poem depicts, as a tragic fait accompli, an English rural landscape now transformed into a 'barren splendour' of cultivated estates and agricultural mass-production where 'One only master grasps the whole domain'. One powerful scene describes economic migration on a massive scale and, with it, the departure of 'sweet Poetry' itself:

> I see the rural Virtues leave the land ...
> And thou, sweet Poetry, loveliest maid,
> Still first to fly where sensual joys invade;
> Unfit in these degenerate times of shame,
> To catch the heart, or strike for honest fame ...
> Farewell, and O! where'er thy voice be tried ...
> Aid slighted truth, with thy persuasive strain
> Teach erring man to spurn the rage of pain
> Teach him that states of native strength possessed,
> Though very poor, may still be very blest ... (pp. 2885–6, ll. 398–426)

This image, near the poem's conclusion, makes clear that 'in these degenerate times of shame', the fate of England's countryside is already sealed. More positively, the speaker glimpses the possible re-emergence of 'rural Virtues' and 'native strength' in foreign climes. Accompanied by 'sweet Poetry', the endeavours of the rural poor in their new homes 'may still be very blest'. There is no implication that this foreign landscape represents a British colony or that its economic migrants labour on behalf of the British empire (as in Thomson's poem). Instead, the speaker's vision implies that the best and most enterprising members of England's rural population leave in order to improve their own livelihoods, taking with them the 'rural Virtues' that will inspire future poetry. Goldsmith's vision suggests a desolate and barren English countryside, notwithstanding its agricultural yields incapable of 'productivity' in the broadest cultural sense.

Politics and Poetry

The political significance of *The Deserted Village* also needs to be considered within the context of its poetic devices. Leo Storm has convincingly argued that Goldsmith's depiction of Auburn's rural pastimes reflects his debt to the Georgic pastoral model and, in particular, the English Georgic model made popular by James Thomson's *The Seasons*. Goldsmith clearly deploys this model to different – indeed, virtually opposite – ends to Thomson's; what they share (from the Georgic model) is the depiction of a rural existence made up mostly of hard labour with occasional interludes of sport and other recreation. These (considered in the Extended Commentary on George Crabbe's *The Village*, below) are precisely the elements of contemporary rural life with which Crabbe takes exception in Goldsmith's poem. In Goldsmith's defence, it is worth noting that they only feature in his portrait of *historic* Auburn – now gone forever – rather than contemporary England.

Goldsmith's depiction of the *contemporary* plight of the rural poor is largely conveyed in anecdotal, sometimes broadly sentimental, terms. Often these take the form of tragic 'vignettes' in which vulnerable rural females, both young and old, suffer destitution and abandonment. The solitary widow who struggles to survive in the ruined landscape of Auburn, for example, finds a direct parallel in Cowper's depiction of Crazy Kate in Book I of *The Task*. A more familiar tale of urban corruption is related through the representation of one such 'poor houseless shivering female':

> Now lost to all; her friends, her virtue fled,
> Near her betrayer's door she lays her head,
> And pinched with cold, and shrinking from the shower,
> With heavy heart deplores that luckless hour,
> When idly first, ambitions of the town,

She left her [spinning] wheel and robes of country brown.
(*The Deserted Village*, p. 2884, ll. 331–6)*

The overwhelming prevalence of this image in relation to the transformation of the English rural landscape attests to its wider symbolic resonance during this period. As we will see, a similar image will be used to very different effect by George Crabbe; the pathos with which it is evoked here reflects a nostalgia for pastoral innocence already as distant from England's contemporary rural landscape as it is from Virgil's Golden Age.

Crabbe's bitter depiction of a poverty-stricken English rural landscape is intended as an antidote to the smug pastoral fantasy idealised by affluent readers – whose collaboration in this moral outrage he challenges directly – since it is an indifference born out of ignorance:

Oh! trifle not with wants you cannot feel,
Nor mock the misery of a stinted meal ...
Ye gentle souls, who dream of rural ease,
Whom the smooth stream and the smoother sonnet please ...[18]

Crabbe – and Cowper – both address the much broader sense of moral and social responsibility that their contemporary readers must now take both towards their global empire and, nearer to home, the English countryside. In this sense, their poetry is deeply concerned with a theme still implicit in the guilt and contradictory impulses of twenty-first-century English middle-class culture: exploitation (particularly of poorer populations and the natural landscape). Though Crabbe and Cowper differ markedly in the extent to which a poetic version of the pastoral idyll may provide spiritual solace – either for readers or the poets concerned – and in their poetic structure, they offer alternative versions of how eighteenth-century poetry sought to address this burgeoning sense of social culpability in the period directly before and during the Romantic period.

---

* Compare this portrait with that of the naive herdsman (who ends up robbed of his savings and infected with venereal disease) in *Gay's Trivia: Or, the Art of Walking the Streets in London* (1716).

Extended Commentary: Crabbe, *The Village* (1783)

A familiar critical response to Crabbe's poem discerns his specific objections to Goldsmith's idyllic view of Auburn and his more general rejection of the pastoral form as both unrealistic and unhelpful. Rather than eschewing the Classical poetic tradition which inspired pastoral works such as Goldsmith's and Thomson's, however, Crabbe worked from within it; thus it is also 'a commonplace of criticism to say that Crabbe was "the last of the Augustans"'. Ronald Hatch has convincingly suggested that Crabbe is something of a poetic revolutionary, one who 'believes that he must begin a new style of poetry … Not only are the themes and forms of the past insufficient to handle the new situations, they are obstacles to a clear presentation of the new problems.'* [19] Regarding the 'obstacles' in question, Crabbe's task in this poem is two-fold; he rejects *both* the Classical and contemporary model of pastoral poetry.

Crabbe's seemingly contradictory position in relation to the pastoral model is not easily understood. In Book I the poem's speaker dismisses Virgil's model of pastoral poetry as one that strays from the truth:

> Must sleepy bards the flattering dream prolong,
> Mechanic echoes of the Mantuan song?
> From truth and nature shall we widely stray,
> Where Virgil, not where Fancy leads the way? (p. 157, ll. 17–20)

The main purpose of these lines is to establish the distance between Virgil's poetry and 'truth and nature'. It is worth noting that, as they appear here, these lines offer a revised version of Crabbe's original. Suggested by Samuel Johnson (and endorsed by Crabbe), the revisions alter the passage's original meaning such that it now asserts that it is specifically the Classical model of pastoral poetry that makes

---

* Hatch also points out, however, that Crabbe was by no means the only 'anti-pastoral poet' during this period, citing Richard Jago's *Edge-Hill* (1767) and William Shenstone's *Rural Elegance* (1750), p. 279.

contemporary poets 'widely stray' from the truth. In Crabbe's original version, the final couplet reads 'From Truth and Nature shall we widely stray,/ Where Fancy leads, or Virgil led the way?'[20] The original version dismisses as false both contemporary pastoral poetry (the universal concept of poetic 'Fancy') and Classical models on equal terms.

Crabbe's poem does, ultimately, seek to dismiss both pastoral models (hence Crabbe's acceptance of Johnson's alterations) but he does so in an extended and systematic manner. As they now stand, Crabbe's lines quickly dismiss the (less relevant) charge of falsity in Classical pastoral poetry in order to concentrate his energies on the far more serious critical charges he subsequently raises against contemporary poetry.

Crabbe's extended consideration of the inadequacies of contemporary poetry is first developed in terms which address the economic necessity of agricultural labour ('peasants now/ ... plod behind the plough,/ And few ... have time/ To number syllables and play with rhyme'). 'Playing' with rhyme is clearly a frivolous activity when compared with the serious task of earning one's livelihood through labour; pastoral verse is further denigrated as a particularly 'easy' form of poetry to write:

> From one chief cause these idle praises spring,
> That, themes so easy, few forbear to sing;
> They ask no thought, require no deep design,
> But swell the song and liquefy the line ...
> But when amid such pleasing scenes I trace
> The poor laborious natives of the place ...
> Then shall I dare these real ills to hide,
> In tinsel trappings of poetic pride? (pp. 158, ll. 31–48)

Crabbe's attack on contemporary pastoral poetry goes far beyond its dismissal on these terms. He makes clear that such poetry offers no practical relief for the suffering of the rural poor:

> To you [poor labourers] the smoothest song is smooth in vain;
> O'ercome by labour and bow'd down by time,

Feel you the barren flattery of a rhyme?
Can poets sooth you, when you pine for bread,
By winding myrtles round your ruin'd shed?
Can their light tales your mighty griefs o'erpower,
Or glad with airy mirth the toilsome hour? (pp. 158–9, ll. 56–62)

By establishing such a stark contrast between the cruel realities of rural poverty and its 'picturesque' pastoral form, Crabbe clears the way for a new poetic mode '[a]s truth will paint it, and as bards will not'. This mode of poetic truthfulness anticipates the clarity of vision exercised by William Wordsworth and John Clare, among other Romantic poets, but Crabbe's poetic rendering of this rural landscape – the 'frowning coast' of his native Aldeburgh in Suffolk – is equally marked by the more formal and structured poetic diction of his predecessors such as Alexander Pope. There is a sustained and regular quality in Crabbe's vision of 'sad splendour' which mocks the meagre practical resources it provides for its inhabitants:

Where the thin harvest waves its wither'd ears;
Rank weeds, that every art and acre defy,
Reign o'er the land and rob the blighted rye ...
There poppies nodding, mock the hope of toil,
There the blue bugloss paints the sterile soil;
Hardy and high, above the slender sheaf,
The slimy mallow waves her silky leaf;
O'er the young shoot the charlock throws a shade,
And the wild tare clings round the sickly blade ... (p. 159, ll. 66–76)

The passage's botanic imagery reflects Crabbe's personal expertise on the subject.* The colourful and varied image of the weed-strewn field of

---

* Before taking orders as an Anglican clergyman, Crabbe had studied medicine and botany; his knowledge of Suffolk and other areas of the English countryside is later reflected in his contribution on natural history to the compendious *History and Antiquities of Leicestershire* (8 volumes, 1795–1815).

rye – aesthetically pleasing in its own right but here an indication of poor agricultural yields – echoes the previous contrast Crabbe discerned between the pointless beauties of pastoral poetry versus the 'truthful' (and therefore, by association, productive) realm of his own verse.

The 'sad splendour' of Crabbe's rye field also reverses the contemporary vision of the English rural landscape that Goldsmith envisaged, in which the 'barren splendour' of a bountiful harvest offered practical value but little aesthetic appeal. Arguably, then, through the metaphor of the English agricultural landscape, Crabbe does engage in the same aesthetic debate as Goldsmith, even though he seeks elsewhere to distance his 'truthful' verse from the contemporary vogue for pastoral poetry.

Significantly, the image of the young girl betrayed and corrupted by man which is employed in Goldsmith's poem is also present here, but is used by Crabbe as a simile to extend the aesthetic misconception of the rye field ('[w]hose outward splendour is but Folly's dress,/ Exposing most, when most it gilds distress'). In other words, the shared image of the corrupted young girl is employed by Goldsmith to represent the urban corruption of rural innocence, but Crabbe's casual reference is made on aesthetic grounds alone. The tone of *The Village* changes dramatically, however, after this point. The remainder of the poem's description focuses on the rural lives and experience of the human population of the (unnamed) village. It is, broadly speaking, an unremittingly negative portrait of 'a wild amphibious race':

> With sullen woe display'd in every face;
> Who, far from civil arts and social fly,
> And scowl at strangers with suspicious eye. (p. 159, ll. 85–8)

Reduced to crime, drunken riot and other vices by 'fruitless toil' on the 'famish'd land', the inhabitants of Crabbe's rural landscape bear little resemblance to the contented self-sufficiency of Goldsmith's Auburn landowners. Anything but sentimental in its depiction of humanity reduced to the last extremes of social degradation, Crabbe's poem progresses through a series of rural scenes in order to survey the manifest effects of poverty. Early scenes contrast the opportunistic violence of strong young men engaged in acts of piracy with the weary resignation of the prematurely-aged labourer who seeks an end to his life of toil, honest but thankless, on other men's land. Powerfully, Crabbe's poem grants the labourer a voice with which he recognises the futility of his own life:

> '... Why do I live, when I desire to be
> At once from life and life's long labour free? ...
> These fruitful fields, these numerous flocks I see,
> Are others' gain, but killing cares to me ...
> A lonely, wretched man, in pain I go,
> None need my help and none relieve my woe ...' (p. 163, ll. 206–23).

In his final wish to 'let my bones beneath the turf be laid,/ And men forget the wretch they would not aid', the labourer resigns his last possession – his bones – to the rich man's land on which he has laboured for years. Like the Irish babies whose flesh provides a nourishing meal for the middle-class English readers of Swift's *Modest Proposal* (1729), Crabbe's rural labourer must relinquish his very body to the same source that has already 'consumed' the rest of his existence.

An overwhelming sense of resignation is also evident in the speaker's bitter evaluation of the parish poorhouse's insane or mentally handicapped residents as having the 'happiest' release from rural suffering. Here too, however, in an extended description of the poorhouse and its inhabitants, the speaker angrily addresses the poem's readers first-hand. Contrasting the 'real pain' and lonely death of the rural poor in the poorhouse with the imaginary ailments of the affluent, the speaker's repeated rhetorical questions suggest a challenging, almost aggressive tone:

> Say ye, opprest by some fantastic woes,
> Some jarring nerve that baffles your repose ...
> Who with sad prayers the weary doctor teaze
> To name the nameless ever-new disease;

Who with mock patience dire complaints endure,
Which real pain, and that alone can cure;
How would ye bear in real pain to lie,
Despis'd, neglected, left alone to die?
How would ye bear to draw your latest breath,
Where all that's wretched paves the way for death? (p. 164,
ll. 250–61)

Crabbe's poem has progressed from denouncing contemporary pastoral poetry, in the earlier passages, to questioning directly the complacent affluence of its middle-class readers. Other passages adopt a more generalised poetic perspective (as suggested by a preceding reference to 'the cold charities of man to man'), but there is little doubt that Crabbe sought to challenge the moral integrity of his first readers' views on rural poverty by presenting them with some harsh social realities.

To this end, the extended passage describing the parish poorhouse features a range of poetic devices to demonstrate that the 'cold charities of man to man' can be hopelessly ineffective. In addition to the poem's direct address to the reader already considered, the poorhouse episode contains two scathing portraits of rural inhabitants employed by parish charity to help the poor – the parish doctor and the parish priest – which provide a stark contrast to their admirable and unceasingly generous counterparts in Goldsmith's Auburn (pp. 164–5, ll. 277 ff.) Here, the sneering and contemptuous parish doctor shows '[i]mpatience ... in his averted eyes' during the most cursory of visits to the poorhouse sickbed. As the time of death draws near, the parish priest – a 'jovial youth' otherwise occupied with hunting, playing cards, feasting and so on – fails to attend the sick man's deathbed.

It is later made clear that this priest considers 'his Sunday's task/ As much as God or man can fairly ask'; at the end of Book I, the funeral bier of the now-departed parishioner and the mourning crowd are portrayed 'waiting long' for the minister's arrival before leaving 'distrest,/ To think a poor man's bones should lie unblest'. Repeating the previous image of the weary labourer's bones laid to rest and forgotten, the final insult to *this* poor parishioner is that his burial in a communal paupers' grave (among the 'mingled relicks of the parish poor') is not even marked by a funeral.* Taken as a whole, the extended poetic episode depicting the inhabitants of the parish poorhouse builds up a moving, if unrelentingly bitter, narrative of charity's failure to relieve rural suffering and poverty.

Crabbe's depiction of the parish poorhouse and its inhabitants' experiences, framed by the larger poem, provides an extended version of the narratives featured in all of the poems considered in this chapter. In Crabbe's case, as well as the opportunity it provides him to 'answer' Goldsmith's Auburn narratives, the poorhouse episode combines the narrative progression of the parishioner's tale (from illness to an ignominious death) with the poignant symbolism of the poorhouse building's physical description:

> Such is that room which one rude beam divides,
> And naked rafters form the sloping sides;
> Where the vile bands that bind the thatch are seen,
> And lath and mud is all that lie between;
> Save one dull pane, that, coarsely patch'd, gives way
> To the rude tempest, yet excludes the day … (p. 164, ll. 262–7)

Like the weed-strewn field of rye, the very fabric of the poorhouse itself conveys the desperation of rural poverty. The building's threadbare construction and single patched window – that manages both to exclude light and allow in foul weather – anticipates how the Romantic poetic perspective often reinterprets its surroundings in a symbolically meaningful manner. In eighteenth-century poetry, the inclusion of progressively elaborate narrative fragments (such as that concerning Crabbe's poorhouse) may reflect the period's increasing taste – most evident in the popular growth of the novel – for narratives generally. In

---

* According to the Protestant liturgy, the act of commemorating the dead is not an official part of the priest's role. Here, the parish priest who '[d]efers his duty till the day of prayer' (i.e. Sunday service) is not technically committing an offence although, as in the twenty-first century, churchgoers would expect a parish priest to attend and pay some respects at the graveside of a parishioner.

the narrative fragments included in all of the poems considered here, it is apparent that their use in poetry develops significantly – in the fifty-five years between *The Seasons* and *The Task* – from Thomson's highly stylised pastoral vignettes to Cowper's tale of Crazy Kate (or Crabbe's poor parishioner) in which evocative physical descriptions are combined with detailed character portraits and rudimentary 'plots' over a passage of time.*

Book II of *The Village* witnesses a profound shift in the tone and intent of Crabbe's poem. The unremittingly gloomy portrait of rural poverty in Book I is immediately mollified with the speaker's acknowledgement that 'oft amid these woes/ Are gleams of transient mirth and hours of sweet repose'. What briefly follows is a more balanced depiction of rural life, considering the Sunday activities of a wider social and economic spectrum, although this, too, soon gives way to a wide-ranging portrait of rural vice as rife and varied as its urban counterpart (pp. 169–70, ll. 33–76.) Surprisingly evocative of Fielding's depiction of the rural landscape in *Tom Jones* (1749), Crabbe's catalogue of rural vices (ranging from slander, drunken fights and 'domestic broils' to the seduction of young women and the theft of a landowner's property) comes to an end with another direct address to the reader which, like Fielding's narrator in *Tom Jones*, allows the speaker to occupy a particular moral high ground in his recognition of both vice and virtue among *all* of the social classes:

> Yet why, you ask, these humble crimes relate,
> Why make the poor as guilty as the great?
> To show the great, those mightier sons of Pride,
> How near in vice the lowest are allied ...
> So shall the man of power and pleasure see
> In his own slave as vile a wretch as he;
> In his luxurious lord the servant find
> His own low pleasures and degenerate mind;

* See, for example, in Thomson's *Summer*, the stories of Celadon and Amelia (ll. 894–944) and Damon and Sacharissa (ll. 966–1036) and the sentimental portrait of the elderly shepherd in *Winter* (ll. 350–95).

And each in all the kindred vices trace
Of a poor, blind, bewilder'd, erring race;
Who, a short time in varied fortune past,
Die, and are equal in the dust at last. (pp. 170–1, ll. 77–100)

This passage serves two purposes. It mitigates the repeated images of death associated with the rural poor in Book I with the Christian image of universal death (which brings equality between all social classes) that Crabbe foregrounds here. In asserting that the realm of human vice – and virtue – are *equally* accessible to rich and poor men, these lines also make the transition which allows Crabbe to celebrate – as he does for the remainder of Book II – the virtues of a rich man. The man in question is the dead military hero Robert Manners, under whose brother Charles, fourth Duke of Rutland (1754–87), Crabbe had served as ducal chaplain since 1782.[21] In Book II, Robert Manners is commemorated in the form of a verse elegy which celebrates his life as a series of heroic glories, the example of which shall live on in future 'guardians of the land':

Oh! Make the age to come thy better care,
See other RUTLANDS, other GRANBYS there;
And as thy thoughts through streaming ages glide,
See other heroes die as MANNERS died … (p. 173, ll. 194–7)

A satisfactory explanation of the incongruous nature of Book II's content (compared with Book I's portrait of rural poverty) remains elusive. Ronald Hatch reasonably observes, however, that the utterly bleak nature of social injustice that Crabbe paints in Book I leaves little room for poetic manoeuvre:

Suppose it had proved impossible to find such a man [as Manners]. The conclusion would be that nothing anyone could do would have meaning. In rejecting the pastoral world in which man lives in harmony with nature, Crabbe developed a world in which nature is either indifferent or hostile to man. Such a 'naturalistic' world places man on the same plane as other animals, and seems to make him the slave of his passions and instincts.[22]

There would be no place, in such a world, for either pastoral poetry or the 'truthful' poetry of social conscience that Crabbe offers his readers. Carried to its logical extreme, Crabbe's stark vision of rural poverty and middle-class indifference in Book I (and universal human vice in Book II) would make all poetry – or any other form of human endeavour seeking social progress and justice – utterly meaningless. As a Christian minister and a poet, Crabbe was highly unlikely to accept this position as his 'final word' on any subject, never mind the pressing moral issue of social injustice he addresses in *The Village*.

This does not suggest that Crabbe's recognition of the heroic virtues of a dead nobleman is itself intended to serve as a poetic 'resolution' to the social injustice and rural poverty presented in Book I. The resolution – perhaps equally as unsatisfactory to many modern readers as the heroism of Manners – comes in the theme of Christian virtue which, in death, unites the heroism of Manners with the suffering of the rural poor:

> Life is not valu'd by the time we live ...
> But 'tis the spirit that is mounting high
> Above the world; a native of the sky;
> The noble spirit, that, in dangers brave,
> Calmly looks on, or looks beyond the grave. (p. 173, ll. 172–80)

Crabbe and Cowper both struggled – as authors continue to do so in the twenty-first century – to integrate their deeply held convictions concerning social inequality and injustice with a need for public recognition. Then, as now, part of the task's challenge is the need to appeal to the sensibility of readers who serve as both the potential reformers of social injustice as well as its perpetrators. The social and moral remit assumed by late eighteenth-century authors such as Cowper and Crabbe, in particular, anticipates the poetic idealism that would be needed to usher in a new age of poetry in the next decade.

Notes

1   On the development of Romanticism, see Jonathan Wordsworth's preface in Jonathan Wordsworth and Jessica Wordsworth (eds), *The New Penguin Book of Romantic Poetry* (London: Penguin Books, 2003), pp. xiii–xxxix.

2   On the general history of the Enclosure Acts during the eighteenth century, see J. R. Wordie, 'The Chronology of English Enclosure, 1500–1914', *Economic History Review*, n.s. 36:4 (November 1983), pp. 483–505; and Michael E. Turner, *English Parliamentary Enclosure: Its Historical Geography and Economic History* (Folkestone: Dawson Press, 1980).

3   On the history of electoral practice in England prior to 1832, see W. A. Speck, *Tory and Whig: The Struggle in the Constituencies 1701–15* (London: Macmillan, 1970); and Frank O'Gorman, *Voters, Patrons and Parties: The Unreformed Electorate of Hanoverian England 1734–1832* (Oxford: Clarendon Press, 1989).

4   William Cowper, *The Task* (London, 1785). All further citations of this primary text refer to this source. Also available through *Eighteenth Century Collections Online*, www.jisc-collections.ac.uk/ecco (hereafter *ECCO*).

5   James Thomson, *The Seasons: Autumn* (London, 1730), pp. 172–3, ll. 113–27. All further citations of this primary text refer to this source. Also available through *ECCO*.

6   See 'Thomson, James (1700–1748)', in H. C. G. Matthew and Brian Harrison (eds), *Oxford Dictionary of National Biography* (Oxford: Oxford University Press, 2004).

7   On the development of the notion of 'the Sublime' in the eighteenth century, see Tom Huhn, 'Burke's Sympathy for Taste', *Eighteenth-century Studies*, 35:3 (Spring 2002), pp. 379–93; and M. H. Abrams, 'From Addison to Kant: Modern Aesthetics and the Exemplary Art', in Ralph Cohen (ed.), *Studies in Eighteenth-century British Art and Aestheticism* (Berkeley: University of California Press, 1985), pp. 16–48.

8   But also see, on this point, Thomas B. Gilmore, 'Implicit Criticism of Thomson's *The Seasons* in Johnson's *Dictionary*', *Modern Philology*, 86:3 (February 1989), pp. 265–73.

9   Earl Miner, 'From Narrative to "Description" and "Sense" in Eighteenth-century Poetry', *Studies in English Literature 1500–1900: The Restoration and Eighteenth-century*, 9:3 (Summer 1969), p. 476.

10   T. E. Blom: 'Eighteenth-century Reflexive Process Poetry', *Eighteenth-century Studies*, 10:1 (Autumn 1976), p. 68.

11   Ibid., p. 60.

12   Oliver Goldsmith, *The Deserted Village,* in Lawrence Lipking and James Noggle (eds), *The Norton Anthology of English Literature*, Volume C: *The Restoration and the Eighteenth Century* (New York and London: W. W. Norton, 2006), pp. 2877–86, at p. 2883, ll. 265–80. All further citations of this primary text refer to this edition.

13   Blom, 'Eighteenth-century Reflexive Process Poetry', p. 55. A similar point is made regarding Crabbe and Goldsmith (and, more surprisingly, Thomson) by Ronald B. Hatch, 'George Crabbe and the Tenth Muse', *Eighteenth-century Studies*, 7:3 (Spring 1974), p. 274.

14   On Goldsmith's political agenda in this poem, see Alfred Lutz, 'The Politics of Reception: The Case of Goldsmith's *The Deserted Village*', *Studies in Philology*, 95:2 (Spring 1998), pp. 174–96, especially p. 178.

15   Ibid., p. 177.

16   Ibid.

17   W. A. Speck, *Stability and Strife: England 1714–1760* (London: Edward Arnold, 1980), p. 68.

18   George Crabbe, *The Village*, in Norma Dalrymple-Champneys (ed.), *The Complete Poetical Works* (Oxford: Oxford University Press, 1988), Volume 1, pp. 155–74. All further citations of this primary text refer to this source.

19   Hatch, 'George Crabbe and the Tenth Muse', p. 276.

20   On this point, see Hatch, 'George Crabbe and the Tenth Muse', pp. 278–9. Johnson's views here also reflect his well-known dismissal (in *The Lives of the English Poets*, published in stages between 1779 and 1781) of Milton's much earlier pastoral elegy *Lycidas* (1637) on charges of artificiality and a lack of 'truth'.

21   Alastair W. Massie, 'Charles Manners, Fourth Duke of Rutland (1754–87)', *ODNB*.

22   Hatch, 'George Crabbe and the Tenth Muse', p. 288.

Fact and Fiction: Defoe, Fielding and Sterne

Novels often focus on how an individual develops in moral, emotional and psychological terms, yet novels – paradoxically – reflect anything but authentic human experience. By their very nature, novels are consciously artificial forms that convey something readers recognise as a semblance of authentic experience. This concept of the novel helps us to understand its development in relation to other literary forms which occupy that uncertain territory between notions of authentic and artificial – or 'true' and 'false', 'fact' and 'fiction' – during this period.

The Authority of the Printed Word

Part of the reason for the novel's success within this uncertain territory is its medium. It has long been established that human beings associate the printed word with a sense of credible authority less readily afforded to other forms of communication. As Ian Watt asserts:

> Print, to the reader, is no fallible specimen of humanity – no actor, bard or speaker who must prove himself worthy of credence: it is a material reality which can be seen by all the world and which can outlive everyone in it. Nothing printed has any of the individuality, the margin of error, the assertion of personal

idiosyncrasy, which even the best manuscript retains; it is more like an impersonal fiat which – partly because the State and the Church print their messages, and so hallow the medium – has received the stamp of universal social approbation. We do not, instinctively at least and until experience has made us wise, question what has appeared in print.[1]

To a large degree, Watt's argument concerning the universal acceptance of the seemingly objective – because impersonal – authority of the printed word is still borne out by twenty-first-century cultural practice. The printed word sustains its authority in legal transactions concerning property, inheritance, marriage and taxation, to name but a few. The very notion of identity itself, at least as defined by documentation such as certificates of birth and death, or passports, may also be considered in this context. The invention of the printing press wrought such profound cultural change that all forms of printed matter gained some degree of implicit authority over their predecessors in the form of oral communication and manuscripts.[2] (This topic is discussed further in Part Four: 'A Culture of Print'.)

A paradox exists at the very heart of this cultural change. In England, at least, there is a widespread cultural assumption that something much older than the English legal system stands behind the way that property, marriage or taxation are regulated. We might describe it as 'custom' or 'tradition'. The relationship between custom and law is ancient and complex but, as J. G. A. Pocock has argued, closer historical scrutiny reveals that the true origins of English law are rather less obscure than might first be thought:

> The ideology of the Ancient Constitution can be accounted for by means of a purely structural explanation: all English law was common law, common law was custom, custom rested on the presumption of immemoriality; property, social structure, and government existed as defined by the law and were therefore presumed to be immemorial. But if we think of it as ideology, as coming into being as social creatures sought new ways of

conceptualizing themselves, we can characterize it as a mode of civic consciousness particularly appropriate to a gentry asserting itself in parliament, in litigation, and in the local administration of the common law.[3]

English law is grounded on a paradoxical 'presumption' that certain social traditions or customs have been in place since time immemorial (perhaps before history first began to be recorded). In reality, English laws concerning property, social structure and government were first inscribed by the English gentry – who were the principal owners of property and the leaders of government – in order to safeguard their own interests. It is *their* particular interests or, as Pocock puts it, their 'ideology', which have been transcribed into English law, politics and social practice. 'Ideology' is a useful term in this context because it encompasses not only a person's political loyalties or affiliations but also their ideals and values concerning religion, morality, economic practice, social hierarchy and decorum.

Readers and authors, then as now, possess their own ideological perception of present reality ('truth') and of past reality ('history'), elements of which they share with other people.[4] An historical account of an event (such as a battle, a monarch's reign, the development of the slave trade) is clearly the product of a particular ideological framework, but so too are the methods by which writers attempt to gain credence for their own version of history or truth. Whether by using eyewitness accounts, or displaying their capacity to cite Classical or contemporary sources, or to seek justification for their beliefs in the Bible, writers – including novelists – demonstrate their ideological commitments to distinct cultural values. An awareness of ideological values will help to inform our reading of any literary genre but it is particularly valuable when considering the genesis of the novel because that genre presents us with a narrative essentially concerned with notions of authenticity, that is the depiction of 'history' and 'truth'.

News, History and the Novel

The English novel emerges out of the ideological upheavals that the Civil War, and its aftermath in the Restoration of the monarchy in 1660, wrought on English popular culture. In particular, the novel's early development is related to the growing availability and diversity of printed 'news' (current events) and 'history' (past events) during this period. As Pocock explains:

> An increase in the capacity of Western men to understand history presented itself in the form of an acute and growing awareness of the potential quarrel between value and history, virtue and history, personality and history; and the growth of theories of progress during the eighteenth century is not to be understood without understanding of this counterpoint.[5]

In other words, the English Civil War brought with it a growing awareness that different ideological 'versions' of recent history could co-exist in print. It is no accident that, in England, the establishment of periodical forms such as the newspaper coincides with the English Civil War. Prior to this period, news of current events had first been circulated orally via the parish pulpit, and was later sold by travelling salesmen or chapmen in cheap printed formats such as chapbooks or ballads.[6] Michael McKeon has argued that the partisan politics of the English Civil War garnered fresh scepticism regarding the authenticity of news reports even while it helped to establish its ascendance as a 'discursive entity' quite distinct from popular ballads:

> The combination of revolutionary politics and a succession of governments whose left-wing Protestantism ensured a relative freedom of the press led to an unparalleled efflorescence of news reporting. The effect of this outpouring was double. On the one hand, it helped validate the new as worthy of attention and to associate news with the historical authenticity of printed

documents. On the other hand, the experience of comparing highly partisan and divergent 'true accounts' of the same events induced a considerable scepticism regarding the ostentatious claims to historicity which had already become quite conventional.[7]

This dialectical pattern in the growth of news reporting – its cultural validation and simultaneous sceptical reception during the Civil War – is central to an understanding of McKeon's wider discussion of the origins of the English novel.[*] [8] Importantly, it also emphasises the political impetus behind the rapid increase and dissemination of printed matter in seventeenth-century England. By the time of the English Civil War, the press provided a well-established (though not necessarily state-licensed) medium through which Royalists and Parliamentarians could articulate their own versions of current events and – significant to our investigation of the novel – recent history. The political upheaval and partisanship of the Civil War period galvanised ideological tensions already extant within English culture and literature concerning notions of 'truth'.

Even before the Civil War, however, there is literary evidence of sceptical responses to the veracity of printed news. Naive Mopsa, in Shakespeare's *Winter's Tale*, is sure that the ballads sold by the roguish Autolycus are 'true' merely because they are printed; Autolycus's own description of the incredible content of his ballads suggests otherwise:

> Here's one to a very doleful tune, how a usurer's wife was brought to bed of twenty money-bags at a burden, and how she longed to eat adders' heads and toads carbonadoed … Here's the midwife's name to't, one Mistress Tail-Porter, and five or six honest wives' that were present. Why should I carry lies abroad?[9]

The ballad's 'news' is clearly fantastical, yet Autolycus supports its authenticity (as is the case with much of today's journalism) with the

---

* A 'dialectical' system is one in which mutually dependent social forces remain in constant opposition to each other. McKeon's introduction gives a substantial overview of dialectical method in literary history as it relates to the origins of the novel, pp. 1–22.

'evidence' of eyewitness accounts and a rhetorical appeal to his audience's common sense. This reference indicates how well-established such journalistic strategies already were by Shakespeare's period; it also provides a glimpse into the origins of the publication and dissemination of news in sixteenth- and early seventeenth-century England.

England's interest in, and taste for, printed news continued to increase during the sixteenth and early seventeenth centuries until what McKeon describes as its 'unparalleled efflorescence' from the period of the Civil War onwards. The regular circulation of printed news brings with it an acute cultural awareness that events in the immediate past and the present are directly related to each other. It is perhaps not surprising, therefore, that the vast majority of early English novelists set their plots in the immediate present or recent past. More than fifty years ago, Ian Watt suggested that the novel broke with the 'earlier literary tradition of using timeless stories to mirror the unchanging moral verities':

> The novel's plot is also distinguished from most previous fiction
> by its use of past experience as the cause of present action: a
> causal connexion operating through time replaces the reliance of
> earlier narratives on disguises and coincidences, and this tends to
> give the novel a much more cohesive structure.[10]

It should also be noted that many early novels, including *Tom Jones* (1749) and *Tristram Shandy* (1759–67), continue to exploit traditional plot devices such as disguise and coincidence but do so in a markedly self-conscious manner. This tendency points to an increasing awareness with which such authors manipulated certain plot conventions, for example the passage of time. As the opening of Book II of *Tom Jones* also demonstrates, such writing continued to take for its literary context a wide spectrum of other popular forms in which claims to historical 'truth' were self-evident:

> Tho' we have properly enough entitled this our work, a history,
> and not a life; nor an apology for a life, as is more in fashion; yet
> we intend in it rather to pursue the method of those writers, who

profess to disclose the revolutions of countries, than to imitate the painful and voluminous historian, who, to preserve the regularity of his series, thinks himself obliged to fill up as much paper with the detail of months and years in which nothing remarkable happened, as he employs upon those notable æras when the greatest scenes have been transacted on the human stage.

Such histories, as these do, in reality, very much resemble a newspaper, which consists of just the same number of words, whether there be any news in it or not … .[11]

Henry Fielding's techniques in his prose fiction also relate to the dramatic genre in which he first established his literary career. For ten years Fielding had written highly successful plays, but his outspoken criticism of Walpole's government led directly to the passage of the Licensing Act in 1737 (and thus the end of his career as a playwright). Character-revealing dialogue, dramatic revelations and a densely packed, highly structured plot feature in all of his novels. A defining feature of his prose fiction, however, is Fielding's use of an omniscient narrator who engages directly – conversationally, even – with the reader. The many prefatory commentaries voiced by this narrator in *Tom Jones* collectively provide a kind of literary 'mission statement'. In the first chapter of Book VIII, for example, the narrator warns against the employment of supernatural or 'marvellous' elements in fiction (ghosts, 'elves and fairies, and other such mummery'):

To say the truth, if the historian will confine himself to what really happened, and utterly reject any circumstance, which, tho' never so well attested, he must be well assured is false, he will sometimes fall into the marvellous, but never into the incredible … It is by falling into fiction, therefore, that we generally offend against this rule, of deserting probability, which the historian seldom if ever quits, till he forsakes his character, and commences a writer of romance. (VIII.i.363–4)

Through this narrator (as elsewhere in his canon, such as his 1742 preface to *Joseph Andrews*), Fielding establishes a detailed framework of literary principles and cultural ideals underpinning his prose fiction. The coolly rational – but entirely genial – tone of the narrator in *Tom Jones* provides a particular kind of authorial companion for readers, a fellow observer of the universal qualities of human nature as revealed through this particular narrative. His presence ensures that Fielding's readers are constantly reminded of the distance that separates the artificial realm being depicted (for all of its 'probability') and the more tangible realm inhabited by readers and authors.

Narrators and Chronological Time in the Novel

All three novels considered in this chapter feature a fictional narrator who speaks directly to his readers. HF, the narrator of Defoe's *Journal of the Plague Year* (1722), is simply presented as an authentic eyewitness who recollects first-hand his memories of the events depicted in the text. The companionable narrator of *Tom Jones* takes the position of an authorial presence who converses directly with his readers; he also acknowledges a wider dialogue concerning specific cultural contexts in which readers and authors are both engaged. Ostensibly presented as a work of autobiography, Sterne's *Tristram Shandy* is narrated by Tristram himself. As both the protagonist of his own narrative, and the mediator between his readers and his dogged efforts to produce a comprehensive textual rendition of his own 'life and opinions', Tristram's position becomes increasingly – though humorously – untenable.

All three authors also engage directly with actual historical episodes in these early novels, although their methods and intentions widely differ. The compendious nature of the footnotes that accompany most editions of *Tristram Shandy* attests to the staggering wealth of cultural information, both ancient and modern, contained within it. The novel incorporates authentic historical events – in particular, the Siege of Namur in 1695 – and past events in the lives of its fictional narrator and his family.* It also addresses fundamental problems concerning the textual depiction of the passage of time in a narrative. On a number of occasions, Tristram's remarkable ability to keep numerous time-frames going – in different but simultaneously narrated stories – leads to memorably comic results.

In the twenty-eighth chapter of Volume VII, for example, Tristram is caught at a kind of chronological crossroads between three separate narratives concerning France. Two relate to memories of separate journeys made to Auxerre (one as a young man with his father and uncle Toby, the other as a middle-aged invalid); the third narrative concerns the 'present moment' in which he is writing:

> I have been getting forwards in two different journies together, and with the same dash of the pen-for I have got entirely out of Auxerre in this journey which I am writing now, and I am got halfway out of Auxerre in that which I shall write hereafter ... I have brought myself into such a situation, as no traveller ever stood before me; for I am this moment walking across the market-place of Auxerre with my father and my uncle Toby, in our way back to dinner---and I am this moment also entering Lyons with my post-chaise broke into a thousand pieces—and I am moreover this moment in a handsome pavilion ... upon the banks of the Garonne ... and where I sit now rhapsodizing all these affairs.[12]

Even while it celebrates the dynamic energy that allows fictional narrative to encompass all conceivable space and time within its creative compass, this passage highlights the artificiality of a narrative that attempts such an impossible task. Human perception of the passage of time is subjective and relative, as are the causal connections between past, present and future events. Conventional practice dictates that the act of reading a page of text is linear and one-directional. In his attempt

---

* The 1695 Siege of Namur was part of the War of the Grand Alliance (also known as the Nine Years' War) between England and France (1688–97). It ended with the signing of the Treaty of Ryswick.

to combine these irreconcilable propositions, Tristram's narrative shifts, in turns slowly or rapidly, forward, backwards and sideways through time and space. If Tristram's narrative, ultimately, expresses the implicit failure of literature to replicate human experience, it is a particularly glorious and energetic failure.

Tristram's earnest intention to produce a truly comprehensive narrative, in all of its digressive and simultaneously progressive complexity, is announced early on. In a tone slightly reminiscent of Fielding's genial narrator in *Tom Jones*, he assures readers that

> as you proceed further with me, the slight acquaintance which is now beginning between us, will grow into familiarity; and that, unless one of us is in fault, will terminate in friendship ... then nothing which has touched me will be thought trifling in its nature, or tedious in its telling. (I.vi.10)

His confident tone in this passage is misplaced, since much of what the reader finds has 'touched' Tristram's life *will* be judged – and enjoyed, in comic terms – as both trifling and tedious. The tacit point that Sterne makes here is a profound one concerning the nature of the novel, if not the nature of all literature: it is for readers to come to their own conclusions concerning the material contained within this narrative, not Tristram. In making this observation, albeit via the trials and tribulations of his hapless narrator, Sterne's work sets a wholly new cultural agenda for the English novel.

Realism and the London Landscape in Defoe's *Journal*

Much of the convincing semblance of realism achieved by Defoe's *Journal* is based in its inclusion of authentic historical data superimposed against a characteristically accurate and detailed depiction of London's landscape. Indeed, for the first thirty years or so after its anonymous publication, Defoe's *Journal* was widely accepted as a genuine historical account of London's Great Plague of

1665 as related by a surviving eyewitness.[13] Known to readers only by his initials ('HF'), the narrator charts each detail of the devastation wrought upon the people and landscape he describes, both as witnessed from his residence 'without Aldgate about mid-way between Aldgate Church and White-Chappel Bars, on the left Hand or North-side of the Street', and from his many journeys around London's parishes and streets. The realism of this narrative, closer to what we might now describe as 'reportage', is also recognisable in Defoe's 1704 work *The Storm* (which considers, through a series of eyewitness accounts, the devastation wrought across Europe by an enormous storm in late November 1703).[14] In both cases, Defoe offers readers an account of a traumatic event still familiar in their memory, as well as the preliminary stages and immediate aftermath as experienced by a wide spectrum of different social classes. The *Journal*'s narrator is entirely fictional, though some critical speculation has suggested that HF may represent at least the historical perspective that was available to Defoe's uncle Henry Foe.[15] The authenticity of diverse voices in *The Storm*, presented as a series of eyewitness reports from letters collated by an editor, is still very much subject to critical debate.[16]

The Storm and *Journal of the Plague Year* clearly demonstrate their author's talent for capitalising on current events with timely works of fiction. By 1720, another outbreak of bubonic plague had returned to Europe, reaching Marseilles on the southern coast of France. Then as now, public anxiety about the possibility of contagion reaching England spreads far more quickly than disease itself. London's booksellers had ample time to exploit the public mood through the re-publication of plague-related literature from the 1665 outbreak. As John Mullan explains in his introduction to the *Journal*:

> Such books were advertised alongside Defoe's *Journal* in the press and would have been available alongside it in the booksellers' shops. Any one of the first readers of Defoe's 'novel' (as we now call it) would naturally take it to be one of this flurry of plague-excited documentary publications. The very circumstances that

probably stirred Defoe's fiction-making thoughts guaranteed that his fake memoir would be taken to be genuine.[17]

Defoe's *Journal* opens with the observation that, by late 1664, the Plague had 'returned to Holland'. In the 1720s, Holland was one of England's closest political and trading allies, thus tacitly emphasising for the text's first readers just how possible were the chances of infection.

One of the most striking aspects of the *Journal's* realism is Defoe's seamless juxtaposition of authentic facts with fictional material. The factual elements are discernible in both the detailed references to actual locations and the frequent inclusion of statistics and legislation related to the epidemic. A great deal of statistical information from the Bills of Mortality (weekly listings of fatalities which occurred in each London parish, categorised by cause of death) offer their own grim narrative of the Plague's increasing hold on the London populace. Mullan notes that the Mortality Bills for the period of epidemic were anonymously published in 1712 as *London's Dreadful Visitation* and were readily employed as a source by Defoe during the composition of his fictional narrative.[18]

For modern readers, the inclusion of Mortality Bills in the *Journal* provides a stark indication of contemporary ignorance concerning the bubonic plague during the seventeenth and eighteenth centuries. Since its true cause – and means of its prevention – were unknown, its occasional outbreak was seen by many contemporaries in terms of its 'providential' (that is, divine) significance.[19] HF's observations record many examples of religious hysteria and superstition occasioned by the Plague. These episodes attest to Defoe's conviction that humanity, facing its greatest fear – the fear of the unknown – will believe in virtually anything:

> But there was still another Madness beyond all this, which may serve to give an Idea of the distracted humour of the poor People at that Time; and this was their following a worst sort of Deceivers than any of these; for these petty Thieves only deluded them to pick their Pockets, and get their Money ... this was in

wearing Charms, Philters, Exorcisms, Amulets, and I know not what Preparations, to fortify the Body with them against the Plague; as if the Plague was not the Hand of God, but a kind of Possession of an evil Spirit; and that it was to be kept off with Crossings, Signs of the Zodiac, Papers tied up with so many Knots... . (pp. 48–9)

HF refers to the myriad of false prophets, soothsayers, quacks, astrologers and other tricksters who operate during the epidemic as 'Oracles of the Devil'. This is not to suggest that they are directly inspired by the Devil, but that they do the Devil's work for him by distracting people from true religious fear and penitence. HF's observations reveal at length his grave disapproval of such trickery as well as the faith he personally places in God's power. Significantly, he also notes that some social classes are more vulnerable to deception than others:

But it was impossible to make any Impression upon the middling People, and the working labouring Poor; their Fears were predominant over all their Passions; and they threw away their Money in a most distracted Manner upon those Whymsies. Maid-Servants especially and Men-Servants, were the chief of their Customers; and their Question generally was, *Oh Sir! For the Lord's Sake, what will become of me? Will my Mistress keep me, or will she turn me off? Will she stay here, or will she go into the Country? And if she goes into the Country, will she take me with her, or leave me here to be starv'd and undone.* And the like of Men-Servants. (p. 48)

He goes on to note that the plight of London servants was particularly 'dismal' as many were left jobless by their employers' departure from London. While such comments reveal the (relatively) elevated social position from which HF views events, they simultaneously provide a socioeconomic dimension, also seen in *The Storm*, to the crisis at hand. Both texts exemplify Defoe's consummate ability to combine emotional intensity with the rational objectivity of economic journalism.

Given the solidly rational stance HF displays here, it is curious that he chooses to stay in London at all, thereby risking the personal danger of infection. His intense desire to bear first-hand witness to the Plague's effects overrides any passing urge to leave, despite his having 'several friends and relations in Northampton' and a sister in Lincolnshire 'very willing to receive' him. Early on, however, HF seeks and finds divine endorsement for staying put when he consults his Bible:

> from that Moment I resolv'd to stay in the Town, and casting myself entirely upon the Goodness and Protection of the Almighty, would not seek any other Shelter whatever; and that as my Times were in his Hands, he was as able to keep me in a Time of the Infection as in a Time of Health; and if he did not think fit to deliver me, still I was in his Hands, and it was meet he should do with me as should seem good to him. (p. 34)

Like Robinson Crusoe, HF engages in a form of bibliomancy, seeking providential guidance at a pivotal moment which subsequently directs the protagonist's actions throughout the rest of the narrative.[20] This religious tendency aligns HF with Defoe's own convictions even while it provides what may be interpreted (by a more secular reader) as questionable justification for risking death.

Beyond his religious conviction and his compulsion to bear witness to the Plague's horrors first hand, HF's character remains almost entirely unknown to the reader. As such, can he be considered as the work's true protagonist? If not (the reader is tempted to wonder), then, who is? It might be argued that the Plague itself occupies this position. In this reading, the text's protagonist is an amorphous and unthinkingly destructive entity that shifts, develops and impacts on the lives of many people during the course of the narrative, before finally departing as mysteriously as it arrived in the first place. Alternatively, Anthony Burgess has suggested that the city of London itself may serve as the novel's protagonist.[21] Against the odds, London survives the pestilence and sustains its characteristic bustling cosmopolitan presence. As in Haywood's *Fantomina* (1725) and Defoe's own *Moll Flanders* (1722),

London as depicted in the *Journal* contains a wide social and economic spectrum of humanity open to the shifts and re-inventions of identity that such an urban landscape makes possible. In the *Journal*, however, this urban presence occupies centre-stage as its communal plight – rather than that of any individual London resident – is the reader's primary focus.

The inclusion of many anecdotes and dramatic vignettes throughout the *Journal* underscores (in the parlance of modern-day journalism) the 'human interest' dimension of the Plague's effects. These 'mini-narratives' relate instances of families torn apart, or a father in tears over the body of a dead child, yet conspicuously absent from these stories is any mention of names or physical descriptions of individuals. Juxtaposed against the bleakly anonymous statistics listed in the Mortality Bills, and related by a narrator who remains very nearly as nameless and faceless as his human subjects, the *Journal*'s many anomalies are strongly indicative of the novel's early stage of development and Defoe's magpie-like tendency to include many contrasting literary elements in his writing. Though set retrospectively, the timely nature of Defoe's subject matter in the *Journal* – as with all of the novels considered in this chapter – foregrounds the early novel's firm commitment to the contemporary issues which interested its first readers.

Tom Jones: The Comic Novel and the Classical Tradition

In comparison to Defoe, Fielding's more selective mode of realism proffers a world in which, as R. P. C. Mutter explains:

> imaginary characters rub shoulders with real people – where Beau Nash can speak to Mrs Western, and the real landlady of the 'Bell' at Gloucester, Mrs Whitefield, can dine with the fictitious Tom Jones and lawyer Dowling. In the background, and sometimes in the foreground, are the events of the Jacobite rising of 1745–6, against which Fielding had inveighed in his weekly papers *The True Patriot* and *The Jacobite's Journal*. Tom, with the Jacobite

Partridge ignorantly in tow, sets off to fight the rebels, and Sophia is mistaken for the Young Pretender's mistress, Jeanie Cameron.[22]

The inclusion of authentic elements situates *Tom Jones* firmly within its own political and historical period; it also provides a secondary means by which the reader may interpret the actions and moral behaviour of fictional characters – such as Tom or Sophia – within the framework of Fielding's own ideological loyalties.

The unfolding narrative of Fielding's great comic novel is observed through the mediating presence of a narrator who also ostensibly occupies the role of author. His story begins with the discovery of a baby in the bed of the revealingly named Squire Allworthy, a genial Somersetshire landowner, who raises the infant Tom as a gentleman despite his apparent illegitimate birth. The novel's primary plot concerns the relationship between Tom and Sophia (the charming daughter of Allworthy's neighbour Squire Western), and the mutual trials and tribulations undergone by both parties. A large cast of secondary and more minor characters also feature, along with an extremely complex series of sub-plots.

All of these elements complement and contribute to a conclusion which leads to the happy union of Tom and Sophia and the unravelling of the mystery concerning Tom's true parentage. Though complex in detail, the plot of *Tom Jones* follows a patterned structure in which eighteen books (comprising about 200 chapters) are split into three groups of six featuring, consecutively, the early lives of the main characters, their journeys to London, and the events that occur within London itself. A series of remarkable coincidences throughout the plot interweaves events from the past (concerning Tom's birth) with the present and emphasises the sense of an overriding structure which dictates the narrative's movement.

Ian Watt rightly notes that plot clearly overrides depiction or development of individual characters in *Tom Jones*, a strong indication of Fielding's debt to the Classical literary tradition.[23] The neoclassical elements of Fielding's canon have long provided a substantial basis for critical debate, not least because, as Nancy Mace argues, 'they affect our understanding of his originality, his use of and place in the literary tradition, and his affinities with other eighteenth-century writers'.[24] Fielding certainly drew heavily from the contemporary tradition of Classical imitation but he also incorporated elements of romance and the prevailing taste for moral literature. Indeed, *Tom Jones* implicitly interrogates the appropriateness of its Classical epic model (an ancient literary form in which plot is constructed through a series of traditional stages and parallel structures) through the depiction of its protagonist. Paradoxically, Tom's youth is marked by numerous bouts of sexual misconduct and foolish naivety although it is in these episodes that he attempts to emulate the model of a Classical hero.[25]

It is worth considering how Fielding's use of satirical irony and comic effect, combined with his imitation of Classical models such as the epic, compares with a mock-heroic work such as Pope's *Rape of the Lock* (1712–14). In the latter, Pope's adherence to his Classical model is strictly observed in terms of form (the heroic couplet, the epic poem) and a refined sense of authorial detachment towards the scenes being depicted. Pope's depiction of mock-battles is grounded in the aesthetic regularity of his writing while Fielding's rely for their humour on the depiction of distinctly non-heroic aspects of contemporary life. In one memorable scene Molly Seagrim, the lascivious daughter of Black George the gamekeeper, engages in a screaming fist fight with a mass of female locals in a graveyard. The mock-battle, 'in the Homerican Stile', evokes the lofty language of the epic tradition, now juxtaposed with scenes of grubby, distinctly rural, violence:

> Recount, O Muse, the names of those who fell on this fatal day.
> First Jemmy Tweedle felt on his hinder head the direful bone.
> Him the pleasant banks of sweetly winding Stower had
> nourished, where he first learnt the vocal art, with which,
> wandring up and down at wakes and fairs, he cheered the rural
> nymphs and swains, when upon the green they interweave the
> sprightly dance ... Next old Echepole, the sow-gelder, received a
> blow in his forehead from our Amazonian heroine, and
> immediately fell to the ground. He was a swinging fat fellow, and

fell with almost as much noise as a house. His tobacco-box dropt at the same time from his pocket, which Molly took up as lawful spoils. (IV.viii.173–4)

Fielding's renderings of the poorer inhabitants of this Somersetshire parish are clearly intended to satirise their unpolished behaviour. His pastoral references and language, however, equally serve another purpose, evoking the charms of the rural scene even as he mocks the locals. As Watt has argued, in this linguistic balancing act, as in his occasional employment of emblematic names (such as 'Allworthy' or 'Thwackum'), Fielding encourages readers to maintain their humorous detachment towards the subjects depicted.[26]

One particular local inhabitant merits closer attention. Goody Seagrim is depicted with typically vigorous humour when she berates her daughter Molly, pregnant out of wedlock, for her actions:

> '[S]he hath brought a disgrace upon us all. She's the vurst of the vamily that ever was a whore.'

> 'You need not upbraid me with that, mother,' cries Molly, 'you yourself was brought to bed of sister there, within the week after you was married.'

> 'Yes, hussy,' answered the enraged mother, 'so I was, and what was the mighty matter of that? I was made an honest woman then; and if you was to be made an honest woman, I should not be angry; but you must have to doing with a gentleman, you nasty slut; you will have a bastard, hussy, you will; and that I defy anyone to say of me.' (IV.ix.177)

The literal approximation of Goody Seagrim's Somersetshire accent adds a theatrical comicality to her idiosyncratic views on premarital sex. Her moral standards, however, pale in comparison to the outright cruelty of characters such as Blifil or Lady Bellaston, whose distinguished birth increases their licence for immorality. Fielding's portrait of human nature is hardly prejudiced in favour of the upper classes; it tacitly asserts that wealth and nobility are no viable substitute for higher virtues – charity, kindness and common sense – as embodied by characters such as Squire Allworthy.*

A central question, never truly resolved, concerns the extent to which birth determines actions in later life. Tom's birth is ultimately revealed as gentle but illegitimate; if, as Ian Watt suggests, the narrator asserts that 'liberality of spirit' is 'scarce ever seen in men of low birth and education', it is rarely seen in Fielding's depiction of the social elite, either.[27] These views may be weighed against some pertinent observations made by Goody Seagrim herself, who notes that the circumstances of her own background and Squire Western's are less distant than their present circumstances might suggest:

> For poor as I am, I am a gentlewoman, And thof I was obliged, as my father, who was a clergyman, died worse than nothing, and so could not give me a shilling of *potion* [sic], to undervalue myself, by marrying a poor man, yet I would have you to know, I have a spirit above all *them* things. Marry come up, it would better become Madam Western to look at home, and remember who her own grandfather was. Some of my family, for ought I know, might ride in their coaches, when the grandfathers of some voke walked a-voot. (IV.ix.178)

Goody Seagrim's lofty defence of her status as a 'gentlewoman' may be read in several ways. Her relative equality with Squire Western is borne out, not for the reasons she intends, but by the fact that Western is also driven by greed in his attempt to coerce Sophia into marrying Blifil. Goody's words, however, also echo the sentiments expressed by other female protagonists in contemporary literature. As a child, Defoe's Moll Flanders expresses an ambition to be a 'gentlewoman' on the external evidence of the genteel life of a neighbourhood prostitute. Mrs Seagrim's insistence that she has a 'spirit above all *them* things' also recalls the

---

* Nor, despite the erudite example set by the narrator himself, is learning a substitute for virtue, as demonstrated by the characterisation of Thwackum and Square.

spirited defence that Richardson's Pamela makes on behalf of her virtue. Fielding's evocation of such sentiments here is surely intentional, mocking as it does the naive misapplication of self-respect in females whose birth or dubious moral character makes such sentiments (in his views) utterly ludicrous.* [28] It was precisely this aspect of Richardson's *Pamela* with which Fielding took such strong exception; it is clear that Fielding's own deployment of a 'new style of writing' provided a satirical antidote to what he saw as Richardson's sanctimonious moralising while it offered his own – equally definitive – moral agenda.

The moral authority and mediating presence of Fielding's narrator in *Tom Jones* anticipates certain elements of the English novel's literary progression into the nineteenth century. In the novels of George Eliot, for example, the narrator's position is often similarly poised midway between the reader's world and the realm occupied by the text's fictional characters. The bawdiness and satirical content of *Tom Jones*, however, situates this novel firmly in a culture which its author shared with Swift and Pope. As we shall see in the next chapter on the novel, Fielding's debt to the popular Restoration theatre of the eighteenth century (particularly evident in his use of characterisation, dialogue and comic action) diverges markedly from the theatrical influences equally apparent in Frances Burney's novel *Evelina* (1778). The point of divergence is, specifically, these two authors' differing moral perceptions of sexual propriety. The sexual escapades of Fielding's protagonist are hardly celebrated in *Tom Jones*, but the frankness with which such behaviour is depicted would become progressively more unacceptable, at least in popular fiction, in the latter decades of the eighteenth century and beyond. Sexual frankness, in *Tom Jones*, is one clear indicator of this novel's relatively early place in the development of the eighteenth-century popular novel. While *Tom Jones* is clearly engaged with the kind of depictions of historical reality that will also feature in later novels, its use of characterisation and its Classically derived and formalised plot structure situate it firmly within Fielding's unique realm of narrative fiction.

---

* Fielding's well-known contempt for Richardson's *Pamela* (1740) is exemplified in his parodic *Joseph Andrews* (1742) and his anonymously published *Shamela* (1741).

Extended Commentary: Sterne, *The Life and Opinions of Tristram Shandy, Gentleman* (1759–67)

Tristram Shandy is a profoundly unusual literary work. Its singularity brought it both immediate commercial success and, in the longer term, cultural longevity. Its form challenges virtually every literary convention associated with contemporary prose fiction, yet it has also famously been described by one eminent critical theorist, Victor Shklovsky, as 'the most typical novel of all world literature'.* [29] These two descriptions at first appear irreconcilable; what *is* evident is that no study of the eighteenth-century novel would be complete without consideration of Sterne's work.

Tristram Shandy is a satirical narrative about the difficulties of composing narratives. It comprises nine volumes which Sterne composed over the course of seven years. Most stories start with a beginning but, as our narrator Tristram demonstrates to us, even beginning to tell the story of one's life is a task fraught with difficulty. Where does the story of an individual's life actually start? Is it at the first moment of remembered consciousness, or the moment of conception, or even before that, with the stories of one's parents or grandparents? Tristram attempts to begin his narrative at what he deems the right point (the moment of his conception) but the opening lines of the text suggest that already things are not quite going to plan. A lengthy quotation is offered in order to demonstrate, from the novel's very outset, the idiosyncratic nature of its protagonist's voice:

> I wish either my father, or my mother, or indeed, both of them, as they were in duty both equally bound to it, had minded what they were about when they begot me; had they duly consider'd how much depended upon what they were doing; - that not only

---

* As a consummate work of eighteenth-century satire, Sterne's work is indebted to a wide reading of many authors, principally François Rabelais (*c.* 1494–*c.* 1553), Miguel de Cervantes (1547–1616), Michel de Montaigne (1533–92), Robert Burton (1577–1640) and Jonathan Swift (1667–1745).

the production of a rational Being was concern'd in it, but that possibly the happy formation and temperature of his body, perhaps his genius and the very cast of his mind; --and, for aught they knew to the contrary, even the fortunes of his whole house might take their turn from the humours and dispositions which were then uppermost: Had they duly weighed and considered all this, and proceeded accordingly, - I am verily persuaded I should have made a quite different figure in the world, from that, in which the reader is likely to see me. (I.i.5)

With this apology for something (or someone) which 'might have been', the bemused reader is immediately presented with several important thematic features of the narrative to come. Here, for example, Tristram makes reference to matters of medicine and physiology: the notion of humours was of Classical origin, discussed in the writings of Hippocrates, but still current well into the eighteenth century.[*] Throughout *Tristram Shandy*, the narrator's many learned medical allusions, particularly to the study of gynaecology and obstetrics, underline a key parallel between the 'birth' of the narrative and the narrator's own birth. In both cases, a very arduous and protracted period of labour must first be endured by the narrator himself.

The work's title establishes certain expectations on the reader's part regarding how autobiographical narratives ought to progress. Here, such expectations are constantly held up for comic scrutiny. Tristram's aggrieved tone towards his parents in the opening passage already cited reflects his larger frustration at being unable to control a burgeoning narrative which slips, repeatedly, away from the matter at hand. His dilemma, resulting in his failure to get the story even to the stage when he is born until well into the third volume, is feelingly expressed:

---

[*] This theory suggests that the balance of characteristics in a human being's makeup, both physically and emotionally, relates to the proportionate amounts of the four cardinal 'humours' they possess – blood, phlegm, choler (yellow bile) and melancholy (black bile) – and that the balance of such humours is decided at the moment of conception.

O ye POWERS! (for powers ye are, and great ones too)-- which enable mortal man to tell a story worth the hearing,-- that kindly shew him, where he is to begin it,--and where he is to end it,-- what he is to put into it,--and what he is to leave out,--how much of it he is to cast into shade,--and whereabouts he is to throw his light! (III.xxiii.164)

As a conscientious and rather pedantic man, Tristram aims to leave out nothing that is relevant to the wider narrative of his 'life and opinions'. In his introduction to the novel, Ian Campbell Ross asserts that the above passage reflects both 'Tristram's exasperation but also Sterne's good sense' since the difficulties of storytelling clearly apply to both entities.[30] Autobiography implies a linear narrative, but human experience – the perception of reality itself in which each passing moment is combined with endless associated memories and speculations about the future – is anything but linear. Its demonstrative foregrounding of this central paradox of literary representation has rightly gained this novel much attention from, in particular, scholars of Russian Formalism such as Victor Shklovsky and Mikhail Bakhtin.[31] Their acknowledgement of *Tristram Shandy*'s importance within the context of the wider literary and novelistic tradition merits further consideration beyond the possible scope of this chapter; here, it must suffice to say that Sterne's ground-breaking text continues to serve, for some scholars, as the quintessential example of a profoundly influential literary genre precisely because it interrogates our understanding of that genre.

In acknowledging the conundrum of narrating human experience in written form, Tristram's efforts also uphold – while simultaneously demonstrating the impossibility of upholding – John Locke's profoundly influential philosophical concept concerning the association of ideas.* [32] While a clearer understanding of many aspects of Locke's philosophy will invaluably inform any appreciation of *Tristram Shandy*, readers will

---

* In 1700 (in the fourth edition of his *Essay*), Locke suggested how ideas can 'come to be so united in some Men's minds, that 'tis very hard to separate them, they always keep company'. See also Part Four: 'Man, Nature and Liberty' for a discussion of Locke.

172

equally realise that Tristram's own wholesale endorsement of Lockean precepts is sometimes at the very root of his difficulties.[33]

In describing the events which make up his own life, Tristram inevitably relates much of what happens in the lives of others. Tristram's immediate domestic circle includes his parents, his Uncle Toby (who, recovering from a war wound, has come to live near Shandy Hall), household servants including Obadiah and Susannah, and Uncle Toby's manservant Corporal Trim. Other local residents include the Roman Catholic Doctor Slop (who botches Tristram's delivery by forceps, damaging his nose in the process), Parson Yorick and the Shandy family's widowed neighbour Mrs Wadman (who has designs on Uncle Toby). In one sense it seems ironic that Tristram's voluminous autobiography produces a far more detailed depiction of others – in particular his father and Uncle Toby – than the protagonist himself. In another sense, however, this irony reflects the impossibility of separating these narratives. In telling the interconnected stories, Tristram repeatedly struggles to pick up the thread of his own narrative; the burgeoning reality of the text before him represents only a small fragment of the 'complete' – potentially infinite – narrative:

> I am this month one whole year older than I was this time twelve-month; and having got, as you perceive, almost into the middle of my fourth volume – and no farther than to my first day's life – 'tis demonstrative that I have three hundred and sixty-four days more life to write just now, than when I first set out; so that instead of advancing, as a common writer, in my work with what I have been doing at it – on the contrary, I am just thrown so many volumes back-- was every day of my life to be as busy as this – And why not? – and the transactions and opinions of it to take up as much description – And for what reason should they be cut short? as at this rate I should just live 364 times faster than I should write- It must follow, an' please your worships, that the more I write, the more I shall have to write– and consequently, the more your worships read, the more your worships shall have to read. Will this be good for your worships' eyes? (IV.xiii.228)

he Long 18th Century

The absurdity of his proposition highlights important differences between the fictional Tristram and the text's actual author. Tristram purports to consider his readers' interests (or at least their eyesight) in his ambitious autobiographical project, but his decision to carry on regardless ('Heaven prosper the manufactures of paper under this propitious reign …') makes clear he feels his authorial intentions should prevail. Sterne, in contrast, was keenly aware that the popular novel was first and foremost a vehicle for the reader's enjoyment. Any lofty intentions espoused by the author – intellectual, moral or otherwise – depend for their success on the willing cooperation of readers.

Early in the novel, Tristram chides a female reader for misconstruing his meaning in the previous chapter and sends her back to reread it more carefully (I.xx.47–8). Such episodes point to the authorial pitfalls of attempting to dictate meaning to one's readers. The relationship between meaning and language is essentially unstable, so a reader's interpretation remains beyond authorial control. This sentiment, with its anticipation of postmodernist thinking, is ably demonstrated through Sterne's use of aposiopesis. In the use of dashes or asterisks to indicate missing words or gaps in the text, or in the breaking-off of sentences midway, leaving implied conclusions unspoken, aposiopesis emphasises the process by which readers 'fill in the gaps' for themselves. Tristram is often rather shocked with the salacious nature of his readers' interpretations of these 'gaps'. In the fifth volume, he recalls a very unfortunate childhood injury involving a full bladder and a sash window:

> ---The chamber-maid had left no ******* *** under the bed: --- Cannot you contrive, master, quoth Susannah, lifting up the sash with one hand, as she spoke, and helping me up into the window-seat with the other,--cannot you manage, my dear, for a single time to **** *** ** *** ******?

> I was five years old. –Susannah did not consider that nothing was well hung in our family,--so slap came the sash down like

lightening upon us;--Nothing is left,--cried Susannah,--nothing is left—for me, but to run my country.— (V.xvii.301)*

In 'filling in the gaps' above, readers will recall that, during the course of the entire narrative, Tristram devotes a great deal of writing to the subject of genitalia in general and injury or trauma to that bodily area in particular.[34] *Tristram Shandy* demonstrably asserts that, in the use of literary devices such as aposiopesis, symbol or metaphor, textual meaning can always move beyond, or even subvert, the intentions of its author. Thus it is that the text never actually reveals the nature of the injury that Tristram sustains in this episode, and yet the reader remains perfectly aware of what has occurred.

Considering metaphor in this way can help to illuminate the strange story of Slawkenbergius, included at the beginning of Volume IV, which tells of a mysterious stranger who rides on a mule from Strasbourg to Frankfurt. The tale's comic significance rests entirely on the possibility that references to the stranger's stupendously large nose might represent another part of his anatomy. The giant nose creates a sensation wherever the stranger appears; women are particularly intrigued and are desperate to get a closer look – and hopefully, a feel – of it. The size of the nose also prompts public debates concerning how it could be sustained with an adequate blood supply, while the sight of it alone keeps several convents of nuns 'tossing and tumbling from one side of their beds to the other the whole night long'. Metaphors (phallic or otherwise) depend on the reader's capacity to see the narrative in the same light as the writer intends, and the inclusion of the tale of Slawkenbergius provides a typically elaborate and bawdy example of how Sterne subverts the idea that language and meaning exist in a stable relationship.†

---

* See also Tristram's reference to aposiopesis in II.vi.81–2.
† Further non-literary devices in *Tristram Shandy* underline this idea. See, for example, the black pages inserted at the end of Volume I, which commemorate the death of Parson Yorick, or the complete absence of Chapter xxiv from Volume IV (which, apparently, was ten pages long, as reflected in the gap in the page numbers).

The story of Slawkenbergius is also included in Tristram's narrative as a means of demonstrating his father's obsessive interest in obscure and esoteric scholarship. Each of the principal characters in turn is preoccupied with a particular subject or interest which guides their outward perception. In the (ironic) case of the utterly benign and gentle Uncle Toby, it is military matters in general and, in particular, his re-enactments of the Siege of Namur where he received his groin wound.* These characteristic obsessions, or 'hobbyhorses', play an extremely important role in Sterne's wider narrative. The extent to which Walter and Toby Shandy tolerate each other's very different hobbyhorses, while continuing to ride their own with such enthusiasm, indicates an important element of human (and humane) conduct upheld by Sterne which appears to contradict Locke's premise that men cannot tolerate each other's differences and personal preoccupations.[35]

If Toby's and Walter's unusually benign mutual toleration tacitly interrogates Locke's premise, it does not actually reject the idea that men find it virtually impossible to perceive each other's point of view. This is ably demonstrated by the episode in Volume II, in which Corporal Trim reads out a sermon which falls out from the pages of a book by Stevinus.† Like the story of Slawkenbergius, the sermon is inserted (or, to use J. Paul Hunter's term, 'interpolated') into the wider narrative. Although its subject (the abuses of conscience) produces markedly different responses on the assembled listeners depending on their own personal hobbyhorses, no one is particularly affected by its moral content.‡ [36] This episode in particular, Hunter concludes, poses '[t]he ultimate question … whether any didactic work – sermon, tract, satire, or novel – can have the desired effect on human beings, or whether in fact all is vanity, and the didactic intentions of the moral philosopher are the greatest vanity of them all'.[37]

---

* Uncle Toby's gentle character is demonstrated by Tristram's recollection of a childhood incident when Toby gently escorts a fly (which had landed on his arm) outside rather than kill it.

† Simon Stevinus (1548–1620) was a Flemish mathematician, engineer and inventor.

‡ The sermon appears in Chapter xvii of Volume II and is, in fact, one of Sterne's own sermons, originally published in York in 1750.

The question of morality in *Tristram Shandy* is best understood through the concept of the hobbyhorse. Given that Toby's injuries were sustained on a battlefield, his military obsession might seem odd at first. What soon becomes clear is that, for Toby, his re-enactment of sieges and manoeuvres help him to recover from both the physical and mental trauma he sustained on the actual battlefield.[38] It is no coincidence that the two strongest examples of hobbyhorses portrayed in this narrative are possessed by men who have both retreated into quiet retirement in the countryside. Seen in this light, hobbyhorses are the necessary and therapeutic means by which the cruelty of the outside world – a world in which wars kill and maim soldiers and Tristram's brother, Bobby, dies while away at school – is kept at bay.

A final 'interpolated' story in Volume VI brings together the theme of retirement with the therapeutic benefits of Toby's hobbyhorse. It also anticipates the late eighteenth-century's growing interest in the literature of sentiment and sensibility, as discussed in the following chapter in relation to Fanny Burney's *Evelina*. This narrative describes how Toby comes to the emotional and financial aid of Le Fever, a wounded lieutenant, who lies bedridden at the village inn near Toby's home. The moral significance of the tale juxtaposes Toby's and Trim's generosity towards Le Fever and his young son with the evidently therapeutic benefits that these charitable actions bestow on Toby's own recuperation.

Tristram's narration imposes many interruptions and digressions onto his telling of Le Fever's tale, thereby heightening the reader's awareness of both the literary currency of the tale's sentimental content and its artifice. Despite this, the moral significance of Le Fever's story remains intact, at least partly because the tale incorporates characters from the central narrative (Toby and Trim). More significantly, this interpolated story explores through these characters, and echoes in the plight faced by Le Fever and his son, the central themes of death, loss and empathy that prevail throughout the text. The ranks of wounded soldiers, fatherless sons and fathers grieving over the loss of a son can only be helped by each other's presence, and the mutual benefits of charitable generosity towards each other.

Seen in this way, the snug domestic walls and gardens of Shandy Hall, where most of the wider narrative takes place, provide the only proper vantage point from which mutual benefits may be derived and sentiments properly considered. As Richard Lanham has convincingly suggested, the juxtaposition and mutual support of the two brothers in *Tristram Shandy* provide the real moral lesson at the heart of this 'drama of sentiment'. For the purposes of this chapter's investigation, *Tristram Shandy*'s playful interrogations of Lockean philosophy, traditional narrative form and novelistic chronology make it perhaps the most comprehensive example of this period's capacity for literary innovation and experimentation with fictional form. The work's real triumph, however, lies in its ability to depict, simultaneously, the complexity and moral obligations of lived human experience. It is the novel's capacity in this second regard that is further considered in the next chapter.

Notes

1   Ian Watt, *The Rise of the Novel: Studies in Defoe, Richardson and Fielding* (London: Peregrine Books, 1963), p. 205.
2   See Elizabeth L. Eisenstein, *The Printing Press as an Agent of Change: Communication and Cultural Transformation in Early Modern Europe* (Cambridge: Cambridge University Press, 1979).
3   J. G. A. Pocock: *The Machiavellian Moment: Florentine Political Thought and the Atlantic Republic Tradition* (Princeton and London: Princeton University Press, 1975), pp. 340–1.
4   On this point, see, in particular, Lennard J. Davis, *Resisting Novels: Ideology and Fiction* (New York and London: Methuen, 1987), pp. 24–51.
5   Pocock, *The Machiavellian Moment*, p. 402.
6   On this subject, see Michael McKeon, *The Origins of the English Novel, 1600–1740* (Baltimore: Johns Hopkins University Press, 1987), pp. 46–7; and Lennard J. Davis, *Factual Fictions: Origins of the English Novel* (New York: Columbia University Press, 1983).
7   McKeon, *The Origins of the English Novel*, p. 47.
8   Ibid., pp. 47–51.
9   William Shakespeare, *The Winter's Tale*, IV.iv. On this point, see also Ben Jonson's play *The Staple of News* (1626).
10   Watt, *The Rise of the Novel*, p. 23.

Fact and Fiction

11   Henry Fielding, *The History of Tom Jones, A Foundling*, edited and with an introduction by R. P. C. Mutter (London: Penguin, 1966), II.i.87. All further citations of this primary text refer to this edition.

12   Laurence Sterne, *The Life and Opinions of Tristram Shandy, Gentleman*, edited and with an introduction by Ian Campbell Ross (Oxford and New York: Oxford University Press, 1983), VII.xxviii.413–14. All further citations of this primary text refer to this edition.

13   For an overview of the contemporary reception of the *Journal*, see John Mullan, Introduction to Daniel Defoe, *A Journal of the Plague Year* (1722), in *The Works of Daniel Defoe*, Volume 7: *The Novels of Daniel Defoe* (London: Pickering & Chatto, 2009), pp. 1–4; all further citations of this primary text refer to this edition. See also Robert Mayer, 'The Reception of *A Journal of the Plague Year* and the Nexus of Fiction and History in the Novel', *English Literary History*, 57 (1990), pp. 531–2.

14   Daniel Defoe, *The Storm: or, A Collection of the Most Remarkable Casualties and Disasters* ..., edited and with an introduction by Richard Hamblyn (London: Allen Lane, 2003).

15   Anthony Burgess, Introduction to Daniel Defoe, *A Journal of the Plague Year* (London: Penguin Classics, 1966), p. 15.

16   Richard Hamblyn, Introduction to *The Storm* (London: Allen Lane, 2003), edited and with an introduction by Richard Hamblyn, pp. xxviii–xxxii.

17   Mullan, Introduction to *A Journal of the Plague Year*, p. 4.

18   Ibid., p. 29.

19   On the subject of providentialism, see Keith Thomas, *Religion and the Decline of Magic* (London: Weidenfeld & Nicolson, 1971); and Alexandra Walsham, *Providence in Early Modern England* (Oxford: Oxford University Press, 2001).

20   Crusoe takes solace and advice from his discovery of a Biblical passage towards the end of his bout of 'ague': Daniel Defoe, *The Life and Strange Surprizing Adventures of Robinson Crusoe* (1719), in W. R. Owens (ed.), *The Works of Daniel Defoe*, Volume 1: *The Novels of Daniel Defoe* (London: Pickering & Chatto, 2008), p. 126.

21   Burgess, Introduction to *A Journal of the Plague Year*, p. 18.

22   Mutter, Introduction to *Tom Jones*, pp. 19–20.

23   Watt, *The Rise of the Novel*, pp. 288–92.

24   Nancy A. Mace, *Henry Fielding's Novels and the Classical Tradition* (London: Associated University Presses, 1996), p. 61.

25   Mace and Watt both suggest that this ambivalence towards elements of Classicism – particularly, the Homeric ideal of heroism – is in fact a prevalent feature of much Augustan literature. See Mace, *Henry Fielding's Novels*, p. 72.

26   See I. P. Watt, 'The Naming of Characters in Defoe, Richardson and Fielding', *Review of English Studies*, 25:100 (1949), pp. 322–38.

27   Watt, *The Rise of the Novel*, p. 281. Fielding's narrator makes this point at IX.i.439.

28   For an overview of the responses to *Pamela*, see Thomas Keymer and Peter Sabor (eds), *The Pamela Controversy: Criticisms and Adaptations of Samuel Richardson's Pamela, 1740–1750*, 6 vols (London: Pickering & Chatto, 2001); on Fielding's response in particular, see Judith Frank, 'The Comic Novel and the Poor: Fielding's Preface to *Joseph Andrews*', *Eighteenth-century Studies*, 27:2 (Winter 1993/4), pp. 217–34.

29   Victor Shklovsky, '*Tristram Shandy*: Stylistic Commentary', in *Russian Formalist Criticism: Four Essays*, trans. L. T. Lemon and M. J. Reis (Lincoln: University of Nebraska Press, 1965), p. 57.

30   Ross, Introduction to *Tristram Shandy*, p. xviii.

31   See Shklovsky, *Russian Formalist Criticism: Four Essays*. Bakhtin's extended discussion of *Tristram Shandy* may be found within his essay entitled 'Discourse in the Novel', in Michael Holquist (ed.), *The Dialogic Imagination: Four Essays by M. M. Bakhtin*, trans. Caryl Emerson and Michael Holquist (Austin: University of Texas Press, 1981), pp. 259–422.

32   John Locke, *An Essay Concerning Human Understanding, An Abridgement*, edited by John Yolton (London: J. M. Dent & Sons, 1976), II.xxxiii ('Of the Association of Ideas'), p. 199.

33   For a full consideration of Lockean philosophy in Sterne's work, see Arthur H. Cash, 'The Lockean Psychology of Tristram Shandy', *English Literary History*, 22:2 (June 1955), pp. 125–35; John Traugott, *Tristram Shandy's World: Sterne's Philosophical Rhetoric* (Berkeley and Los Angeles: University of California Press, 1954).

34   On the relationship between language and physical deficiency in *Tristram Shandy*, see Ross King, '*Tristram Shandy* and the Wound of Language', *Studies in Philology*, 92:3 (Summer 1995), pp. 291–310.

35   Locke, *An Essay Concerning Human Understanding*, II.xxxiii.198.

36   J. Paul Hunter explores this and several other Shandean 'interpolations', and compares them with Fielding's incorporation of the tale of the Man of the Hill in *Tom Jones*, in his essay 'Response as Reformation: *Tristram Shandy* and the Art of Interruption', *Novel*, 4:2 (1971), pp. 132–46.

37   Ibid., p. 137.

38   The last section of this critical discussion draws extensively for its arguments on Richard A. Lanham, '*Tristram Shandy*': *The Games of Pleasure* (Berkeley and London: University of California Press, 1973).

The Novel and the Individual: Bunyan, Haywood, Richardson and Burney

The long eighteenth century witnesses much development of the literary genre which has, arguably, come to dominate the popular imagination and our prevailing understanding of English literature. There are a staggeringly large number of definitions for the term 'novel' and, consequently, critical opinions endorsing texts as the 'first English novel' abound.[1] This discussion has further widened in the past few decades to acknowledge many important works (particularly by female authors) written before 1740.[2] If defined too rigidly, the term 'novel' itself can hinder every step of its own critical discussion; it must suffice to say that all the texts considered here offer a profound sense of the novel's cultural heritage.

The moral, emotional and psychological demands that early modern English society placed on the individual – even the development of the concept of 'the individual' itself – are key novelistic concerns during the long eighteenth century. Individualism, as a social construct, informs Western notions of modernity and implicitly challenges older, community-centred, cultural models in its revaluation of the nature of duty and social responsibility. As conceived during the long eighteenth century, individualism reflects post-Reformation changes in the religious conscience of Protestant individuals, with profound implications for social institutions such as the family, marriage and inheritance, as well as for human relationships within wider social communities (in particular, the congregation, the parish and the town).[3]

Protestantism upholds the idea of a direct relationship between each individual human being and God, and in which the Bible (the word of God made manifest on earth) serves as the key instrument through which to understand the nature of one's duty to God. Protestantism recognises no mediating forces (such as the Pope) which stand between God and the individual Protestant soul; no instruments of ecclesiastical authority (such as the Roman Catholic practice of private confession) may intervene in the individual's direct engagement with their Maker. The Protestant Reformation did not remove or deny the spiritual authority of the Christian 'church' (either in its sense as an institution or as a gathered community of the faithful) but it did limit and qualify that authority.

The Protestant Reformation is one of many powerful cultural factors which helped to fashion the notion of the individual during the long eighteenth century. Given that individualism is a social construct that is subject to cultural change, it is worth reconsidering how we read early novels. Our instinctive tendency to 'identify' with their protagonists can actually be a reductive process if we choose to ignore the inherent cultural differences evident in these texts. It is consistently important that we interrogate what our literary expectations are when we read a particular genre – such as the novel – and remain open-minded towards texts that confound our expectations.

The Early Novel and Other Contemporary Genres

Cultural traffic moves in both directions. As a genre essentially defined by its responsiveness to popular tastes (the need for success in the literary marketplace), the early novel both reflected and influenced its readers. Although the full extent to which, for example, Samuel Richardson's *Pamela* (1740) would have coloured contemporary notions and expectations concerning marriage may never be known, there is little doubt that such works contributed to the formation of eighteenth-century culture in a very real sense.[4]

A key aspect of the novel's popular success during the long eighteenth century was its capacity to endorse and simultaneously challenge earlier literary forms. Works we now consider as 'novelistic' were written from within other well-established traditions and justified their presence in the literary marketplace on these terms. Other, older, literary genres which contribute to the genesis of the novel include a vast array of religious and didactic writing including Protestant spiritual biographies such as Lucy Hutchinson's *Memoirs of the Life of Colonel Hutchinson* or John Bunyan's *Grace Abounding* (1666) as well as conduct works, published sermons and Newgate biographies.* Another important literary influence, the romance, also has a very long literary ancestry.[5]

From the late seventeenth century onwards, however, a new and distinctly English form gained popular precedence in the amatory fiction of authors such as Aphra Behn, Delarivier Manley and Eliza Haywood† and a role in the development of the novel.‡ Their writing dramatically extended the remit of earlier works of continental amatory fiction, largely concerned with sexual and courtly intrigue, to also reflect on England's contemporary political scene as well as the period's growing readership of both genders. Ros Ballaster argues:

> [T]he early woman writer was far from the modest and amateur lady of letters most histories would have her be. She was rather a prostitute of the pen, trafficking in desire for profit and, in this respect, no different from many of her male contemporaries. Behn, Manley and Haywood reveal themselves to be far from subjected by the imposition of an emergent philosophy of 'separate spheres' (politics and romance, masculine and feminine, the coffee-house and the boudoir). Indeed, they exploit this

---

* Lucy Hutchinson's biography of her husband, the regicide and staunch Parliamentarian Colonel John Hutchinson, was written between 1664 and 1671 although it was not published until 1806. Bunyan's spiritual autobiography *Grace Abounding* was composed during one of his extended periods of imprisonment for Nonconformity.

† Aphra Behn (*c.* 1640–89), Delarivier Manley (*c.*1670–1724) and Eliza Haywood (*c.* 1693–1756) were three of the most popular and versatile authors – of either gender – in the earlier part of the long eighteenth century.

‡ For a discussion of the romance genre, see below and Part Four: 'A Culture of Print'.

division in order to construct ... a specifically female writing identity for themselves. Their experimental texts dramatize the seduction of the female reader by amatory fiction, exploring alternatives that offer models for the female victim to come to the 'mastery' of or resistance to the fictional text through the figure of the heroinized female writer.[6]

As Ballaster suggests, the importance of this particular contribution to the genesis of the novel is that it negates the boundaries emerging in late seventeenth-century culture between political, economic and gender spheres of influence in order to construct a new 'species' of authorial identity. Behn, Manley and Haywood engage head-on with established literary conventions (amatory fiction, the seduction plot), thereby challenging the reader's expectations even while they appear to bow to the demands of popular readership.

Like religious or didactic forms, amatory fiction in this period often focuses on the individual's moral and emotional conduct. As it is consciously presented by Behn, Manley and Haywood, however, its agenda is largely deconstructive rather than didactic, often challenging and questioning traditional modes of authority, or foregrounding the creative power of the author behind the text. That such assertiveness was often met with open hostility from male authors – their direct competitors in the literary marketplace – is perhaps the best indication of the contemporary impact of such writing.* [7] Richardson once famously described *Pamela* as a

> new species of writing that might possibly turn young people into a course of reading different from the pomp and parade of romance-writing, and dismissing the improbable and marvellous, with which novels generally abound, might promote the cause of religion and virtue.[8]

---

* Haywood was famously lampooned in Pope's *Dunciad* in all of the work's revisions between 1729 and 1743 (attesting to the longevity of her public recognition).

Richardson's comments also reflect the contemporary ambiguity with which the term 'novel' – as then loosely aligned with 'romance' – was viewed. In this sense, 'romances' were fictional works of both poetry and prose, popular in England and on the continent in the seventeenth century and earlier, which derived from the medieval courtly tradition. Such works often contained fantastical plots, heroic battles, and idealised a pure and necessarily unrequited love rooted in the Christian virtues. Amatory fiction shares elements of the courtly tradition with romance while it also addresses more explicitly the realms of sexual intrigue and power. Richardson's greatest work, *Clarissa* (1747–8), is derived from the Protestant and didactic tradition he publicly endorsed as well as from the tradition of amatory fiction and romance from which he publicly wished to distance his writing.

The Protestant tradition in which Richardson consciously wrote his works of prose fiction had a profound impact on early novels. Many Protestant genres centre on the intrinsic spiritual value to be gleaned from written accounts of the lives – and often deaths – of godly individuals.[9] Such works also draw heavily on the Bible's richly allusive language and literary devices such as symbol and allegory. These features compel readers to see beyond the immediate text to deeper levels of meaning; details of everyday life experience can reveal powerful divine truths hidden to less attentive readers. So great is the importance of the cultural impact of religious didactic writing on the early novel that a religious work which anticipates the novel is the subject of the next part of our discussion in this chapter.

Narrative, Allegory and the *Progress* of the Individual

A profoundly important precursor to the novel and the quintessential classic of the Puritan tradition, *The Pilgrim's Progress* is – after the Bible – one of the most widely read books ever printed in English. It takes the form of a religious allegory which, the narrator tells us in his opening sentence, he 'dreamed in a dream'. The narrative is a simple one. At the outset the terrified protagonist Christian flees to escape the 'fire from Heaven' which he has read will shortly engulf the City of Destruction where he lives with his family. Unable to persuade his wife and four children to join him, Christian sets off on his journey to find safety and a means to remove the heavy burden he carries upon his back. The remainder of the narrative charts Christian's eventful journey towards salvation and the Celestial City.

A fundamental tenet of Protestant Christianity is the individual's responsibility to conduct his own spiritual journey towards spiritual salvation. Bunyan's text depicts this journey in the form of a richly elaborate allegory; his clear didactic intention is to illuminate this spiritual path. In Part I, the protagonist Christian confronts the hideous monster Apollyon, who in turn recognises him as 'one of my subjects'. Apollyon attempts to persuade Christian to turn back and renew his former allegiance, but Christian replies:

> What I promised thee was in my noneage; and besides, I count
> that the Prince under whose banner now I stand is able to absolve
> me; yea, and to pardon also what I did as to my compliance with
> thee: and besides (O thou destroying Apollyon), to speak truth, I
> like his service, his wages, his servants, his government, his
> company, and country better than thine: and therefore leave off to
> persuade me further.* [10]

Christian asserts that his former allegiance, a sign of his youthful ignorance, can now be absolved by his faith in God. In this episode it is possible to see that the character Christian is already being described in terms of his individual experience (which comprises, among other things, a youthful and mistaken alliance to the demon Apollyon). Though by no means as well-rounded as characters whose experiences are depicted in later novels, Christian's character has a discernible past history as well as the capacity for change.

---

* 'Noneage' means here, literally, 'non-age', or having not yet reached full maturity. In *Revelations* 9:11, Apollyon the Destroyer is a fallen angel who presides over a bottomless pit of monstrous beasts. Bunyan's narrator describes him as a monster 'hideous to behold, he was clothed with scales like a fish … wings like a dragon, feet like a bear, and out of his belly came fire and smoke, and his mouth was as the mouth of a lion'.

A straightforward allegorical reading of *The Pilgrim's Progress* – in which every character and element of the physical landscape on Christian's journey precisely matches its doctrinal equivalent – is entirely possible. A rich patchwork of Scriptural language and imagery, Bunyan's text conveys a strong sense of Puritanism's vision of human fallibility and the urgent need for conversion and steadfast faith. Such a reading, however, would fail to convey any sense of the text's rich literary heritage and its own resonance as a fictional narrative which anticipates the novel. The Puritan tradition and author which produced *The Pilgrim's Progress* were not impervious to secular cultural influences; Bunyan's text may even claim among its literary ancestors forms far more ancient than Christianity itself in, for example, its employment of the dream device and the quest narrative.* It combines Scriptural allusion with occasionally surprising flashes of realism (particularly in its depiction of human nature) and Bunyan's own distinctive colloquial style. As Roger Sharrock suggests:

> His language has the life of speech, salted with proverbs and vigorous provincial turns of phrase; it is the plain colloquial manner that he has no doubt also employed in the pulpit … It is the manner of generations of popular preachers using parables to point their case, but in *The Pilgrim's Progress* it is wrought to the pitch of art.[11]

Bunyan's text inhabits a special place in the development of the novel because it is the powerfully imaginative sum of many seemingly conflicting parts. Crucially, it is related to literary forms whose interests

---

* The dream device, for example, may be found in *The Dream of the Rood*, one of the oldest narratives in Old English literature whose creation goes back to at least the seventh century AD: see Michael Swanton (ed.), *The Dream of the Rood* (Manchester: Manchester University Press, 1970). The poem also contains thematic elements which pre-date Christianity, such as the notion of heroic sacrifice and the spiritual powers of the natural world. The quest narrative is one of the oldest narrative patterns of the Anglo-Germanic literary tradition. Examples include the heroic quest *Beowulf*, an Old English poem which survives from a tenth-century manuscript, classic literary works such as Miguel de Cervantes's *Don Quixote* (1605–15) or Herman Melville's *Moby-Dick* (1851), and fairy tales.

are both secular *and* religious. Indeed, Michael McKeon argues that its very shortcomings – when considered singly as either a novel or an allegorical narrative – constitute its strength:

> Despite the intrusions, the gaps, the glaring 'incompleteness' of the narrative, Bunyan's literal plot makes a powerful imaginative claim on our attention. And its seemingly treacherous pull toward an exclusive self-sufficiency may be seen not simply as a failure, but as a fulfilment of allegorical form so successful that it strains toward a different form entirely – different, but intimately related in spirit and purpose.[12]

McKeon goes on to suggest that 'Bunyan's increasing proximity to the epistemology of the early novelists' is also evident in the opening of Part II of *The Pilgrim's Progress* (added in 1684).* [13] In the second part of the text, Christian's wife (Christiana) and four sons embark on their own pilgrimage to the Celestial City. McKeon's argument relates to the self-conscious linking device employed by Bunyan in order to give credence to the continuation of the original narrative. In a second dream in the opening of Part II, the narrator has a discussion with 'an aged gentleman' which reveals what has transpired since Christian's triumphant pilgrimage (pp. 219 ff.). McKeon observes that Bunyan's employment of Mr Sagacity may be read as a 'rather startling claim to historicity', in other words, a conscious effort on the part of the author to provide a self-affirming internal history for his narrative's plot for the purposes of credibility.[14] This device thus aligns the two-part narrative of Bunyan's text more closely to secular works of early prose fiction where similar devices are employed (for example, Daniel Defoe's *Robinson Crusoe*, published in 1719 and often cited as the 'first English novel', or McKeon's example of *Oroonoko* in 1688).†

---

* Epistemology (meaning, literally, a theory of knowledge) in this context refers to the manner in which the writing of early novelists demonstrates its own system of ideas concerning how knowledge and understanding are acquired and developed.

† On Aphra Behn's profoundly important work of prose fiction *Oroonoko, or The Royal Slave* (1688), see Part Four: 'A Culture of Print'.

Beyond the linking device with which it commences, the second part of *The Pilgrim's Progress* taken as a whole both affirms and undermines its relationship to more secular forms of prose fiction, such as the early novel, and overtly didactic forms, such as the spiritual biography. Its narrative serves to confirm the allegorical resonances of Christian's original pilgrimage as Christiana and her children revisit the sites where many of his struggles and triumphs took place. Christian's position, once he departs from his family and the City of Destruction, is largely representative of Everyman, or any spiritual pilgrim who treads the path towards salvation. The form of Part II, however, is not allegorical in its own right; Christiana and her sons encounter different problems and impediments on their path to salvation. Sharrock identifies in Bunyan's professional experience as a minister some possible reasons for the changes in concern between the narrative's two parts:

> The interest has shifted from the lonely epic of the individual to the problems of the small urban community of Nonconformists: problems of mixed marriages, the need for cohesion, and the difficulty certain members have (Fearing, Feeble-mind) in fitting into the life of the church. Bunyan had now been many years an administrator and a pastor of souls … As most novelists do, he has passed from an autobiographical first novel to an external, more calculated subject.[15]

Notwithstanding the importance of Bunyan's ministerial role to our reading of *The Pilgrim's Progress*, to describe the narrative's second part as a novel of any kind (or its author as a novelist) tends to overshadow its equal debt to popular religious genres such as the spiritual biography. In its specific depiction of a pious female pilgrim, the narrative of Christiana's journey recalls the authentic lives of such women while it also anticipates the more secular concerns of what Sharrock describes as the 'bustling social novel'.[16]

Christiana's identity and journey – like the second part of the narrative itself – are dependent on an understanding of her husband's narrative; as such, her reputation precedes her. The episode in which she visits the House of the Interpreter provides a useful example of how this differing notion of identity may be perceived. In response to the Interpreter's inquiry ('Art thou that Christiana whom Christian, the good man, left behind him, when he betook himself to the pilgrim's life?'), she must both affirm and deny the true nature of her identity:

> I am that woman that was so hard-hearted as to slight my husband's troubles, and that left him to go on in his journey alone, and these are his four children; but now I also am come, for I am convinced that no way is right but this. (p. 246)

Christiana is Christian's wife, but now she has repented. Within the wider social context, the nature of identity itself is dependent on just such forms of recognition which must constantly both affirm and deny aspects of the individual's relationship to others. In other words, Christiana's position more closely resembles those shifting and subjective identities, necessarily immersed in the wider social context, found both in earlier didactic genres (such as the conduct work and spiritual biography) as well as in the novel.

The Family, Conduct and Morality

The influence of family relationships on the formation of individual experience is always important in novels, but it is often important by virtue of its conspicuous absence. It is no coincidence that so many early novels feature protagonists whose immediate family is absent, distant or deceased. All of Defoe's protagonists are either orphaned or abandoned as children or choose, like Robinson Crusoe, to run away from home. Richardson's Pamela is employed far away from the protection of her doting parents while, as we shall see, Clarissa is alienated by her indifferent relations. In Fanny Burney's and Henry Fielding's novels, the mysteries surrounding the true parentage of Evelina and Tom Jones provide a key theme. The unnamed female protagonist in *Fantomina*

(1725, the subject of this chapter's Extended Commentary), whose mother is abroad at the opening of the narrative, is acutely vulnerable in her isolation:

> young, a stranger to the world, and consequently to the dangers of it; and having nobody in town, at that time, to whom she was obliged to be accountable for her actions, did in everything as her inclinations or humours rendered most agreeable to her ... She depended on the strength of her virtue to bear her fate through trials more dangerous than she apprehended ...[17]

Even Bunyan's protagonist Christian begins his eventful pilgrimage by fleeing from his home with his fingers in his ears to block out the cries of his wife and children.* The essential nature of the protagonist is that of an individual in conflict who is isolated or removed – by choice or circumstance – from conventional sources of emotional and moral guidance. This dual sense of liberation and isolation is a form of psychological tension characteristic of most protagonists in early novels. Their experience relates directly to what Lawrence Stone describes as 'affective individualism', a culturally determined notion which first emerges in the late seventeenth century:

> The most powerful influence ... was the overpowering sense of sin and the preoccupation with individual salvation that was the hallmark of the Puritan personality in the seventeenth century, and was greatly stimulated by literacy and the habit of private reading and meditation ... Puritanism, introspection, literacy and privacy form a single affinity group of characteristics.[18]

Introspection, literacy and privacy are the very qualities most desirable in readers seeking the advice provided by didactic literature. The popular success of conduct works during this period (often directed at particular social groups, such as young men and women) suggests an avid

---

* Later, at the House of the Lord of the Hill, Charity affirms Christian's decision to leave behind his wife and children and deliver his own soul (pp. 84–5).

readership of this type.[*] [19] Some took the form of dialogues, but were distinctly thin in terms of 'non-didactic' features such as character delineation and imagery.[†] Both before and after the publication of *Robinson Crusoe* (1719), however, the conduct works of Daniel Defoe provide a fascinating glimpse into the increasing attention this author devotes to the portrayal of subjective experience.[‡] His fictional subjects become more complex and unique, more the reflection of their cumulative experience and therefore less easily assimilated into predictable patterns of behaviour seen in other conduct works.

The incorporation of 'literary' (or non-didactic) features within didactic works was justified as a means to both entertain and instruct readers who might otherwise not attend to the moral message behind the narrative. Defoe makes this clear in the introduction to his 1715 conduct work, *The Family Instructor*:

> we live in an age that does not want so much to know their duty as to practice it; not so much to be taught, as to be made obedient to what they have already learnt … The way I have taken for this, is entirely New, and at first perhaps it may appear something Odd, and the Method may be contemned; But let such blame their own more irregular Tempers, that must have every thing turned into new Models; must be touch'd with Novelty, and have their Fancies humour'd with the Dress of a Thing; so that if it be what has been said over and over a thousand times, yet if it has but a different colour'd Coat, or a new Feather in its Cap, it pleases and wins upon them, whereas the same Truths written in the divinest Stile in the World, would be flat, stale and unpleasant without it.[20]

---

[*] Notable among these works were advice guides meant specifically for women; see, in particular, George Savile, *The Lady's New-year's Gift: or, Advice to a Daughter* (1688).

[†] See, for example, William Darrell, *The Gentleman Instructed* (1704) and Richard Baxter, *The Poor Man's Family Book* (first published in 1674 but frequently reprinted).

[‡] Defoe's conduct works include *The Family Instructor* (2 vols, 1715 and 1718) and *Religious Courtship* (1722).

The Novel and the Individual

Read today, Defoe's unapologetic defence of his 'new Model' may seem surprising in light of his later prolific career as a novelist. The conduct work, however, was only one of many popular forms which an avid contemporary readership apparently accepted on the premise of its 'improving' content. The dire consequences of criminal activity, for example, were outlined by criminal (or Newgate) biographies, which readily combined some factual content with hearsay or imaginative speculation on the part of the author. Many of these narratives derived from the 'Newgate Calendar', a collection of popular periodicals and broadsheets which chronicled the exploits of infamous Newgate criminals throughout the eighteenth century and beyond. In all these narratives (both fictional such as Defoe's *Moll Flanders* (1722) or ostensibly 'factual' such as the Newgate Calendar), protagonists were usually notable criminals whose imminent or recent execution provided both an extra frisson in the consideration of their moral downfall and a stern warning to readers.

The lurid details of criminal activity revealed in these texts would, like the exploits of Moll Flanders, have attracted readers just as strongly – if not more so – than the underlying moral lesson. *Moll Flanders* is an interesting literary hybrid of many forms including the criminal biography and the picaresque tale. The latter was first popularised in Spain during the sixteenth century and related in episodic form the adventures of a *picaro* (Spanish for 'rogue'), a protagonist more morally dubious and less noble than the traditional or Classical hero. Paul Salzman suggests the form's English counterpart has a distinct political and economic history:

> The English Rogue reflects tensions generated by the changing role of commerce, and the new relationship between individuals in a city like London. It appeared only a few years after the Interregnum ended, and it embraces some of the comic and satirical implications of 'the world turned upside down' – a literary motif which became very real during the Civil War. The eclectic nature of English picaresque and rogue literature may

account for its long, vigorous life, which makes it a barometer of social, as well as literary, change.[21]

Salzman's description reflects the economic dimension of the moral ambiguity inherent in characters such as the Newgate criminal or the English Rogue. Through disguise or a change of address within the urban landscape, such characters could reinvent their identities (as Moll and Roxana repeatedly demonstrate) and thus move seamlessly up or down the socioeconomic ladder. No longer confined to a rural community in which public identity is based on time-honoured associations with land and kinsmen, protagonists become increasingly exposed to the opportunities, and concomitant dangers, of the urban environment.

Indeed, urban landscapes depicted across texts as chronologically distant as Defoe's novels in the 1720s and Burney's *Evelina* in 1778 provide a startlingly consistent indication of how the nation's capital was represented to contemporary readers during the long eighteenth century. The enormous growth of London during this period presented many temptations and dangers to the influx of new arrivals arriving from the country in search of employment. Such threats included both the practical dangers of increased population density (such as disease, fire and crime) as well as the expansion of sexual possibility. If, however, London represented the fascination and allure of sexual possibility, it also represented its potential dangers. In popular literature, the risk to men is represented by the prospect of contracting venereal disease from one of Gay's or Swift's Drury Lane prostitutes. For women, however, the risks are greater still and more diverse, ranging from illegitimate pregnancy (*Fantomina*) to rape and death (*Clarissa*). As the long eighteenth century progresses, the sanctification of female virtue and marriage – key Richardsonian themes – becomes an integral aspect of English social propriety across many genres including the novel.

Clarissa and the Preservation of Female Virtue

At more than a million words long, Richardson's masterpiece, *Clarissa* (1747–8), at first appears a daunting prospect to all but the most devoted students of this period's literature. The story is vividly contemporary in its depiction of a mid-eighteenth-century cultural landscape while it harks back to the moral pattern of amatory fiction from the previous century. It is also a fable, and the virtues of its eponymous heroine (like the cruelty and hypocrisy of those who destroy her) are emblematic and timeless.

Clarissa is the second of Richardson's three works, all of which took the form of an epistolary novel.* [22] The first, *Pamela, or Virtue Rewarded* (1740–1) received phenomenal and immediate popular recognition. Broadly, both *Pamela* and *Clarissa* consider the tribulations inherent in the preservation of female virtue when confronted by an all-powerful male sexual prerogative.† As well as the somewhat predictable qualities of beauty, youth and impeccable moral virtue, her correspondence reveals that Clarissa also has a strong intellect, personal warmth and sound moral judgement. Although the correspondence of some twenty individuals is related during the course of the text, the lion's share of the narrative consists of letters between Clarissa and her friend Anna Howe, and between Lovelace and his friend John Belford. The novel's tragic ending confirms its moral and didactic intentions but leaves unanswered even more compelling questions concerning the mutual sexual fascination that escalates between Clarissa and Lovelace.

Clarissa's first misfortune comes in the form of a greedy, callous family who strive to force her to marry against her will. Her refusal leaves her vulnerable to Lovelace, the charming but sexually dangerous

---

* Despite Richardson's famous claim to have invented in the English epistolary novel a 'new species of writing', Aphra Behn's *Love-letters between a Nobleman and his Sister* (1683) provides a much earlier example of this form.

† Richardson's last novel, *Sir Charles Grandison* (1754), addresses similar thematic concerns but instead takes for its eponymous protagonist a man of unimpeachable moral integrity.

male protagonist, who helps her escape from the family home. Angus Ross provides a usefully brief summary of the remainder of the novel's plot:

> At the centre of a web of lying harassment, [Clarissa] is imprisoned in a brothel, defies Lovelace, escapes, but is lured back to captivity, drugged and raped. She again escapes, and having been isolated from her family and friends turns to the consolations for the oppressed virtuous of the future life, and dies. Lovelace himself is killed in a duel with her cousin.[23]

These bald facts of the novel's plot conceal a complex duet of conflicting motivations and identities for Richardson's two protagonists. The error of judgement that Clarissa makes in accepting Lovelace's initial offer – to assist her in escaping from her parents' insistence that she marry the odious but wealthy Solmes – is based on her attraction to Lovelace's positive qualities (intelligence and charm) combined with her conviction that she can reform his negative ones (promiscuity and sexual aggression). In the London brothel, Lovelace's increasingly coercive attempts to seduce Clarissa are met by a resistance which serves only to increase his love – and lust – for her. In turn, like Milton's Eve in dialogue with the serpent in *Paradise Lost* (1667), the imprisoned Clarissa variously finds herself delighted, suspicious and bewildered by Lovelace's charm. She fails to reform him but the keen depiction of their opposing perspectives provides a conclusion that is at once shocking and, equally, inevitable.

The novel's sustained epistolary form – absenting the authoritative position of an omniscient narrator – invites readers to construe their own final meanings for the text. This 'open-ended' quality (or textual indeterminacy) at first might seem to contradict the author's avowed didactic intentions.[24] Unsurprisingly, Richardson's monumental text has provoked a gratifyingly diverse range of critical responses.[25] Beyond the text's presentation of female sexual subjection at the hands of a male oppressor lies a form of symbolic oppression evident in Lovelace's 'literal' interference with Clarissa's textual discourse (as seen in his manipulation of her correspondence).*

The elaborate textual representation of Clarissa's oppression in these terms – the battle of the sexes conducted through language – contrasts markedly with the curt acknowledgement of the novel's central act of sexual violence. An alternative reading of Lovelace's cursory announcement in Letter 257 ('And now, Belford, I can go no farther. The affair is over. Clarissa lives.') remains strangely prophetic. The 'affair' *is* now over in the sense that the rape cancels all chances of reparation and thereby the possibility of sustaining the *balance* of perspectives and mutual power struggles previously depicted between Clarissa and Lovelace. In this sense alone, and as Lovelace would have it, the sexual prerogative of masculine domination brings to an end the language and with it the more ambiguous powers of female expression.

At the same time, and despite Lovelace's 'ending' of the affair, Clarissa *does* live. She briefly survives the act of rape but, more importantly, her physical death is clearly depicted as a pious Christian's triumph over mortality (L.481, pp. 1360–3). In the Postscript to the novel's fourth edition, Richardson's third-person justification of his literary form – still rejecting the term 'novel' – closely echoes Defoe's arguments from thirty-six years earlier concerning his 'new way' in *The Family Instructor*:

> [Richardson] imagined that in an age given up to diversion and entertainment, he could *steal in*, as may be said, and investigate the great doctrines of Christianity under the fashionable guise of an amusement ... The author of the History (or rather Dramatic Narrative) of *Clarissa* is therefore well justified by the *Christian System* in deferring to extricate Suffering Virtue to the time in which it will meet with the *Completion* of its Reward.[26]

---

* Lovelace's discourse constantly and imaginatively 'pushes' at the confines and conventions of the letter-form; this may be seen in his use of false or edited letters (for example, L.239.1, pp. 811–14), his inclusion of pictorial markers (L.229.1, pp. 743–52) and the use of alternative genres such as playscripts or contracts (L.232, pp. 762–7; L.254, pp. 871–4).

Notwithstanding Richardson's didactic intentions, Clarissa's deathbed scene may be read as a form of saintly Protestant martyrdom while the lengthy series of posthumous letters sent after her death may also be seen as a form of 'textual immortality' (LL.488–92, pp. 1371–7). Ultimately, while 'Clarissa lives', it is Lovelace who is silenced and 'can go no further'. Even the circumstances of his death are depicted to the reader at the distance of several (textual) removes, thus reiterating the Christian motif of a sinner's death (L.537, pp. 1486–8).[*] As a whole, *Clarissa* offers the most substantial evidence that the Protestant tradition of didactic literature continued to bear fruit well into the eighteenth century.

Virtue, Marriage and Manners: *Evelina*'s Progress

Nearly four decades after the publication of Richardson's *Pamela*, the longevity of the epistolary form's popularity is borne out by the immediate success enjoyed by *Evelina* (1778), Burney's first (anonymously published) novel. As in *Pamela* and *Clarissa*, the central theme of *Evelina* is a virtuous young woman's engagement with a larger world which threatens both immediate dangers (in the form of masculine sexual aggression) and a wide spectrum of subtler risks (ranging from hypocrisy and betrayal to impoliteness and faux pas).

Richardsonian parallels, however, end there. As the novel's extended title consciously implies, the author was wholly aware that her chosen genre would invoke certain literary expectations in her readers.[†] This is a highly self-conscious text. It looks back, rather cynically, to the Richardsonian narratives of the 1740s while it also starts to navigate some of the subtler – if no less perplexing – notions of propriety, taste and refinement that its female readers faced in the latter part of the eighteenth century.

---

[*]   The circumstances of his death are related in a letter from Trent to Belford which, translated from French, was penned by the French valet who attended Lovelace's final moments.

[†]   The full title is *Evelina, or the History of a Young Lady's Entrance to the World*.

While still broadly representative of the temptations and dangers that it posed for Fantomina and Clarissa, the urban landscape now comes into sharper focus. Evelina's London consists of the specific venues – opera houses, pleasure gardens and theatres – attended by both the elite and some lower members of the social pecking order. Evelina navigates through the panoply of diversions on offer in the city; her experience, presented as both necessary and desirable, presents a series of obstacles that must be overcome on the path towards marital bliss.

As we have seen, protagonists in early novels often possess a personal history in which impediments and errors – in both the past and future – play a vital role in their development. As such, Evelina's errors of judgement and faux pas while in London are necessary steps towards her social refinement, as are the various impediments encountered along her path to a happy and advantageous marriage with Lord Orville. Clearly the trials faced by Evelina in the fashionable circles of late eighteenth-century London are very different to those encountered by Christian in *The Pilgrim's Progress*. Hers are the mistakes of an innocent young woman, raised wholly in the countryside, newly exposed to the challenges presented by London's sophisticated urban landscape. The journey is made all the more exciting for Burney's contemporary readers by its plethora of authentic detail. What the protagonists of Bunyan's and Burney's texts share, however, is their capacity to learn from their exposure to both positive and negative influences – through the examples of kindness versus cruelty, or hypocrisy versus sincerity – that are presented to them.

Along with the disappointments and crushing social embarrassments that Evelina undergoes during the course of the narrative, she is periodically delighted by London's many diversions. It is no coincidence that the playhouse is reserved for Evelina's first and most effusive praise.* [27] Running through Burney's novel is a rich vein of references to theatrical performance. Evelina's account of the

* See, for example, Evelina's raptures over Garrick's performance at the Drury Lane Theatre. Evelina's relatively refined taste for the 'higher' forms of entertainment, and the novel's debt to theatrical performance in general, reflects the cultural milieu in which Burney herself moved.

performance of Congreve's *Love for Love* (first performed in 1695), for example, provides for the reader heightened and dramatic elements of character description discernible through the responses of her companions. In other words, *Evelina*'s readers may glean additional layers of information from the intertextual elements of the novel (in the reactions of the fictional characters to known cultural forms, such as plays or operas). For Burney's contemporary readers, the timely nature of the theatrical events witnessed by Evelina and her companions would have made such episodes even more culturally resonant.

Certain characters, such as Evelina's grandmother Madame Duval or her friend Maria's father Captain Mirvan, recall stock characters from Restoration comedies and comic operas, as do the heightened melodrama and slapstick of their more farcical encounters (for example, the Captain's mock-robbery and the subsequent tumble taken by Madame Duval into a muddy ditch):

> The rage of poor Madame Duval was unspeakable; she dashed the candle out of his hand, stamped upon the floor, and, at last, spat in his face.

> This action seemed immediately to calm them both, as the joy of the Captain was converted into resentment, and the wrath of Madame Duval into fear; for he put his hands upon her shoulders, and gave her so violent a shake, that she screamed out for help; assuring her, at the same time, that if she had been one ounce less old, or less ugly, she should have had it all returned to her own face. (p. 67)

Evelina's journal-letters demonstrate that she is a masterful mimic of speech idioms and idiosyncratic behaviour as well as a social critic. The depiction of her London relatives, the Branghtons, demonstrates their brashness while simultaneously revealing her personal contempt for their ill-bred vulgarity:

This ceremony over, the young ladies began, very freely, to examine my dress, and to interrogate me concerning it. 'This apron's your own work, I suppose, Miss? But these sprigs a'n't in fashion now. Pray, if it is not impertinent, what might you give a yard for this lutestring? –Do you make your own caps, Miss? –' and many other questions equally interesting and well-bred. (p. 71)[*]

Despite – or perhaps because of – her rural upbringing, Evelina makes clear that her understanding of decorum surpasses that of her urban cousins. At the same time, however, Burney's depiction of London demonstrates a city where such matters are increasingly problematised because the higher echelons of polite society – towards which Evelina is both propelled and naturally attracted – often frequent the same venues as the more vulgar social ranks. Put another way, wealth and good breeding do not necessarily go hand in hand (witness Madame Duval) or even necessarily run in the same family (Captain Mirvan versus Mrs Mirvan and Maria); even the well-bred Lady Louisa, sister to Lord Orville, is affected and peevish.

These are the lessons which Evelina must glean from experience alone. They contrast markedly with the physical and sexual dangers lurking in the more abstracted urban landscapes of Haywood's and Richardson's fiction. The tragic tale of Evelina's mother, Caroline, evokes but also historicises the nature of these, older, threats to female virtue. Similarly, Burney's narrative, in a manner akin to theatrical transformation, changes Lord Belmont from a callous Lovelace-like rake into a repentant and sentimental father.

The curious sub-plot concerning Mr Macartney presents interesting questions for the student of the eighteenth-century novel. As the plot uncovers, Mr Macartney is Evelina's half-brother and has also suffered the emotional and financial repercussions of being disowned by their father, Sir John Belmont. As a post-Richardsonian narrative, the novel's depiction of Mr Macartney's anguish may be read as an indication that

***

[*] Dress aprons were worn during the daytime in this period as a matter of course; lutestring (or lustring) was a type of silk dress-fabric.

males, too, will suffer for the sexual transgressions of their fathers. Taken as a whole, the narrative concerning Evelina's relationship with her wider biological family presents far more questions than it answers; these mysteries anticipate the growing complexities of family relationships which will feature heavily in Austen's novels in the early nineteenth century. Mr Macartney's tale bears some resemblance to that of the tearful protagonist of the contemporary sentimental novel *The Man of Feeling* (1771) by Henry Mackenzie, as well as to Sarah Fielding's (much earlier work) *The Adventures of David Simple* (1744). As with so many other elements of contemporary popular culture, Burney's novel here reflects the growing trend for sentiment and sensibility in both the literature and plays of the late 1770s.* [28]

Evelina contextualises and, to an extent, historicises the plight of Richardson's heroines for a late eighteenth-century readership. Nevertheless, it presents its heroine with a new series of social challenges. Indeed, Evelina's experience represents a much wider paradox inherent throughout eighteenth-century constructions of female conduct, as Joanne Cutting-Gray observes:

> Though Evelina incarnates artlessness in a world of duplicity and evil, she nonetheless requires 'observation and experience' to make her 'fit for the world' ... Her private innocence is disrupted when she sallies forth into a disjunctive, public world where, affronted by male assertiveness, she, as a female, becomes a problem to herself. Unless one hears in Evelina's discourse a misguided effort to maintain the 'simplest attire' of innocence, one will see only female compliancy. Yet as long as she insists upon preserving her Innocency-passivity (a symbol for the stasis of her being) she cannot be compelled to assimilate experience fully. [29]

---

* Sensibility, within the context of eighteenth-century English literature, refers to a concept derived from moral philosophy in which the cultural importance of fellow-feeling, charity (in an emotional as well as financial sense) and sympathy are foregrounded in social relationships.

Though it will be articulated most succinctly in the first decades of the nineteenth century, particularly in Jane Austen's oeuvre, Evelina's paradox provides a relatively early example of the key theme which will continue to sustain the narratives of English novels for many years after the conclusion of the long eighteenth century.

Extended Commentary: Eliza Haywood, *Fantomina; or, Love in a Maze* (1725)

The contemporary success of a novel can provide a worthwhile indicator of its cultural significance. With this in mind, it should be noted that, during the first half of the eighteenth century, sales of Haywood's first work of prose fiction, *Love in Excess* (1719), were equalled only by *Robinson Crusoe* (1719), *Gulliver's Travels* (1726) and *Pamela* (1740–1). Given her intensely prolific output and the level of popular recognition that Haywood enjoyed during her lifetime, it is hardly surprising that her more recent critical 'rediscovery' has gleaned such rewarding and diverse interpretation.

Like many of her contemporaries, Haywood's literary output encompassed a wide range of genres including political writing (satires, essays and works of fiction), poems, translations, plays, criticism, periodicals and conduct books. She was also an actress and, during the 1740s, a publisher in her own right. While hardly exceptional, Haywood's versatility attests to a cultural atmosphere which encouraged authors to adapt and respond to the fickle demands of the literary marketplace. (For an extended discussion of this particular aspect of the literary culture of the period, see Part Four: 'A Culture of Print'.) Meeting demands, however, does not necessarily mean merely imitating popular literary models, since, as Paula Backscheider and John Richetti argue:

> [E]ven in her more formulaic tales of tumultuous passion the corruption of the male establishment is a given. Taken all together, Haywood's novellas are as much a critique of patriarchal

arrangements as they are often enough a celebration of female emotional intensity. Pathos and anger share the stage with erotic arousal and explorations of women's sexuality. To gain this effect, she sometimes creates the perspective of women watching men and construing them an alien, secret society. She can also meld class privilege with gender power in ways that have startling, contemporary resonance.[30]

Fantomina reflects many of the thematic and stylistic features typical in contemporary amatory fiction. Then, as now, lurid speculation concerning the sexual dalliances of London's fashionable and wealthy elite was a popular cultural pastime, as was the undoing of females whose passion leads them astray from the path of virtue. Like the hapless Beauplaisir in the text, however, readers should be wary of outward appearances. On closer examination, the narrative's depiction of a remarkably dynamic and resourceful female protagonist is anything but conventional.

An unnamed 'young lady of distinguished birth, beauty, wit, and spirit' finds that her elevated class makes it impossible for her to become acquainted with the handsome but fickle Beauplaisir through conventional means (p. 2566). As such, she adopts the disguise of a wealthy London courtesan and soon finds herself enjoying 'a vast deal of pleasure in conversing with him in this free and unrestrained manner' (p. 2567). Very quickly, however, the inevitable dilemma arises concerning how far she will carry on the disguise – and the subsequent role of the high-class prostitute – that she has assumed. A compelling combination of fierce determination, desire and sexual innocence leads her to devise a rather precarious plan in order to meet Beauplaisir again in private. The sexual encounter depicted underlines the problematic intersection, in gendered terms, between language – the 'charming conversation' of lovers – and physical consummation:

> She had now gone too far to retreat. –*He* was bold; -he was resolute. *She* fearful – confused, altogether unprepared to resist in such encounters, and rendered more so by the extreme liking she

had to him. –Shocked, however, at the apprehension of really losing her honour, she struggled all she could, and was just going to reveal the whole secret of her name and quality, when the thoughts of the liberty he had taken with her, and those he still continued to prosecute, prevented her, with representing the danger of being exposed, and the whole affair made a theme for public ridicule. –Thus much, indeed, she told him, that she was a virgin, and had assumed this manner of behaviour only to engage him. But that he little regarded, or if he had, would have been far from obliging him to desist; -nay, in the present burning eagerness of desire, 'tis probable that had he been acquainted both with who and what she really was, the knowledge of her birth would not have influenced him with respect sufficient to have curbed the wild exuberance of his luxurious wishes, or made him in that longing, that impatient moment, change the form of his addresses. (p. 2569)

Like *Clarissa*'s Lovelace, Beauplaisir in 'that impatient moment' negates the female's use of language (either as a means to preserve her virginity, or expose her identity): 'In fine, she was undone' (ibid.). Unlike Richardson, Haywood's narrator provides a detailed exposition of the differing, gendered, perceptions of the episode, revealing in turn the female protagonist's profound ambivalence and Beauplaisir's probable indifference regarding her true identity, anyway. Here and elsewhere in the narrative, true 'power' is in the hands of this omniscient narrator.

The rakish Beauplaisir is quick to accept the deception offered by the female protagonist as an explanation for her actions (she tells him that she is Fantomina, the 'daughter of a country gentleman' attempting to satisfy her curiosity concerning the experience of mistresses). Significantly, Beauplaisir's complacence is based on his own narrow understanding of females since he 'did not doubt by the beginning of her conduct, but that in the end she would be in reality the thing she so artfully had counterfeited' (p. 2570). Ironically, the narrator goes on to inform us, he 'had good enough nature to pity the misfortunes he imagined would be her lot' (ibid.). Despite his own role in her 'undoing', Beauplaisir's judgement of female conduct leads him to imagine that his new lover will end up, like most heroines of contemporary amatory fiction, a tragic victim. In revealing Beauplaisir's thoughts, the narrator emphasises the hypocrisy of the conventional rake figure even while he is simultaneously being outwitted at his own game.

As a typical rake, Beauplaisir '[v]aried not so much from his sex as to be able to prolong desire to any great length after possession', yet the intrepid female protagonist proves herself to be anything but the conventional passive victim of amatory fiction. Now fully aware that she seeks rather more than Beauplaisir's charming conversation ('to be compelled, to be sweetly forced to what she wished with equal ardour'), she adopts a series of disguises in order to repeatedly seduce (in the guise of being seduced by) her hapless lover.

The stratagem sees Fantomina transformed, in turn, into a pretty maid in Bath called Celia, a charming young widow named Mrs Bloomer, and finally into the utterly mysterious Incognita. Disguise and masquerade are prevalent themes in much eighteenth-century literature (and amatory fiction in particular); here and elsewhere, they offer the protagonist a liberating and empowering ability to control both her own identity and sexual agency.[31] The fluidity with which she moves between social realms, and transforms her appearance, recalls the cultural significance of theatrical performance as a contemporary motif; it is no coincidence that the protagonist first notices Beauplaisir, and carries out her first deception, at the theatre.

The protagonist is eventually brought to an important self-realisation concerning her use of disguise, one that allows Haywood to overwrite the formulaic model of amatory fiction itself. Though initially motivated simply by her love for Beauplaisir, the protagonist becomes aware that the true source of her pleasure is the ever-changing novelty of Beauplaisir's passion, and the thrill of manipulative power itself:

> She could not forbear laughing heartily to think of the tricks she
> had played him, and applauding her own strength of genius and
> force of resolution, which by such unthought-of ways could

triumph over her lover's inconstancy … the most violent passion, if it does not change its object, in time will wither. Possession naturally abates the vigour of desire, and I should have had, at best, but a cold, insipid, husband-like lover in my arms; but by these arts of passing on him a new mistress whenever the ardour, which alone makes love a blessing, begins to diminish for the former one, I have him always raving, wild, impatient, longing, dying. –O, that all neglected wives and fond abandoned nymphs would take this method! (p. 2580)

In her realisation that her plight is 'the same' as that of other females, Haywood's protagonist is presented as the female protagonist in all amatory fiction – in which knowing males manipulate innocent and passive females – who consciously rejects this position. This is not to suggest that Haywood merely inverts the model and posits the 'triumph' of the female sex over the male. Beauplaisir is a willing – if also unwitting – accomplice to his own seduction. Moreover, the narrative's conclusion witnesses a sort of downfall for the protagonist; she is 'undone' by neither the sexual impropriety of her behaviour nor by Beauplaisir but, instead, by external factors – the unexpected arrival of her mother and the biological imperative of pregnancy. Despite these factors, however, as Ballaster and other critics have suggested, 'the conclusion of *Fantomina* is one of the least melancholy of Haywood's endings'.[32]

That this is the case is due in part to Haywood's challenge to the literary conventions of amatory fiction; it is also due, arguably, to the narrative's foregrounding of the creative authority of the writer herself over all other forms of power. Haywood's manipulation of literary form in *Fantomina* – the deeply contrived nature of this narrative – consciously interrogates the relationship between literary representation and the reader's expectations. The reader *is* Beauplaisir, endlessly and *willingly* diverted by novelty and artifice in pursuit of other pleasures. As Beauplaisir is duped by Fantomina's cursory changes in appearance, so the reader is happy to accept the highly contrived nature of Haywood's settings and plot. In parallel with the conventions of amatory prose fiction, Haywood's urban landscapes and interior scenes represent little more than theatrical backdrops to the narrative's action while the plot progresses through a series of seduction episodes. The reader's expectations are constantly titillated by additional narrative details that Haywood can contrive at a moment's notice: for example, a bed is instantly and conveniently situated in the room where the Widow Bloomer faints, and the protagonist's Bath country dialect is particularly convincing because 'having been bred in these parts, [she] knew very well how to imitate' it (p. 2572).

This reading gains further significance in the final seduction episode in which Beauplaisir finds himself being quite literally 'kept in the dark' by the mysterious masked Incognita. He resolves to wake early, to catch a glimpse of her face before she dons the mask, only to find himself outwitted again as she has contrived to keep him in an artificially darkened bedroom. Turning day into night, she once again slips away unrecognised (pp. 2581–2).

Despite the 'disappointment of his curiosity' concerning his lover's true identity, the narrator informs us that Beauplaisir continues the affair with Incognita 'for about a fortnight'. His plight is the reader's own. In order to satisfy their own ends, readers knowingly suspend their disbelief and submit to any number of literary contrivances and stratagems in the hope of delaying the moment which concludes their reading pleasure. It is a pleasure based, in part, on the knowledge that texts have the power to manipulate the emotional responses of individual readers even as they present scenes, plots and characters that are deeply implausible. Put another way, a consciously artificial literary text does not deny the presence of a realm in which diverse individual experience exists, it merely places a beautifully elaborate and curious mask in front of that experience. The conclusion of *Fantomina* may mark the final 'unmasking' of this remarkable female protagonist, but leaves firmly in place the creative power of the author herself.

Notes

1   Of the many critical studies of the novel's origins, two of the most
     influential are Ian Watts, *The Rise of the Novel: Studies in Defoe, Richardson
     and Fielding* (London: Peregrine Books, 1963); and Michael McKeon, *The
     Origins of the English Novel, 1600–1740* (Baltimore: Johns Hopkins
     University Press, 1987).
2   In particular, see Jane Spencer, *The Rise of the Woman Novelist: From Aphra
     Behn to Jane Austen* (Oxford: Blackwell, 1986); and Janet Todd, *The Sign of
     Angellica: Woman, Writing and Fiction 1660–1800* (London: Virago, 1989).
3   The most influential text on the development of the early modern concept
     of the individual within this period is Lawrence Stone, *The Family, Sex and
     Marriage in England 1500–1800*, abr. edn (London: Penguin Books, 1979).
     See also Christopher Flint, *Family Fictions: Narrative and Domestic Relations
     in Britain, 1688–1798* (Stanford: Stanford University Press, 1998).
4   For a sense of the profound cultural impact of *Pamela* on contemporary
     readers and authors, see Thomas Keymer and Peter Sabor, *'Pamela' in the
     Marketplace: Literary Controversy and Print Culture in Eighteenth-century
     Britain and Ireland* (Cambridge: Cambridge University Press, 2006); and
     Thomas Keymer and Peter Sabor (eds), *The 'Pamela' Controversy: Criticisms
     and Adaptations of Samuel Richardson's 'Pamela', 1740–1750*, 6 vols
     (London: Pickering & Chatto, 2001).
5   On the history of romance, see Tomas Hägg, *The Novel in Antiquity*
     (Berkeley and Los Angeles: University of California Press, 1983); and Ben
     E. Perry, *The Ancient Romances: A Literary–Historical Account of their Origins*
     (Berkeley and Los Angeles: University of California Press, 1967).
6   Ros Ballaster, *Seductive Forms: Women's Amatory Fiction from 1684 to 1740*
     (Oxford: Clarendon Press, 1992) pp. 29–30.
7   An overview of contemporary public responses to female authorship may
     be found in Vivien Jones (ed.), *Women in the Eighteenth Century:
     Constructions of Femininity* (London and New York: Routledge, 1990),
     especially Section 4.II (Writing: Public Images), pp. 170–92.
8   From a letter to Aaron Hill, probably from January 1741, as cited in
     George L. Barnett, *Eighteenth-century British Novelists on the Novel* (New
     York: Meredith Corporation, 1968), p. 72.
9   See, in particular, G. A. Starr, *Defoe and Spiritual Autobiography* (Princeton,
     New Jersey: Princeton University Press, 1965); and J. Paul Hunter, *The
     Reluctant Pilgrim: Defoe's Emblematic Method and Quest for Form in
     'Robinson Crusoe'* (Baltimore: Johns Hopkins University Press, 1966) and

Before Novels: The Cultural Contexts of Eighteenth-century English Fiction (New York and London: W. W. Norton, 1990).

10   John Bunyan, *The Pilgrim's Progress*, edited and with an introduction by Roger Sharrock (Harmondsworth: Penguin Books, 1965), p. 91. All further citations of the primary text refer to this edition.

11   Sharrock, Introduction to Bunyan, *The Pilgrim's Progress*, pp. 23–4.

12   McKeon, *The Origins of the English Novel*, p. 297.

13   Ibid., pp. 312–14.

14   Ibid.

15   Sharrock, Introduction to Bunyan, *The Pilgrim's Progress*, p. 23.

16   On the literature of pious female experience, see Ann Hughes, 'Puritanism and Gender', in John Coffey and Paul C. H. Lim (eds), *The Cambridge Companion to Puritanism* (Cambridge: Cambridge University Press, 2008), pp. 294–308.

17   Eliza Haywood, *Fantomina; or, Love in a Maze*, in Lawrence Lipking and James Noggle (eds), *The Norton Anthology of English Literature*, Volume C: *The Restoration and the Eighteenth Century* (New York and London: W. W. Norton, 2006), pp. 2566–84, at pp. 2567–8. All further citations of this primary text refer to this edition.

18   Stone, *The Family, Sex and Marriage*, p. 152; see pp. 151–80 for an overview of the concept of affective individualism.

19   The profound cultural impact of Savile's and other conduct works, particularly on the formation of the early novel, is the subject of Nancy Armstrong, *Desire and Domestic Fiction: A Political History of the Novel* (New York: Oxford University Press, 1987).

20   Daniel Defoe, Introduction to *The Family Instructor*, Volume 1: *A Facsimile Reproduction*, edited by Paula Backscheider (New York: Scholars' Facsimiles and Reprints, 1989), pp. 2–3.

21   Paul Salzman, *English Prose Fiction 1558–1700: A Critical History* (Oxford: Clarendon Press, 1985), p. 240.

22   For a consideration of Richardson's use of the epistolary form, see Chapter 2, 'Richardson's Sources', in Cynthia Griffin Wolff, *Samuel Richardson and the Eighteenth-century Puritan Character* (Hamden: Archon, 1972), pp. 14–58; on the form generally, see Janet Gurkin Altman, *Epistolarity: Approaches to Form* (Columbus: Ohio State University Press, 1982).

23   Angus Ross, Introduction to Samuel Richardson, *Clarissa* (London: Penguin Books, 1985), p. 18. All further citations of the primary text refer to this edition.

24   But also see Tom Keymer, *Richardson's 'Clarissa' and the Eighteenth-century Reader* (Cambridge: Cambridge University Press, 2004).

25   For a comprehensive overview of some of the critical responses to *Clarissa* (particularly but not exclusively those associated with the study of gender and sexuality), see Sue Warrick Doederlein, 'Clarissa in the Hands of the Critics', *Eighteenth-century Studies*, 16:4 (Summer 1983), pp. 401–14.

26   As cited in Barnett, *Eighteenth-century British Novelists on the Novel*, pp. 76–7.

27   See Vivien Jones's Introduction to Frances Burney, *Evelina* (Oxford: Oxford University Press, 2002), pp. x–xii, xx–xxiv. All further citations of the primary text refer to this edition.

28   See G. J. Barker-Benfield, *The Culture of Sensibility: Sex and Society in Eighteenth-century Britain* (Chicago and London: University of Chicago Press, 1992); and John Mullan, *Sentiment and Sociability: The Language of Feeling in the Eighteenth Century* (Oxford: Clarendon Press, 1988).

29   Joanne Cutting-Gray, 'Writing Innocence: Fanny Burney's *Evelina*', *Tulsa Studies in Women's Literature*, 9:1 (Spring 1990), pp. 43–57, at p. 43.

30   Paula R. Backscheider and John J. Richetti (eds), Introduction, *Popular Fiction by Women 1660–1730: An Anthology* (Oxford: Clarendon Press, 1996), p. xx.

31   In particular, see Terry Castle, *Masquerade and Civilisation: The Carnivalesque in Eighteenth-century English Culture and Fiction* (Stanford: Stanford University Press, 1986), and 'The Carnivalization of Eighteenth-century English Narrative', *PMLA*, 9 (1984), pp. 903–16.

32   Ballaster, *Seductive Forms*, p. 192.

Part Four
Critical Theories and Debates

Man, Nature and Liberty

When Charles II was restored to the English throne in May 1660, most of the adult population would still have been able to recall his father's execution eleven years earlier. Some did so with a sense of satisfaction (in that the King's abuse of his royal authority had finally been curtailed); others remembered this pivotal historical event as a tragic miscarriage of justice. All would have recognised in it the extent to which, when provoked, an elected English parliament could wield remarkable power.

If the English Civil War and its aftermath had provoked deadly arguments concerning the appropriate nature of civil government, the social and political upheaval of the period equally posed many questions about the nature of society itself. Philosophical and political contexts will illuminate any period of history but, during the long eighteenth century, questions about how human beings first formed together into social groups – and how those groups or 'societies' acquire political structures – gained particular urgency.

Much of the most influential philosophical and political writing during this period possesses literary merit in its own terms; well-structured arguments and a fundamental belief in rational thought were valued across many cultural disciplines. Succinct writing is often the most memorable: from a well-known aphorism used to describe man's life in a state of nature (prior to the formation of societies) as being 'solitary, poor, nasty, brutish, and short', for example, we can quickly see how Thomas Hobbes means to depict the miserable conditions of life for human beings deprived of the benefits of civil society.[1]

Hobbes and His Influence

Despite their shared use of key terms (including 'state of nature'), the philosophical model of Thomas Hobbes (1588–1679) differed significantly from that of John Locke (1632–1704) (see below). Now best known for his *Leviathan* (published in 1651 in English, with a definitive Latin edition in 1668), Hobbes argued that human appetite was driven by the need for self-preservation; man is in essence a selfish animal, motivated primarily by the desire to survive. Hobbes argued, like Locke, that the basis of all human knowledge is sensation, but he also suggested that man acquires knowledge solely to preserve himself and his own self-interest (rather than for any 'higher' – more philanthropic or spiritual – aim). Although capable of rational thought, men employ reason purely for self-gain or self-preservation.

Mankind first existed, according to Hobbes, in an isolated 'state of nature' before forming into social groups for the purposes of mutual self-benefit; societies in turn developed organised power structures and all forms of political and social control, from monarchies to legal justice and the democratic process, are derived in this way. The populace are willing to remain subject to political power only because – and for as long as – the demands of self-interest dictate that their needs are better served by submission than by rebellion (for example, the King may use his authority to protect them and their offspring during a period of war). The memorable image of the kingly figure associated with *Leviathan* illustrates this concept in its depiction of a multitude of people formed into the single body of the sovereign, the 'body politic', with its leader at its 'head'.

Hobbes's broadly cynical conception of human nature raised several disturbing implications for contemporary readers; if certain behavioural 'norms', for example morality, were just artifices which stopped men from killing each other through a mutual contract of self-preservation, then what role did God play? Or did He even exist? Hobbes's writing was widely viewed throughout the long eighteenth century as deeply controversial and even atheistical.[2] The cultural longevity of his ideas, however, can be seen in authors as diverse as the Earl of Rochester, Aphra Behn, Jonathan Swift, Daniel Defoe and even George Crabbe (all of whom are discussed in Part Three of this volume). Rochester, in particular, upholds Hobbesian arguments concerning the pre-eminence of bodily sensation as the only means by which man can attain knowledge. His typically misanthropic depiction of mankind as creatures wholly devoted to self-interest, lacking the higher faculties needed for spiritual devotion to God, even suggests that humans are worse than other animals because man alone is capable of betraying his own kind ('Man undoes man, to do himself no good').[3]

Rochester's rejection of any notion of spiritual integrity in human nature is powerfully nihilistic. The influence of the Hobbesian model, however, is variously discernible in diverse contemporary literature including that of authors readily known for their religious conviction. Jonathan Swift, Dean of Dublin's St Patrick's Cathedral, created a hero who encounters a race of filthy, irrational and morally depraved beings (the Yahoos) whose behaviour reminds Gulliver of his human counterparts back in England. At the same time, and interpreting Hobbesian ideas of human nature very differently, Swift's Houyhnhnms, and their coldly rational indifference towards the Yahoos, evokes the callous 'inhumanity' of absentee English landlords towards their destitute Irish tenants.[4]

More closely aligned to the Puritan tradition of spiritual biography than Swift's work, Defoe's novels express the profound influence of Hobbes's rational philosophy in ambiguous terms. This is particularly apparent in his repeated depiction of protagonists who relentlessly pursue material gain. Scholarly consideration of the Hobbesian model of human nature, applied to Defoe's fiction, has rewardingly revealed the extent to which these texts' protagonists offer excellent scope for psychological, including psychoanalytic, analysis. As early as 1971, for example, Homer O. Brown usefully explored the relationship in Defoe's fiction between the 'strong fear of the menace of other wills, a pervasive fear' and the extent to which it may be explained through the 'notion of radical egocentricity'.[5]

Most powerfully symbolised through Robinson Crusoe's isolated state on his island, this psychological tension is equally evident in the burning desire to steal which continues to motivate Moll Flanders long after the risk of starvation has passed. Such a tension may also be seen to represent the energy which drives capitalism itself; it is the desire to accumulate wealth for its own sake rather than for any benefits derived from it. It is hardly surprising that all of Defoe's novels have also provided rich analytical sources for Marxist literary interpretation. Lois A. Chaber has suggested, for example, that Moll's desperate escape through London's back alleys after her first theft provides an 'emblem for the novel' itself in its evocation of 'the twisted course laid out for Moll in an unjust society'.[6] In its purest form and in Defoe's last novel, Roxana's excessive accumulation of material wealth offers her no ultimate solace in the contemplation of a life of sin and deceit:

> [A]fter some few Years of flourishing, and outwardly happy Circumstances, I fell into a dreadful Course of Calamities ... and I was brought so low again, that my Repentance seem'd to be only the Consequence of my Misery, as my Misery was of my Crime.[7]

Unlike Defoe's earlier protagonists, Roxana is unable to bridge the profound gap between her 'outwardly happy Circumstances' and the 'Calamities' and 'Misery' caused by her relentless pursuit of material wealth. This narrative provides the most powerful example of a tension which Defoe's fiction – and, more broadly, the eighteenth-century novel in general – implicitly highlights. It is a tension born out of the irreconcilable discrepancies between a new world view of rational, individual and materialist perception of reality – the model broadly associated with the rational philosophy of Hobbes and Locke, among others – and a more traditional perspective in which God, the King, the community and the family (often but not necessarily in that order) took precedence over individual or private interests. This tension is a definitive aspect of English literature and culture during the long eighteenth century.

The novel is by no means the only literary form that concerns us in the long eighteenth century, but it offers perhaps the most accessible example of the 'tension' described above because its defining concern is individual experience (see also Part Three: 'The Novel and the Individual'). The cultural identity of the individual (as we continue to recognise it in social, economic and even psychological terms) emerges during the course of the long eighteenth century. Christopher Flint has suggested:

> Amplifying the scientific and philosophic rationalism synthesized by Locke and championed by others such as Bacon, Descartes, Hobbes, and Newton, eighteenth-century writers of fiction began to address the problems associated with the newly-conceived social, political, and economic status of the individual without necessarily transforming the social contexts that produce individuals. They were concerned with the effect of these intellectual changes on the fabric of everyday life, on how individuals juggled their own interests with those of the family, the magistrate, the landowner, the mob, and the crown. At the same time, such writers also wanted to diminish some of the power of the individualism they were, in theory, promoting.[8]

The remainder of this chapter explores the complex cultural interface between what Flint refers to as 'scientific and philosophic rationalism' – the very nature of intellectual development most readily associated with the European Enlightenment as a whole – and the deeply ambiguous 'power of individualism' which concerned writers throughout the long eighteenth century. Individualism is an ambiguous form of power because, in the broadest possible sense, it alludes to both the breaking-down of traditional systems (of religious and political authority, in particular) and the foundation of new concepts of human 'progress' or 'modernity'.

Locke and the 'Power of Individualism'

Beyond its manifestation in the literature of the long eighteenth century, the ambiguous 'power of individualism' – defined in this broad sense, at least – might also be associated with the very disparate versions of political revolutionary fervour which chronicle the whole of the period. It is impossible to gauge the full extent to which Locke's philosophy influenced this cultural period, but literary evidence suggests that the epistemological theories in his *Essay Concerning Human Understanding* (1689) had the greatest impact whereas his *Two Treatises of Government* (1690) was equally valuable for its reflections on the political atmosphere of its period.[9] Although the two works are not entirely consistent (in, for example, his discussion of the law of nature and the concept of moral certainty), there are useful and important correlations between his political philosophy and his description of the originating principles of human nature (the operation of the mind, the senses, language, instinct, and so on) which are briefly considered.

Fundamentally, Locke's *Essay* suggests that the mind of a human being, when first born, is like a piece of 'white paper void of all characters, without any *ideas*'.[10] Humans possess no innate sense of self or identity but, instead, they derive all knowledge and understanding from sense-impressions received after birth:

> The senses at first let in particular ideas and furnish the yet empty cabinet; and the mind by degrees growing familiar with some of them, they are lodged in the memory, and names got to them.[11]

This seemingly simple concept has many profound implications. Fundamentally, it implies that social hierarchies (such as class or other aspects of social identity) are not fixed and innate; kings and paupers are therefore made, not born. While his *Essay* therefore tacitly suggests the fundamental equality of all men, the full political – and potentially revolutionary – implications of this idea are explored in his *Two Treatises of Government*.

Locke's model of sense-derived human understanding goes on to suggest that the relationship between knowledge (in the form of ideas and language) and the tangible, external world is also derived from sense-impressions:

> It may also lead us a little towards the Original of all our Notions and Knowledge, if we remark, how great a dependance our *Words* have on common sensible *Ideas*; and how those, which are made up of to stand for Actions and Notions quite removed from sense, *have their rise from thence, and from obvious sensible* Ideas *are transferred from more abstruse significations*, and made to stand for *Ideas* that come not under the cognizance of our senses … .[12]

The complex process by which ideas are associated with each other in the human mind is separately considered by Locke in the previous section of the *Essay*. His assertion that ideas can 'come to be so united in some Men's minds, that 'tis very hard to separate them, they always keep company' was humorously explored by Sterne in *Tristram Shandy*; it also has profound implications that would later be considered by Freudian psychology.[13] The primary notion of human communication – language – is described by Locke in terms that emphasise nature as both quintessentially social ('whereby [men's ideas] might be made known to others, and the thoughts of men's minds be conveyed from one to another'), yet also individual and idiosyncratic:

> … the knowing and the ignorant, the learned and unlearned, use the words they speak (with any meaning) all alike. They, in every man's mouth, stand for the ideas he has, and which he would express by them … they suppose their words to be marks of the ideas in the minds of other men, with whom they communicate.[14]

On this basis, language is an imperfect means of communication because human beings rarely or never share the same precise significations for the words they learn although they share

certain articulate sounds very perfectly and have them readily on
our tongues and always at hand in our memories, but yet are
not always careful to examine or settle their significations
perfectly, [thus] it often happens that men, even when they
would apply themselves to an attentive consideration, do set
their thoughts more on words than things ... therefore some,
not only children but men, speak several words no otherwise
than parrots do, only because they have learned them and have
been accustomed to those sounds.[15]

Profoundly interesting in its own right as well as within the wider
context of the history of linguistics, Locke's theory of language provokes
intriguing political questions. His assertion of men's tendency to 'set
their thoughts more on words than things' tacitly questions the validity
of legal procedures such as the swearing of oaths to the monarch or to
the Church (which played a fundamental role in state legislation). His
observations concerning the imperfect or inconsistent transmission of
words' signification in language implicitly questions the 'unshakeable'
authority of texts such as the Bible or a piece of parliamentary legislation.
On this point, it is worth observing that much of Locke's writing was
attacked both during and after his lifetime for its theological
implications, a point which makes it even more difficult to gauge the
true scale of his contemporary influence. Locke himself was widely
accused of deism (that is, the belief that Jesus Christ was human rather
than divine). There is little doubt that his religious views were
controversial; his profound scepticism concerning Scriptural authority
is explicitly expressed in *The Reasonableness of Christianity as Delivered in
the Scriptures* (1695), in which he asserts that faith and good works are
sufficient means by which *most* people can achieve salvation; the
contents of the Scriptures are largely superfluous to their needs and are
only suitable for 'learned men':

Though all divine Revelation requires the obedience of Faith; yet
every truth of informed Scriptures is not one of those, that by the
Law of Faith is required to be explicitly believed ... any other

Proposition contained in the Scripture, which God has not thus made a necessary part of the Law of Faith, (without an actual assent to which he will not allow any one to be a Believer) a Man may be ignorant of, without hazarding his Salvation by a defect in his Faith.[16]

Scriptural authority was held in high regard by Protestants both within and outside the Protestant establishment; the Bible provided the direct means by which Christians could understand God's 'word'. In questioning that authority – and the concept of language itself – Locke consciously excluded himself from the intellectual mainstream.

Locke broadly rejects the Classical philosophical model of the mind as essentially separate from the body (Platonic idealism) because knowledge, in his model, is derived from sensory (bodily) experience. The image of the individual human body stands at the centre of Locke's philosophy, as the conduit through which all knowledge is derived, and (he argues in the second *Treatise*) as the original source of labour through which humanity, in a state of nature, first obtained sustenance. Locke and Hobbes both depend on different narratives in which a 'state of nature' is created in order to explain the subsequent origins of human society. Following principles first suggested by the sixteenth-century theologian Richard Hooker, John Locke argues that, within the state of nature, men enjoyed equality and freedom. This equality provides 'the foundation of that obligation to mutual love amongst men, on which [Hooker] builds the duties they owe one another, and from whence he derives the great maxims of justice and charity'.[17]

This state of mutual love and charity might at first appear as a contradiction to Locke's latter observation that 'in that state of perfect equality', 'all men may be restrained from invading others' rights', yet both here and throughout the second chapter of his second *Treatise*, his emphasis remains upon the protection of *others'* rights ('justice') rather than the self-interest and instinct towards self-preservation foregrounded in Hobbes's state of nature (defined in Chapter 14 of *Leviathan* as a state 'without a common power to keep them all in awe').[18]

Beyond the state of nature, Locke's principal concern in the second *Treatise* is to describe what happens when mankind gathers together into groups, or 'political societies'.* He argues that the act of voluntarily joining a political society is tantamount to agreeing to abide by its rules and accept the decisions of the majority; this act of voluntary consent is known as the 'compact', or social contract:

> Whosoever therefore out of a state of nature unite into a community, must be understood to give up all the power, necessary to the ends for which they unite into society, to the majority of the community … this is done by barely [merely] agreeing to unite into one political society, which is all the compact that is, or needs be, between the individuals, that enter into, or make up a commonwealth … thus that, which begins and actually constitutes any political society, is nothing but the consent of any into such a society. And this is that, and that only, which did, or could give beginning to any lawful government in the world.[19]

Locke's concept of the social contract is intended to provide a powerful rejection of the patriarchal model of absolute monarchy proposed by Sir Robert Filmer (*c.* 1590–1653). Filmer's *Patriarcha, or the Natural Power of Kings* (published in 1680) had argued – as did Hobbes – that a sovereign possessed absolute power over the lives and property of their subjects, in the same manner that a father possessed absolute power over his wife, children and servants (as the head of his household). Filmer also asserted that, paralleling the Biblical precedent of Adam's power in the Garden of Eden, sovereignty is divinely ordained. Locke's second *Treatise* clearly asserts that 'absolute monarchy … is indeed inconsistent with civil society, and so can be no form of civil government at all.[20]

---

* He maintains that human beings opt to join political societies because, although the state of nature represents a state of liberty, it is unstable and subject to war.

A Turbulent History

Locke had a tendency to rework his manuscripts; as such, the original dating of his writing remains notoriously problematic.[21] Nevertheless, extensive scholarly research has ascertained that Locke's rejection of the patriarchal model of monarchy was directly inspired by the series of turbulent events which, from 1678, dominated English political life. Long-standing concerns that Charles II had produced no legitimate Protestant heir (combined with the public knowledge of his brother's conversion to Roman Catholicism) flared into mass panic when Titus Oates, a Catholic convert, provided sworn testimony of the existence of a Catholic assassination plot to remove Charles and place his brother James, Duke of York, on the throne. The highly dubious testimony of Oates – detailing the mass-murder of Protestants and the reinstatement of Catholicism, all at the behest of James and Charles's Catholic wife – might, by itself, have come to nothing. Shortly afterwards, however, the murdered body of a Middlesex magistrate involved in Oates's case (Sir Edmond Berry Godfrey) was discovered. Only after the execution of fifteen men and the torture of many more (most or all of whom were probably entirely innocent), and a political crisis nearly resulting in a second English Civil War, were the outrageous claims of Oates finally dismissed and Oates himself imprisoned.

Anthony Ashley Cooper, first Earl of Shaftesbury (1621–1713), had served as the Lord Chancellor from 1672 but fell out of favour with the King over his efforts to pass an Exclusion Bill (barring Roman Catholics from succeeding to the throne of England). He was also a close friend and employer of John Locke (who had first met Shaftesbury in 1666 and subsequently served in his household as a political adviser and tutor). Now the head of the opposition (Whig) party, Shaftesbury and the Whigs took advantage of the public hysteria against Roman Catholicism to promote popular support for the Exclusion Bill. They approached Charles's eldest illegitimate son, James Walter, the Protestant Duke of Monmouth, as the most viable candidate to succeed his father (despite the fact that Charles refused to legitimise his birth).

The efforts of the Whigs to pass the Exclusion Bill on two occasions only narrowly failed; on the third attempt in 1681, after it was passed in the House of Commons but before it could proceed to the House of Lords, Charles dissolved Parliament. Now secretly in receipt of subsidies from the French king and thus no longer financially dependent on his ministers, Charles refused to allow the formation of a new Parliament during the remainder of his lifetime. Commemorated in many contemporary works such as John Dryden's *Absalom and Achitophel* (1680) and Sir Thomas Otway's verse tragedy *Venice Preserv'd* (1682), Shaftesbury was lucky to survive his imprisonment in the Tower (on charges of high treason) at all; he died shortly afterwards in Holland. Monmouth was less adept at learning from political failure and was executed for his part in leading a disastrous Protestant rebellion against his uncle, King James II, in 1685.

The turbulent political events that occurred between 1678 and 1688 – culminating in James's forced abdication from the English throne – highlight the tensions inherent within a form of government which combined patriarchal monarchy with a representative parliamentary system. The long-held notion of divinely ordained and absolute monarchical authority ('divine right' or 'Jure divino') increasingly came to be questioned during the reigns of Charles II and James II, although their staunchest Tory allies continued to support the Stuart cause – and the hereditary rights of James's successors – long after 1688. Questions surrounding legitimate patrimony and patriarchal succession – and the very concept of English identity itself – are a key thematic concern across the entire literary period. Earlier works such as Aphra Behn's *Oroonoko* (1688) reflect the author's Tory sympathies in its tragic depiction of a heroic prince who, along with his pregnant wife, is betrayed into slavery by the greedy and hypocritical English authorities; in the same year the Catholic wife of James II, Mary of Modena, gave birth to a son shortly before the King's abdication. The Jacobite rebellions of 1715 and 1745 reflected continuing public support for the Stuart succession through the hereditary claims of James's exiled son James Francis Edward Stuart (1688–1766) and grandson Charles Edward Stuart (or 'Bonnie Prince Charlie', 1720–88).

As outlined in Part Two: 'A Cultural Overview', the 'Glorious Revolution' of 1688 brought the Protestant Dutch King William of Orange and his wife, Mary (the daughter of James II by his first, Protestant, wife, Anne Hyde), to the English throne. It also brought John Locke back to England after approximately a decade in political exile (in France and Holland) and, in 1690, saw the publication of his *Two Treatises*. By this time, Locke's refutation of Filmer's *Patriarcha* (the principal subject of the first *Treatise*) was less important than his discussion of natural law and the origins of property.[22] Locke had argued that, within the state of nature, mankind had enjoyed perfect and complete liberty. Liberty does not, however, mean complete licence to do anything one wishes; mankind within the state of nature must still observe certain principles of moral integrity. The basis of morality is natural law, handed down to man from God; as all men are equal in the eyes of God, He commands that men do not harm others in terms of their 'life, health, liberty, or possessions'.

John Locke and America

The role of possessions, or property, is essential to an understanding of Locke's argument concerning civil government and the compact. While in the state of nature, all men held land 'in common', but when an individual mixes his labour with the raw materials provided by nature (by picking fruit off the tree, or tilling a piece of land), his investment of labour makes those materials and that land his rightful property. Moreover, those who could achieve better yields from their investment of labour (such as colonial settlers who bring more efficient methods of farming to their new settlements) have a superior claim to that property. Among other things, Locke's argument provides clear justification for the English appropriation of land in colonial America from the native population on the basis of their 'improvement' of the land; in *Two Treatises*, Locke relies heavily on the notion of 'America', both as an example of a location where limitless fertile common land awaits cultivation and as a template for the 'state of nature' in which primitive groups of men lived under 'the law of nature'. Other social concepts, including the origins of money (a commodity which would not waste or decay and which men could store or trade with others) and the differences between slavery and servitude are systematically defined in Locke's plain and forthright prose.[23]

Locke's political philosophy continued to exert a profound influence after his death in 1704. In the last quarter of the eighteenth century, in their bid for political representation and, ultimately, self-rule, American revolutionaries such as Thomas Jefferson and Thomas Paine turned again to Locke's writing to justify their authority to claim independence from English colonial power. One of the most influential political documents of the eighteenth century, the *American Declaration of Independence* (1776), bears a striking resemblance in both its prose style and political orientation to Locke's *Second Treatise*. The *Declaration* reads:

> When in the Course of human events it becomes necessary for one people to dissolve the political bands which have connected them with another and to assume among the powers of the earth, the separate and equal station to which the Laws of Nature and of Nature's God entitle them, a decent respect to the opinions of mankind requires that they should declare the causes which impel them to the separation.*

Revolution was a key European cultural movement in the latter part of the eighteenth century, not just in the American colonies but also in France, Holland, Poland and parts of modern-day Italy. While powerful arguments for political independence and social equality feature in much of the philosophical writing from this period, it is equally apparent that the definition of 'equality' remains wholly subjective. Locke's state of nature accommodated the concept of slavery, for example, and made clear that, while parental power over children was neither absolute nor extended beyond the children's age of minority, fathers retained authority over their wives and children.[24]

---

* *The American Declaration of Independence* was signed on 4 July 1776. It is generally believed that Thomas Jefferson was responsible for writing the Declaration. See also Thomas Paine, *On Common Sense* (1776).

Mary Astell and the Marriage Contract

Mary Astell (1666–1731) systematically dismantled Locke's political model. A staunch Tory who upheld the principles of absolutism and divinely ordained monarchical power, Astell was a devout Anglican who defended the constitutional rights of ecclesiastical power in government. Equally – and perhaps surprisingly – she embraced the principle of universal human reason, a belief which underpinned her lifelong campaign for social equality and rationally expressed political debate. Unlike most of her female contemporaries, Astell received an education that was rigorous and highly intellectual. In her first published work, *A Serious Proposal to the Ladies* (published in parts in 1694 and 1697), she argued that, denied a proper education, women were unjustly confined to an ornamental and petty existence. By a 'proper' education, Astell meant adequate exposure to the works of moral and religious philosophy which would teach women to understand their higher spiritual purpose in life.

Astell's work is remembered now primarily because she was an early and articulate campaigner for the education of women but, within the context of political philosophy, she provides a thought-provoking rejection of the principle of social contract as put forward by Hobbes and Locke.[25] Her contribution to the social contract debate helps to underline how, in the long eighteenth century, it became increasingly important that political and philosophical writing (and its discussion of abstract concepts such as human nature, social equality and political power) needed to be expressed in ways that were readily accessible to a receptive and growing public readership.

For Locke and Hobbes, the social contract refers to an agreement by which subjects obey and submit to a ruler in exchange for protection of their lives and livelihood. Patricia Springborg has observed that such a concept 'relied for its force on the only form of legal contract with which ordinary people had experience, the marriage contract'.[26] In opposition to this analogy, Astell outlined what she saw as fundamental differences between the marriage contract and the social contract which, she argued in *Reflections upon Marriage* (1700), emphasised the legal and social inferiority of women's status. 'If all men are born free,' she famously asks Locke in the preface, 'how is it that all women are born slaves?' Hobbes and Locke had drawn parallels between the voluntary submission of subjects to their rulers in the social compact and the voluntary submission of wives to their husbands, stressing in both cases the freedom and equality of those who willingly entered into either contract. Refuting this, Astell pointed out that the rights of wives within the marriage estate were anything but equal to those of their husbands, and that their vulnerable position bore no resemblance to the legal and civil protection enjoyed by subjects bound to their sovereign.

Astell's clarification of the compact as a political, rather than social, theory helps to underline her recognition of fundamental gender inequalities within marriage. Elsewhere in *Reflections*, however, she employs the political/social analogy in order to compare the sanctity of marriage vows with the oaths of loyalty and obedience that subjects swear to their divinely ordained monarch. In doing so, her purpose is to emphasise the holy sanctity of both kinds of vows (such as were broken, for example, by those subjects of James II who betrayed their former loyalties by swearing allegiance to William III in 1688). Here, Astell's exploitation of the marriage/social contract analogy demonstrates both the depth of her Tory political convictions and the internal coherence of her Christian rationalist belief system as it concerned social, religious, moral and political conduct.

Two Influential Societies

Notwithstanding Astell's views, the reign of William and Mary is generally associated with an increasing moral and religious rectitude and projects for social reformation. There is little question that the courtly vogue for libertine excess and sexual promiscuity most readily aligned with the reign of Charles II – and, by association, those members of the Stuart royal family who had lived in exile during the Interregnum – gave way to a completely different cultural atmosphere from the last decade of the seventeenth century. This change is particularly apparent in the foundation of the Society for the Reformation of Manners, in 1691 under the patronage of Queen Mary, in order to suppress profane and immoral activity in London (particularly prostitution).[27]

The Society maintained a rigid structure in which a top layer of management (made up of eminent professionals such as lawyers, judges and parliamentary ministers) advised and funded the prosecution of cases of immorality. A secondary group was appointed to suppress and discourage vice amongst those they employed (this group mostly consisted of tradesmen and merchants); a third group of constables was responsible for raiding brothels and arresting offenders. Within the fourth and final Society group, a wide network of informers gathered the names and misdeeds of those within their jurisdiction whose activities were deemed immoral or profane. If such a social concept now seems insidious and itself vulnerable to abuse (particularly given the Society's use of funding to bring about successful prosecutions), it is worth noting that its efforts spread beyond London to other cities and it sustained its royal patronage with Queen Anne as well as John Tillotson and Thomas Tension, two Archbishops of Canterbury.*

In 1698, the Society endorsed the publication of Jeremy Collier's influential pamphlet, *A Short View of the Immorality and Prophaneness of the English Stage*; the impact of Collier's work on the English comedy of manners reflects a wider and growing sense of public distaste for the licentiousness of earlier Restoration comedies. During the second and third decades of the eighteenth century, the Society remained an active prosecutor of vice and 'immoral activities', particularly in London; its activities provide an early and vigorous example of a wider project for moral reformation which grew over the course of the eighteenth century.

---

* Queen Anne, the younger Protestant daughter of James II (and the last of the English Stuart monarchs), reigned 1702–14. None of her children survived her and the English throne passed to a distant German cousin (George I). John Tillotson (1630–94) was Archbishop of Canterbury 1691–4; he was succeeded by Thomas Tenison (1636–1715).

From the beginning of the period, social reform on a much broader scale – in the general sense of human progress or the advancement of knowledge for the general benefit of mankind – was ambitiously proclaimed by the Royal Society of London for the Improving of Natural Knowledge.[28] The concept of 'natural knowledge' or 'natural philosophy' encompasses what today would be called 'science'. Like the modern scientific establishment, Society members and the institution itself encountered both admiration and considerable public criticism. Their religious integrity, in particular, was frequently called into question by authors who saw the pursuit of natural knowledge as an unnecessary (and possibly sinful) prying into the secrets of God's creation.[29] Ultimately, the extensive public recognition gained by the Society and its members, both in the contemporary press and other literature, stands as a testament to its cultural significance.

The Society originated with a series of informal meetings between like-minded intellectuals before and during the Interregnum.[30] From the time of the Restoration onwards, this august institution has been associated with some of the most brilliant English intellects of the long eighteenth century, including Robert Boyle, Sir William Petty, Sir Christopher Wren and Sir Isaac Newton.[*] Its public reputation now rests on the many achievements of its illustrious members, but the political power and authority wielded by the Society's elite membership during the reign of Charles II are regarded with scepticism by some historians.

The Royal Society based its principles for empirical investigation of the natural world (broadly speaking, the use of systematic observation and experimentation to prove or disprove theories) on methods first

---

[*]   Robert Boyle (1627–91) was a pioneering scientist whose experiments with air, with his technical assistant Robert Hooke, led to the formulation of 'Boyle's Law'. Sir William Petty (1623–76) was a political economist principally remembered for his early work in statistics. Sir Christopher Wren (1632–1723) designed numerous buildings and is principally remembered for St Paul's Cathedral. The intellectual achievements of Sir Isaac Newton (1642–1727) in mathematics, optics, astronomy and associated fields remain foremost in most scholarly assessments of the European Enlightenment.

established in the early seventeenth century by Francis Bacon.* The Baconian legacy added intellectual gravitas and at least the external appearance of political neutrality to the scientific efforts of its collection of (largely) gentlemanly scholars. At the same time, however, the Society's royal charters (obtained in 1662 and 1663) publicly aligned its project of social reform with the political and religious authority of Charles II. There was no other option; the Society sought and gained wider public recognition during a time in which divided political and religious loyalties – which had polarised members of the public during the Civil War and Interregnum period – were still prevalent. As such, the Society was obliged to make its alliances with the restored monarchy and Church of England very clear indeed. As Antonio Perez-Ramos illustrates:

> The English Restoration of 1660 saw the adding of institutional flesh to the programmatic bones already perceptible during the Interregnum … On the one hand, Royalist historians were anxious to conceal the achievements of Cromwellian Baconians, so that experimental science could be made politically unobjectionable … and hence could be linked to the established Church of England and the monarchical settlement … the Baconian strict separation of the domains of scientific and religious knowledge as expressed in the *Novum organum* becomes crystallized in an institutional shape. In Hooke's own words, the business of the Royal Society was: 'To improve the knowledge of natural things and all useful arts, manufactures, mechanic practices, engines and inventions by experiments – not meddling with divinity, metaphysics, morals, politics, grammar, rhetoric or logic.'[31]

---

* Francis Bacon (1561–1626) had a successful political career culminating in his appointment as Lord Chancellor of England; he fell from public grace after admitting to taking bribes. His scientific legacy is most often associated with his *Advancement of Learning* (1605) and *Novum Organum* (1620); other notable works include his Utopian *The New Atlantis* (published posthumously 1627) and his collected *Essays* (1597 onwards).

Some members of the Royal Society addressed the difficult question of religion by 'compartmentalising' the branches of knowledge they pursued such that religion ('divinity') remained outside their realm of study. Hooke's listing of 'divinity, metaphysics, morals' and so on alludes to a centuries-old traditional syllabus for scholastic and university learning; the Society's project to improve knowledge of 'natural things and all useful arts' reflected their endorsement of a new, more practical and utilitarian, agenda for future study and social reform. Other members, such as William Derham and John Ray, offered treatises which employed rational arguments to 'prove' God's presence and power; their writing suggests a belief that natural religion (knowledge of God derived from logical deduction or external observation) was a fundamental component of natural philosophy.* Although, today, the term 'scientific' has almost become synonymous with the idea of secular thinking, many of the Royal Society's early members were ordained ministers who discerned no conflict between their religious and 'scientific' principles of belief.[32]

Given their ambitious agenda of 'useful' knowledge and social reform, however, Michael Hunter remarks that 'on the whole the contribution of [Royal Society] scientists to technology in this period was disappointing in comparison with the interest in the subject that they expressed'.[33] Hunter sees a direct correlation between this lack of practical scientific progress and the Society's failure to recruit members from the mercantile and trading classes (in other words, those members of society best informed to know which practical measures were required):

> [D]espite the hopes of Sprat and others that science would advance hand in hand with commerce, few practising merchants were Fellows of the Royal Society ... In so far as one can find a significant social connection for science it is not directly with commerce but more with a nexus between landed wealth, trade

---

* The principal work on natural religion by William Derham (1657–1735) is *Physico-Theology* (1713). John Ray (1627–1705) was a biologist and botanist, author of *The Wisdom of God Manifested in the Works of Creation* (1691).

and government ... which helps to explain the indolently utilitarian character of science at the time ... and its actual tendency to fail to realise these hopes and instead settle down as a primarily intellectual activity to which men of affairs devoted their leisure in common with scholars and dilettantes.[34]

The Royal Society sustained contemporary criticism, too, from a Warwick physician named Henry Stubbe in a pamphlet entitled *The Plus Ultra reduced to a Non Plus* (1670).* In a prefatory section, Stubbe accuses members of the Royal Society of trying to block the publication of his work. He makes a second, even more serious, accusation against the Royal Society when he suggests that his recent proposal to Parliament (intended to improve elements of English colonial trade in Jamaica) was rejected out of hand – by a parliamentary council made up entirely of Royal Society members – because he himself was not a Society member:

> They that know the Men, know their meaning: and whosoever understands the Constitution of our Parliaments, is assured that they need not look out of their own number for indifferent judicious persons, to inform the House what the Reality, Usefulness, or Newness, &c. is of Inventions ... .[35]

Stubbe goes on to suggest that the Society's parliamentary council may influence the appointment of 'university preferments' and other positions. It is impossible, now, to ascertain how far Stubbe's implications – that the Royal Society council was anything but 'indifferent' and 'judicious' – constitute sour grapes on his part. What his comments do imply is the potentially enormous level of political influence that the Royal Society exercised, in its capacity as government adviser, over parliamentary decisions concerning trade and new inventions.

---

* Stubbe's pamphlet was a response to the writings of Joseph Glanville (1636–80), a Royal Society member and King's chaplain, whose *Plus Ultra: or, The Progress and Advancement of Knowledge since the Days of Aristotle* (1668) had defended his and the Society's scholarly practices.

Within the political context, Stubbe's criticism of the powerful influence of the Royal Society – arguably serving as a state-sponsored apparatus to control scientific and intellectual progress – presents a useful focal point to consider the changing relationship between public versus state authority. The Society's project of social reform and pursuit of the 'useful arts' are idealistic goals, though no less admirable for being so. Such intentions merit consideration in their own terms as well as in the light of twenty-first-century examples of scientific and scholarly projects which have, in turn, had to justify their aims to accommodate the wider context of political and economic reality.

Philosophy and Education

Beyond this, the example of the Royal Society inspired contemporary authors to pose some profound philosophical questions. What, precisely, is the relationship between man, the natural world and God? How far should mankind strive for knowledge hidden from his view? Is mankind truly capable of universal understanding (between cultures, languages, religions) and, if so, would such understanding bring universal peace? The true cultural contribution of the Royal Society during the long eighteenth century encompasses these questions along with the ambitious spirit of human progress and intellectual endeavour that it helped to foster.

The Royal Society's intention to broaden its membership beyond the most privileged members of the upper classes implies – in principle at least – their belief that the true advancement of human knowledge requires wider educational opportunities for rigorous, practical and multi-disciplined courses of study. This humanist ideal of a more practical (and universal) form of learning had been embraced in principle as far back as the Protestant Reformation itself; by its very definition, Protestantism conceives a much closer relationship between the individual and God based on that individual's capacity to understand the word of God – to read the Bible, in other words.

The origins of English educational reform belong to the Renaissance period. Early Protestant reformers on the continent, including Jean

Calvin* and Pierre de la Ramée (1515–72, often known by the Latin version of his name, Petrus Ramus), had always seen the reform and accessibility of education as part and parcel of Protestantism's larger project; reformers of the English educational system (such as Sir Henry Savile) adopted some of the principles of Ramus for teaching in England's two universities (Oxford and Cambridge).[36] Educational reform during this period was not always religious (or essentially Protestant) in nature; the reforms suggested ranged from the introduction of new and arguably more 'practical' subjects (such as mathematics, medicine or natural philosophy) to refinements in the teaching of the traditional (Classically derived) syllabus of rhetoric, as well as employment of new 'textbooks' such as those of Ramus.

During the first half of the seventeenth century, the writings of John Amos Comenius were highly influential in further extending the remit of English education reform in social terms. Comenius embraced the principle of wider access to learning as well as (along with Francis Bacon) the teaching of subjects of a practical and tangible – rather than abstract and theoretical – nature.[37] His efforts in particular were embraced by English Puritans, including John Milton, who saw the provision of a practical and rigorous education to be the responsibility of a reformed Church and Commonwealth state. Indeed, Cromwell's government was demonstrably committed to educational reform and improvement. It planned the construction of new universities in Durham and London, and provided substantial grants for the improvement of educational facilities in schools throughout England and Scotland. Irene Parker argues:

> The Commonwealth, then, may be described as a time of considerable educational activity ... The work done between 1640–1660 was the natural outcome of the attempts made in those and the preceding years to influence public opinion in the direction of demanding educational reform ... Men felt that the dream of Bacon and Comenius, and of the early Protestants

* Jean Calvin (1509–64), a French theologian, was a profoundly influential reformer of early Protestantism.

indeed, was about to be realised, and that learning which had been the monopoly of the upper classes was at last within the reach of every individual who desired it.[38]

Parker goes on to make the somewhat dramatic observation that '[p]robably no event in English history has had so far-reaching and disastrous an effect upon education as the Restoration'.[39] Specifically, she is referring to the profound impact of the Clarendon Code on the education of English dissenters (Protestants who worshipped outside the Church of England).* From December 1661 onwards, Charles II's 'Cavalier Parliament' passed the first of a series of measures now collectively known as the 'Clarendon Code' (named after Lord Chancellor Edward Hyde, Earl of Clarendon), which severely curtailed the civil and religious liberties of dissenters, enforced through the use of heavy fines and imprisonment.[40] Amongst other restrictions, the Clarendon Code excluded dissenters from teaching in schools, and also from attending the universities at Oxford and Cambridge.

These measures prompted some dissenting teachers and ministers to found new educational academies; before 1690 (when the Toleration Act removed or relaxed many of the Clarendon Code's measures) most were small and private institutions which taught the standard university-level subjects – law, divinity and medicine – both to dissenters and Anglican students. One, founded in Newington Green, London, is now best remembered for its most famous pupil (Daniel Defoe, who attended between 1674 and 1681) and the role of its founder, Charles Morton, in the later foundation of Harvard.[41]

The Newington Green Academy syllabus incorporated Latin, Greek, Hebrew, Logic, Mathematics and Science as well as modern languages, geography and history. This impressive range of disciplines reflects the scholarly talents of Morton who, like virtually all of the other dissenting

* The term 'dissenter' covered a wide range of denominations, from the most moderate Presbyterians (who wished to be accepted into Anglican congregations) to separatist groups such as the Quakers (whose worship diverged radically from the Anglican liturgy). There is no way of calculating accurately the English population – or its percentage of dissenters – during this period; scholarly estimates approximate that dissenters made up 10 to 20 per cent of the English population.

ministers who founded academies, were graduates if not also former teachers at Oxford or Cambridge. Other, smaller, academies – for which less detailed records exist – probably taught a less comprehensive choice of subjects, but evidence suggests that several (including one in Rathmell, Yorkshire, and another in Sheriffhales, Shropshire) continued to operate as prodigious centres of rigorous learning for several decades. Moreover, from the twenty-two (known) establishments founded in 1663–90, dissenting academies multiplied and flourished throughout the eighteenth century, expanding their subject ranges and continuing to attract students from both aristocratic and more middle-class families.[42]

The Scottish Enlightenment

Notwithstanding the academic opportunities made available by England's dissenting academies, eighteenth-century dissenters could also look to the neighbouring country of Scotland for an excellent university education. In 1583 the University of Edinburgh had received its royal charter from James VI of Scotland (who became, following the death of Queen Elizabeth I in 1603, James I of England). The University of Glasgow is older still; its foundation was granted by papal bull to James II in 1451. Despite sharing a monarch since 1603, several attempts to unite England and Scotland under one parliament had failed before protracted political negotiations finally brought about the Act of Union (uniting England, Scotland and Wales as the kingdom of Great Britain) in 1707. Scotland regained its own parliament in 1999 but had always retained its own legislative system and, more generally, an independently rich cultural and intellectual tradition. During the eighteenth century, a particularly prolific period of Scottish intellectual achievement – sometimes referred to as the Scottish Enlightenment – extended and refined many of the principles of social reform and rational philosophy, as well as practical advances in scientific thinking, that characterised the wider European Enlightenment.[43]

Of particular interest in this context are the writings of Francis

Hutcheson, David Hume and Adam Smith. The philosophical model of human nature proposed by David Hume (1711–76) in his *Treatise on Human Nature* (1739) explores its subject with a rigorous logic more often associated with scientific investigation. Regarding his concept of the 'universe of the imagination', for example, Hume argued that the human mind is only capable of grasping 'perceptions' and then (based on preconceived notions in the mind) turning those perceptions into 'ideas'. As such it is

> impossible for us to so much as conceive or form any idea of any
> thing specifically different from ideas and impressions ... we
> never really advance a step beyond ourselves, nor can conceive
> any kind of existence, but those perceptions, which have appear'd
> in that narrow compass.[44]

In turn, the human mind considers ideas, and through 'custom, or, if you will, by the relation of cause and effect ... it forms them into a new system, which it likewise dignifies with the title of *realities*'.[45] Arguably, since reality is the product of human perception, everything that the human mind is capable of conceiving – including God – is reduced via Hume's rigorous application of logic (in the *Treatise* and more explicitly in later works such as his *Enquiry Concerning Human Understanding*, published in 1748) to 'nothing but ideas'. Unsurprisingly, Hume's work met with considerable hostility from contemporary and later theologians; the full extent of some of his ideas (on, for example, the subject of suicide) did not appear in print until the twentieth century.[*] Nevertheless, and like Hobbes a century before him, such hostility itself indicates how far the contemporary religious establishment recognised Hume's philosophy as a threat. At the same time, Hume's rational philosophy was greatly admired during his lifetime by friends such as

---

[*]   Hume's *Five Dissertations* (1755) contained two highly controversial essays, 'Suicide' and 'Of the Immortality of the Soul', which Hume's publisher was later obliged to withdraw. Various anonymous and pirated versions of the essays circulated during the late eighteenth century but the final versions (as revised by Hume) appeared in the press only in the twentieth century.

Adam Smith and James Thomson, and has ultimately helped to secure his reputation amongst the most influential philosophical thinkers of the eighteenth century.

The moral philosophy of Francis Hutcheson (1694–1746) presented less of a threat to the moral and religious establishment.* He proposed a detailed model of the complex relationship between man's 'senses' – encompassing the five external senses along with features such as consciousness or self-perception, beauty, moral sense and honour – and the quality and nature of his actions and emotions. Hutcheson's concept of the human 'affections' – emotional attachments to other members of mankind – was inspired by the aesthetic philosophy of Anthony Anthony Cooper, third Earl of Shaftesbury (1671–1713), whose influence may also be discerned in the Romantic concept of the 'sublime'. As explored in his best-known work, *An Inquiry into the Original of our Ideas of Beauty and Virtue* (1725), Hutcheson developed Shaftesbury's ideas to realise more fully the relationship between the aesthetic and moral/emotional elements of human perception. This subject, in turn, forms part of a much wider cultural survey of human nature, 'a deep and profound discernment of all the mazes, windings and labyrinths which perplex the heart of man'.[46] Such exploration is equally evident in both the period's moral philosophy and works of contemporary literature such as Sarah Fielding's *The Adventures of David Simple* (1744) and Henry Mackenzie's *The Man of Feeling* (1771).[47]

At Glasgow University, Hutcheson served as professor of moral philosophy from 1729 until his death; his most famous student, Adam Smith (1723–90), held the same position between 1752 and 1764 but is now far better remembered for his virtual invention of the modern study of economics. Smith's groundbreaking work, *An Inquiry into the Nature and Causes of the Wealth of Nations* (1776), explores the impact of free trade on the structure and behaviour of society at precisely the same cultural moment as the early stages of the Industrial Revolution

---

* The religious controversy provoked by Hume's writing, and Hutcheson's objections, were both factors in Hume's failure to attain the moral philosophy chair at the University of Edinburgh (held both by Hutcheson and, later, Hume's friend and Hutcheson's student, Adam Smith).

began to realise the validity of his socioeconomic theories on a global scale.

Smith's work represented the wider implications of economic development, both in positive and negative terms, on human civilisation. Of particular interest in the latter context is his consideration of how unjust practices of commercial exploitation (for example, through slavery) are themselves indications of a regressive society. Free trade, then, is not so much unquestioningly celebrated by Smith as it is analysed as a potential source of human and social progress (or misery). Alfred Lutz has intriguingly suggested that one of the profound cultural influences of Smith's work was that it created a more distinct division between the realm of economics and contemporary poetry which addressed ethical subjects. 'Ethics,' he observes,

> began to play a less significant role in economic thought because the economy began to be considered as a self-regulating and internally coherent system. Poetry, largely concerned with what political economists considered trivial, was no longer, as it still had been in Pope's *Moral Essays*, a viable medium for the discussion of economic issues. The separation of economics from poetry had been completed.[48]

Lutz's point might be supported by the point that poetry in the last quarter of the eighteenth century is increasingly concerned with ethical concerns such as social injustice – slavery or rural poverty, for example, as illustrated in this volume by the verse of Goldsmith, Crabbe and Cowper (see Part Three: 'Pastoral and Anti-pastoral Poetry'). Such subjects are clearly not entirely distinct from the realm of 'economic issues'. In poetry, however, social injustice is most movingly depicted in portraits of individual human suffering (often in vignettes or self-contained 'narratives') rather than the global scale of free trade. In addition, and as has already been suggested in Part Three: 'The Novel and the Individual', the period's general movement towards a literature of sentiment, and more rigid standards of moral conduct, is also concerned with the scale of human experience (particularly in the novel form). If 'the separation of economics from poetry' – or other literature – in this period is partly due to the burgeoning scale of England's self-regulating political economy, it is equally evident in literary portrayals of the expanding moral complexity of individual experience.

Notes

1 Thomas Hobbes, *Leviathan, or the Matter, Form, and Power of a Commonwealth Ecclesiastical and Civil*, in William Molesworth (ed.), *The Collected Works of Thomas Hobbes*, Volume 3 (London: John Bohn, 1839), pp. 112–14.

2 See, for example, Mark Goldie, 'The Reception of Hobbes', in J. H. Burns and M. Goldie (eds), *The Cambridge History of Political Thought 1450–1700* (Cambridge: Cambridge University Press, 1994), pp. 589–615; and H. Warrender, *The Political Philosophy of Hobbes: His Theory of Obligation* (Oxford: Clarendon Press, 1957).

3 John Wilmot, Earl of Rochester, *A Satire Against Reason and Mankind*, in Lawrence Lipking and James Noggle (eds), *The Norton Anthology of English Literature*, Volume C: *The Restoration and the Eighteenth Century* (New York & London: W. W. Norton, 2006), p. 2175, l. 132.

4 On the relationship between *Gulliver's Travels* and Hobbesian philosophy, see Ann Cline Kelly, 'Swift's Explorations of Slavery in Houyhnhnmland and Ireland', *PMLA*, 91:5 (October 1976), pp. 846–55; and T. O. Wedel, 'On the Philosophical Background of *Gulliver's Travels*', *Studies in Philology*, 23:4 (October 1926), pp. 434–50.

5 See, for example, Homer O. Brown, 'The Displaced Self in the Novels of Daniel Defoe', *Journal of English Literary History*, 38 (1971), pp. 564–5.

6 Lois A. Chaber, 'Matriarchal Mirror: Women and Capital in MF', *PMLA*, 97:2 (March 1982), p. 212.

7 Daniel Defoe, *The Fortunate Mistress*, also known as *Roxana* (1724), in P. N. Furbank (ed.), *The Works of Daniel Defoe*, Volume 9: *The Novels of Daniel Defoe* (London: Pickering & Chatto, 2009), p. 267.

8 Christopher Flint, *Family Fictions: Narrative and Domestic Relations in Britain, 1688–1798* (Stanford: Stanford University Press, 1998), p. 14.

9 On the contemporary impact of Locke's philosophy, see Lois G. Schwoerer, 'Locke, Lockean Ideas and the Glorious Revolution', *Journal of the History of Ideas*, 51:4 (1990), pp. 531–48; and Jonathan Barnes, 'Mr Locke's Darling Notion', *Philological Quarterly*, 22:88 (July 1972), pp. 193–214.

10 John Locke, *An Essay Concerning Human Understanding, An Abridgement*, edited by John Yolton (London: J. M. Dent & Sons, 1976), II.i.33.
11 Ibid., I.ii.11.
12 John Locke, *An Essay Concerning Human Understanding*, edited by Peter H. Nidditch (Oxford: Oxford University Press, 1975), III.i.403.
13 Locke, *An Essay Concerning Human Understanding, An Abridgement*, II.xxiii.199. On Locke and Freudian psychology, see Erling Eng, 'Locke's *Tabula Rasa* and Freud's "Mystic Writing Pad"', *Journal of the History of Ideas*, 41:1 (1980), pp. 133–40.
14 John Locke, *An Essay Concerning Human Understanding, An Abridgement*, III.ii.208.
15 Ibid., p. 210.
16 John Locke, *The Reasonableness of Christianity as Delivered in the Scriptures* (London, 1695), p. 300.
17 John Locke, *Second Treatise of Government*, edited by Mark Goldie (London and Rutland: J. M. Dent, 1993), Ch. 2, 'Of the State of Nature', p. 116.
18 Ibid., pp. 116, 118; see also Mark Goldie's introduction, pp. xxiii–v; Hobbes, *Leviathan*, pp. 111–16.
19 Goldie (ed.), *Second Treatise of Government*, pp. 164–5.
20 Ibid., p. 159.
21 On the dating of the *Two Treatises*, see Goldie (ed.), *Second Treatise of Government*, pp. xix–xxiii.
22 Ibid., Chs 2–5, pp. 116–40.
23 According to Locke, the 'perfect condition of slavery' exists when the life of the enslaved (a prisoner of war or a man condemned to death) is held in the possession of another; the enslaved still retains the power, 'by resisting the will of his master, to draw on himself the death he desires': *Second Treatise of Government*, Ch. 4, 'Of Slavery', p. 126; see also Ch. 7, 'Of Political or Civil Society', pp. 156–7.
24 Regarding paternal power and duty, see ibid., Ch. 6, pp. 140 ff.
25 On Mary Astell's political writing, see Patricia Springborg, *Mary Astell: Theorist of Freedom from Domination* (Cambridge, Cambridge University Press, 2005).
26 Patricia Springborg, 'Mary Astell and John Locke', in Steven Zwicker (ed.), *The Cambridge Companion to English Literature 1650–1740* (Cambridge: Cambridge University Press, 1998), pp. 276–306.
27 On the history of the Society for the Reformation of Manners, see E. J. Burford, *Wits, Wenchers and Wantons – London's Low Life: Covent Garden in the Eighteenth Century* (London: Robert Hale, 1986), p. 260; and Alan Hunt, *Governing Morals: A Social History of Moral Regulation* (Cambridge: Cambridge University Press, 1999).

28   For a description of the Society's aims, see Thomas Sprat, *The History of the Royal Society* (1667), edited by Jackson I. Cope and Harold Whitmore Jones (London: Routledge & Kegan Paul, 1959).

29   On the religious controversy provoked by the Royal Society, see Roslynn D. Haynes, *From Faust to Strangelove: Representations of the Scientist in Western Literature* (Baltimore and London: Johns Hopkins University Press, 1994), pp. 36–49; and R. H. Syfret, 'Some Early Reactions to the Royal Society', *Notes and Records of the Royal Society of London*, 7 (1950), pp. 207–58.

30   See Dorothy Stimson, *Scientists and Amateurs: A History of the Royal Society* (New York: Henry Schumann, 1948).

31   Antonio Perez-Ramos, 'Bacon's Legacy', in Markku Peltonen (ed.), *The Cambridge Companion to Bacon* (Cambridge: Cambridge University Press, 1996), pp. 315–16.

32   For biographical details of the ministers who were also members of the Royal Society, see Wilbur Samuel Howell, 'Voices of the Royal Society', in *Eighteenth-century British Logic and Rhetoric* (Princeton: Princeton University Press, 1971), pp. 448–502.

33   Michael Hunter, *Science and the Shape of Orthodoxy: Intellectual Change in Late Seventeenth-century Britain* (Woodbridge: Boydell Press, 1995), p. 107.

34   Ibid., p. 111. Regarding the Royal Society's early membership, see also Michael Hunter, *The Royal Society and Its Fellows 1660–1700: The Morphology of an Early Scientific Institution* (Oxford: British Society for the History of Science, 1982), pp. 8–11.

35   Henry Stubbe, *The Plus Ultra reduced to a Non Plus, or, A Specimen of some Animadversions upon the Plus Ultra of M. Glanvill , wherein sundry Errors of some Virtuosi are discovered ...* (London, 1670), no page numbers in this section.

36   For a detailed discussion of the writings of Pierre de la Ramée, see Walter J. Ong, *Ramus, Method, and the Decay of Dialogue* (Cambridge: Harvard University Press, 1958, repr. 1974); and Howell, *Eighteenth-century British Logic and Rhetoric*. On the work of early English educational reformers such as Sir Henry Savile (1549–1622) and Sir William Temple (1554/5–1627), see Irene Parker, *Dissenting Academies in England: Their Rise and Progress and Their Place among the Educational Systems of the Country* (Cambridge: Cambridge University Press, 1914), Chs 2 and 3.

37   On the educational reforms of John Amos Comenius (1592–1670), see Benjamin de Mott, 'Comenius and the Real Character in England', *PMLA*, 70 (1955), pp. 1068–81.

38   Parker, *Dissenting Academies in England*, pp. 42–3.

39 Ibid., p. 43.

40 For a detailed discussion of the measures imposed upon dissenters by the Clarendon Code, see Michael Watts, *The Dissenters: From the Reformation to the French Revolution* (Oxford: Clarendon Press, 1978), pp. 221–62.

41 For a detailed discussion of Morton's establishment, see Lew Girdler, 'Defoe's Education at Newington Green Academy', *Studies in Philology*, 50:4 (1953), pp. 573–91.

42 In addition to Parker's text, on the history of the dissenting academies see also Herbert McLachlan, *English Education under the Test Acts: Being the History of the Non-Conformist Academies 1662–1820* (Manchester: Manchester University Press, 1931); and J. W. Ashley Smith, *The Birth of Modern Education: The Contribution of the Dissenting Academies, 1660–1800* (London: Independent Press, 1954).

43 On the Scottish Enlightenment, see David Daiches, Peter Jones and Jean Jones (eds), *The Scottish Enlightenment, 1730–90: A Hotbed of Genius* (Edinburgh: University of Edinburgh Press, 1986).

44 David Hume, *A Treatise of Human Nature*, edited by L. A. Selby-Bigge, 2nd edn revised by P. H. Nidditch (Oxford: Clarendon Press, 1975), pp. 67–8. See also D. F. Norton (ed.), *The Cambridge Companion to Hume* (Cambridge: Cambridge University Press, 1993), in particular, R. J. Fogelin, 'Hume's Scepticism', pp. 90–116.

45 Hume, *A Treatise of Human Nature*, p. 108.

46 Henry Fielding, Preface to *The Adventures of David Simple* (1744), in George L. Barnett (ed.), *Eighteenth-century British Novelists on the Novel* (New York: Meredith Corporation, 1968), p. 53.

47 See G. J. Barker-Benfield, *The Culture of Sensibility: Sex and Society in Eighteenth-century Britain* (Chicago and London: University of Chicago Press, 1992); and John Mullan, *Sentiment and Sociability: The Language of Feeling in the Eighteenth Century* (Oxford: Clarendon Press, 1988).

48 Alfred Lutz, 'The Politics of Reception: The Case of Oliver Goldsmith's *The Deserted Village*', *Studies in Philology*, 95:2 (Spring 1998), p. 184.

Gender and Sexuality

It is only in the past thirty or forty years that two of the most talented authors of the long eighteenth century, Aphra Behn and Eliza Haywood, have begun to receive even a fraction of the critical attention enjoyed by male contemporaries such as Dryden, Swift and Pope. Since that time, the critical 'rediscovery' of many other important female authors has continued to increase the sense that female authorship proliferated during the long eighteenth century on an unprecedented scale in English literary culture.

This relatively recent process, in scholarly terms, is long overdue and will undoubtedly continue. If for no other reason, the critical attribution of anonymously published texts – highly prevalent during the long eighteenth century due to state-imposed censorship and prejudice against female authors, among other things – provides enormous critical scope for the discovery of 'new' authors of both genders. At the same time, the very question of an author's gender immediately raises related questions concerning the wider practices of literary and historical investigation. Should we be – necessarily – concentrating on the gender of authors in the first place? Is there not a danger that, in recognising female authorship as a long-neglected aspect of how we read texts written during this period, we construct a separate literary canon or canons? (And how do the newer and older models relate to each other?) Are our notions of a 'female canon' adequately inclusive, given the very real historical presence of a majority of the female population excluded from representation in – or access to – contemporary literature?

These and many other questions signify the uneasy relationship being negotiated between this problematic, but very exciting, area of critical study and the more traditional canon of 'dead white males' active during the long eighteenth century. Female authors during the long eighteenth century were motivated to publish their writing for specific reasons (some of which, such as the need to earn a living, they shared with men). There is little doubt, however, that theirs was the more challenging task and they were keenly aware that in fulfilling it they subjected themselves to public criticism. Countless authors, from Behn to Wollstonecraft, have acknowledged this social reality in terms which justify the products of their own pen but also find it necessary to defend, repeatedly, the place of women's voices in the public sphere.

The rediscovery of female authors active during the long eighteenth century has also contributed to our deeper understanding of the historical and political period as a whole. They engaged directly in contemporary social and political issues far beyond the remit of ostensibly 'feminine' concerns such as marriage and childbirth. Authors such as Mary Astell, Catherine Macaulay and Mary Wollstonecraft are now best known for their writing on educational reform but they also addressed the political significance of events such as the Glorious Revolution (which, for Astell, was anything but glorious) and the French Revolution with a forthright and rational prose style that directly challenged their adversaries.

This dual perspective reflects the observation made by Vivien Jones that questions of 'whether, and how, women should be educated are always part of wider political debates'.[1] The changing ideals envisaged for female education in this period were structured, initially, in the form of a challenge to received notions of male intellectual superiority. Extensive debates concerning the precise capacities of the female mind reveal, inevitably, the political agenda of their authors. Whether women merited better education in order to improve their chances (and their children's chances) for spiritual salvation, or to provide superior companionship for their husbands, the primary question concerning the need for improved education is one of the projected social contribution that females would be able to make.

Anne Finch and Female Authorship

In the long eighteenth century, both genders engaged in very public debates, both good-natured and otherwise, concerning female authorship; the amiable poetic exchanges between Anne Finch and Alexander Pope may be considered in this context.* [2]

Perhaps reluctant to adopt the more direct political stance implied by the pamphlet genre, Anne Finch expressed her political views through the subtler metaphors of poetry (as did Aphra Behn) when obliged to mask her Royalist loyalties during the turbulent political milieu of the 1680s.[3] Recognised with praise after her death by Wordsworth, Anne Finch in particular was adept at writing verse consciously presented from the stance of a life retired from the public milieu. Although this stance is a recognisable feature of much verse written before and after the long eighteenth century period, Finch's spare poetic style skilfully incorporates into this perspective the (multiple) concerns of a Royalist in political retreat after 1688, an artist who seeks the intellectual solitude necessary for creative inspiration, and an individual – perhaps neither male nor female – who reflects in isolation on the universal human qualities which unite the genders. As she writes in 'A Nocturnal Reverie' (1713):

> In such a night let me abroad remain,
> Till morning breaks, and all's confused again;
> Our cares, our toils, our clamors are renewed,
> Or pleasures, seldom reached, again pursued.[4]

---

* Of relevance here is London's Blue Stocking Circle, an informal gathering of highly educated men and women, who met periodically for learned and sociable discussion after 1750. Members included Elizabeth Vesey (?1715–91) and Elizabeth Montagu (1720–1800).

As Carol Barash has observed, however, Finch's political beliefs (like those of Katherine Philips* before her) are also metonymically expressed *through* the female poetic perspective:

> Finch often generates a female community which brings together the female poet's friends, contemporary political figures, and ideal heroic women from history and myth. For numerous women writers between Phillips and Finch, the guise of safe, domestic affiliations between women upholds the idea – and figuratively protects the body – of the exiled monarch. But the diversity of women's writing, as well as the importance of the women's community as a political trope ... has been largely ignored since the eighteenth century.[5]

Finch's example is significant because it indicates the extent to which (before 1700) female authors are already manipulating their position in relation to disparate aspects of their identity (as females, as poets, as Royalists). Of course, in doing so, it may be argued that female authors occupied precisely the same spheres of literary activity as males. This is particularly notable in the early part of the period, before the point when the 'feminine realm' of domestic fiction – the novel – became the acceptable face of 'women's literature'.

In the previous paragraph, the uncomfortable self-consciousness with which phrases such as 'feminine realm' and 'women's literature' are employed already demonstrates how the relationship between the female gender and literature in *any* historical period is fraught with difficulty. A large proportion of this chapter is necessarily taken up with clarification and definition of terms in order to address the different but related problems of considering female readership, female authorship and the representation of females in eighteenth-century literature. Regarding the last and largest of these subjects, Vivien Jones outlines the difficulties that challenge critical readers in the introduction to her thought-

---

* Katherine Philips (1631–64), familiarly known as the 'Matchless Orinda', was a Royalist poet and translator who was much admired by her contemporaries; she died of smallpox aged 33.

provoking anthology, *Women in the Eighteenth Century: Constructions of Femininity*:

> 'Women in the Eighteenth Century' is an impossibly general title
> (a similar anthology on 'Men in the Eighteenth Century' would
> be self-evidently absurd) … Apart from the obvious impossibility
> of ever fully knowing 'women' in any period, its subject is written
> culture, and its concern … is with representation, with 'women'
> as a culturally defined category which women had to negotiate
> and suffer.[6]

Even after clarifying her subject as the representation of '"women" as a culturally-defined category', Jones rightly notes that her discussion is necessarily restricted, in terms of social class, which further limits its perspective:

> Given eighteenth-century literacy levels, the focus is therefore
> predominantly on middle-class discourses of femininity,
> discourses which restricted middle-class women to the role of
> domestic consumers and subjected working-class women to a
> double repression, erasing them culturally and economically by
> projecting leisured domesticity as general.[7]

Following her example, it is worth clarifying here, too, that the allocation of a privileged critical space in which to consider 'women in the eighteenth century' (whatever that means), or – as in this chapter – related topics such as gender and sexuality, is inevitably based on a limited analysis of textual representation. There is no question that the literary representation of female identity is diverse and subject to change during the period between 1660 and 1790, but it would be impossible to determine if females of any class themselves changed in any or all of these ways.

The study of female readership during the long eighteenth century also presents many obstacles. Beyond (the pertinent question of) even the most rudimentary levels of literacy, the quality and content of education accessible by females in this period can neither be taken for granted, nor can it be generalised on the basis of class. Affluence, now as then, is not in itself an indication of astute learning for either gender. It is generally apparent that higher levels of literacy, education and the leisure time necessary for reading are associated with middle and higher levels of social class for both men and women but the period in question is (by definition) one of transition in which notions of a 'middle class' first began to emerge. As such, the highly specialised historical study of female readership during the long eighteenth century remains outside the scope of this chapter. Assumptions concerning general readership will be made (for example, a correlation between a book's 'success' or 'popular recognition' and its publication in multiple editions) but not female readership.

Gender, Identity and Power

The term 'gender' is employed in this chapter's title in order to tacitly acknowledge the shifting and unstable boundaries between representations of male and female identity during this period. 'Gender', in this sense, refers to social rather than anatomical distinctions between male and female identity; certain activities or modes of behaviour are socially deemed to be 'masculine' or 'feminine' and these socially determined gender codes may change over time.

The term also alludes to an important critical approach to interpreting the cultural period spanned by the long eighteenth century. This approach allows us to consider the practice by which certain gendered notions of identity become, from the second half of the eighteenth century onwards, culturally 'set in stone' to the extent that they still remain recognisable today. Through this practice, the traditional spheres of female versus male influence – private versus public life – become rigidly formalised, arguably through the powerful cultural influence of literary genres such as the novel, but also ratified by wider legal, economic and political factors.

Within this context it is worth noting the importance of Michel Foucault (1926–84), a French philosopher, whose theories concerning the origins of political and institutional power within Western culture have profoundly influenced modern cultural studies including literary criticism. His ideas are reflected in some of the most important critical work on the literature of the long eighteenth century over the past few decades, particularly concerning the development of the novel.[8] Extending some of Foucault's ideas, Judith Butler's highly influential critical work *Gender Trouble: Feminism and the Subversion of Identity* (1990) presents the notion of human gender as a performative, and culturally relative, mode of social identity. Butler's work calls for subversive and creative action such that the cultural configuration of gender may be liberated from hegemonic prescription and, instead, become a 'free floating' element of human identity.[9]

Foucault did not directly address the question of gender difference but considered the means by which human sexuality has been transformed, over the centuries, into a subject for scientific investigation (as has crime).[10] Decipherable by the ruling cultural institutions (science, the law, the church, literature), sexual activities may be deemed as either 'licit' or 'illicit', 'normal' or 'perverse', and so on. Foucault's system depends on the notion of Western political power in the sense of prevailing cultural ideology as exerted by the institutional forces of society. Such power, he asserts, manifests itself in a negative manner (seeking to negate, control or stop) and, as such, the desire to resist power is implicated in the prevailing notion of power itself (for example, a law forbidding theft is predicated on the knowledge that the desire to commit theft exists).[11]

Clearly Foucault's ideas have implications beyond any single cultural period, but they resonate powerfully within the context of English literature in the latter part of the eighteenth century when notions of 'feminine' behaviour, in particular, become culturally delineated so distinctly. Foucault's notion of (negative) power aptly addresses the controlling energies by which public and private/male and female spheres of influence regulate each other in terms of, for example, moral conduct. At the same time, Foucault's failure to acknowledge the fundamental legal, economic and political subordination of the female gender within the social order itself – long before and after the long eighteenth century – arguably limits the scope of its effectiveness.

Another critical perspective might consider how the entire cultural period in question (1660–1790) may be interpreted through the concept of gender. Beginning with the 'masculine' realm of Restoration culture (dominated by images of military and sexual prowess, libertinism and patriarchal kingship), literature moves towards the 'feminine' realm represented by the literature of sentiment and sensibility and the domestic novel. The long eighteenth century, however, rightly resists this process of gendering. Such a simplistic model does a disservice to the presence of literary genres which do not fit easily into its tidy pattern. How, for example, does it accommodate the complexities of gender and political power relations in scandal works such as Delarivier Manley's *The New Atalantis* (1709)?* [12] At the other end of the period, how does a 'feminised' and domestic literary phase account for the rising contemporary vogue for Gothic fiction, so often characterised by deep-seated anxieties concerning family relationships and domestic harmony?

Notwithstanding the importance of these questions, the notion of this cultural period's progressive 'feminising' can, nevertheless, help to clarify our understanding of how gender and power relations shift during the course of the long eighteenth century.[13] A 'gendered' model of literary culture is not necessarily simplistic, and different critical perspectives work, cumulatively, to contribute to an ongoing debate which continues to yield invaluable benefits for literary scholarship as a whole. Consensus has never been the purpose of this debate. Its engagement with both primary sources (of eighteenth-century literature) and a potentially vast array of secondary sources (encompassing critical, historical, philosophical and other texts) suggests that such a consensus remains unlikely at any time in the future.

---

* Delarivier Manley, *Secret Memoirs and Manners of Several Persons of Quality … from the New Atalantis* (1709) was published with a key to the 'true identities' of its fictional characters; the work provides a thinly veiled political diatribe against notable contemporary Whigs. Following its publication, Manley was briefly imprisoned for the work's libellous content.

Sexuality and Literature

The secondary term in this chapter's title also needs clarification. Again, the intended definition must be considered on two levels. 'Sexuality' is employed here to mean 'sexual activity' – or at least any proclivity towards it – rather than the more specific sense of a sexual preference for both or either sex. Perhaps more than in any other literary period, the textual representation of *any* discernible proclivity towards sexual activity, for both sexes, becomes less apparent as the eighteenth century progresses. In this broad sense, one could argue that the long eighteenth century becomes 'desexualised' or, at least, confines its sexual activities firmly behind the bedroom doors of married couples where it will remain until the twentieth century.

As has already been suggested in relation to the period's drama and poetry, literary representations of passion and love (intense and shared but largely cerebral emotions, in other words) eventually come to replace almost entirely the earlier period's (sometimes very frank) acknowledgement that sexual intercourse takes place both within and outside of marriage. One need only compare Aphra Behn's works of prose fiction, such as *Oroonoko*, with works such as Frances Burney's *Evelina* or Jane Austen's *Sense and Sensibility* in order to see this progression.

This development indicates some of the longer-term implications of social and economic changes wrought upon the family and the status of the individual as the period progresses. These changes increasingly valued affective or companionate marriage as the ideal form of moral and economic participation in English society. By the last quarter of the eighteenth century, the domestic realm of family life (tacitly incorporating consensual sexual intercourse between married couples) begins to be institutionalised within literary forms such as the novel as well as contemporary English law. This period heralds the point at which the middle-class family values and standards of moral conduct, still recognisable today, begin to emerge.

There is another, more complex, manner in which this chapter addresses 'sexuality' during the long eighteenth century. Though now over twenty years old, Nancy Armstrong's excellent introduction to *Desire and Domestic Fiction: A Political History of the Novel* provides a highly pertinent description of the critical obstacles of writing about gender and power from *within* a culture which still – perhaps inevitably – associates them together. As Armstrong writes:

> [N]o one has thoroughly examined the figure, or turn of cultural logic, that both differentiates the sexes and links them together by the magic of sexual desire. And if we simply assume that gender differentiation is the root of human identity, we can understand neither the totalizing power of this figure nor the very real interests such power inevitably serves. So basic are the terms 'male' and 'female' to the semiotics of modern life that no one can use them without to some degree performing the very reifying gesture whose operations we would like to understand and whose power we want to historicize ... Once one thinks within such a structure, sexual relationships appear as the model for all power relationships.[14]

Armstrong's point is that we reiterate, or at least assert, the social convention of male authority merely by engaging with a system which recognises either female subordination or resistance to male repression. Fundamentally, the notion of sexual desire, the 'magic' which links males and females together, oscillates around and through the notion of power itself. Although Armstrong's particular focus is on the development of the novel, her conclusion that 'to remove oneself from the field of consideration is finally impossible' also rings true for how we approach the literature of the long eighteenth century. In other words, the fundamental structure of eighteenth-century culture is, essentially, male-dominated and centred on models of male authority; in either accepting or rebelling against that model, and in constructing models of desire in relation to it, authors of both genders reconfirm the model itself.

Rakes and Libertines

Notwithstanding the power relationships that underlie human relations generally, it may be argued that social and historical changes affect male and female members of society in equal measure. The provocative assertion that Pope makes in his 1735 *Epistle to a Lady* – that 'ev'ry Woman is at heart a Rake' (ll. 216) – may be used to demonstrate this. The aggressively universal nature of the statement – particularly in the hands of Pope – is open to interpretation as being straightforwardly ironic or, more ambiguously (as is also the case with Austen's opening line in *Pride and Prejudice*), purposely intended to make readers of both sexes question their own values and assumptions in relation to glib universalities concerning male and female 'norms' of behaviour.[15]

Unstable boundaries between notions of gender are transmitted through the use of gendered terms. In this context, Pope's use of the word 'rake' is particularly interesting. It is a term overwhelmingly associated with masculine conduct during the whole of the period in question but that changes its social connotations dramatically during that time.[*][16] In the earlier stages of the period, beginning with the restoration of Charles II, a 'rake' was generally synonymous with a 'libertine' (a man of aristocratic or upper-class background who indulged in self-conscious acts of sexual licence). Significantly, Daniel Statt has observed that 'there is no received definition of this type' during this period as it relates to *real* people. Directly relevant to the charges of misogyny (that is, hostility towards *real* women) levelled at Pope's poetic assertion is the fact that definitions for 'rake' in this period depend 'almost entirely on literary representations of rakes and libertines' (particularly in Restoration drama).[17]

By the time that Pope's poem was published, the moral representation of rakes in drama and other literature had changed noticeably, reflecting

---

* The concept of the 'female rake' was not unknown during the period but was largely employed for its novelty rather than any stable notion of female behaviour. See, for example, Joseph Dorman's comic play entitled *The Female Rake; or, a Modern Fine Lady* (1735).

in turn the public's growing preference for morally upright and sexually continent male heroic behaviour. By 1735, the figure of the heroic rake was – if not necessarily emasculated – reformed, and made answerable for his moral transgressions. In this volume, the earlier stage of this transition is demonstrated in differences between the figures of Behn's Willmore in *The Rover* (1677–81) and Congreve's Mirabell in *The Way of the World* (1700) but is increasingly apparent across other literary genres as the period progresses.* By 1755, as Statt also observes, 'rake' and 'libertine' part company; Samuel Johnson

> defined the rake in much more denunciatory language, as a 'loose, disorderly, vicious, wild, gay, thoughtless fellow' addicted to pleasure, than he used to describe the libertine, who was defined in terms of irreligion and licentiousness.[18]

The process continues during the eighteenth century such that Charles Surface, the rake-hero figure of Sheridan's *The School for Scandal* (1777), shows little evidence of his rakish ancestry beyond his forthright conversation and a taste for gambling (he is soon to be reformed by his virtuous wife). Even by the time that Pope published his *Epistle to a Lady*, 'rake' is arguably already a term describing a recognisable but outmoded model of male behaviour that had come to be considered as undesirable in either males or females concerned with notions of social propriety.† Pope's conscious use of a 'masculine' term in this context emphasises the fact that both males and females are subject to the representational modes that contemporary language and society impose on them, and usefully reiterates the need – both then and now – to clarify the distinction between satires concerning 'the characters of women' and the textual representation of women's characters.

---

* See, for example, the discussion of the character of Lord Belmont (Evelina's father) in Burney's novel and the analysis of sexual conduct in *Fantomina*.
† The phrase 'a rake's progress' is defined in relation to Hogarth's highly popular series of engravings of the same name (1735), as 'a progressive deterioration, especially through self-indulgence': Elizabeth Knowles (ed.), *A Dictionary of Phrase and Fable* (Oxford: Oxford University Press, 2006).

Satire and Moral Conduct

Satire, including Pope's *Epistle to a Lady* – with all of its correspondent features of ambiguity and irony across an interpretative spectrum – formed a very large proportion of eighteenth-century literature; it relies for much of its effect on the use of contemporary social stereotypes, both as a means to endorse or to undermine them. At the same time, satires on the 'characters of women' were such a prevalent aspect of eighteenth-century literature that their sheer multitude alone suggests far more than a conscious use of irony.[19]

It would be wrong to assume that all eighteenth-century satire which took female character as its subject was wholly misogynistic in its intention. Nevertheless, as Vivien Jones's anthology aptly demonstrates, there is ample evidence of genuine misogyny in contemporary texts that were not essentially 'literary' in nature but instead asserted their authority as treatises on medicine, education, philosophy, social reform, and so on. Such texts were arguably more damaging because they could endorse damaging sexual stereotypes from a position of seemingly objective 'authority'. In 1743, for example, Dr James's *Medicinal Dictionary* asserts that the disease of 'hysterica'

> more particularly seizes Virgins, before their first menstrual Discharge, such as are marriageable, young Widows, and Wives; especially if they are full of Blood and Moisture, and have not borne Children: As, also, such as are brought up in Idleness, or are of soft Texture, and delicate Constitution …[20]

Dr James's work is not openly misogynistic but it clearly implies that certain pathological conditions, such as 'hysterica', are to be avoided through the healthy social channels of marriage and lawful sexual intercourse.

While Dr James's *Medicinal Dictionary* is ostensibly intended for medical reference, it is worth noting that, during this early cultural period, the lack of perceivable boundaries between genres makes it difficult to determine finally what is 'literary' and what is not. This is particularly evident in the case of conduct works which adopted the form of fictional dialogues or narratives. The relationship between these works and the development of the novel has already been discussed within the context of Defoe's two volumes of *The Family Instructor* (1715 and 1718) and *Religious Courtship* (1722), but the practice of incorporating fictional dialogue into conduct works is also previously evident in Thomas Brooks's highly popular *Apples of Gold for Young Men and Women, and a Crown of Glory for Older Men and Women* (1662) and Richard Baxter's *Poor Man's Family Book* (1674). From about the turn of the century, Nancy Armstrong has suggested, a massive increase in the number of conduct works aimed specifically at women offered advice across a fairly wide social spectrum:

> Taken together, these local voices [in female conduct books] comprise a text displaying obvious distinctions between town and country, between old money and new, among income levels and various occupations, and particularly among the different amounts of leisure time people had to occupy ... By dividing the social world on the basis of sex, this body of writing produced a single ideal of the household.[21]

Interestingly, Armstrong argues that the increasing popularity of the form, along with the broad social spectrum accommodated by its intended readership, are factors which 'helped to generate the belief that there was such a thing as a middle class with clearly established affiliations before it actually existed'. If so, 'then it is also reasonable to claim that the modern individual was first and foremost a female'. Substantial literary evidence supports Armstrong's observations (not least of which is the fact that the female protagonist takes precedence over the male in the early novel). At the same time, it is important to acknowledge that the origins of 'modern individualism' *and* the English middle class, while certainly associated with this historical period, are also derived from multiple economic factors including the growing cultural status of the mercantile class and the importation of foreign 'luxuries' from an expanding international market (see 'Part Four: Trade, Colonial Expansion and Slavery'). This observation is made not to contradict Armstrong's point so much as to recognise in it a classic 'chicken and egg' historical scenario (in the impossibility of determining which of these factors 'came first').

Armstrong's work also addresses the complex issue of female readership during the long eighteenth century in a compelling way. It implies an aspirational quality in readers of female conduct books, whether those aspirations are directed towards the 'improvement' of their personal conduct or their domestic environment. Perhaps it goes without saying that readers of conduct books (or the 'self-help' book that constitutes its twenty-first-century equivalent) seek to 'improve' themselves, but the nature of what they seek to improve reveals a great deal about the contemporary culture they inhabit. Central to this volume is the fact that the foremost ideal progressively upheld by the female conduct book during the eighteenth century was the sanctity of female virtue as enshrined by the institution of marriage. Marriage was not always venerated in this way; a significant amount of historical scholarship has considered the changing fortunes of marriage in England during the seventeenth and eighteenth centuries, with particular emphasis on the deeply divisive legislation commonly referred to as Hardwicke's Marriage Act of 1753.[22]

Hardwicke's Marriage Act

The regulation of marriage was the object of legislation during the course of the eighteenth century; in both literature and legislation, the cultural recognition of marriage's economic and social value was realised and exploited more thoroughly through the idealisation of female virtue and companionate marriage. Hardwicke's Marriage Act, 'for the better preventing of clandestine Marriages', was named after its primary supporter Philip Yorke, first Earl of Hardwicke (1690–1764) who served as Lord Chancellor (1737–56). Its main intention, as Erica

Harth explains, was 'to close up loopholes on existing legislation on marriage that allowed minors to marry without parental (read, paternal) consent'. Harth continues:

> [A] marriage was clandestine if contracted without banns or license. Despite statutes going back to 1694 to restrict such marriages, they were nevertheless quite common. There were two main types of so-called clandestine marriage: 1) the betrothal, or self-marriage; 2) the irregular marriage.[23]

'Betrothal' refers to an ancient form of lay marriage which took the form of a couple's private mutual agreement; until 1753, it was still recognised as binding by the Church. Derived from ancient Roman law, betrothal had been accepted since the twelfth century into English canonical law.[24] 'Irregular' marriages were performed by (usually less than scrupulous) clergymen who complied with the couple's request to dispense with preliminary public announcements of the marriage (banns) for a fee. Harth and David Lemmings have both discussed how this secondary practice was particularly associated with the 'roaring trade' in clandestine marriages which flourished, between approximately 1660 and 1753, in the area around Fleet Prison.[25]

Thus it was that the English laws concerning marriage had 'degenerated into a confused and contradictory mess by the early eighteenth century'. As Lemmings asserts, clandestine marriages were

> out of control, despite several legislative attempts to discourage it, a failure of the law which enabled adventurers, courtesans and social inferiors to marry underage heirs and heiresses against the wishes of their families, without any possibility of annulment. Even more frustratingly, the uncertainty of the law of marriage facilitated secret bigamy, whether intentional or unintentional, and the courts were in the invidious position of sometimes having to admit or even enforce legal rules which disinherited regularly married couples and bastardized their children.[26]

This description of previous legal efforts to restrict marriage of 'underage heirs and heiresses against the wishes of their families' – what was ultimately achieved by Hardwicke's Marriage Act – is particularly revealing. It points fundamentally to the economic agenda which motivated the passage of perhaps one of the most divisive acts of legislation enforced during the eighteenth century.[27]

Historians' views are divided regarding what the Act's passage finally tells us concerning the social and demographic nature of contemporary English society. Most agree that Hardwicke's Marriage Act was intended to benefit the economic interests of the landed classes (families whose wealth was retained through property). Intervention in an offspring's choice of a marital partner ensured that wealthy property owners could dictate how best their wealth would be settled in succeeding generations of the family.

A further source of debate between historians, however, is the specific means by which property was inherited in wealthy families. The relatively new practice of 'strict settlement' ensured that property was passed, in its entirety, to the eldest son (with younger children receiving smaller 'portions' of capital). This replaced the much older practice whereby property was divided between siblings.[28] The historical debates centre around the fact that this period is also associated with a period of 'demographic crisis' in which, as Lawrence Stone has observed, the landed classes' increasing tendency to marry late or not at all meant that they were failing to provide sufficient heirs in the first place.[29] As Lloyd Bonfield and others have suggested, however, the passage of Hardwicke's Marriage Act made it easier for wealthy families to dictate advantageous marriages for their children which would help provide the capital required to fund younger siblings' portions in the process of strict settlement.[30]

It seems clear from the question of strict settlement alone that, as Harth concludes, contemporary debates over the passage of Hardwicke's Act reflect wider economic concerns about the regulation of wealth and 'the spoils of an industrious nation with a developing capitalist economy'.[31] This is significant because the legislation impinged on all levels of society, even if its benefits were solely directed towards the interests of the moneyed classes. The protection of wealth was hardly an issue for poor people hoping to marry, but the Act's stipulation of a licence and banns incurred costs (over and above the wherewithal required to set up house together), a fact which might be implicated in the significant increase in illegitimate births that Stone generally associates with lower-class members of English society during the latter part of the eighteenth century.[32]

This lengthy discussion of Hardwicke's Marriage Act is intended to give a sense of its profound cultural impact but, even more importantly, how the heated debates both supporting and opposing its passage serve to articulate representations of female virtue and marriage still recognisable in English culture today. It seems obvious that the Act serves the mercenary interests of wealthy families seeking to control the marriage of their children. Significantly, while serving the same interests, the Act was promoted as a means to prevent another sort of mercenary marriage in which fortune hunters – or members of lower social orders – took advantage of underage heirs and heiresses. Attorney-General Sir Dudley Ryder expressed this view most succinctly when he suggested that 'young gentlemen and ladies of fortune' could be drawn into clandestine marriages with 'sharpers', 'bawds' and 'strumpets'.[33]

Long before 1753, the practice of marrying for money – whether at the behest of parents or the personal choice of unmarried individuals – had been censured in the press as a sure means of obtaining mutual misery. Mary Astell expressed this view in 1700 in *Some Reflections upon Marriage*, although she equally warns against the practice of marrying

> for love, an heroic action, which makes a mighty noise in the world, partly because of its rarity, and partly in regard of its extravagancy, and what does his marrying for love amount to? … the man does not act according to reason in either case, but is governed by irregular appetites.[34]

Later authors expressed increasingly different values concerning the importance of love between a couple intending to marry but the potential misery of a marriage founded on mercenary interests is universally deplored.* [35] Perhaps surprisingly, the context of heightened economic value implied by the passage of Hardwicke's Marriage Act increases the stakes concerning unhappy (mercenary) marriages; marital unhappiness brought with it the dangers of abandoned wives (vulnerable to seduction) and profligate husbands who strayed from the marriage bed. Both incurred the potential risk that carefully consolidated wealth could be dispersed among illegitimate children, or venereal disease which threatened to destroy the reproductive process altogether.† [36]

Divorce

Divorce was not a viable solution to marital unhappiness during the long eighteenth century. Until 1858, divorce was solely obtainable through a (prohibitively expensive) Act of Parliament and was the very last refuge only for England's wealthiest couples. One of the most famous divorces during this period involved one of the richest men in Europe, the Duke of Mazarin, and Hortense Mancini, an Italian aristocrat. The couple's marriage in 1661 proved to be disastrous; extensive rumours circulated in private and public concerning the Duke's mental instability and insanely jealous suspicions of his wife (which kept her confined as a virtual prisoner in the early years of their marriage). Hortense Mancini was widely rumoured to be a bisexual who engaged in numerous lesbian and heterosexual affairs before and after her divorce. She made several attempts to escape from her husband before eventually settling in London in 1675 (her cousin was Mary of Modena, the second wife of James, Duke of York); she

---

*   See also, for example, the essay by the pseudonymous Philogamus, *The Present State of Matrimony: Or, the Real Causes of Conjugal Infidelity and Unhappy Marriages* ... (1739). One of the earliest and most obvious literary examples in which couples marry for love rather than mutual financial benefit is Samuel Richardson's *Pamela* (1740).

†   William Hogarth's series of engravings entitled *Marriage A-la-Mode* (1743–5) depicts precisely these implications for an arranged mercenary marriage between the daughter of a wealthy merchant and the aristocratic (but penniless) son of Lord Squanderfield. For reproductions and commentaries on the engravings, see *The Norton Anthology*, pp. 2658–63.

subsequently became one of the mistresses of Charles II. Mancini's autobiographical memoirs were offered as evidence in the divorce proceedings.[37]

Only very slightly lower down the social spectrum, another divorce case which merited attention in the literary press involved Sir William Yonge, whose acrimonious split from his first wife, Mary, was obtained when he presented evidence of her adultery (with Colonel Thomas Norton) to a public court. The divorce settlement stipulated that Yonge should receive his wife's dowry and most of her considerable fortune; a further parliamentary petition won him the right to remarry.

What this bald statement of historical facts does not record (as is also the case with his biographical entry) is that Yonge was, himself, a serial adulterer.[38] The plight of Mrs Yonge is considered in a poem, probably written around 1724 by Lady Mary Wortley Montagu, which takes the form of an imaginary letter from Mrs Yonge to her estranged husband.[39] In it, a number of references to other notable contemporary figures associated with adultery (either directly or through their spouses), including Sir Robert Walpole, clearly implies the widespread nature of such practices in the highest echelons of English society. Montagu's poem also reflects cynically on the network of political friendships which flourished between England's male social elite (Yonge himself was a politician and baronet, and a friend of Walpole's) and inevitably favoured the male participant of the divorce case; moreover, his political cronies might provide an even greater advantage in the form of a wealthy new wife:

> Beneath the shelter of the law you stand,
> And urge my ruin with a cruel hand,
> While to my fault thus rigidly severe,
> Tamely submissive to the man you fear [that is, Walpole] ...
> Go: court the brittle friendships of the great,
> Smile at his board, or at his levee wait ...
> Your high ambition may be gratified,
> Some cousin of her own may be your bride ... (ll. 55–78)

Given Montagu's cynical (but, arguably, informed) view of mercenary marriage amongst the nation's social elite, the effective *endorsement* of such practices through Hardwicke's Marriage Act – promoted on the basis that marriage between couples of similar class backgrounds better ensured their mutual happiness – seems all the more remarkable. What emerges, increasingly, from both sides of contemporary debates is the importance of virtuous and mutual love as the *only* prevailing interest which would sustain a happy marriage.[40]

For the purposes of this chapter, this is the real significance of Hardwicke's Marriage Act. Historians have differently assessed its impact in relation to the wider cultural drive towards affective individualism (as manifest in a personal, rather than parental, choice of marriage partner) and the very notion of romantic love within marriage itself.[41] Indeed, it might never be possible to determine, objectively and finally, the real relationship between the 1753 Act and the state of companionate or loving marriage during the eighteenth century. David Lemmings reveals the ongoing nature of the historical debate itself:

> Whether love and affection were on the increase at the level of individual families during this period is a question which remains debatable. But it is clear that romantic individualism was not to be allowed to prevail in the age of Walpole and the Pelhams ... the controversy which surrounded [the Act] suggests that among the eighteenth-century elite of landowners and power-brokers marriage was viewed primarily as a way of achieving material or political advantage.[42]

The reconciliation of this legislative and economic context with the cultural evidence of contemporary literature (and further emphasised by the structural paradigm of the novel's 'happy ending' of marriage) remains challenging. Nevertheless, the idealisation of companionate marriage remains too prevalent a cultural feature to be ignored. Richardson's *Pamela* may present a marriage of social inequality – much to the dismissive contempt of its many critics – but undoubtedly upheld marriage as the final, happy, 'destination' of its virtuous protagonist.[43] Equally, *Tom Jones* demonstrates marriage's reforming virtues as well as, in the negative depiction of Blifil, the disastrous progeny of a loveless marriage. Both works, published before 1753, demonstrate the contemporary prevalence of female virtue and companionate marriage before the passage of Hardwicke's Marriage Act.[44]

Sexual Danger and the 'Vulnerable' Female

This chapter has suggested that female virtue and loving marriage are increasingly sanctified within literature despite changes to English marriage law after 1753, and that this cultural movement in turn reflects the wider economic processes by which England's growing economy consolidated and preserved its wealth. This may be further demonstrated by considering the implied sexual dangers that threatened female virtue excluded from the 'security' of loving or companionate marriage. In the previous chapter, the impact of the Society for the Reformation of Manners was discussed within the context of a wider project of social reform principally directed at the eradication of prostitution. Its efforts continued well into the second half of the eighteenth century but were gradually and finally subsumed by the gentler objectives of charitable institutions such as the Magdalen Hospital for the Reception of Penitent Prostitutes (founded in 1758).* [45]

The Magdalen Hospital sought to reform, rather than arrest, prostitutes. Its efforts may be associated with the sweeping measures of social reform actively sought by a large number of philanthropic and charitable institutions established in England during the second half of the eighteenth century. This movement, considered in Part Four: 'Trade, Colonial Expansion and Slavery', is itself linked to the period's rapidly

---

* The Magdalen Hospital was founded by philanthropist Jonas Hanway (1712–86), a devout Anglican and successful merchant with the Russia Company. He was also instrumental in the foundation of Thomas Coram's Foundling Hospital and the Marine Society (for the financial support and training of delinquent boys to join the Navy as officers' servants).

expanding capitalist economy and, in religious terms, the growing tendency towards Christian evangelism. Within the context of prostitution, the efforts of the Magdalen Hospital need to be placed in stark contrast with a justifiably infamous pamphlet by Bernard Mandeville which proposes a state-regulated 'service' whereby prostitutes may be supplied to meet the lustful needs of male members of society:

> It is Lust, not Love: And, therefore, the natural Impatience of Lust will prompt [men] to take the speediest way for present Gratification, and make them prefer the ready and willing Embraces of a Courtezan, before the doubtful and distant Prospect of enjoying a modest Damsel.[46]

Regarding male lust, Mandeville asserts that all men's needs are consistent ('for Love ever was and will be the same in all Men, and in all Ages'). Moreover, he assumes that their taste in sexual partners is indiscriminate, since the services of 'a Courtezan' will suffice if readily available. He also notes that the practical means to instigate this system would require 'necessary Recruits' via 'Supplies of young Women, which we may reasonably expect from the Northern and Western parts of these Kingdoms' (though, failing this, he proposes the expedient measure of an 'Act for encouraging the Importation of Foreign Women').

What makes Mandeville's scheme so extraordinary – if it were not enough so already – is that it is justified in terms of the protection of (middle-class) female chastity. Mandeville argues that since females possess a 'violent natural desire' (clearly sexual, at least in Mandeville's estimation, since it can be satisfied only by 'the Application of the Male Organ'), the preservation of their chastity prior to marriage is achieved only through the combined effects of both natural and 'artificial' chastity (notions of honour). The inherently precarious nature of female chastity 'built upon a very Ticklish Foundation' therefore also requires the concerted efforts of males:

> The only Way to preserve Female Chastity is to prevent the Men from laying Siege to it: But this Project of the Publick Stews

[brothels] is the only Way to prevent Men's laying Siege to it: Therefore, this Project is the only Way to preserve Female Chastity. (p. 66)

The admirably circular logic of Mandeville's proposition appears, on first reading, to contrast markedly with a contemporary proposal by Daniel Defoe in *Some Considerations upon Street-walkers with a Proposal for Lessening the Present Number of Them* (1726) to reduce prostitution by providing government incentives, including tax exemptions for marital status, and 'certain Privileges' for parents of three or more children.[47] Significantly, however, both Mandeville *and* Defoe place the spectre of middle-class females, reduced to sexual or moral depravity, before the reader's eyes in order to emphasise the social and economic importance of preserving female virtue within marriage. Mandeville's scheme presents only the 'dangerous' possibilities of middle-class female sexual frustration (the loss of chastity); Defoe's educated and articulate prostitute has been reduced to the trade (and, like Moll Flanders, awaits her execution by hanging on charges of theft in Newgate) after being seduced and forsaken by a nobleman. The misfortunes of both scenarios would have been 'resolved', implicitly, by middle-class companionate marriage.

Clearly, the most abhorrent aspect of Mandeville's scheme is his vision of a society in which a female underclass operates as sex workers servicing the 'social reality' of middle-class male lust. It is a vision made all the more disturbing by its resemblance to the sex trade in modern-day Western culture. Clearly, the ongoing cultural relevance of prostitution in Western society is deeply complex and merits consideration far beyond the scope of this volume.[48] The social history of prostitution in the eighteenth century, however – or even the history of its literary representation – is an infinitely more challenging task than might first appear. If defined in the simplest terms, relating to the exchange of sexual contact for money, prostitution incorporates countless figures, including (at one end of the social spectrum) Swift's bedraggled Drury Lane Corinna and Mandeville's serried ranks of state-sponsored sex workers.* At the other end of the spectrum, within the context of a wealthy elite for whom marriage was largely an economic transaction, the possibilities are truly endless.

In previous chapters consideration has been given to, individually, the wealthy courtesan Angellica Bianca in Behn's *The Rover* (as well as Behn's conscious paralleling of the writer's and prostitute's professions), and Betty, the prostitute whose contempt for the Swiftian figure in Lady Mary Wortley Montagu's poem provides literally the 'last word' on his performances in print. Defoe's letter-writing prostitute in Newgate regrets her father's provision of a middle-class education which has since proved to be her 'greatest Curse, as it has enabled me to feel more bitterly the Ills which I have undergone'.[49] There is little or no common ground between these individual representations of females. Through their and other literary representations may be discerned, instead, a vast plethora of contemporary social anxieties. These include (but are not limited to) moral corruption, the proliferation of crime, venereal disease, the possibilities of disguise and masquerade, female sexual agency and illegitimacy. If the literary history of the prostitute in eighteenth-century England *is* ever written to the full extent of its cultural implications, it will be a very long story.

Such a story can only complement the gratifyingly rich and complex qualities of the period's current scholarship. It has already been suggested in this chapter that pluralism, rather than consensus, is the key to our critical understanding of female experience during the course of the long eighteenth century. Perhaps, more than in any other area of study, the example of gender and sexuality has served to refashion the critical arena in which the texts of this period are best appreciated, and has helped to set the precedent for its future scholarship.

---

* Swift's satirical poem, *A Beautiful Young Nymph Going to Bed* (1734), famously depicts a poverty-stricken Drury Lane prostitute who – in the process of undressing for bed – 'dismantles' a series of artificial aids to her beauty, including a glass eye, false eyebrows and false teeth.

Notes

1   Vivien Jones (ed.), *Women in the Eighteenth Century: Constructions of Femininity* (London and New York: Routledge, 1990), p. 98. The chapter which precedes this quotation offers an excellent introductory overview to eighteenth-century writing on female education, pp. 98–139.

2   See the poetic 'correspondence' between Finch and Pope in Lawrence Lipking and James Noggle (eds), *The Norton Anthology of English Literature*, Volume C: *The Restoration and the Eighteenth Century* (New York and London: W. W. Norton, 2006), pp. 2596–7.

3   For an insight into female Royalist poets in this period, see Carol Barash, 'The Political Origins of Anne Finch's Poetry', *Huntingdon Library Quarterly*, 54:4 (Autumn 1991), pp. 327–51.

4   Anne Finch, from 'A Nocturnal Reverie', in Lipking and Noggle (eds), *Norton Anthology of English Literature*, Volume C, p. 2298, ll. 47–50.

5   Barash, 'The Political Origins of Anne Finch's Poetry', p. 329. On the subject of female Royalist poets, see her monograph entitled *English Women's Poetry, 1649–1714: Politics, Community, and Linguistic Authority* (Oxford: Oxford University Press, 1997).

6   Jones, *Women in the Eighteenth Century*, pp. 6–7.

7   Ibid.

8   See, in addition to Nancy Armstrong's monograph cited in Note 14 below, John Bender, *Imagining the Penitentiary: Fiction and the Architecture of the Mind in Eighteenth-century England* (Chicago and London: University of Chicago Press, 1987); and Thomas Laqueur, *Making Sex: Body and Gender from the Greeks to Freud* (Cambridge: Harvard University Press, 1992).

9   Judith Butler, *Gender Trouble: Feminism and the Subversion of Identity* (London: Routledge, 1990).

10   Michel Foucault, *The History of Sexuality*, Volume 1, trans. Robert Hurley (London: Penguin, 1978), pp. 81–102.

11   Also important to a wider understanding of Foucault's notion of the 'negative' manifestation of power in culture is his *Discipline and Punish: The Birth of the Prison*, trans. Alan Sheridan (New York: Vintage, 1979).

12   For a detailed discussion of this text, see Ros Ballaster, *Seductive Forms: Amatory Fiction from 1684 to 1740* (Oxford: Clarendon Press, 1992), pp. 114–23.

13   For a more complex model of this cultural period's progressive 'feminisation', see, for example, Carey McIntosh, *The Evolution of English Prose 1700–1800: Style, Politeness and Print Culture* (Cambridge: Cambridge

University Press, 1998), pp. vii and 195–220; and Terry Eagleton, *The Rape of Clarissa: Writing, Sexuality and Class Struggle in Samuel Richardson* (Oxford: Basil Blackwell, 1982.

14 Nancy Armstrong, *Desire and Domestic Fiction: A Political History of the Novel* (Oxford: Oxford University Press, 1987), p. 24.

15 On Pope's famous assertion and the (related) subject of female sexual behaviour in the eighteenth century, see Patricia Meyer Spacks, 'Ev'ry Woman is at Heart a Rake', *Eighteenth-century Studies*, 8:1 (Autumn 1974), pp. 27–46; and Terry Castle, 'The Female Thermometer', *Representations*, 17 (Winter 1987), pp. 1–27.

16 The subject of 'female rakes' is treated differently by Martha Vicinus in her study of the representation of lesbian sexuality entitled *Intimate Friends: Women Who Loved Women 1779–1928* (Chicago: University of Chicago Press, 2004).

17 Daniel Statt, 'The Case of the Mohocks: Rake Violence in Augustan London', *Social History*, 20:2 (May 1995), p. 180. 'Mohocks' refers to a club or gang of aristocratic young men who, from 1712, terrorised London with a series of drunken and violent night-time rampages. Statt considers how the example of their conduct interrogates the social term 'rake' as it applied to literary representations versus authentic examples of male behaviour.

18 Statt, 'The Case of the Mohocks', p. 181.

19 See Ellen Pollak: *The Poetics of Sexual Myth: Gender and Ideology in the Verse of Swift and Pope* (Chicago: University of Chicago Press, 1985); for a useful guide to eighteenth-century satire, see Arthur Pollard, *Satire* (London: Methuen, 1970).

20 R. James, M.D., from *A Medical Dictionary* (1743) in Jones, *Women in the Eighteenth Century*, pp. 85–6.

21 Armstrong, *Desire and Domestic Fiction*, p. 66.

22 See, for example, Erica Harth, 'The Virtue of Love: Lord Hardwicke's Marriage Act', *Cultural Critique*, 9 (Spring 1988), pp. 123–54. The literary implications of the 1753 Act are considered by Katherine Sobba Green in 'The Heroine's Blazon and Hardwicke's Marriage Act: Commodification for a Novel Market', *Tulsa Studies in Women's Literature*, 9:2 (Autumn, 1990), pp. 273–90. The historical importance of the previous (briefly enforced) Marriage Act of 1653 (which expired in 1660) is discussed by Dorothy McLaren in 'The Marriage Act of 1653: Its Influence on the Parish Registers', *Population Studies*, 28:2 (July 1974), pp. 319–27.

23 Harth, 'The Virtue of Love', p. 123.

24 David Lemmings, 'Marriage and the Law in the Eighteenth Century: Hardwicke's Marriage Act of 1753', *Historical Journal*, 39: 2 (1996), p. 344.

25   Harth, 'The Virtue of Love', p. 125; Lemmings, 'Marriage and the Law in the Eighteenth Century', p. 345.
26   Lemmings, 'Marriage and the Law in the Eighteenth Century', p. 344.
27   The divisive nature of the Act, and the means by which it was promoted or opposed, is discussed in detail by Lemmings and Harth throughout the course of their excellent articles.
28   Harth notes that strict settlement 'arose shortly after the beginning of the hundred years or so between the mid-seventeenth and mid-eighteenth centuries' in 'The Virtue of Love', pp. 128–30; see also Lemmings, 'Marriage and the Law in the Eighteenth Century', p. 357. The subject was first prompted by H. J. Habbakuk's discussion of it in 'Marriage Settlements in the Eighteenth Century', *Transactions of the Royal Historical Society*, 4:32 (1950), pp. 15–30.
29   See Lawrence Stone, *The Family, Sex and Marriage in England 1500–1800*, abridged edn (London: Penguin, 1979), pp. 166–7.
30   Lloyd Bonfield, *Marriage Settlements, 1601–1740: The Adoption of the Strict Settlement* (Cambridge: Cambridge University Press, 1983).
31   Harth, 'The Virtue of Love', p. 139.
32   On the increase in illegitimate births in the second half of the eighteenth century, see Belinda Meteyard, 'Illegitimacy and Marriage in Eighteenth-century England', *Journal of Interdisciplinary History*, 10:3 (Winter 1980), pp. 479–89; and Stone, *The Family, Sex and Marriage in England*, pp. 397–8, 402.
33   Support for the Act is further demonstrated in William Cobbett, *The Parliamentary History of England, from the Earliest Period to the Year 1803* (London: Longman, 1813), p. xv, as cited in Lemmings, 'Marriage and the Law in the Eighteenth Century', p. 347.
34   Mary Astell, *Some Reflections upon Marriage*, in Lipking and Noggle (eds), *Norton Anthology of English Literature*, Volume C, pp. 2286–7.
35   See an extract from Philogamus, *The Present State of Matrimony: Or, the Real Causes of Conjugal Infidelity and Unhappy Marriages* ... (1739) in Jones, *Women in the Eighteenth Century*, pp. 77–81, discussed in Harth, 'The Virtue of Love', pp. 140–1.
36   These fears are expressed in Philogamus, *The Present State of Matrimony*.
37   Hortense and Marie Mancini, *Memoirs*, ed. and trans. Sarah Nelson (Chicago: University of Chicago Press, 2008). See also Toivo David Rosvall, *The Mazarine Legacy: The Life of Hortense Mancini, Duchess Mazarin* (New York: Viking Press, 1969).
38   H. T. Dickinson, 'Yonge, Sir William, Fourth Baronet (*c.* 1693–1755)', *Oxford Dictionary of National Biography* (Oxford University Press, 2004).
39   Lady Mary Wortley Montagu, *Epistle from Mrs Yonge to her Husband*, in

Lipking and Noggle (eds), *Norton Anthology of English Literature*, Volume C, pp. 2587–8.

40   Keith Thomas provides a useful contextual background, as well as substantial historical evidence of the increasing trend towards companionate marriage in this period, in *The Ends of Life: Roads to Fulfilment in Early Modern England* (Oxford: Oxford University Press, 2009), pp. 216–17.

41   For example, according to Harth in 'The Virtue of Love', p. 132, Alan MacFarlane concludes that, the Act's passage represented 'a brief aberration in the long tradition of individual choice and romantic love in English marriage'. MacFarlane depicts England's long cultural tradition of companionate marriage, going back to the thirteenth century, in *Marriage and Love in England: Modes of Reproduction 1300–1840* (Oxford: Basil Blackwell, 1986), pp. 182 ff.

42   Lemmings, 'Marriage and the Law in the Eighteenth Century', p. 359.

43   For a discussion of *Pamela*'s reception, see Thomas Keymer and Peter Sabor, *'Pamela' in the Marketplace: Literary Controversy and Print Culture in Eighteenth-century Britain and Ireland* (Cambridge: Cambridge University Press, 2006).

44   In *The Ends of Life*, p. 214, Thomas briefly traces the English cultural tradition of companionate marriage back to Plutarch (AD *c.* 50–125), a Greek philosopher whose discussion of friendship within marriage in his *Moral Essays* (variously translated into English during the sixteenth century) also found currency in English Puritan moral treatises.

45   See J. S. Taylor, *Jonas Hanway: Founder of the Marine Society: Charity and Policy in Eighteenth-century Britain* (London: Scolar Press, 1985).

46   'Colonel Harry Mordaunt' (Bernard Mandeville), from *A Modest Defence of Public Stews: or, an Essay Upon Whoring* (1724; 1740 edn) in Jones, *Women in the Eighteenth Century*, pp. 66–7.

47   Daniel Defoe, from *Some Considerations upon Street-walkers with a Proposal for Lessening the Present Number of Them* (1726), in Jones, *Women in the Eighteenth Century*, pp. 69–72.

48   On the global history of prostitution, see Nickie Roberts, *Whores in History: Prostitution in Western Society* (London: HarperCollins, 1992); and Nils Johan Ringdal, *Love for Sale: A World History of Prostitution*, trans. Richard Daly (New York: Grove Press, 2004).

49   Daniel Defoe, from *Some Considerations*, in Jones, *Women in the Eighteenth Century*, p. 71.

Trade, Colonial Expansion and Slavery

In terms of physical landmass, Britain is a small country. The enormous increase of its imperial and economic power during the course of the long eighteenth century therefore represents dual aspects of the same process. Global imperial and economic supremacy – the exalted position achieved by imperial Britain during the period of industrialisation which followed – were built on the foundations of Britain's colonial expansion and the exploitation of those colonial resources during the course of the eighteenth century. As Suvir Kaul has recently observed:

> [T]he rapid socio-economic transformation of Britain that economists have labeled capitalism was sparked off and intensified by trade to the Spice Islands, Asia, and in the Mediterranean, and even more so by colonial and plantation settlements in the Caribbean and North America, including the trade in slaves, sugar and rum, tobacco, and manufactured goods across the Atlantic.[1]

During the long eighteenth century England (or, after 1707, Britain) began to compete in earnest for its own share of colonial and economic power (mostly with Holland and, increasingly, France) across the globe. As it did so, a newly expanded sense of British cultural identity began to be formulated, through the printed word.[2] Imaginative or 'literary' works, newspapers and magazines, essays and treatises all contributed to this process. Profound cultural change is never realised without some sense of anxiety. This new sense of cultural identity sometimes celebrated and sometimes deplored Britain's burgeoning colonial and economic presence.[3] It might even be argued that the modern sense of ambiguity which still characterises Britons' regard for their national identity has some of its origins in the imperial expansion of this period.

In terms of contemporary literature, Britain's past and present sense of national identity is predicated on how it regards both itself and other nations. During the course of the long eighteenth century, many changes to Britain's imperial borders and shifting trade relations with other nations and cultures meant that emerging notions of 'British' or 'English' identity also contended with (equally emerging) notions of 'foreign', 'Turkish', 'Indian', 'American' identity, and so on.[4] Contemporary literature represents objects and individuals associated with this process. This (differently) applies to nations that came to be incorporated directly into Britain's imperial realm (in Scotland and Ireland, in North America, India, and so on), nations which had long contributed to Britain's wealth through exploitation of their resources (in the nations of western Africa, in particular), and nations which had engaged – sometimes for centuries – in a myriad of trading relationships with the British empire (including Turkey and the Ottoman empire, and Far Eastern nations such as China).

A brief overview of some of the period's key developments will provide a useful historical context for this discussion. England was a slow starter in the European race to colonise the world.[5] Although an English trading presence had been established on the eastern coast of North America, in India and in the Caribbean during the reigns of Elizabeth I and James I, these early colonial outposts were dwarfed by Spanish, Portuguese, French and Dutch interests around the world during the sixteenth and early seventeenth centuries. England also traded with the Islamic realm and the Far East during this period in well-established global trading centres such as Constantinople (modern-day Istanbul).

In 1655, Oliver Cromwell failed to oust Spanish traders from their colonial stronghold in Hispaniola (modern-day Haiti and the

Dominican Republic) although he succeeded in adding Jamaica to Britain's existing colonial territories in the Caribbean (including Barbados, Montserrat, Nevis and St Kitts). From this period to the middle of the 1670s, a repeated succession of trade treaties and wars marked the struggles between England and Holland over trading concerns in the West Indies. The accession of a Dutch king to the English throne in late 1688 brought the beginning of an extended period of Anglo-French hostilities over the (related) subjects of trade and the balance of Protestant (versus Roman Catholic) power in Europe.

Britain's extensive conflicts with French forces throughout the eighteenth century, both within Europe and in colonial territories, were an enormous drain on national resources. In 1695, the foundation of the Bank of England was specifically intended to raise funds for King William's French campaigns.[6] Nearer to home, the 1707 Act of Union brought England and Scotland together into a national empire whose cultural and political centre remained indisputably in London (as noted with due resentment by numerous Scottish nationalists over the centuries).[7]

Two of the most momentous events in Britain's colonial history occurred in the last half of the eighteenth century. The first, Robert Clive's triumphant victory at Plassey (modern-day Palashi in West Bengal) in 1757, began the process of securing not only the British East India Company's domination of Indian trade, but also its government.[8] The second, the signing of the Declaration of Independence in July 1776, marked the beginning of a lengthy period by which Britain's thirteen American colonies began the process of securing their national independence. The war came to an end in 1781 and America's independence was formally recognised in 1783 via the Treaty of Paris. Only in September 1787 was the American Constitution – in many ways the most important document in the foundation of the new republic – adopted as the fundamental agreement of what constitutes federal legislative power (versus jurisdiction at the level of individual states or districts within states). General George Washington was inaugurated as the first American President in 1789.

The Transatlantic Slave Trade

It has previously been suggested that Lockean principles of civil equality may have inspired the principles and language that Thomas Jefferson incorporated into the American Declaration of Independence.* As many of his biographers have noted, however, Jefferson himself was an owner of slaves throughout his lifetime.[9] There are many such, seemingly bewildering, discrepancies in eighteenth-century culture (both British and American) which must remain outside the scope of this volume. Suffice to say, the cultural assumption of white racial supremacy in eighteenth-century British literature is so widespread as to be effectively universal but does not, in itself, offer sufficient explanation for the success and longevity of the slave trade.

The transatlantic slave trade brought immense wealth to Britain.[10] From approximately the middle of the sixteenth century, as part of a wider commercial exploitation of material goods acquired from their voyages to western Africa, British traders became involved in the lucrative business of capturing, trading and selling its human inhabitants to labour on the Spanish plantations of Hispaniola in the Caribbean. In 1632, Charles I granted a licence to a group of London merchants for the transportation of enslaved people from West Africa and the trade grew at an exponential rate. Estimates have suggested that nearly 200,000 Africans were transported in British slave trips during the 1720s; by the 1790s, slightly less than half a million African slaves laboured in British colonies in the Caribbean.

In colonial America, a form of bonded labour had been in practice as early as 1600; this generally took the form of indentured servitude whereby an individual served a period of hard (usually agricultural) labour in exchange for the cost of their transport to the colonies and their (eventual) freedom. Indentured servants tended to come from either northern Europe (including English, Scottish, Irish and German immigrants) or Africa. When the convicted thief Moll Flanders 'pleads her belly' (pregnancy) at her trial, her sentence of execution is exchanged

---

* See Part Four: 'Man, Nature and Liberty'.

for one of transportation as an indentured servant to the colony of Virginia. Many of Defoe's contemporaries would have judged transportation as the less desirable option.

In Britain's American colonies, indentured servitude gradually gave way to the more lucrative and regulated system of human trafficking that the transatlantic slave trade became during the eighteenth and nineteenth centuries. The establishment of state-relevant Slave Codes stipulated the (sometimes widely divergent) civil legislation that slave-owners had to observe concerning their 'property'. From around the last quarter of the eighteenth century, on both sides of the Atlantic, public voices condemning the practice of slavery began to increase in number and urgency. Slavery was abolished in England in stages between 1772 and 1833; in America, abolition was finally achieved on a national scale with the Thirteenth Constitutional Amendment (after the Civil War) in 1865. Estimates vary, but most suggest that the transatlantic slave trade involved 11 to 12 million Africans; the number that died during the process of capture, incarceration or transport can never be known.

The transatlantic slave trade constituted a lucrative and largely efficient means of realising high profits from the triangular journey between Europe, the west coast of Africa and numerous ports in the Caribbean or South and North America. On the first leg of the journey, European manufactured goods (including guns, gunpowder, alcohol and metal goods) were exchanged for captured Africans. In the early stages of the slave trade, African tribal leaders managed the entire process whereby prisoners were gathered, incarcerated in warehouses awaiting transport, and eventually sold to European traders. As the trade became more established and streamlined, European traders took over the management of many of the largest slave warehouses themselves.

The so-called 'Middle Passage' of the triangular trade took enslaved Africans (and other commercial goods from Africa, including ivory and gold) across the Atlantic. The human cost of slave trafficking under these conditions is not easily imaginable; it is worth noting that conditions in the utterly filthy holds of slave ships (in which the slaves were transported, tightly packed together for maximum profit) were generally considered unsuitable for the storage of goods being imported into Europe on the journey's third leg (such as sugar, tobacco and rice). It has been estimated that, on average, 10 per cent of the human cargo died en route while a bad voyage might incur 30 per cent losses. Within the context of the transatlantic slave trade's longevity, these bleak statistics stand as a bitter testament to the enormous potential profits that justified such a high level of 'wastage'.

The barbarity of slavery presents a moral theme which inspired numerous literary representations of social and ethical injustice throughout the course of the long eighteenth century. One tale tells the story of an English trader and castaway named Thomas Inkle whose certain death at the hands of savages is prevented by a beautiful and virtuous Indian maiden named Yarico. After a period of blissful loving attachment, the pair are rescued by a passing English ship but, on reaching (the British slave colony of) Barbados, the duplicitous and cruel Inkle sells his now-pregnant former lover into slavery. The narrative first appeared as early as 1657 in Richard Lygon's *History of the Island of Barbados* but was repeatedly refashioned in periodical literature, fiction and drama over the course of the next century. Its most famous versions appear in Richard Steele's *Spectator* in 1711 and in George Colman the Younger's very popular comic opera (with a revised 'happy ending') in 1787.[11] Beyond its general relevance to the contemporary issue of slavery during the long eighteenth century, the markedly differing versions of this tale's plot, characterisation and related moral precepts attest to the cultural process by which a central theme such as slavery could be manipulated to suit the prevailing tastes of its potential audience.*

In the last quarter of the eighteenth century, the theme of slavery was given new and more specific cultural impetus in the form of several autobiographical accounts detailing first-hand experience of the horrors of the transatlantic journey and the experience of capture. These early

---

* A similar observation can be made concerning Aphra Behn's well-known tragic prose fiction entitled *Oroonoko, or, The Royal Slave: A True History* (1688). For a closer discussion of this, see Part Four: 'A Culture of Print'.

depictions convey (for the white middle-class readers who would have had primary access to them) some of the intense cruelty suffered by the enslaved.[12] Two autobiographical accounts which fall into this category were attributed to Olaudah Equiano (*c.* 1745–97) and Ottobah Cugoano (b. *c.* 1757). Beyond their cultural importance as two of the earliest African authors to be published in English, Cugoano and Equiano express very different affiliations to the late eighteenth-century Christian Evangelical movement which gave momentum to the project of abolition on both sides of the Atlantic. Cugoano's political treatise *Thoughts and Sentiments on the Evil and Wicked Traffic of the Commerce of the Human Species* (1787) offers an impassioned diatribe against the cruelties of the slave trade. He declares that Africans had a moral duty to resist enslavement:

> If any man should buy another man, and compel him to his service and slavery without any agreement of that man to serve him, the enslaver is a robber and a defrauder of that man every day. Wherefore it is as much the duty of a man who is robbed in that manner to get out of the hands of his enslaver, as it is for any honest community of men to get out of the hands of rogues and villains.[13]

Cugoano's polemical prose is presented within a detailed context of Christian humanist political philosophy and traces the aberration of slavery through history (including Biblical history) as well as considering his personal experience of capture and enslavement. Despite their shared use of autobiographical narrative, Cugoano's work contrasts significantly in tone and intention with Olaudah Equiano's *Interesting Narrative* (1789) which, reminiscent of works such as *Robinson Crusoe*, is firmly rooted in the English literary tradition of spiritual autobiography and travel narratives.[14] A committed Evangelical Christian, Equiano (who lived for a period of his enslavement under the name of Gustavus Vassa) provides a vivid account of his life before, during and after the experience of slavery as well as his conversion and experiences as a Christian social reformer.[15]

Significant critical speculation continues to question the veracity (and possibly the attribution) of parts of this text.[16] There is little doubt, however, that Equiano's *Interesting Narrative* provided a powerful piece of abolitionist propaganda which occasioned no fewer than nine editions during the course of Equiano's lifetime; it continues to provoke diverse critical debates concerning African identity, voice and authority within the context of colonial literature.[17] Considering the Christian Evangelical motivation behind texts such as Equiano's *Interesting Narrative*, Suvir Kaul has suggested:

> Evangelical Christianity, with its powerful narratives of and insistence upon witnessing and personal conversion, offered black Africans – enslaved and free – a tenuous community, and the only self-definition, ratified by white society. Writing, then, becomes a crucial, and difficult, exercise in belonging and alienation.[18]

What emerges clearly from the highly articulate and 'civilised' prose of Equiano's narrative is the European education and Christian sensibility which he shared with the white, middle-class readership whose sympathies were being courted so assiduously:

> Are the dearest friends and relations, now rendered more dear by their separation from their kindred, still to be parted from each other, and thus prevented from cheering the gloom of slavery …?
> … Surely this is a new refinement in cruelty, which, while it has no advantage to atone for it, thus aggravates distress.[19]

Christian abolitionists, as Kaul notes elsewhere, sought the end of slavery but not the end of British imperial rule, nor indeed the tacitly upheld cultural superiority of white Europeans that it implied.* [20]

It is worth briefly considering the general significance of post-colonial studies like Kaul's in relation to eighteenth-century literature as a whole. In this context, post-colonial scholarship seeks to acknowledge the wider

---

* Kaul makes this point with reference to Samuel Johnson, an early Christian abolitionist who did not support the American bid for independence, p. 133.

cultural implications of the process of European colonialism, accommodating not only the historical project of colonialism itself (on both the coloniser and the colonised) but *also* the subsequent processes which reject or revise aspects of colonialism (in movements towards abolitionism, independence and 'social equality'). Anti-colonial/ independence movements which succeed in gaining precedence over once-colonised nations themselves often adopt 'many of the legacies and institutions of colonial rule, and thus maintained many of the economic and social divides (within and across nations) enforced by colonialism'.[21] Contemporary literature is not excluded from this wider cultural tendency and can be indicative – even in the ostensible process of rejecting imperialist ideology – of the same institutional influences which were employed to justify colonial aggression.[22] The application of post-colonial theory to certain themes in this volume is intended to give a sense of the broad critical spectrum available to readers of eighteenth-century literature. These ideas are proposed in conjunction – rather than opposition – to the volume's prevailing discussions of economic and political contexts for changes in British culture during the long eighteenth century.

In its mission to 'civilise' the unconverted people of the globe, Christianity offers a prime – though hardly isolated – example of a European cultural institution which contributed to both the enslavement, and liberation, of millions of Africans during the course of several centuries. The ultimate success of the Christian abolitionist project in Britain was relatively early in European terms although it was still not complete by the end of the period considered by this volume. Britain's imperial project was far from over by 1790. The East India Company governed India on behalf of the British government for a century from 1757 before the country came under British Crown rule (1858–1947). As Philip Lawson and John Phillips argue, in the earlier part of the period actual and fictional representations of wealthy British merchants, or 'nabobs',* who returned to Britain laden with the spoils of their trading

---

* *The Concise Oxford Dictionary*, 8th edn (Clarendon Press: Oxford, 1990), p. 786, defines 'nabob' as '(formerly) a conspicuously wealthy person, especially one returned from India with a fortune'. Its origins relate to the Urdu word *nawab*, a term once used to describe a Muslim official or governor under the Mughal Empire.

281

interests in India reflect the 'considerable misgivings over the many effects that an empire of conquest in the east would have on Britain':

> [I]n the decades immediately preceding the battle of Plassey in 1757 nabobs found themselves caricatured, slandered, and vilified in the press, in parliament, on the London stage, and in a host of private diaries and letters.[23]

This is certainly evident in, for example, Samuel Foote's depiction of the 'rapaciously mercantile' Matthew Mite in his satirical play *The Nabob* (1772) although, by this time, depictions such as that of Sir Oliver Surface in Sheridan's *The School for Scandal* (1777) reflect more positively on the new influx of wealth that Indian colonisation brought with it.[24] The literary depiction of nabobs reflects yet another facet of the profound ambiguity with which Britain continued to regard its newly expanded national identity as, by the close of the period, the largest and wealthiest of European empires.[25]

Investment, Speculation and Luxury

The generation of new English wealth, leading in some cases to unprecedented levels of affluence, began in earnest in the first decades of the eighteenth century. The English government and its advisers came up with numerous – and increasingly inventive – schemes to generate the finances needed to fund the ongoing wars with France. For investors, these schemes exploited the exciting opportunities for investment and speculation that went hand in hand with global trade. Although the East India Company had been founded much earlier (in the last years of Queen Elizabeth's reign) its trading activities increased significantly during this period; the South Sea Company was first established in 1711, creating new sources of public investment to speculate in the lucrative trading markets of South America.

Investors came to realise – the hard way – that prices can go down as well as up. In 1720 the 'South Sea Bubble', now widely recognised as the first stock market crash, 'burst'. This followed a frenzied year of speculation which saw shares in the South Sea Company rise tenfold in value before a combination of factors (including the simultaneous 'bursting' of speculative bubbles in the French and Dutch stock markets) led to a crisis in investor confidence and a scramble to sell shares; prices plummeted and the fortunes of a wide social spectrum of shareholders – from servants to the gentry – were ruined overnight.* Perhaps unsurprisingly, this period of England's economic history coincides with some of the earliest literary references to the insidious corrupting forces of luxury. John Sekora has observed the wide scale and longevity of such references over the course of the eighteenth century.[26]

The expanding commercialism of British culture was often directly associated with the importation of 'luxury' goods from abroad, but Sekora observes several phases within the period's literature that address related political, moral and social aspects of luxury's growth.[27] Related to speculative disasters like the South Sea Bubble was a deepening sense of public unease concerning the expanding system of public credit which detached the traditional concept of wealth from its physical manifestation in the solid economic realities of the past (property and agricultural goods). Associated with these concerns were worries about other novel features of the rapidly expanding economic climate; these included the growth of stock-jobbing (artificial inflation of share prices by unscrupulous City traders) and repeated calls to raise taxes to fund a standing army (to protect the nation's security even in times of peace).[28] Swift vehemently rejected the second proposition in a popular pamphlet entitled *The Conduct of the Allies* (1711) which sold over 11,000 copies in its first few months of publication:

---

*   In the wake of the South Sea Bubble, the new Lord Treasurer Robert Walpole was obliged to take a series of decisive measures to restore public confidence. A number of South Sea Company directors were found fraudulent and fined, and government ministers (including the Chancellor of the Exchequer) were impeached or imprisoned. The Company itself was restructured; through the redistribution of its stock into the Bank of England and East India Company, it continued to play an important role in the speculative generation of wealth – and the provision of government funds – for another century.

We have been Fighting for the Ruin of the Publick Interest, and the Advancement of a Private. We have been Fighting to … enrich Usurers and Stock-jobbers; and to cultivate the pernicious Designs of a Faction, by destroying the Landed Interest. The Nation now begins to think these Blessings are not worth Fighting for any longer, and therefore desires a Peace.[29]

In broad terms, then, the condemnation of luxury in eighteenth-century literature is split along political as well as newly delineated cultural lines. After 1688 and William's accession to the throne in place of his Stuart (and Roman Catholic) father-in-law James II, Tory interests were associated with members of the landed gentry (whose wealth had been accumulated the 'old-fashioned' way, through the realisation of profits from agriculture or tenants' rents). With Tory interests may also be associated the later prevalence in a growing sense of nostalgia centred around images of the English countryside and gentlemen's country estates.[*] Tories viewed with increasing suspicion the visible evidence of new Whig wealth, largely generated through City speculation and overseas trade:

[For Tory sympathisers] the Revolution of 1688 was a Pandora's box setting loose a spirit of luxury the natural order could not contain … Luxury was begetting a new, false, and artificial wealth, a new and noxious economic order, and a new and sinister breed of men whose sole office was to multiply by some nefarious means the new man-made values.[30]

This suspicion was not only directed at the luxury imported goods that represented cultural change but, more disturbingly, towards the veneer of social respectability that came with Whigs' buying power. If wealth and social position could be acquired within a generation, what 'value'

---

[*] Regarding this sense of Tory nostalgia, consider the images of rural simplicity and castigation of luxury depicted in Goldsmith's poem *The Deserted Village* (1770) as well as his essay against luxury entitled *An Enquiry into the Present State of Polite Learning* (1759), as also discussed by Sekora, pp. 96–7.

were ancient bloodlines and heavily mortgaged country estates? This is clearly reflected by Swift's observation:

> Let any man observes the equipages [expensive carriages] in this town, he shall find the greatest number of those who make a figure [that is, an ostentatious display of wealth], to be a species of men quite different from any that were even known before the Revolution [of 1688].[31]

The tone of class hostility is difficult to miss. Nevertheless, it would be unwise to assume too wide a division between Tories and Whigs, old and new money, or gentlemen and the moneyed classes of City merchants, across the whole period. As the financial value of English property dropped in relation to the market value of City and overseas investments, increasing numbers of the landed gentry were obliged to marry their noble offspring to 'new money' as represented by cash-rich City Whigs and an aspiring mercantile class who had benefited from the expanding global market. In this sociological trend must be recognised the fact that people's values – then as now – rarely divide into neat categories.[32]

Luxury goods came to represent not only the country's new source of wealth but universal indicators of a 'polite' urban society on both sides of the political divide. The 'consumer revolution' that occurred in eighteenth-century England has been vividly described by Neil McKendrick, John Brewer and J. H. Plumb in terms of its influence on virtually every level of society:

> Objects which for centuries had been the privileged possessions of the rich came, within the space of a few generations, to be within the reach of a larger part of society than ever before … 'luxuries' came to be seen as mere 'decencies', and 'decencies' came to be seen as 'necessities'. Even 'necessities' underwent a dramatic metamorphosis in style, variety and availability.[33]

This observation makes clear that such profound cultural changes impinge even on the level of language itself. The rejection of luxury which Sekora observes across the period needs to be understood in relation to the 'revolutionary proportions' of commercialisation that English society had undergone by the last quarter of the eighteenth century. Its social implications were such that the display of fashionable luxury goods gave ready indicators of the intricate class hierarchies that increasingly characterised English society. In turn, according to McKendrick, Brewer and Plumb:

> These characteristics – the closely stratified nature of English society, the striving for vertical social mobility, the emulative spending bred by social emulation, the compulsive power of fashion begotten by social competition – combined with the widespread ability to spend (offered by novel levels of prosperity) to produce an unprecedented propensity to consume: unprecedented in the depth to which it penetrated the lower reaches of society and unprecedented in its impact on the economy.[34]

It is important to stress, once again, the ambiguity with which this cultural change is reflected in literature. To ignore this fact would imply that Britain embraced, wholeheartedly and unquestioningly, its emerging identity as a powerful trading empire. This is hardly the case. At the same time, however, Kaul notes:

> The creative thirst for novelty was sharpened by the quickened stream of chinoiserie, textiles, spices, dried fruits, sugar, tobacco, rum, and other goods that flowed into Britain … English merchandizing benefited, of course, as did the shipbuilding and outfitting industries, as an armed navy expanded. The enlargement of trade also resulted in the creation of a domestic network of wholesalers and retailers, linked now to the great world beyond.[35]

It would have been impossible to ignore the direct relationship between Britain's colonial expansion and its financial expansion. Consumption of luxury imports could be perceived as an act which – then as now – interrogated the consumers' (ethical and political) relationship to the products they consumed. This volume's discussion of the period's satirical literature in Part Three: 'Political and Social Satire' addresses this ambiguity in relation to Pope's famous portrait of Belinda's dressing table in *The Rape of the Lock* (1712–14). The related themes of female vanity and cosmetic artifice are equally evident (if less flatteringly depicted) in Swift's poem *The Lady's Dressing Room* (1732). In relation to these images, Laura Brown has suggested how the authors' depiction of female capriciousness and vanity is aligned with their role as consumers of colonial markets (which in turn deflects the reader's consideration away from the acts of colonial exploitation which secured the goods in the first place).[36]

In Issue 69 of *The Spectator* in 1711, the famous depiction of a woman's dress by Addison and Steele makes even more explicit the global market that stands behind consumer goods, but here these features are indicative of the wearer's 'Quality' (wealth) and sophistication:

> The single dress of a Woman of Quality is often the Product of an hundred Climates. The Muff and the Fan come together from the different Ends of the Earth. The Scarf is sent from the Torrid Zone, and the Tippet [a fur stole] from beneath the Pole. The Brocade Petticoat rises out of the Mines of Peru, and the Diamond Necklace out of the Bowels of Indostan.[37]

A more ambiguous example of female apparel is presented in Roxana's 'Turkish Dress'. Defoe provides this singular article of clothing with an intriguing narrative of its own exotic origins:

> The Habit I had got at Leghorn, when my Foreign Prince bought me a Turkish slave … the Malthese Man of War had, it seems, taken a Turkish Vessel going from Constantinople to Alexandria,

in which were some Ladies bound for Grand Cairo in Egypt; and as the Ladies were made Slaves, so their fine Cloaths were thus expos'd; and with this Turkish Slave, I bought the rich Cloaths too ....[38]

As is equally the case with Roxana herself, both the Turkish ladies and their 'fine Cloaths' are marketable goods capable of being bought, sold or taken as the spoils of conquest by Maltese privateers. Roxana wears this dress on a number of occasions to impress the London guests who attend her masked balls, and the costume is altered on several occasions:

> the Dress under it, was ... set with Pearl in the Work, and some Turquois Stones ... and on both Ends where it join'd, or hook'd, was set with Diamonds for eight Inches either way, only they were not true Diamonds ... on the front ... was a good Jewel, which I had added to it.

> This Habit, as above, cost me about sixty Pistoles in Italy, but cost much more in the Country from whence it came ... . (p. 150)

Like a South Sea Company share, the value of the Turkish dress is clearly subject to change. Significantly, later in the narrative, the revelation of Roxana's true identity as the mother of her maid Susan is intimately connected with Susan's recognition of the Turkish dress itself.[39] This singular article of clothing, so intimately connected with Roxana's immoral past as a courtesan, contains within it the potential for both triumph and disaster in the fashionable urban world of London society. It is also associated – as is Roxana's later assumption of a Quaker costume – with her penchant for disguise and reinvention but its overseas origins and the story of its acquisition are linked with the realm of colonial trade. Roxana's Turkish dress provides a compelling example, from an author who so frequently expressed his wholehearted endorsement of Britain's colonial project, of the powerful cultural ambiguity with which such objects must be perceived.

Defoe's canon demonstrates his general endorsement of British colonialism and mercantile interests.[40] This is evident in his numerous depictions of honest merchants whose scrupulous conduct in financial transactions and other matters serves as a credit to the mercantile profession as a whole. Defoe's *New Family Instructor* (1722) and *Complete English Tradesman* (1726) also demonstrate his commitment to this subject. Trade, Defoe famously noted in the final issue of his nine-year periodical *The Review* (1704–13), was the 'Whore I really doated upon, and design'd to have taken up with'.[41] The growing prevalence of positive representations of merchants in contemporary literature attests not only to the rising affluence and social status afforded to mercantile traders but, perhaps more importantly, their pivotal position in maintaining the lifeblood of the British economy.* [42]

In the twenty-first century, British consumers are increasingly curious about their cultural relationship with the plethora of manufactured goods they desire, purchase and reject on a daily basis. That relationship may be interrogated in political, ethical or psychological terms. Perhaps this ongoing curiosity explains why new questions are also being posed about *why* the consumer revolution in latter eighteenth-century Britain occurred in the first place. Colin Campbell, for example, has suggested that the received explanation of emulative motives in eighteenth-century British consumers remains 'unproven':

> [I]t is important to stress that many goods are desired for their own sake rather than for any prestige which may be attached to them … something which is especially likely to be the case with products such as coffee, tea, chocolate and sugar which yield their own immediate and obvious satisfactions.[43]

Coffee has a very special cultural relationship with eighteenth-century Britain which extends far beyond its 'immediate and obvious' restorative powers (see further consideration of its significance in 'Part Four: A Culture of Print'). Here, the reason for making a distinction between

---

* Another positive portrayal of the mercantile profession is the figure of George Barnwell, the protagonist of George Lillo's play *The London Merchant* (1731).

specific consumer products (such as those suggested by Campbell) and trade imports generally is not necessarily to endorse his point as it is to note the differently desirable nature of such products. Coffee provides a useful case in point because its popularity in eighteenth-century Britain in some ways relates to its original use in Islamic culture (specifically, in Turkey, where coffee supplies were first purchased by British traders).[44] John E. Willis notes that coffee was

> a product of the world of Islam … By the mid-sixteenth century it was well-established in the cities of the Ottoman Empire, and the coffee house as a place of male sociability and discussion had become a basic feature of Muslim urban culture. Europeans lived and traded in these cities – Constantinople, Aleppo, Alexandria, Cairo – and reports on their coffee-drinking habits can be found in many accounts of sixteenth-century European travellers in the Near East.[45]

In contrast, 'the growth of the consumption of tea [in Britain] carried little or no Chinese or Japanese cultural baggage'.[46] Increased tea and coffee consumption in Britain from the 1690s onwards has a fascinating history. What is relevant to *this* investigation is that the urban culture of trade – implying with it a sort of worldly sophistication and openness to new intellectual ideas gleaned from a wider (global) cultural context – could be imbibed by British traders engaging with the well-established trading cultures of the Near East (along with the coffee). Coffee was widely extolled (and sometimes berated) by British authors during the eighteenth century for its stimulating qualities, as well (as an anonymous work of comic prose from 1732 makes clear) its associations with the decadent ennui of 'coffee house saunterers': 'I have been sauntering about from Coffee-House to Coffee-House; and have wearied those drowsy Asylums of the Indolent and Enervate. I am really fatigued with having nothing to do.'[47] However, coffee was also always associated with the social and intellectual engagement of ideas and urban culture (see Part Four: 'A Culture of Print').

To what extent does *this* cultural feature of coffee relate to its origins – from a British perspective – in Turkish trade? Moreover, given the previously discussed image of Roxana's Turkish dress, is there something fundamentally different about the cultural representation of coffee versus other 'Turkish' objects in eighteenth-century British culture? In an article which considers the setting for Defoe's novel, Rodney M. Baine has suggested that a particular vogue for Turkish culture and dress may be associated with the early eighteenth-century period:

> [P]robably the most telling evidence for a Georgian setting of Roxana's London is her Turkish costume ... When George I came to the throne [in August 1714] he brought with him his two Turkish personal servants, Mustapha and Mahomet ... Then from about 1719 Lady Mary Wortley Montagu, upon her return from Constantinople, helped to popularise Turkish customs like small-pox vaccinations and woman's (fictional) freedom – and Turkish dress.[48]

Montagu's trip to Constantinople (and numerous other locations abroad) between 1716 and 1718 were taken while accompanying her husband on his ambassadorial posting. She was reluctant to publish her *Turkish Embassy Letters* which relate to those travels (they were not published until 1763, the year after her death) but undoubtedly the prominence of her social position and influence would have helped to popularise the practice of smallpox inoculation which she brought back from Turkey (a disease which had killed her brother and nearly killed her).[49] Her letters are now frequently remembered for their efforts to dispel popular stereotypes concerning Turkish culture and habits (particularly towards women); some commentators have suggested that Montagu's observations may have established other cultural misconceptions in the process.[50] In any event, the descriptions in her *Turkish Embassy Letters* and her famous efforts to reform British medical practice concerning smallpox both suggest an active comparison between aspects of Britain and Turkey which engages with the intellectual and social province of culture (not merely aesthetic mimicry of clothing).

Baine's historical observations concerning George I go some way towards explaining the contemporary interest in Turkish culture, but not the manner in which different aspects of that culture – smallpox vaccinations and dresses being obvious examples – are represented in contemporary British literature. From a British perspective, Turkey's geographical position between Europe and Asia has repeatedly endorsed the received cultural perception that Turkey is partly representative of an eastern, 'exotic', 'Oriental' and non-Christian culture while also associated with recognisably European cultural traits.[51] Roxana's dress is a sumptuously exotic 'Curiosity' while the use of smallpox vaccinations implies a forward-thinking and progressive attitude towards medical practice. Coffee is imbibed by urban sophisticates keen to engage socially or intellectually with a like-minded global milieu (or is often represented in British literature in these terms).

In the eighteenth century, literary representations of Britain's perception of certain elements of Turkish culture are evident in works which thereby interrogate aspects of British culture. This may be demonstrated by Defoe's prose work entitled *The Conduct of Christians Made the Sport of Infidels* (1716). This work provides, as its elaborate preface explains, an account of British current events as seen from the perspective of a particularly well-travelled merchant:

> Kara Selym Oglan, Merchant of Amsterdam, is by Birth an Armenian of Lesser Georgia, on the Confines of Persia ... But being taken away young by his Mother's Brother, and carry'd into Aleppo; he was then bred a Mahometan: And his said Unkle being a very considerable Merchant, he remov'd him afterwards to Constantinople ... he settled in Holland; where he grew in Wealth and general Correspondence, to an exceeding Degree ... his Curiosity, led him at length to come over to England; where, it seems, by the Tenour of his Correspondence, he resided ....[52]

It would be impossible to ascribe a cultural background for Kara Selym Oglan as precisely 'Turkish' (or any other single nationality). His 'culture' is global trade itself and this perspective informs his opinions concerning English modes of behaviour. The real purpose of Defoe's text is to castigate participants on both sides in the ongoing Bangorian controversy (a contemporary political dispute largely involving religious differences between members of the Anglican clergy); his narrator's Muslim faith and experience of trade between many disparate nations of the world usefully provides a 'neutral' and objective stance concerning the English religious controversy at hand.[53] At one point, Kara Selym Oglan observes of the contentious British ministry:

> Sure the Gods of these Christians are going to … bring them to Destruction by the Agency of their own Follies: Seeing they suffer them to fall into such Breaches and such continual Quarrels as are not consistent with their being as a Nation … While I was among them, such a Feud began among their Dervices [*sic*] or Priests, as had adminster'd Matter of Laughter to all the World ….(pp. 34–5)

It is his neutral but shrewd objectivity which makes Defoe's narrator a potent commentator on British folly, not his 'exotic' foreign origins. As its title suggests, another work, *A Continuation of Letters from a Turkish Spy* (1718), presents its narrator, Mahmut, as a Turkish spy who (ostensibly) offers his judgement on English political affairs between 1687 and 1693. Max Novak has discussed how both Defoe's narrator and his 'historical' subject are being deployed to consider events much closer – in both time and location – to Britain. The format and title of this text merely indicate Defoe's wish to exploit a type of popular narrator familiar from a series of anonymously published French works from 1684.[54] From the conveniently detached – if wholly artificial – stance of a Turkish spy, writing about a period in recent history, what actually emerges is a contemporary and very damning portrait of British political and religious folly.

This concluding example demonstrates the potential complexity, as early as 1718, of the notion of cultural representation in eighteenth-century English literature. As readers, we ignore such complexity at our peril; even as key cultural concepts (such as 'British', 'colonial' or

'Turkish') are being formulated, they are simultaneously interrogated or undermined within a wider forum of debating discourses. The next chapter further considers how the rapidly expanding scale of contemporary print – reflecting British's domestic and colonial culture back at itself in a myriad of forms – came to assume its own cultural representation during the course of the long eighteenth century.

Notes

1   Suvir Kaul, *Eighteenth-century British Literature and Postcolonial Studies* (Edinburgh: University of Edinburgh Press, 2009), p. 86; see also p. 155. For a detailed economic overview of Britain's economic expansion in this period, see M. J. Daunton, *Progress and Poverty: An Economic and Social History of Britain 1700–1850* (Oxford: Oxford University Press, 1995).

2   For an overview of the formation of British nationalism during this period, see Linda Colley, *Britons: Forging the Nation, 1707–1837* (New Haven: Yale University Press, 1992) and *Captives: Britain, Empire and the World 1600–1850* (London: Pimlico, 2003); and Gerald Newman, *The Rise of English Nationalism: A Cultural History, 1740–1830* (London: Weidenfeld & Nicolson, 1987).

3   On this subject, see Bruce McLeod, *The Geography of Empire in English Literature 1580–1745* (Cambridge: Cambridge University Press, 1999); and Stephen H. Gregg (ed.), *Empire and Identity: An Eighteenth-century Sourcebook* (Basingstoke: Palgrave Macmillan, 2005).

4   See Kathleen Wilson, *The Sense of the People: Politics, Culture, and Imperialism in England, 1715–1785* (Cambridge: Cambridge University Press, 1995).

5   On England's place in the European drive for colonial expansion, see Jerry Brotton, *The Renaissance Bazaar: From the Silk Road to Michaelangelo* (Oxford: Oxford University Press, 2002).

6   On the formation of the Bank of England, see Patrick Brantlinger, *Fictions of State: Culture and Public Credit in Britain, 1694–1994* (Ithaca: Cornell University Press, 1996).

7   On this subject, see Lawrence Brockliss and David Eastwood (eds), *A Union of Multiple Identities: The British Isles c. 1750–1850* (Manchester and New York: Manchester University Press, 1997).

8   John Keay, *India: A History* (London: Harper Collins, 2001), pp. 391 ff.

9   See, for example, Richard B. Bernstein, *Thomas Jefferson* (New York: Oxford University Press, 2005).

10 Useful resources about British involvement in the transatlantic slave trade include Douglas Hamilton and Robert J. Blyth (eds), *Representing Slavery: Art, Artefacts and Archives in the Collections of the National Maritime Museum* (Farnham and London: Lund Humphries and the National Maritime Museum, 2007); and S. I. Martin, *Britain's Slave Trade* (London: Macmillan, 1999). Other resources are listed in Part Five of this volume.

11 On the cultural impact of the Inkle and Yarico tale over the course of the long eighteenth century and beyond, see Frank Felsenstein (ed.), *English Trader, Indian Maid: Representing Gender, Race, and Slavery in the New World. An Inkle and Yarico Reader* (Baltimore: Johns Hopkins University Press, 1999).

12 For an overview of this genre, see Peter Fryer, *Staying Power: The History of Black People in Britain* (London: Pluto Press, 1984); and Keith A. Sandiford, *Measuring the Moment: Strategies of Protest in Eighteenth-century Afro-English Writing* (Selinsgrove: Susquehanna University Press, 1988).

13 Ottobah Cugoano, *Thoughts and Sentiments on the Evil and Wicked Traffic of the Commerce of the Human Species ...* (London, 1787), p. 73. Also available through *Eighteenth Century Collections Online*, www.jisc-collections.ac.uk/ecco (hereafter *ECCO*). The definitive and most accessible modern edition of Cugoano's *Thoughts and Sentiments* is edited by Vincent Carretta (London and New York: Penguin, 1999).

14 Specific consideration of the *Interesting Narrative*'s relationship to the literary tradition of conversion narrative may be found in Adam Potkay, 'Olaudah Equiano and the Art of Spiritual Autobiography', *Eighteenth-century Studies*, 27:4 (Summer 1994), pp. 677–92; and Helen Thomas, *Romanticism and Slave Narratives: Transatlantic Testimonies* (Cambridge: Cambridge University Press), pp. 226–54.

15 Substantial numbers of literary anthologies for this period contain selections from Equiano's *Interesting Narrative* but the definitive modern edition is Olaudah Equiano, *The 'Interesting Narrative' and Other Writings*, edited by Vincent Carretta (London and New York: Penguin, 2003); also see Vincent Carretta, *Equiano, the African: Biography of a Self-made Man* (Athens: University of Georgia Press, 2005) for a detailed historical biography of Equiano.

16 As well as Carretta (ed.), *Equiano, the African*, see S. E. Ogude, 'Facts and Fiction: Equiano's Narrative Reconsidered', *Research in African Literatures*, 13 (Spring 1982), pp. 31–43; and Paul E. Lovejoy, 'Autobiography and Memory: Gustavus Vassa, alias Olaudah Equiano, the African', *Slavery and*

Abolition, 27:3 (December 2006) and ensuing responses by Carretta and Lovejoy in the subsequent edition of *Slavery and Abolition*, 28:1 (April 2007).

17   In particular, see Robin Sabino and Jennifer Hall, 'The Path Not Taken: Cultural Identity in the Interesting Life of Olaudah Equiano', *Melus*, 24:1 (2000), pp. 5–19; and Roxann Wheeler, 'Domesticating Equiano's *Interesting Narrative*', *Eighteenth-century Studies*, 34:4 (Summer 2001), pp. 620–4.

18   Kaul, *Eighteenth-century British Literature and Postcolonial Studies*, p. 145, makes the point in specific relation to *A Narrative of the Most Remarkable Particulars in the Life of James Albert Ukawsaw Gronniosaw...* (1774). Gronniosaw (*c.* 1705–75) lived in colonial America; Kaul's discussion of his *Narrative*, pp. 143 ff., raises questions concerning attribution, voice and identity which broadly parallel aspects of critical investigation of Equiano's *Interesting Narrative* (see Notes 15–16 above).

19   Olaudah Equiano, *The Interesting Narrative* ... in Lawrence Lipking and James Noggle (eds), *The Norton Anthology of English Literature*, Volume C: *The Restoration and the Eighteenth Century* (New York and London: W. W. Norton, 2006), pp. 2850–9, at p. 2855.

20   For a broader consideration of Christian Evangelism and abolitionism in this period, see David Turley, *The Culture of English Anti-slavery, 1780–1860* (London: Routledge, 1991); and Frank Lambert, '"I Saw the Book Talk": Slave Readings of the First Great Awakening', *Journal of Negro History*, 77:4 (Autumn 1992), pp. 185–98.

21   Kaul, *Eighteenth-century British Literature and Postcolonial Studies*, p. 2.

22   For a more in-depth discussion of post-colonial studies, see ibid., pp. 1–3. See also Roxann Wheeler, *The Complexities of Race: Categories of Difference in Eighteenth-century British Literature* (Philadelphia: University of Pennsylvania, 2000); and Charlotte Sussmann, *Consuming Anxieties: Consumer Protest, Gender, and British Slavery, 1713–1833* (Stanford: Stanford University Press, 2000).

23   Philip Lawson and John Phillips, 'Our Execrable Banditti: Perceptions of Nabobs in Eighteenth-century Britain', *Albion*, 16:3 (Autumn 1984), p. 225. This reluctance is also reflected in the (actual) reception that Sir Robert Clive met from Parliament, on his victorious return to England; see C. H. Philips, 'Clive in the English Political World, 1761–64', *Bulletin of the School of Oriental and Asian Studies*, 12:3/4 (1948), pp. 695–702.

24   For a general discussion of Foote's writing, see Terence M. Freeman, 'Best Foote Forward', *Studies in English Literature, 1500–1900*, 29:3 (Summer 1989), pp. 563–78.

25   See Sudipta Sen, *Empire of Free Trade: The East India Company and the*

Making of the Colonial Marketplace (Philadelphia: University of
Pennsylvania Press, 1998); and Robert Travers, *Ideology and Empire in
Eighteenth-century India* (Cambridge: Cambridge University Press, 2007).

26   'For the period [between] 1721–71 ... the British Museum and London
School of Economics possess more than 460 books and pamphlets in
English that discuss luxury; for the whole century the number would nearly
double [which] ... does not include the vast numbers of comments in
periodicals. If comments of all types during the century were counted, the
number would be several thousand': John Sekora, *Luxury: The Concept in
Western Thought, Eden to Smollett* (Baltimore: Johns Hopkins University
Press, 1977), p. 66.

27   Ibid., pp. 63 ff.

28   Ibid., p. 68.

29   Jonathan Swift, *The Conduct of the Allies, and of the late ministry*, 1st edn
(1711), p. 52. Also available through *ECCO*. See also Ann Cline Kelly,
Swift and Popular Culture (New York and Basingstoke: Palgrave, 2002),
p. 39.

30   Sekora, *Luxury*, p. 68.

31   In his *Examiner* for 2 November 1710, as cited by Sekora, *Luxury*,
pp. 84–5.

32   Sekora, *Luxury*, p. 76.

33   Neil McKendrick, John Brewer and J. H. Plumb, *The Birth of a Consumer
Society: The Commercialisation of Eighteenth-century England* (Bloomington:
Indiana University Press, 1982), p. 1.

34   Ibid., p. 37.

35   Kaul, *Eighteenth-century British Literature and Postcolonial Studies*, p. 86.

36   Laura Brown, *Ends of Empire: Women and Ideology in Early Eighteenth-
century English Literature* (Ithaca: Cornell University Press, 1993). For an
in-depth consideration of one female consumer in this period, see Amanda
Vickery, 'Women and the World of Goods: A Lancashire Consumer and
Her Possessions, 1751–81', in John Brewer and Roy Porter (eds),
Consumption and the World of Goods (London: Routledge, 1993),
pp. 274–301.

37   As cited by Kaul, *Eighteenth-century British Literature and Postcolonial
Studies*, p. 90. See Donald Bond (ed.), *Critical Essays from the 'Spectator'*
(Oxford: Clarendon Press, 1965).

38   Daniel Defoe, *The Fortunate Mistress* (also known as *Roxana*) (1724), in P.
N. Furbank (ed.), *The Works of Daniel Defoe*, Volume 9: *The Novels of Daniel
Defoe* (London: Pickering & Chatto, 2009), p. 150.

39   Rodney M. Baine also makes this point in 'Roxana's Georgian Setting',
Studies in English Literature, 1500–1900, 15:3 (Summer 1975), p. 464.

40   Two articles which cast light on notions of credit and masquerade in
      Roxana are Terry Castle, 'The Carnivalisation of Eighteenth-century
      Narrative', *PMLA*, 99:5 (October 1984), pp. 903–16; and John F.
      O'Brien, 'The Character of Credit: Defoe's "Lady Credit", "The Fortunate
      Mistress" and the Resources of Inconsistency in Early Eighteenth-century
      Britain', *English Literary History*, 63:3 (Fall 1996), pp. 603–31.

41   Defoe makes the remark in the *Review* for 6 June 1713; as cited in Max
      Novak, *Daniel Defoe: Master of Fictions* (Oxford and New York: Oxford
      University Press, 2001), p. 431.

42   On the cultural history of the British merchant capitalist in the early
      modern period, see also John McVeagh, *Tradefull Merchants: The Portrayal
      of the Capitalist in Literature* (London: Routledge & Kegan Paul, 1981).

43   Colin Campbell, 'Understanding Traditional and Modern Patterns of
      Consumption in Eighteenth-century England: A Character-action
      Approach', in Brewer and Porter (eds), *Consumption and the World of Goods*,
      pp. 40–57. On a related point, Carole Shammas observes that 'the reason
      why people make economic development decisions may not be knowable,
      because it requires information about motivation': 'Changes in English and
      Anglo-American Consumption from 1550 to 1800', in Brewer and Porter
      (eds), *Consumption and the World of Goods*, p. 177. The 'emulative' concept
      of consumerism that Campbell refers to is often associated with the theories
      of social economist Thorstein Veblen in his *Theory of the Leisure Class: An
      Economic Study of Institutions* (London: George Allen & Unwin, 1925).

44   'The coffee trade was dominated by Muslim traders from the north, whose
      activities in the Red Sea were linked to the great pilgrimage trade to
      Mecca': John E. Willis, 'European Consumption and Asian Production in
      the Seventeenth and Eighteenth Centuries', in Brewer and Porter (eds),
      Consumption and the World of Goods, p. 142.

45   Ibid., p. 140.

46   Ibid.

47   Anonymous, 'On Coffee-house Saunterers', in *A Council of Women* …
      (1732), not paginated but between p. 51 and p. 54. Also available through
      ECCO.

48   Baine, 'Roxana's Georgian Setting', p. 464.

49   Isobel Grundy, 'Montagu, Lady Mary Wortley (*bap.* 1689, *d.* 1762)', *Oxford
      Dictionary of National Biography* (Oxford University Press, 2004). See
      Robert Halsband (ed.), *The Complete Letters of Lady Mary Wortley Montagu*
      (Oxford: Clarendon Press, 1965).

50   For a discussion of Montagu's *Turkish Embassy Letters*, see Mary Jo
      Kietzman, 'Montagu's Turkish Embassy Letters and Cultural Dislocation',
      Studies in English Literature, 1500–1900, 38:3 (Summer 1998),

pp. 537–51; and Srinivas Aravamudan, 'Lady Mary Wortley Montagu in the Hammam: Masquerade, Womanliness, and Levantization', *English Literary History*, 62:1 (Spring 1995), pp. 69–104.

51   The best-known and most comprehensive consideration of the representation and perception of eastern cultures from the British/European imperial perspective is Edward Said's important but controversial critical work entitled *Orientalism: Western Conceptions of the Orient* (New York: Pantheon, 1978). See also Victor Kiernan, *The Lords of Humankind: European Attitudes to Other Cultures in the Imperial Age* (London: Serif, 1969, 1995), pp. 112 ff. Said extends his investigation, and responds to some of his (many) critics, in 'Orientalism Reconsidered', *Cultural Critique*, 1 (Autumn 1985), pp. 89–107.

52   Daniel Defoe, *The Conduct of Christians Made the Sport of Infidels* (1717), in David Blewett (ed.), *The Works of Daniel Defoe*, Volume 5: *Satire, Fantasy, and Writing on the Supernatural* (London: Pickering & Chatto, 2005), p. 25.

53   On the Bangorian controversy, see W. A. Speck, *Stability and Strife: England 1714–1760* (London: Edward Arnold, 1980), pp. 94–5, 151.

54   On Defoe's employment of the Turkish spy narrator, see Novak, *Master of Fictions*, pp. 528–30; and David Blewett's Introduction to *Satire, Fantasy and Writings on the Supernatural by Daniel Defoe*, pp. 48 ff.

A Culture of Print

Imitation, the old saying goes, is the sincerest form of flattery. This might be the case for faithful acts of mimicry but other imitative functions – such as translation or adaptation – are much more ambivalent procedures, selective acts of self-presentation through which the perceiver reveals their own standards, tastes and expectations in the process of 'imitating' someone or something else.

Throughout the long eighteenth century, translation and adaptation of printed matter were two of the many ways in which this cultural period consciously shaped distinct methods of reading texts and, by extension, 'reading' the wider world of external experience. In this context, 'translation' incorporates the rendering of other languages (especially Latin and Greek) into English as well as Dryden's 'translation' of Chaucer for his contemporary readers.* Jonathan Brody Kramnick has observed:

> By *Dryden's Fables Ancient and Modern, Translated into Verse* (1700) the narrative of refinement had set ... Dryden defended his 'translation' of Chaucer into 'modern English' by suggesting

---

* Consider, within this context, John Dryden's extensive career as a translator of many Greek and Roman authors, and Pope's translations of Homer's *Iliad* (1715–20) and *Odyssey* (1725–6). Dryden's *Fables, Ancient and Modern* (1700) contained versified selections from Ovid, Boccaccio and Chaucer.

that Chaucer's language had become foreign, and that 'turning some of the *Canterbury Tales* into our language as it is now refined' presented an improved and readable text.[1]

The notion of 'improving' literature, as well as refining the modes of perception used to read it, are constant cultural strands that run through the long eighteenth century. Related to this is the formation of a national tradition – a canon – of 'great' literature which includes some authors of the past and more recent times (such as Shakespeare and Milton) and excludes others. In his preface to *Fables, Ancient and Modern* (1700), Dryden depicts a kind of mystical English literary genealogy:[*]

> Milton was the Poetical son of Spencer [*sic*], and Mr Waller of Fairfax; for we have our Lineal Descents and Clans, as well as other Families: Spencer more than once insinuates, that the Soul of Chaucer was tranfus'd into his Body; and that he was begotten by him Two hundred years after his Decease. Milton has acknowledg'd to me, that Spencer was his Original.[2]

The English Canon

The process of canonising English literature begins in earnest during the long eighteenth century, and is influenced not only by Dryden, but also by Addison, Pope, Johnson[†] and numerous others now less familiar to modern-day readers (such as Charlotte Lennox and Clara Reeve). All of these authors helped establish a cultural precedent which continues to inform notions of literary 'quality' and literary criticism itself. Even as it recognised the pantheon of English literary excellence in ancient and modern writing, however, the period simultaneously created, in

---

[*]   In this work, Dryden greatly admired the 'modern' poetry of both Edmund Waller (1606–87) and Sir John Denham (1615–69); he also praised the poetic translation of Tasso undertaken by Edward Fairfax (d. 1635).
[†]   See, for example, Samuel Johnson's monumental *Lives of the English Poets* (1779–81).

'Grub Street', a subculture of literature whose inferior quality derived from its authors' mercenary, rather than 'higher' or 'artistic', aims.*

As Kramnick notes, 'modernity generates tradition'; English culture fashions its own sense of a national heritage as traceable through the 'great works' in its literary past. Anyone who makes decisions concerning the inclusion or exclusion of texts on an undergraduate literature syllabus is presented with a miniature version of the same conundrum. What are we trying to *say* about the literature and culture of a specific period? In putting forward certain texts, are we expressing ideas about literary value that were held in the past, or merely selecting the literature that reflects our own cultural priorities as transmuted through the prism of history?

Ancients versus Moderns

Relevant to these questions is the quarrel between the 'ancients and moderns', an important cultural debate waged during the early decades of the eighteenth century. The controversy originated in France, but began in England with an essay by Sir William Temple (1628–99) entitled *Of Ancient and Modern Learning* (1692). In it, Temple gives effusive praise to the 'ancient' epistles of Phalaris, a tyrannical Sicilian ruler from the sixth century BC. Temple's essay and learning were derided by a learned Classical scholar, Richard Bentley (1662–1742), and the debate was extended when Sir William Wotton (1666–1727), also a prodigious Classical scholar and author, responded in *Reflections upon Ancient and Modern Learning* (1694 and 1697).† Wotton provides a mediating point between Temple's support for the merits of 'modern'

---

*   'Grub Street' was a London street which operated as an early centre of literary production. *The Grub Street Journal* (1730–7) was a largely anonymous, weekly, satirical periodical which targeted many of the figures that Pope memorialised in his *Dunciad* (published 1728–43), including Shakespearian scholar Lewis Theobald (1688–1744), actor and later Poet Laureate Colley Cibber (1671–1757) and bookseller Edmund Curll (1683–1747).

†   Bentley proved conclusively that the Phalaris epistles were not ancient at all (and also questioned the authenticity of Aesop's *Fables*).

learning versus Bentley's pedantic defence of Classical culture as the repository of all worthwhile knowledge.[3]

Though the controversy had come to an end by 1697, when a second version of Wotton's essay was published, it was at this point that Swift was inspired to write *The Battle of the Books* (1704).[*] Swift's intention was to satirise the controversy itself, rather than the sources evoked in its disputation, as a prefatory admonition 'from the Bookseller to the Reader' makes clear:

> I must warn the Reader, to beware of applying to Persons what is here meant, only of Books in the most literal Sense. So, when *Virgil* is mentioned, we are not to understand the Person of a famous Poet, call'd by that Name, but only certain Sheets of Paper, bound up in Leather, containing in Print, the Works of the said Poet, and so of the rest.[4]

In making this point, Swift indicated that he had no wish to extend a controversy which, as Temple's secretary, he had seen first-hand and which represented deeper cultural tensions concerning England's intellectual heritage.

The text begins with a brief narrative about a spider living in a corner of St James's Library, 'swollen up … by the Destruction of infinite Numbers of Flies, whose Spoils lay scattered before the Gates of his Palace', who catches a passing bee in his web. Their ensuing dialogue represents Swift's central allegory for the way that modern thinkers 'spin' knowledge out of their own minds (as a spider spins its web from within its own body) while the ancients gather knowledge (like honey) directly from nature.[5] Their dispute in turn provokes a battle between books written by some of the principal intellectual figures of Classical antiquity (e.g. Homer, Aristotle, Plato) waged against the 'modern' troops of great thinkers (including Bacon, Descartes, Dryden and

---

* The full title of Swift's work is *A Full and True Account of the Battel* [*sic*] *Fought last Friday, Between the Ancient and Modern Books in St James's Library*. It was published along with his *Tale of a Tub* (an allegorical tale about religious contentions between the three principal branches of Christianity).

Boyle), led by Sir William Temple. Swift leaves the battle's ending unresolved at the text's conclusion, suggesting his reluctance to favour any one side in this controversy.[6]

Both the ancients and moderns debate and Swift's textual response reflected wider public concerns about the nature of knowledge and education in the early eighteenth century. Debates about the relative merits of ancient versus modern culture and learning were, in principle at least, also debates about the appropriate curriculum of study for a gentleman. They took place within the changing context of education and social status, made possible by new institutions such as dissenters' academies, and the 'new wealth' produced in Britain's expanding economic climate. They reflected underlying transitions in how eighteenth-century Britain perceived its cultural – and political – heritage. Debates about ancient versus moderns are also therefore debates about the nation's cultural identity, following either Classical models (as, for example, an authoritarian state, imperial power, archival source of traditional learning, and so on) or Enlightenment ideals (such as intellectual and social 'progress', electoral representation and free trade).

Politeness and Aesthetics

Eighteenth-century British writing presents a progressively self-conscious literary culture, a turning inward to interrogate its own standards and precepts. This is particularly evident in its gathering preoccupation with principles of taste, decorum and the complicated notion of 'politeness'.[7] These concern not only aspects of moral conduct (such as sexual propriety) – though these are prominent enough – but also increasingly prescriptive standards of language usage and 'style', and notions of aesthetic judgement as they apply to both literature and external experience in general. Within the context, two Scottish intellectuals from the latter end of the eighteenth century merit particular notice. A highly influential series of lectures on rhetoric and *belles-lettres*, given by Hugh Blair (1718–1800) of Edinburgh University, was extensively reprinted during and after this period;* James Beattie (1735–1803) contributed to the contemporary field of moral philosophy and aesthetics via his *Essay on the Nature and Immutability of Truth* (1770).[8]

From Steele and Addison to Blair and Beattie, Pope and Johnson to Shaftesbury and Burke, eighteenth-century thinkers put forward increasingly elaborate and specialised criteria for the delicate matter of literary and aesthetic judgement. From its outset, this complex area of cultural analysis incorporated diverse fields of creative and scientific study; eighteenth-century thinkers increasingly pursued the serious and systematic investigation of how abstract concepts such as 'beauty' relate to wider moral and intellectual ideas. [9]

Questions about aesthetic judgement – relating to literature and other aspects of lived experience – inevitably raise related questions about the perspective and identity of the judge. There are class implications, for example, in the very act of contemplating a natural landscape in aesthetic terms (as Crabbe's poem *The Village* suggests) since those who labour on the land to survive perceive its contours in very different terms from middle-class, disinterested and detached, aesthetes. At the same time, it could be argued that (the social privilege implied by) aesthetic detachment is a useful and necessary cultural tool in bringing about the reformations and improvements only possible in a 'civilised', democratic society. The status of artists (including authors) as social and political reformers therefore becomes deeply implicated in questions about aesthetic judgement. In the very last years of this period, such contemporary debates gave new urgency to British writers caught up in the political and social turmoil of the French Revolution.[10]

Print obviously played a profoundly important role in how British culture developed in this period; its cultural impact across European civilisation, from about the middle of the fifteenth century onwards, was wide-ranging and unprecedented.[11] Scholarly consensus suggests

---

* The term *belles lettres* is broadly equivalent to 'literary criticism' (particularly in the form of essays), but its origins in Blair's influential lectures on style, rhetoric and literary refinement are meaningful in pointing out the cultural context in which the practice of literary criticism began in earnest in eighteenth-century Britain.

that the first printing press with movable type was developed by Johann Gutenberg (*c.* 1400–68) in his Mainz workshop sometime around 1450. The clear origins of the printing press therefore remain partly concealed in historical uncertainty. There is less doubt, however, that the ongoing efforts of scholars such as James Raven have helped to qualify and analyse the growth of print culture as it relates to eighteenth-century English culture, highlighting along the way the many questions and obstacles which continue to challenge its study.[12]

The Reading Experience and the Print Market

Despite its (inherently) problematic nature, the study of print culture has reaped rich scholarly rewards in recent years. These investigations include, for example, statistical and historical analysis of readership based on literacy rates, marginalia (annotations or markings made by readers on textual margins) and evidence from contemporary private writing (such as diaries and correspondence).[13] Diverse investigation of the history of the book (regarding print runs, textual distribution, booksellers, and so on), legal history and economic analysis has also contributed to our understanding of readers' perceptions in this historical period.[14]

At the same time, analysis of historical readership is, at best, fraught with difficulty and tends to rely on assumptions concerning shared characteristics of readers (based on small groups or individuals). Did individual readers in the past (or now) respond to the experience of reading in the same way? Is it possible to find out? Critical study of reader response or 'reception theory' considers these questions;* this complex field of study offers much food for thought but perhaps less specific insight into the realm of readers in a specific historical period or,

---

* Reception theory, related to reader response theory, broadly argues that modes of textual interpretation are dependent on the subjective experience of the reader, and therefore that the act of reading is comprised of contributions from both the author and any individual reader. Reader response theory is primarily associated with the critical writing of Wolfgang Iser (b. 1926), Stanley E. Fish (b. 1938) and Hans Robert Jauss (1921–97).

arguably, the distinct experience of reading possessed by individual human beings.[15]

Even reader responses as seemingly direct as marginal annotation are not unmediated by the possibility (and the writer's self-conscious awareness of it) that others may read the comments. This is even more the case with diary entries and, obviously, letters. Moreover, some forms of literature are less conducive to marginalia and, therefore, such forms of analysis. Joad Raymond has observed within the context of news-related literature:

> Some readers read and annotate as if conscious of an audience ... For news publications, however, there is a shortage of this kind of evidence ... dense and significant marginalia are particularly rare in pamphlets and newsbooks. Readers ... [left] few traces to posterity.[16]

Notwithstanding the profoundly difficult questions presented by analysis of reader responses during the eighteenth century, it is possible to return to the reassuringly material evidence of its rapidly expanding and diversifying print market. What is discernibly changing here, however, is the traditional relationship between authors and aristocratic patrons which featured so prominently in printed literature during the sixteenth and seventeenth centuries. The traditional system did not give way overnight, however, to a scenario in which professional authors were immediately able to realise for themselves the potentially vast financial gains of meeting their readers' demands head-on.[17] In reality, the eighteenth-century's increasingly capitalist system of publishing went through what has been described as an 'uneven development'. Legislative changes, such as the passage of the 1709 Copyright Act, did little to regulate the print market effectively; widespread practices such as pirating (the distribution and sale of cheaply printed and unauthorised copies of popular texts) existed throughout the period, as did the monopolies operated by the most powerful booksellers (who were also the principal publishers).[18]

Moreover, until 1774, booksellers retained the ability (if not technically the legal right) to buy perpetual copyright, thereby ensuring that the upper hand in the print industry was generally retained by booksellers rather than authors.[19] Other systems, such as subscription (pre-ordering of texts prior to publication), harvested potentially greater profits for all concerned but were largely restricted to works whose success could be calculated on the basis of an author's established reputation.

If few authors reaped enormous profits from their pen during the earlier decades of the eighteenth century, some (like James Thomson) did.[*] Moreover, the capitalist system of print opened doors for many writers who would have been hard-pressed to attract aristocratic patrons. Within this context may be considered, for example, Defoe's employment as a political propagandist for both Godolphin's Whig and Harley's Tory ministries, or the many female authors arguably 'liberated' by the practice of anonymous publication. According to E. J. Clery, Caroline Franklin and Peter Garside:

> Women writers had not thrived under the old-style patronage
> systems, founded on homosocial bonds. Catherine Gallagher …
> has proposed that female authors from Aphra Behn to Maria
> Edgeworth pioneer and then consolidate a new style of abstract
> or 'disembodied' authorship in line with the growth of the
> capitalist market for books and the accompanying
> commodification of literature … the perceived 'nothingness' of
> feminine identity gave them a chameleon-like ability to adapt
> their authorial personae to suit a variety of circumstances.[20]

Notwithstanding the opportunities that eighteenth-century print culture presented for new authors, the shadowy presence of Grub Street attests, equally, to a brutally competitive economic climate driven by gain. Its best-known and most scathing satirical portrait in Pope's *Dunciad* (published in four versions 1728–43), according to Clery, Franklin and

---

[*] The publication of Thomson's poem *The Seasons* is discussed in Part Three: 'Pastoral and Anti-pastoral Poetry'.

Garside, 'chiefly takes aim at those abject writers who collude in their own exploitation, and prostitute themselves to the public appetite for libel, scandal, and sensation':

> [U]nder the aegis of the Goddess of Dulness, writers and booksellers perform like puppets, jockeying and backbiting, swimming in ordure, producing reams of unreadable print or catering to the lowest forms of public taste, all for uncertain gain … But … [t]he *Dunciad* is a war on more than one front; it targets not only low booksellers who exploit writers but political patronage of writers.[21]

Despite its tacit acknowledgement of wider power struggles behind the contemporary print market, Pope's *Dunciad* is the product of an author who had never known the penury of the 'abject writers' he castigated.* [22] Another term for 'the lowest forms of public taste' might, in this context, be 'market conditions'. The literary versatility so characteristic of many eighteenth-century authors reflected, in some cases, an admirable commercial savvy (in being able to adapt their craft to meet the demands of the market). This was also helped by the fact that, in the earlier decades of the period, literary genres (and thus readers' expectations) were less rigidly formalised.

Eliza Haywood presents an excellent example of just such a versatile author. Her diverse career (as an actress, bookseller, playwright, poet, periodical writer and editor, and writer of sexually suggestive works of amatory prose fiction such as *Love in Excess* and *Fantomina*) demonstrates the sort of professional adaptability necessary to thrive in such a marketplace. In the latter half of her career, after her infamous depiction in Pope's *Dunciad*, Haywood re-invented her literary identity to become the 'reputable' writer of highly moral prose fiction such as *The History of Betsey Thoughtless* (1751).[23]

---

*   Pope's commercial success was sustained throughout his career, but his translations of Homer's *Iliad* and *Odyssey*, through subscription and general sales, were particularly lucrative.

Market Forces versus Literary Quality

The process of naming and shaming mercenary authors is essentially another aspect of literary canonisation; Pope's *Dunciad* provides a contemporary 'anti-canon' of inferior writers or hacks for readers' derision and thereby reiterates the idealisation of other, 'refined', literature. His was merely the most famous version of the kind of literary criticism that thrived in the first decades of the eighteenth century, judging 'high' from 'low' literature and thereby assigning an author's motivation (as artistic or mercenary) in the process. Within the context of a market-driven print trade, this practice raises important questions about writing 'quality' and 'popularity' that still occupy modern readers. Do 'best-selling' authors – such as Dan Brown, J. K. Rowling or Stephenie Meyer – present the *only* literary criteria by which the first decade of the twenty-first century would like to be remembered by posterity? Alternatively, do the winners of literary prizes – such as the Man Booker or Costa Book of the Year Award – represent our finest literary 'achievements'?

The intervening two centuries have done little to remove the cultural divisions between 'literary' and 'popular' writing. This process gained a great deal of momentum through the wide-ranging debates carried out in the English periodical press, the output of which experienced phenomenal growth during the course of the eighteenth century. It would, indeed, be difficult to exaggerate the cultural importance of periodical literature in this period. The passage of the first Stamp Act in 1712 attests to both the growth of print, generally, and periodical print in particular. Its legislation added a penny tax on all printed material of fewer than 100 pages, thereby ensuring that governmental coffers could also benefit from the increase in print; meanwhile, Parliament's failure to renew the Licensing Act (after it expired in 1695) marked the beginning of a period when political opinions could be disseminated rather more freely in contemporary literature such as early political periodicals and related 'news' publications.

The Growth of Periodical Writing

In Part Three: 'Fact and Fiction' it was suggested that the earliest 'news' publications in England circulated long before 1642 (in ballads and chapbooks, for example) but the Civil War period witnessed significant expansion of the genre through the combined effects of improved print technology (with more printing presses, and therefore circulation, outside London) and the increased dissemination of 'news' from both sides of the political divide. The publication of English 'news' in diverse printed forms, including the periodical essay, thus developed from within a nexus of fact versus fiction, and political difference – a cultural inheritance which arguably continues to inform its production in the twenty-first century.

A widespread feature of eighteenth-century periodicals was the assumption by an author of a recognisable 'persona' (potentially combining aspects of political, aesthetic or intellectual characteristics), as described by Denise Gigante:

> Inhabiting a pseudo-fictional space somewhere between a public sphere marked by cultural change and a more private, self-enclosed world, the essayists took on the most contested topics of their day, pursuing them through all the nooks and crannies of experience. In essays ranging from taste and aesthetic principles to war, from natural history to fashion and gender roles and relations, these writers invented a number of stylistic techniques.[24]

Genre divisions between these wide-ranging periodical essays are – earlier on, particularly – far less relevant than the establishment of distinct personae which readers could associate with a particular publication. This is evident from early titles such as Defoe's *Review*, which ran from 1704 to 1711, ostensibly dedicated to the 'unbiased' discussion of the ongoing threat which French hostilities posed to

English security. (In truth, Defoe acted under instruction and payment from Sir Robert Harley, to gain popular support for the war effort against France.)* In addition to its consideration of current political events at home and abroad, the *Review* was supplemented by the *Mercure Scandale, or, Advice from the Scandal Club*, a correspondence column through which a gathered 'club' of learned individuals provided advice to readers on a wide range of ethical and social dilemmas.†

Many of the personae presented in eighteenth-century periodical essays are reflective and urbane individuals whose observations on contemporary life and manners were intended to provide both entertainment and moral instruction for their readers. The established reputation of Samuel Johnson as a leading author and thinker of the age preceded his later fame as the distinguisher compiler of the *Dictionary* (1755); his personae in periodicals such as *The Rambler* (1750–2) and *The Adventurer* (1753–4) gave voice to a speaker whose observant perspective is also notably urban:

> [T]hose who have passed much of their lives in this great city look upon its opulence and its multitudes, its extent and variety, with cold indifference; but an inhabitant of the remoter parts of the kingdom is immediately distinguished by a kind of dissipated curiosity, a busy endeavour to divide his attention amongst a thousand objects, and a wild confusion of astonishment and alarm.[25]

---

* Sir Robert Harley (1661–1724) was a moderate Tory statesman who served as Queen Anne's First Lord of the Treasury in 1711–14. He was instrumental in obtaining Defoe's release from Newgate after the author was imprisoned on charges of seditious treason following the publication of his inflammatory treatise *The Shortest Way with the Dissenters* (1703).

† This embryonic 'agony aunt' column took its example from John Dunton's *Athenian Mercury* (1691–7) which, in turn, had given popular currency to the periodical's use of the question and answer format. The parallels between Dunton's *Athenian Mercury* and Defoe's *Mercure Scandale* in combination with the disputation of complex moral questions (known as casuistry) in previous Puritan literature attest to the popularity of such content with English readers some decades before the advent of the novel.

The Adventurer's acute powers of observation also reflect on the subtler ways that contemporary culture impinges on human experience, some of which still seem strikingly apt today:

> [E]very man, in surveying the shops of London, sees numberless instruments and conveniences, of which, while he did not know them, he never felt the need, and yet, when use has made them familiar, wonders how life could be supported without them. (p. 30)

Some personae are further distinguishable by their political loyalties, recreational or literary tastes and even their characteristic locations. The diversification of English periodicals in the eighteenth century must therefore be understood in relation to tangible 'sites of discourse', mostly in London, associated with 'types' in contemporary society: the City merchant, the country squire, the cosmopolitan 'man about town', and so on. Such types came to be personified through personae such as Will Honeycomb and Sir Roger de Coverley in Addison's and Steele's highly popular *Spectator* series (1711–14); they in turn were refined versions of simpler and cruder characterisations from earlier periodicals such as Ned Ward's *Weekly Comedy* (May–July 1699, with a later version in 1707).

The Coffee House and Habermas's Public Sphere

In the 'siting' of personae and their topics, Ward's and later Steele's more popular *Tatler* (1709–11) concentrated on the proliferating centres of social and commercial contact within London's urban milieu.[26] Gigante notes that, from its first number in 1709, the *Tatler* associated certain topics of discussion with specific London locations:

> Steele announced that all accounts of gallantry, pleasure, and entertainment would be dated from White's Chocolate-house; all discussion of poetry and the arts from Will's Coffee House; all

learned commentary from the Graecian; all observations on foreign and domestic news from Saint James's ... Addison's Spectator culled his Speculations from visits to places like Westminster Abbey, Hay-Market Square, the Royal Exchange, and Drury Lane Theatre.* [27]

Deservedly prominent among these sites are the London coffee houses (many of which grew up as extensions of specific business activities). The story of the London coffee house, from 1652 onwards, contributes a great deal to our understanding of Britain's broader cultural and commercial history during the long eighteenth century.[28] Coffee houses were not only sources of hot beverages and current debates; periodicals were generally available for reading on the premises (which implies, in turn, much wider if unrecoverable levels of readership than can be gleaned from sales figures or print runs).

The coffee house's cultural importance as a site of 'refined' assembly, as well as its relationship to the emergence of popular literary forms such as the periodical, has been widely recognised. Highly influential among these discussions is the work of German social theorist Jürgen Habermas (b. 1929), whose *Structural Transformation of the Public Sphere* (originally published in 1962 with an English translation in 1989) continues to provoke scholarly investigation in relation to eighteenth-century cultural studies.[29] Broadly, Habermas suggested that both literal and symbolic sites of eighteenth-century discourse (including the coffee house, club and periodical) represent, within the context of eighteenth-century bourgeois and civil society in British and French culture, a 'public sphere' in which private individuals came together as a public and engaged in debates relevant to their shared experience (in political, economic and other terms).

The political dimension of Habermas's model of the public sphere is borne out by the fact that Charles II (unsuccessfully) attempted to

---

* Will's Coffee House (at the corner of Bow and Russell Street) was known for its literary clientele including Dryden, Congreve and Wycherley. The Grecian (in Devereux Court, Essex Street, Strand) was frequented by members of the Royal Society as well as Addison and Steele.

suppress coffee houses, by royal proclamation in 1675, as potentially disruptive sites of public assembly. During the eighteenth century, their cultural and commercial importance rapidly established coffee houses as a diverse and integral feature of urban Britain's landscape. More than two decades ago, Peter Stallybrass and Allon White stressed the importance of the physical manifestation of sites of public assembly in which specific modes of discourse were engendered:

> Alehouse, coffee-house, church, law court, library, drawing room of a country mansion: each place of assembly is a different site of intercourse requiring different manners and morals. Discursive space is never completely independent of social space and the formation of new kinds of speech can be traced through the emergence of new public sites of discourse and the transformation of old ones.[30]

The Habermas-inspired model of the public sphere of Stallybrass and White directly addresses how public sites of assembly in eighteenth-century urban Britain transformed in relation to the emerging significance of 'polite' discourse and 'refined' social intercourse:

> Augustan England witnesses a particular phase of the change ... The festive calendar was altogether too dirty, too disruptive, and rooted in a network of sites and places which the urban bourgeoisie was rejecting in favour of new sites of assembly, like the coffee-house and the spa ... this was a move from outdoors to indoors ... Street culture ... is a source of fascination and fear on the part of a bourgeois culture which must risk contamination by the low-Other, dirt, and danger whenever it steps down into the street.[31]

The 'rational' pleasures and refinement of public discourse, as presented by the coffee house or club, are usefully distinguished here from the – equally frequently depicted, and equally public – dirty and dangerous street encounters of eighteenth-century literature. In works such as

Swift's famous *Description of a City Shower* (1710), for example, the speaker urges the reader to stay at home:

> Returning home at night, you'll find the sink [sewer]
> Strike your offended sense with double stink.
> If you be wise, then go not far to dine;
> You'll spend in coach hire more than save in wine.[32]

The poem ends with the image of London's irrational chaos and filth converging into an unstoppable flood, while in Gay's *Trivia, or the Art of Walking the Streets of London* (1716) the speaker makes a tour of the city by day and night, pausing only to note the many potential hazards to the sight, body and sensibility of readers along the way.

Even more significant for this investigation is the fact that numerous authors make a direct link between such scenes – irrational, dangerous, chaotic, filthy – and contemporary print culture itself, as seen in the 'pissing contest' which takes central stage in Book II of Pope's *Dunciad*. As Stallybrass and White note, Swift relates this 'excremental interest' to the critical process of reading itself in *A Tale of a Tub*; the critics who peruse books in order to find errors and defects are cautious in the same manner as the man who watches his step in order to 'spy out the filth in his way' and 'come out as cleanly as he may'.[33] Such satirical presentations place their authors 'above' the seemingly sordid process of critical engagement with 'low', or inferior, writing while allowing them to engage in a more refined process of judgement from their own – lofty and detached – perspective.*

Polite Literature and the Advent of Literary Criticism

This discussion of 'high' versus 'low' literary culture therefore relates to Habermas's model of the public sphere. As a means of analysing eighteenth-century print culture, however, the model has been usefully

---

*   The 'high' versus 'low' model of criticism is also exemplified by Pope's satirical treatise *Peri Bathous, or, The Art of Sinking in Poetry* (1727).

challenged by subsequent studies which interrogate how much (or little) we actually understand about the different groups or 'communities' of readers that emerged during this period.[34] Investigation of eighteenth-century readership must also consider, therefore, the emergence of new ways that readers obtained access to printed matter. One important new source of readers was gained through the growing popularity of circulating libraries.[35] Though first viewed with suspicion – if not outright hostility – by authors and booksellers, circulating libraries became an increasingly influential feature of the contemporary print market. Such institutions made popular literature accessible to a much wider readership, both beyond London and other urban centres and to people who would not have been able to afford, or gain access to, new titles. As such libraries began to command the lion's share of sales for particular authors or certain 'types' of writing, the tastes of circulating library users began to be recognised and accommodated by authors (and booksellers commissioning their works).

Much of the expanding clientele of the circulating libraries was female or lived outside London, although it would be unwise to make too broad assumptions about the contemporary readership of certain authors based on this fact. In the same way, the diversifying periodical press (which also heavily influenced literary tastes and preferences for contemporary authors) was rarely if ever clearly directed at specific 'types' of reader in terms of either gender or location. In other words, not only male Londoners read news periodicals. Nor, for that matter, did only females read the 'scandal' sheets or 'female' periodicals (as evinced by the presence of 'scandal' writing in the *Review*) although periodicals which targeted a growing audience of female readers certainly existed, as indicated by titles such as the *Female Tatler* (1709–10) or Eliza Haywood's *Female Spectator* (1744–6). Their presence did not preclude the involvement of female authors or editors on the popular 'mainstream' periodicals (Delarivier Manley, for example, replaced Swift as propagandist and editor on the Tory *Examiner* between 1711 and 1714).

As the period progresses, an increasing interest in manners, social refinement and 'polite' taste (particularly in literature) is evident across virtually all periodicals. A few early titles such as Giles Jacob's *Poetical Register* (1723) passed critical judgement on contemporary literature but interest in the topic expands progressively. Moreover, many of the period's best-known contemporary novelists, poets and playwrights contributed (often anonymously) to such periodicals in parallel with their writing in other genres. Authors such as Henry Fielding, James Boswell and William Cowper all made sustained contributions to contemporary periodicals; that such authors are now more readily associated with other genres provides a significant indication of how critical and popular tastes regarding literary genres change over time.*

Periodical writing helped to generate the expectant communities of readers whose tastes would be catered for by contemporary literature (such as poetry, essays and novels) even as it dictated to them what should – or should not – be read.[36] Evidently, as the proliferation of periodical titles devoted to the discussion of literary taste suggests, this was a form of guidance that readers actively sought. The desire for literary guidance should, however, be compared with a twenty-first-century cultural environment now saturated with critical opinions and reviews to guide our choices (in everything including contemporary literature). Publicity and other 'consumer advice' also contribute, sometimes seamlessly, to a genre now so ubiquitous as to be almost unrecognisable.

It is within this context that we should consider the sustained contemporary success of *Essays, Moral and Literary* (first published 1778), written by minister and educational reformer Vicesimus Knox (1752–1821), which went through fourteen editions by 1795.[†] [37] Here, Knox echoes the now familiar critical sentiment that much contemporary writing is degraded by the mercenary motives of

---

* This is usefully demonstrated by Denise Gigante's anthology of English periodical essays, *The Great Age of the English Essay* (2008) which lists its contents on the basis of author as well as periodical title. Authorial selections are not only from Steele's and Addison's famous *Tatler* and *Spectator* series but also Samuel Johnson's *Rambler* (1750–2) and *Idler* (1758–60), Henry Fielding's *Covent Garden Journal* (1752), William Cowper's *Connoisseur* (1754–6) and Oliver Goldsmith's *Bee* (1759).

† As well as literary criticism, Knox compiled several extremely popular anthologies of literature on works of prose, poetry and letters.

authors (the 'inconvenience of hunger' rather than 'the hope of immortality'):

> [I]t is a known truth, that avarice narrows the mind, and renders it incapable of elevated sentiments and generous enterprises. It ceases therefore to be a matter of wonder, that [such] works are destitute of spirit, when they proceed not from the noble ardour inspired by the love of fame, but from the frigid incitements of the love of money.[38]

Such lofty observations recall Pope's *Dunciad*, but Knox goes on to suggest that another reason for the poor quality of much modern writing is 'the depraved taste of readers' (by which he means unlearned or coarse):

> In vain are [modern authors'] compositions formed on the model of the best writers, and regulated by the precepts of the most judicious critics, if they conform not to the popular caprice and the mistaken judgement of the vulgar. In an age when the taste for reading is universal, many works, contemptible in both design and execution, will be received, by some readers, with distinguished applause. (p. 39)

Knox makes clear distinctions between 'some readers', with capricious and 'popular' or 'vulgar' tastes, and (in the other corner) 'the most judicious critics' and their preference for 'the best writers'. His critical views extend beyond these general distinctions to consider the merits and faults of specific literary genres and authors. Knox is broadly contemptuous of one relatively new cultural form (he observes that '[f]ifty years ago there was scarcely a Novel in the kingdom'), suggesting that its 'extreme insipidity' suits the 'insipid minds [which] find in them entertainment congenial to their own nature' ('On Novel Reading', p. 191). Notwithstanding this dismissive view, Knox's qualified praise for individual novelists suggests that the practice of reading novels is not without its own hazards (particularly for the young or those of 'early virtue'). Samuel Richardson provides a case in point; Knox acknowledges that Richardson's novels are intended to promote virtue, but questions the moral propriety of certain scenes for 'inexperienced' readers. Tobias Smollett, despite his 'great merit', possesses a 'coarse humour' which Knox deems only advisable for readers of 'mature judgement', while Laurence Sterne's 'languishing and affectedly sentimental' writing contains the very different hazard of a tendency 'to give the mind a degree of weakness, which renders it unable to resist the slightest impulse of passion'.*

Knox's opinions are generally indicative of how, in the eighteenth century, the act of reading was perceived as a potential source of moral instruction. The utility and suitability of certain texts – particularly as they apply to younger and therefore more morally impressionable readers – were judged by the increasingly strict standards of moral propriety that featured within the literature itself. Through the dual processes of prescription and proscription, such critical writing continued to uphold and extend the notion of a British canon by directing readers towards certain writers and literary works.

It is not too cynical to suggest that the contemporary popularity of 'literary' writing of this kind was inevitably subject to exploitation by those who had a vested interest in the commercial success of certain literary works. As Richard Taylor has suggested, booksellers such as James Harrison initiated their own periodicals (such as *The Novelist's Magazine*, from 1779 and serialised throughout the 1780s).[39] The burgeoning popularity of the British novel, in particular, must be considered within the context of an equally burgeoning body of critical opinion and publicity being disseminated at the same time.† In this sense, broadly, eighteenth-century literary criticism represents a self-fulfilling – and self-sustaining – process.

---

* Knox further notes that only the right sort of readers will fully appreciate the 'cultivated genius' of Fielding: 'The man of application may find agreeable refreshment, after severer study, in the amusing pages of Fielding; but the fungous growth of the Novel-wright will be too insignificant to attract his notice' ('On Novel Reading', pp. 185–92).

† Taylor also considers later 'literary magazines' such as (bookseller James) *Ballantyne's Novelists's Library* (1821–4).

The 'right sort of reading', for Knox and his contemporaries, was that which improved or educated the reader's capacity for moral virtue. Robinson Crusoe needed only one source of Protestant moral and spiritual guidance – the Bible – on his desert island, but later protagonists in eighteenth-century literature (such as Rousseau's Emile) needed the text of *Robinson Crusoe* itself.[*] [40] Even relatively modern literary works such as Defoe's came to be taken as a kind of cultural shorthand, in the latter eighteenth century, for their morally 'useful' content. Allusions to contemporary texts (in other contemporary texts) indicates a culture which shares – or at least mutually recognises – the 'merit' of works in its literary canon among growing numbers of readers.

The Romance and the Novel

The pitfalls of 'the wrong sort of reading' are more various and difficult to specify. One way of approaching this complex issue is to consider how contemporary literary critics consider two important – but confusingly related – literary forms: the 'romance' and the 'novel'. Both forms of prose fiction present potential moral hazards for readers although the clear relationship between them remains elusive. In 1752, Charlotte Lennox considered the dangers of youthful reading of romances within – ironically enough – the very genre which Knox will see (twenty-six years later) as both 'insipid' and a potential moral hazard for young readers. Lennox's use of the novel form in *The Female Quixote* therefore indicates a different critical stance from Knox's, but the conclusion of that novel makes clear that she shares with him a desire to warn readers against the 'wrong sort of reading'.

In Lennox's novel, Arabella, the young female protagonist, has read extensively and exclusively from the many works of romance she finds in her father's study. 'Romance', in this context, refers to a broad genre of fictional writing (from France, Italy, Spain and England) which

---

[*] In Jean-Jacques Rousseau's, *Emile, or On Education* (1762), *Robinson Crusoe* is proposed as the only text needed for the ideal education of a self-sufficient young person who needs to be shielded from the harmful effects of 'civilisation'.

originated with medieval courtly poetry but became progressively popular in works of prose. Romances were largely tales about passionate – often unrequited – love, heroic bravery and virtue, and fantastic adventure. Arabella's excessive and isolated reading in this genre (while growing up in her father's remote castle) gives her a strangely heightened – and often absurd – sense of perception in relation to the real world.

Lennox's subject echoes aspects of Richard Steele's play *The Tender Husband* (1705) as well as, more obviously, Cervante's classic tale *Don Quixote* (1605). Lennox's Arabella develops a unique code of conduct which is heavily indebted to the melodramatic tales of fantasy, romance and intrigue she has read. In doing so, she fails to conduct herself in a manner that best facilitates her very real need to marry advantageously and so avoid losing her father's fortune.

Unlike Steele's *The Tender Husband*, Lennox's text relies on the reader's more sympathetic understanding of this unwitting heroine's predicament. Arabella has gained some benefits from her reading of romances (including her well-developed – if rather vigorously defended – sense of female virtue, and her superior knowledge of Classical history). She is also highly intelligent. Lennox's text makes clear that Arabella's flaws derive entirely from her blinkered, romance-induced perception of human nature rather than any intrinsic weakness of character.[41] As has been much more widely considered in relation to Jane Austen's later work *Northanger Abbey* (begun in 1798, but not published until after her death in 1818), Lennox's novel finds resolution in its heroine's literary 'conversion' (her rejection of romances in favour of more rational artforms). Moreover, as the heroines of their own courtship novels, both Catherine Morland and Arabella attain the kind of moral judgement necessary to recognise the 'right sort' of husband.[42]

Arabella achieves this level of understanding through the offices of an elderly clergyman (known as 'the Doctor', implying a distinguished and learned man of many years' experience) who is introduced in the closing chapters of the novel. Their extended dialogue (on the pros and cons of reading romances) quickly convinces Arabella of the error of her ways. As a work of fiction, Lennox's novel has been criticised for this use of a fairly unconvincing device by which her heroine is 'converted';

for our purposes, however, their dialogue provides a useful insight into how contemporary authors and literary critics (so often one and the same) viewed a specific literary genre. As will later be the case with *Northanger Abbey*, the central themes of *The Female Quixote* interrogated (as early as 1752) the extent to which the English novel was already beginning to present its readers with exemplary forms of female conduct and female aspiration regarding courtship and marriage.

Early on, the Doctor rejects romances as works of fantasy in which 'Writers have instituted a World of their own ... nothing is more different from a human Being, than Heroes or Heroines.' Arabella, in turn, justifies the escapist and idealistic qualities of romance in comparison with the distinctly inferior qualities of present-day experience: 'if [romances] do not describe real Life, give us an Idea of a better Race of Beings than now inhabit the World'. Significantly, the Doctor's pious response suggests that the real dangers of reading romances lie elsewhere (in the reader's emotional response to such works):

It is of little Importance, Madam ... to decide whether in real or fictitious Life, most Wickedness is to be found. Books ought to supply an Antidote to Example ...[whereas t]he immediate Tendency of these Books ... is to give new Fire to the Passions of Revenge and Love; two Passions which, even without such powerful Auxiliaries, it is one of the severest Labours of Reason and Piety to suppress. (p. 380)

Here, the Doctor's point is that the reading of books should provide an 'Antidote' to suppress the moral shortcomings of human behaviour ('the Passions of Revenge and Love'). Equally, the preservation of female virtue itself is endangered by such books, which 'soften the Heart to Love' while leaving female readers vulnerable to the 'danger of being betrayed to the Vanity of Beauty, and taught the Arts of Intrigue'. Such dangers contrast with the superior merits of 'natural softness, or early Education' that female readers should instead pursue through their experience of reading (p. 381).

There is much support, in the Doctor's sentiments, for Nancy Armstrong's claim that the English domestic novel came to replace (from about the mid-eighteenth century) the female conduct book.[43] Beyond the specific dangers to female virtue outlined in Lennox's novel, however, in both *The Female Quixote* and Knox's *Essays* there are indications that males are also subject to the perils of literary misinterpretation.[44] Moreover, the suggestion that 'Books ought to supply an Antidote to Example' does not warn readers to stop reading altogether, but encourages them to exercise suitable judgement in their choice of reading material.

Clara Reeve, a successful novelist in her own right and contemporary of Knox, provides in the preface to her *Progress of Romance* (1785) what at first appears to be a more balanced summary of the pros and cons of reading 'romance':

> Romances are of universal growth, and not confined to any particular period or countries ... containing ... both good and evil things. They are not to be put into the hands of young persons without distinction and reserve, but under proper restrictions and regulations they will afford useful instruction, as well as rational and elegant amusement ... they are equally entitled to our attention and respect, as any other works of Genius and literature.[45]

Significantly, however, Reeve's concept of 'romance' incorporates far more than the works read so avidly by Lennox's Arabella; it would, indeed, encompass many of Knox's 'modern novels'. In *The Progress of Romance*, Reeve attempts to trace the development of an elusive and universal literary quality (across centuries, cultures and genres) shared alike by both ancient literature and the modern novel which 'sprung up out of its ruins' (p. 8). It is less easy to identify precisely what this elusive literary quality entails. It certainly relates to the broader realm of 'fiction' (and she considers the attendant critical complexities of interpretation posed by its resemblance to 'real life') but also clearly responds to Reeve's own criteria for literary merit (including 'useful instruction' and 'rational and elegant amusement').

Are these criteria, however, any more or less valid than more apparently 'objective' or 'systematic' criteria applied by analysts of English literature in the twenty-first century? Critical analysis in any period is – like the literature it considers – the cultural product of its times. The literary views expressed by Reeve and Knox present, very near the end of the period under investigation, valuable cultural indicators of how contemporary readers responded to the growing significance of relatively new literary genres (such as the novel) in relation to older forms (such as the romance). Their ambivalent judgement of the novel's moral utility presents a recognisable process of cultural assimilation equally apparent, in more recent times, in early responses to the advent of television or the internet.

Unlike Knox, however, Reeve acknowledges the critical difficulty of defining literary terms – such as 'romance' – themselves. Her work takes the form of twelve three-way fictional dialogues between Hortensius, Sophronia and their literary adviser Euphrasia. Early on, Euphrasia asks her companions for their definitions of 'romance'; the differences in their responses prompt her observation that such discrepancies demonstrate how critics are 'running in hazard, to praise or to decry in general terms, without being perfectly acquainted with the whole extent of the subject under consideration' (pp. 6–9). Reeve's *Progress of Romance* identifies a deeply ambiguous aspect of contemporary literary criticism (the crossover between historical romance and modern literature) and proceeds to address it:

> [T]his Genus of composition has never been properly
> distinguished or ascertained ... it wants to be methodized, to be
> separated, classed, and regulated ... a work of this kind would be
> both entertaining and useful. (p. 8)

Her work fails to accomplish the first – impossible – task, but provides an invaluable insight into the critical process undertaken by Reeve in her broad survey of literary merit through the ages. Inevitably, perhaps, this critical process upholds much of what has already been associated with late eighteenth-century British culture, including a strong sense of moral propriety. Through Euphrasia's brief discussion of Aphra Behn and the narrative of *Oroonoko*, however, Reeve ascribes literary merit to the inclusion of scenes of strong emotional content. That she should draw attention to Aphra Behn at all, in 1785, merits particular consideration:

> Among our early novel-writers we must reckon Mrs. Behn. – There are strong marks of genius in all this lady's works, but unhappily, there are some parts of them, very improper to be read by, or recommended to virtuous minds, and especially to youth. – She wrote in an age, and to a court of licentious manners, and perhaps we ought to ascribe to these causes the loose turn of her stories. Let us do justice to her merits, and cast the veil over her faults. (pp. 117–18)

Euphrasia's description of this author's 'strong marks of genius' implies a clear desire to include Behn in the pantheon of great British authors but, equally, that she finds it necessary to ignore the impropriety of a body of literature intended for an age with such 'licentious manners'. Euphrasia goes on to note Behn's burial in Westminster Abbey (and famous epitaph) as further indicators of the author's literary status during her lifetime. Less precise are Euphrasia's vague allusions to the 'many fine and amiable qualities, besides her genius of writing' that Behn possessed; these comments may or may not reflect Reeve's personal sense of admiration for another female author, and one who managed to achieve professional success in a very different literary climate. This supposition is borne out by Euphrasia's later observation – concerning Delarivier Manley – that she would rather be 'spared the pain of disgracing an Author of my own Sex' (although she still mentions her). Like Behn, Manley is an author whose work 'partakes of the Style of the Romance, and the Novel' and was 'once in fashion'. Unlike Behn, Manley's name is 'gradually sinking into oblivion' since (according to Euphrasia) her writing has few redeeming qualities to prevent its being excluded from the English canon.

To Reeve's credit, her passing consideration of Behn (and Manley) in 1785 alludes to two areas of critical investigation that were apparently not properly 'discovered' until the twentieth century (namely, popular recognition enjoyed by eighteenth-century female authors, and the relationship between novels and earlier genres such as the romance or amatory prose fiction). Less fortunately, Reeve's subsequent comments reveal the precise manner by which Aphra Behn is to be remembered by literary posterity:

Euphrasia	… Mrs Behn will not be forgotten, so long as the Tragedy of *Oroonoko* is acted, it was from her story of that illustrious African, that Mr Southern wrote that play, and the most affecting parts of it are taken almost literally from her.
Hortensius	Peace be to her *manes*! – I shall not disturb her, or her works.*
Euphrasia	I shall not recommend them to your perusal, Hortensius. (p. 119)

Despite the 'marks of genius' in Behn's writing, the reading of her original works is emphatically *not* recommended. Instead, Behn herself is to be remembered through the adaptation of her *Oroonoko* (1688) in a play by Thomas Southerne (or Southern), originally published in 1695 but frequently revived during the course of the eighteenth century. Notwithstanding the profound differences between Behn's and Southerne's versions of this narrative, Euphrasia's recommendation implies that the best features of *Oroonoko* therefore consist of the 'most affecting parts' retained in both the original and Southerne's dramatic adaptation. The selective process at work here indicates what (in the latter eighteenth century) constitutes literary merit – and thus deserves to be remembered from the past – and what deserves to be forgotten.

* The Latin *manes* refers to the spirits of the dead, particularly used in relation to dead poets.

In the twentieth and twenty-first centuries, it is Behn's original *Oroonoko* which commands the lion's share of critical attention. This work is predominant amongst a number of important seventeenth-century fictional prose works written by female authors, the presence of which have considerably revised the model of the male authorial triumvirate (of Defoe, Fielding and Richardson) so often associated with the 'rise' of the novel.[46] Behn's story tells the tragic tale of a princely African hero whose cruel betrayal at the hands of English mercenaries leads to his (and his wife's) enslavement, torture and death; it is also a powerful political allegory reflecting Behn's Royalist sympathies for the recently deposed James II.[47]

Behn's Oroonoko represents everything noble and heroic in the face of the cruel injustice he suffers at the hands of duplicitous and mercenary English slave traders. Paradoxically, he also possesses 'all the civility of a well-bred great man ... [and] in all points addressed himself as if his education had been in some European court'.* [48] At the same time, Behn's sympathetic depiction of the cruel repression of African slaves needs to be put into perspective. Prior to his betrayal at the hands of the English sea captain, Oroonoko himself is an experienced slave trader; his humiliating enslavement therefore seems ironic but also presents certain implausible scenarios (for example, the jubilation and awe with which, when he lands at Trefry's plantation, the chained Oroonoko is greeted by the other plantation slaves who recognise him as the military leader who enslaved them in the first place).

The conclusion of Behn's *Oroonoko* sees the cruel torture and dismemberment of its enslaved protagonist. The scene may well have recalled, for contemporary readers, the tragic execution of Charles I, but also consciously draws on the imagery of the Christian crucifixion. In the objectification of Oroonoko's body through the dismantling of its parts, the text itself becomes foregrounded as the sacred and immortal commemoration of his tragic heroism. The themes of subjection and slavery in Behn's *Oroonoko* have been read in conjunction with

---

* Behn's text reveals that, as a young man, Oroonoko was tutored by a Frenchman and had learned the languages (and delighted in the company) of English and Spanish visitors to his kingdom.

328

considerations of female (political, economic and social) subjection. The text's early stages, set amongst the romantic and political intrigues of the Otan's court, also reflect the complex and gendered power relations of early amatory prose fiction (see Part Three: 'The Novel and the Individual' for discussion of Eliza Haywood's *Fantomina*). Behn's *Oroonoko* continues to present substantial critical scope for its interrogation of the intersecting studies of politics, gender and power in the literature of the late seventeenth century.[49]

There are many, sometimes startling, discrepancies between Behn's and Southerne's narratives, not least of which is the conclusion in which Oroonoko's torture, dismemberment and execution are replaced by his act of suicide.* Southerne's *Oroonoko* is very much a work of contemporary tragedy, echoing themes addressed (rather more effectively) in, for example, Dryden's *All for Love*.[†] The play certainly does exploit the emotional potential of some 'affecting parts' in Behn's original narrative (particularly in several tender love scenes between Oroonoko and Imoinda). It also, however, possesses dramatic devices which – though ostensibly popular with theatrical audiences during the eighteenth century – might now be seen as serious shortcomings (chief among which is an unrelated serio-comic sub-plot concerning courtship among the white colonial settlers on the plantation).[‡] Though broadly contemporary, and similarly focused upon the brave African hero who finds it 'nobler still to

---

* The brutal torture and execution of Oroonoko (and murder of Imoinda at his hands) in Behn's tale is replaced entirely while a sub-plot concerning the deputy-governor's lust for Imoinda assumes great significance (leading to his murder at Oroonoko's hands) in Southerne's play. Southerne's Imoinda is the daughter of a white European; at the outset of the play she has already married Oroonoko and is carrying his child.

† *All for Love, or, The World Well Lost* (1678) is the best-known play written by (Southerne's friend and contemporary) John Dryden. Unlike Shakespeare's *Antony and Cleopatra* all of the dramatic action in Dryden's play on the same subject takes place within the last few hours of the ill-fated lovers' lives. Southerne's *Oroonoko* shares with it – rather than Behn's original work of prose fiction – a focus on the hero's conflicting interests (between love and duty), and a tragic concluding scene of Shakespearian proportions featuring multiple suicides and a murder.

‡ For example, Oroonoko appears for the first time on stage bound in chains (in the middle of Act I, Scene ii) and often speaks in the blank verse most befitting a noble hero. Oroonoko also has a lengthy soliloquy on the nature of honour as it conflicts with the oppression of slavery at the end of Act III.

dye/ Than drag the galling yoke of slavery', the works of Behn and Southerne have far less in common than first meets the eye.[50] There is an obvious irony in Reeve's observation that the memory of Aphra Behn and her *Oroonoko* will only live on in Southerne's (now largely forgotten) tragedy. This does not, however, undermine the cultural importance of late eighteenth-century critical analysis itself. The collective processes of literary analysis and criticism – the selective remembering and forgetting of authors, works and even whole genres from an ever-accumulating 'history of English literature' – continue to expand in new directions all the time. As they do so, the opportunities to 'discover', critically and culturally, important works like Behn's *Oroonoko* (which was, thankfully, never really lost in the first place) also grow.

Notes

1   Jonathan Brody Kramnick, *Making the English Canon: Print-capitalism and the Cultural Past* (Cambridge: Cambridge University Press, 1998), p. 18.
2   John Dryden, Preface to *Fables, Ancient and Modern* ... (1700), in *The Works of John Dryden* (Ware: Wordsworth Editions, 1995), pp. 267–8.
3   On the quarrel between the ancients and moderns, see Joseph M. Levine, 'Ancients and Moderns Reconsidered', *Eighteenth-century Studies*, 15:1 (Autumn 1981), pp. 72–89, and *The Battle of the Books: History and Literature in the Augustan Age* (Ithaca and London: Cornell University Press, 1991); John F. Tinkler, 'The Splitting of Humanism: Bentley, Swift, and the English Battle of the Books', *Journal of the History of Ideas*, 49:3 (July–September 1988), pp. 453–72.
4   Jonathan Swift, from 'The Bookseller to the Reader', in *A Tale of a Tub* ... (London, 1710) in Louis Landa (ed.), *Gulliver's Travels and Other Writings by Jonathan Swift* (Boston: Houghton Mifflin, 1960), p. 359.
5   Christopher Flint considers the contemporary use of 'speaking objects' and authorial detachment, as demonstrated in Swift's text and elsewhere, in 'Speaking Objects: The Circulation of Stories in Eighteenth-century Fiction', *PMLA*, 113:2 (March 1998), pp. 212–26.
6   In addition to the previously cited works on the ancients and moderns (most of which refer to Swift's *Battle*), see Maurice J. Quinlan, 'Swift's Use

of Literalization as a Rhetorical Device', *PMLA*, 82:7 (December 1967), pp. 516–21.

7   On politeness in the eighteenth century, see Carey McIntosh: *The Evolution of English Prose, 1700–1800: Style, Politeness and Print Culture* (Cambridge: Cambridge University Press, 1998); and Philip Carter, *Men and the Emergence of Polite Society, Britain 1660–1800* (Harlow: Longman, 2000).

8   See, in particular, Hugh Blair, *Lectures on Rhetoric and Belles Lettres* (1784); and Lois Agnew, 'The Civic Function of Taste: A Re-assessment of Hugh Blair's Rhetorical Theory, *Rhetoric Society Quarterly*, 28:2 (Spring 1998), pp. 25–36.

9   For the development of notions of the aesthetic during the eighteenth century, see Kramnick, *Making the English Canon*, pp. 64–84; Barbara Warnick, 'The Bolevian Sublime in Eighteenth-century British Rhetorical Theory', *Rhetorica*, 8:4 (Autumn 1990), pp. 349–69; Carole Fry, 'Spanning the Political Divide: Neo-palladianism and the Early Eighteenth-century Landscape', *Garden History*, 31:2 (Winter 2003), pp. 180–92.

10   Much scholarly writing on the French Revolution and the responses to it by English authors has a post-1790 focus but a useful overview for the earlier period is provided in Marilyn Butler, *Romantics, Rebels and Revolutionaries: English Literature and its Background, 1760–1830* (Oxford and New York: Oxford University Press, 1981), pp. 1–68. See also Clifford Siskin, *The Work of Writing: Literature and Social Change in Britain, 1700–1830* (Baltimore and London: Johns Hopkins University Press, 1998); and Jerome J. McGann, *The Romantic Ideology: A Critical Investigation* (Chicago and London: University of Chicago Press, 1983).

11   The established scholarly source for this subject is Elizabeth L. Eisenstein, *The Printing Press as an Agent of Change: Communication and Cultural Transformation in Early Modern Europe* (Cambridge: Cambridge University Press, 1979).

12   A useful excellent overview of this field of study is provided in James Raven, *Judging New Wealth: Popular Publishing and Responses to Commerce in England, 1750–1800* (Oxford: Clarendon Press, 1992), and 'New Reading Histories, Print Culture and the Identification of Change: The Case of Eighteenth-century England', *Social History*, 23:3 (October 1998), pp. 268–87; see also Paul Fritz and David Williams (eds), *The Triumph of Culture: Eighteenth-century Perspectives* (Toronto: Hakkert, 1972).

13   See, for example, James Raven, Helen Small and Naomi Tadmore (eds), *The Practice and Representation of Reading in England* (Cambridge: Cambridge University Press, 1996); and Kevin Sharpe, *Reading Revolutions: The Politics of Reading in Early Modern England* (New Haven and London: Yale University Press, 2000).

14   See, for example, John Feather, *A History of British Publishing* (London: Croom Helm, 1988); and R. C. Alston (ed.), *Order and Connexion: Studies in Bibliography and Book History* (Woodbridge: Boydell & Brewer, 1997).

15   See, in particular, W. Iser, *The Act of Reading: A Theory of Aesthetic Response* (Baltimore: Johns Hopkins University Press, 1978); and S. E. Fish, *Is There a Text in This Class? The Authority of Interpretative Communities* (Cambridge: Harvard University Press, 1980).

16   Joad Raymond, 'Irrational, Impractical and Unprofitable: Reading the News in Seventeenth-century Britain', in Kevin Sharpe and Steven N. Zwicker (eds), *Reading, Society and Politics in Early Modern England* (Cambridge: Cambridge University Press, 2003), pp. 185–212, at p. 185. Raymond's observations are made in relation to works from the seventeenth century but are equally relevant for later news publications and demonstrate some of the shortcomings of the systematic analysis of a reader's marginalia.

17   On the history of patronage in eighteenth-century England, see Dustin Griffin, *Literary Patronage in England 1650–1800* (Cambridge: Cambridge University Press, 1996); and Paul Korshin, 'Types of Eighteenth-century Literary Patronage', *Eighteenth-century Studies*, 7 (1974), pp. 453–73.

18   See Mark Rose, *Authors and Owners: The Invention of Copyright* (Cambridge: Harvard University Press, 1993); and John Feather, *Publishing, Piracy and Politics: An Historical Study of Copyright in Great Britain* (London: Mansell, 1994).

19   On these points, see Introduction, E. J. Clery, Caroline Franklin and Peter Garside (eds), *Authorship, Commerce and the Public: Scenes of Writing, 1750–1850* (Basingstoke and New York: Palgrave Macmillan, 2002), pp. 9–16.

20   Ibid., pp. 12–13. See also Catherine Gallagher, *Nobody's Story: The Vanishing Acts of Women Writers in the Marketplace, 1670–1820* (Berkeley: University of California Press, 1994). Defoe's career as a political propagandist is discussed by Max Novak in *Daniel Defoe: Master of Fictions* (Oxford and New York: Oxford University Press, 2001), pp. 189–212, 262–88.

21   Clery, Franklin and Garside (eds), *Authorship, Commerce, and the Public*, pp. 10–11.

22   See Howard Erskine-Hill's essay on Pope, *Oxford Dictionary of National Biography* (Oxford University Press, 2004).

23   On Eliza Haywood's literary reputation and career, see Robert W. Jones, 'Eliza Haywood and the Discourse of Taste', in Clery, Franklin and Garside (eds), *Authorship, Commerce, and the Public*, pp. 103–19.

24   Denise Gigante, Introduction, *The Great Age of the English Essay: An Anthology* (New Haven and London: Yale University Press, 2008), p. vx.

25   Samuel Johnson, *The Adventurer*, 67 (Tuesday, 26 June 1753), in Charles
      Peake (ed.), *'Rasselas' and Essays* (London: Routledge & Kegan Paul, 1967),
      p. 127.

26   See Joseph Chaves, 'Social and Textual Circulation in *The Spectator*', *Media
      History*, 14:3 (December 2008), pp. 293–308, and Notes 27–8 regarding
      the cultural history of the coffee house.

27   Ibid. For detailed consideration of individual London coffee houses, see
      Aytoun Ellis, *The Penny Universities: A History of the Coffee-houses* (London:
      Secker, 1956); and Bryant Lillywhite, *London's Coffee Houses: A Reference
      Book of Coffee Houses of the Seventeenth, Eighteenth and Nineteenth Centuries*
      (London: Allen & Unwin, 1963).

28   See Markman Ellis, *The Coffee-house: A Cultural History* (London:
      Weidenfeld & Nicolson, 2004) and (as editor), *Eighteenth-century Coffee-
      house Culture* (London: Pickering & Chatto, 2006). For discussion of the
      commercial heritage of the coffee house, see Larry Stewart, 'Philosophers
      in the Counting-house: Commerce, Coffee-houses and Experiment in Early
      Modern London', in Patrick Karl O'Brien (ed.), *Urban Achievement in Early
      Modern Europe: Golden Ages in Antwerp, Amsterdam and London*
      (Cambridge: Cambridge University Press, 2001), pp. 326–45; and Warren
      Dawson, 'The London Coffee-houses and the Beginnings of Lloyds',
      Journal of the British Archaeological Association, 40:2 (1935), pp. 104–34.

29   Jürgen Habermas, *The Structural Transformation of the Public Sphere*, trans.
      Thomas Burger and Frederick Lawrence (Cambridge: MIT Press, 1989).
      Within the context of eighteenth-century English literature, Habermas's
      theory gained much attention through its investigation by Marxist literary
      theorist Terry Eagleton; see his work *The Function of Criticism: From the
      'Spectator' to Post-Structuralism* (London: Verso, 1984). For a brief, recent
      overview of how Habermas's theory of the public sphere has been taken up
      by scholars of eighteenth-century English print culture, see Kramnick,
      Making the English Canon, pp. 4–7.

30   Peter Stallybrass and Allon White, *The Politics and Poetics of Transgression*
      (London: Methuen, 1986), p. 80. This work relies heavily on aspects of
      Bakhtin's concept of the 'carnivalesque' elements of eighteenth-century
      British culture; see the Introduction regarding the influence of Bakhtin's
      literary theories.

31   Ibid., pp. 106–7.

32   Jonathan Swift, *A Description of a City Shower*, in Lawrence Lipking and
      James Noggle (eds), *The Norton Anthology of English Literature*, Volume C:
      The Restoration and the Eighteenth Century (New York and London: W. W.
      Norton, 2006), p. 2303.

33   Stallybrass and White, *The Politics and Poetics of Transgression*, pp. 108–9.

34   Of particular interest, in this context, is Benedict Anderson's highly influential *Imagined Communities: Reflections on the Origins and Spread of Nationalism* (London: Verso, 1983, revised 1991), whence comes the term 'print-capitalism'.

35   On the history of circulating libraries and their practices, see James Raven, 'From Promotion to Proscription: Arrangements for Reading and Eighteenth-century Libraries', in Raven, Small and Tadmore (eds), *The Practice and Representation of Reading in England*, pp. 175–201; and Robert Clark, 'Circulating Libraries', *The Literary Encyclopedia*, 11 April 2005, at www.litencyc.com.

36   On the diversification of literary periodicals during this period, see Walter Graham, *English Literary Periodicals* (New York: Thomas Nelson & Sons, 1930). For discussion of the cultural importance of periodicals and other print in eighteenth-century England, see John Brewer, *The Pleasures of the Imagination: English Culture in the Eighteenth Century* (Chicago: University of Chicago Press, 2000), Part 2; and Jeremy Black, 'Books and Newspapers', in *Culture in Eighteenth-century England: A Subject for Taste* (London and New York: Hambledon Continuum, 2005), pp. 147–69.

37   On his prolific and highly influential career, see Philip Carter and S. J. Skedd, 'Vicesimus Knox (1752–1821)', *ODNB*.

38   Vicesimus Knox, 'On Modern Literature', in *Essays, Moral and Literary*, (London, 1778–9), I.ii.38. Also available through *Eighteenth Century Collections Online* (hereafter *ECCO*), www.jisc-collections.ac.uk/ecco.

39   Richard C. Taylor, 'James Harrison, *The Novelist's Magazine*, and the Early Canonizing of the English Novel', *Studies in English Literature, 1500–1900*, 33:3 (Summer 1993), pp. 629–43.

40   See Denise Schaeffer, 'The Utility of Ink: Rousseau and *Robinson Crusoe*', *Review of Politics*, 64:1 (Winter 2002).

41   On this subject, see Margaret Doody's Introduction to Charlotte Lennox, *The Female Quixote* (Oxford: Oxford University Press, 1989), pp. xi–xxii.

42   On Austen's *Northanger Abbey* and Lennox's novel, see Elaine M. Kauvar, 'Jane Austen and *The Female Quixote*', *Studies in the Novel*, 2 (Summer 1970), pp. 211–21; and Debra Malina, 'Rereading the Patriarchal Text: *The Female Quixote, Northanger Abbey*, and the Trace of the Absent Mother', *Eighteenth-century Fiction*, 8 (January 1996), pp. 271–92.

43   Nancy Armstrong, *Desire and Domestic Fiction: A Political History of the Novel* (Oxford: Oxford University Press, 1987). This work is further discussed in Part Four: 'Gender and Sexuality'.

44 See, for example, Knox's discussion of suitable texts for boys' recreational reading at the conclusion of 'On Modern Literature', and the Doctor's warning that the reading of romances teaches men to 'execute vengeance', *The Female Quixote*, p. 380.

45 Clara Reeve, Preface to *The Progress of Romance ... in a course of evening conversations ...* (Colchester, 1785), I.ii, pp. xv–xvi. Also available through *ECCO*.

46 On this extremely broad subject, see (for example) Ros Ballaster, *Seductive Forms: Women's Amatory Fiction from 1684 to 1740* (Oxford: Clarendon Press, 1992); and Gallagher, *Nobody's Story*.

47 See, for example, George Guffey, 'Aphra Behn's *Oroonoko*: Occasion and Accomplishment', in George Guffey and Andrew White, *Two English Novelists: Aphra Behn and Anthony Trollope* (Los Angeles: William Andrews Clark Memorial Library, 1975); and Robert Markley and Molly Rothenberg, '"Contestations of Nature": Aphra Behn's "The Golden Age" and the Sexualizing of Politics', in Heidi Hutner (ed.), *Rereading Aphra Behn: History, Theory and Criticism* (Charlottesville: University Press of Virginia, 1993), pp. 301–21.

48 Aphra Behn, *Oroonoko, or The Royal Slave*, in Lipking and Noggle (eds), *The Norton Anthology of English Literature*, Volume C, pp. 2185–6.

49 See, for example, Susan B. Iwanisziw (ed.), *Troping 'Oroonoko' from Behn to Bandele* (Farnham: Ashgate, 2004).

50 Thomas Southerne, *Oroonoko: A Tragedy...* (The Hague, 1712), III.iv.68. Also available through *ECCO*.

Part Five
References and Resources

Timeline

	Historical events	Literary events
1660	(29 May) Charles II restored to the English throne	(1 January) Samuel Pepys begins writing diary; he continues until 31 May 1669 (failing eyesight prevents further entries)
1660	(onwards) Imposition of the Clarendon Code, restricting religious worship, resulting in widespread civil and religious persecution of English dissenters	
1662	Royal Society of London receives its royal charter	The Licensing Act grants joint monopoly for licensed theatrical productions in London to Thomas Killigrew and Sir William D'Avenant; it also decrees that women must take the part of female characters on stage
1665	(June–September) Great Plague of London kills over 100,000 Londoners in four months; overall mortality rate may have been twice this figure	
1666	(2–5 September) Great Fire of London destroys London landscape; few are killed but thousands left homeless	
1667		John Milton, *Paradise Lost*
1668		John Dryden becomes Poet Laureate

Historical events	Literary events
1673 Conversion to Catholicism by James (Duke of York, brother to Charles II and his successor); he marries his second wife, Mary of Modena, an Italian (and Roman Catholic) princess	
1674	Death of John Milton
1675 Charles II unsuccessfully attempts (by royal proclamation) to suppress coffee houses as sites of public assembly	
1677	Aphra Behn, Part One of *The Rover*
1678 Popish Plot	John Bunyan, Part One of *The Pilgrim's Progress*
1679–81 Exclusion Crisis, together with Popish Plot, heightens growing public fear of impending Catholic rule for England	
1680	Death of John Wilmot, Earl of Rochester
1681	John Dryden, *Absalom and Achitophel*
1681–5 Following third and final Exclusion Parliament (which lasted only one week in October 1681) Charles II flouts constitutional law by refusing to call Parliament to session for the remainder of his reign	
1682	Political turmoil in London leads to the combining of the city's two theatrical companies; they split in 1695
1685 (February) Charles II dies and is succeeded by his brother, James II; (July) Duke of Monmouth (illegitimate, Protestant son of Charles) stages unsuccessful rebellion to take the English throne	

	Historical events	Literary events
1685–8	James II's reign marked by his repeated efforts to extend the civil liberties for English non-Protestants, both dissenters and Catholics; most of these are thwarted by Parliament	
1687		Isaac Newton, *Principia Mathematica*
1688	(December) In the 'Glorious Revolution' senior parliamentary ministers invite William of Orange (the Dutch king) and his wife, Mary (James II's eldest daughter by his first marriage), to take the English throne; James II abdicates, fleeing to France	Death of John Bunyan; Aphra Behn, *Oroonoko*
1689	The Bill of Rights establishes constitutional government in England, curtails powers of the monarch and bars Roman Catholics from the throne	Death of Aphra Behn
1690		John Locke, *An Essay Concerning Human Understanding*
1692		William Temple, *Of Ancient and Modern Learning*
1698		Jeremy Collier, *A Short View of the Immorality and Prophaneness of the English Stage*
1700		Death of John Dryden; William Congreve, *The Way of the World*
1701	War of the Spanish Succession (continues until 1713), leading to rapid growth of speculation (as a means of raising war revenue)	
1702	William dies and is succeeded by Anne of Denmark (James II's second daughter by his first marriage)	

Timeline

Historical events	Literary events
1703	Death of diarist Samuel Pepys
1704	Jonathan Swift, *A Tale of a Tub* and *The Battle of the Books*
1704–9 England triumphs against the French and their allies in the War of the Spanish Succession, including in the Battle of Blenheim (1704)	
1704–11	Daniel Defoe, *The Review*
1707 The Act of Union between England, Scotland and Ireland creates 'Great Britain'	
1709–11	Richard Steele, *The Tatler*
1710 Tory ministry of Sir Robert Harley takes control of Parliament	
1711	Jonathan Swift's *The Conduct of the Allies*, a staunchly Tory anti-war pamphlet, sells over 11,000 copies in the first few months of publication
1711–14	Joseph Addison and Richard Steele, *The Spectator*
1711–20 Rapid growth of speculative investment in England begins with formation of the South Sea Company (1711)	
1712	The first Stamp Act adds a penny tax on the sale of all printed material of fewer than one hundred pages
1714 Queen Anne dies without issue and is succeeded by her distant cousin, George I of Hanover	
1714–27 George I's reign marked by a strong reliance on his ministry and the subsequent development of party-based governmental politics	

	Historical events	Literary events
1715	The first Jacobite Rebellion in Scotland; the 'Old Pretender' (James Stuart, son of James II, born 1688 to Mary of Modena) leads unsuccessful attempt to claim the throne for the Stuart bloodline	
1716–18		Lady Mary Wortley Montagu writes her letters from Turkey (not published until 1763)
1717		Alexander Pope, *The Rape of the Lock*, final version
1719		Daniel Defoe, *Robinson Crusoe*; Eliza Haywood, *Love in Excess*
1720	The South Sea Bubble 'bursts' with massive financial losses for many	
1721–42	Sir Robert Walpole's Whig ministry	
1722		Daniel Defoe, *A Journal of the Plague Year*
1725		Eliza Haywood, *Fantomina*
1726		Jonathan Swift, *Gulliver's Travels*
1727–60	George II's reign characterised by peace on English soil but long, expensive wars with European neighbours, particularly France and Spain, and steady expansion of the British Empire; England becomes the European leader in the transatlantic slave trade	
1728		John Gay, *The Beggar's Opera*
1729		Death of William Congreve
1730		James Thomson, *The Seasons* (in complete form)
1731		Deaths of Daniel Defoe and Mary Astell

Timeline

	Historical events	Literary events
1737		The Licensing Act imposes strict censorship on dramatic writing and theatrical production; London's many playhouses reduced to only two; repealed in the 1960s
1740		Samuel Richardson, *Pamela*
1743		William Hogarth, *Marriage A-la-Mode*; Alexander Pope, final version of *The Dunciad*
1744		Death of Alexander Pope
1745	The second Jacobite Rebellion; the 'Young Pretender' (Charles Stuart, eldest son of James Stuart and grandson of James II) returns to Scotland from France to claim the throne	
1746	(April) Bonnie Prince Charlie defeated at the Battle of Culloden and escapes to France	Death of Jonathan Swift
1747		Samuel Richardson, *Clarissa*
1748		Death of James Thomson
1749		Henry Fielding, *Tom Jones*; Samuel Johnson, *The Vanity of Human Wishes*
1753	Hardwicke's Marriage Act passed, increasing parental control over inheritance and property rights of heirs	
1754		Death of Henry Fielding
1755		Samuel Johnson, *Dictionary*
1757	Robert Clive's triumph at the Battle of Plassey gains Bengal in the first stage towards British control of India	
1759	James Wolfe captures Quebec from the French leading to British control of Canada	
1759–67		Laurence Sterne, *Tristram Shandy*

	Historical events	Literary events
1761		Death of Samuel Richardson
1762		Death of Lady Mary Wortley Montagu; Jean-Jacques Rousseau, *Emile, or On Education*
1764		Death of artist William Hogarth
1768	Captain James Cook voyages to Australia and New Zealand	Death of Laurence Sterne
1760–1820	George III's reign, remembered for increasing unrest in the American colonies culminating in the American War of Independence (1775–81) and ongoing battles with France	
1770		Oliver Goldsmith, *The Deserted Village*
1776		Adam Smith, *The Wealth of Nations*
1777		Richard Sheridan, *The School for Scandal*
1778		Fanny Burney, *Evelina*
1783	William Pitt becomes Prime Minister; signing of Treaty of Paris in which Britain formally recognises American independence	George Crabbe, *The Village*
1784		Death of Samuel Johnson
1785		William Cowper, *The Task*
1787	The American Constitution fully ratified as federal law	Ottobah Cugoano, *Thoughts and Sentiments on the Evil and Wicked Traffic of the Commerce of the Human Species*
1789	The French Revolution begins; George Washington becomes first American president; nearly half a million African slaves labour in British colonies in the Caribbean	Olaudah Equiano, *The Interesting Narrative*

Further Reading

Anthologies and General Resources

Lipking, Lawrence and James Noggle (eds), *The Norton Anthology of English Literature*, Volume C: *The Restoration and the Eighteenth Century* (New York and London: W. W. Norton, 2006)
Comprehensive and highly accessible range of primary texts plus useful introductory, historical and biographical contexts

Zwicker, Steven N. (ed.), *The Cambridge Companion to English Literature 1650–1740* (Cambridge: Cambridge University Press, 1998)
Excellent range of essays providing a sound historical and critical context in which to consider many of the period's principal cultural themes

Useful Websites

British Society for Eighteenth-Century Studies (www.bsecs.org.uk)
Promotes the study of this period across a broad range of cultural disciplines. The website provides useful links to a range of scholarly resources including *Jack Lynch's Eighteenth-Century Resources Page* (http://andromeda.rutgers.edu/~jlynch/18th/pro.html)

Eighteenth Century Collections Online (www.jisc-collections.ac.uk/ecco)
An invaluable source of eighteenth-century primary writing, available via subscription at many UK universities and learning institutes

JSTOR (www.jisc.ac.uk/jstor.html)
A digital archive of over one hundred scholarly journals, available via subscription at many UK universities and learning institutes

The Literary Encyclopedia (www.litencyc.com)
As its name suggests, an encyclopaedic reference tool which catalogues biographical and cultural information on all aspects of global literature, available via subscription at many UK universities and learning institutes

Oxford Dictionary of National Biography (www.oxforddnb.com)
The most comprehensive source of biographical information for British culture and history, available via subscription at many UK universities and learning institutes

Understanding Slavery (www.understandingslavery.com)
An extremely useful resource to extend historical understanding of British involvement in the transatlantic slave trade

Historical and Social Background

Before 1660 (The English Civil War and The Interregnum)

Fletcher, A., *The Outbreak of the English Civil War* (New York and London: New York University Press, 1981)
Charts the origins of the Civil War as it reflects the changing relationship between London and the provinces in sixteenth- and seventeenth-century England

Hill, Christopher, *Puritanism and Revolution: Studies in Interpretation of the English Revolution of the Seventeenth Century* (London: Panther, 1968)
Detailed and vivid account of the more (and less) radical Protestant religious sects instrumental in the early stages of the Civil War

Russell, C. S. R. (ed.), *The Origins of the English Civil War* (Basingstoke and London: Macmillan, 1973)
Wide-ranging collection of essays considering different aspects of pre-Civil War social and political tensions

Social, Cultural and Domestic History

Black, Jeremy, *Culture in Eighteenth-century England: A Subject for Taste* (London and New York: Hambledon Continuum, 2005)
Wide-ranging discussion of contemporary popular culture and the arts (including literature, fine arts, landscape gardens and opera)

Brewer, John, *The Pleasures of the Imagination: English Culture in the Eighteenth Century* (Chicago: University of Chicago Press, 2000)
Explores the 're-invention' of culture during the eighteenth century; particularly effective on the growth of the print trade and consumer culture

Cressy, David, 'Literacy in Seventeenth-century England: More Evidence', *Journal of Interdisciplinary History*, 8:1 (Summer 1977), pp. 141–50
Useful analysis of the problems and challenges facing scholars who seek to understand the nature of readership and literacy in this period

Flint, Christopher, *Family Fictions: Narrative and Domestic Relations in Britain, 1688–1798* (Stanford: Stanford University Press, 1998)
Explores eighteenth-century anthropological and social concepts such as 'family' and 'kinship' in direct relation to contemporary fiction

Pocock, J. G. A., *The Machiavellian Moment: Florentine Political Thought and the Atlantic Republic Tradition* (Princeton and London: Princeton University Press, 1975)
Invaluable discussion which traces the development of concepts associated with the European Enlightenment, such as civic 'virtue', and the growth of print culture

Porter, Roy, *English Society in the Eighteenth Century* (London: Penguin, 1982)
Excellent introductory overview to the social and cultural history of the period

Sekora, John, *Luxury: The Concept in Western Thought, Eden to Smollett* (Baltimore: Johns Hopkins University Press, 1977)
Combines thematic analysis of the depiction of luxury in contemporary literary texts with useful historical context

Shoemaker, Robert, *The London Mob: Violence and Disorder in Eighteenth-century England* (London: Hambledon, 2004)
Uses court records and other historical evidence to chart the decline in street violence during the course of the eighteenth century

Stone, Lawrence, *The Family, Sex and Marriage in England 1500–1800*, abridged edn (London: Penguin Books, 1979)
Definitive historical and economic analysis of the formation of the cultural concept of the 'individual' in early modern England

Thomas, Keith, *The Ends of Life: Roads to Fulfilment in Early Modern England* (Oxford: Oxford University Press, 2009)
> Wide-ranging and anecdotal exploration of historical evidence; thought-provoking as a consideration of cultural and historical 'difference'

Wrightson, Keith, *Earthly Necessities: Economic Lives in Early Modern Britain, 1470–1750* (London: Penguin Books, 2002)
> Useful historical analysis of economic changes to English culture and life, across the class spectrum, both before and during the long eighteenth century

Political and Religious Contexts for History

Clark, J. C. D., *English Society 1688–1832: Ideology, Social Structure and Political Practice during the Ancien Regime* (Cambridge: Cambridge University Press, 1985)
> Revisionist exploration of this period which questions the more established and progressive Whig model of history

Coffey, John and Paul C. H. Lim (eds), *The Cambridge Companion to Puritanism* (Cambridge: Cambridge University Press, 2008)
> Detailed and wide-ranging series of essays which provides a strong sense of the cultural diversity of Protestant religious conviction in early modern England

Langford, Paul, *A Polite and Commercial People: England 1727–1783* (Oxford: Oxford University Press, 1993)
> Comprehensive social and political history of Georgian England in the second half of the eighteenth century, powerfully depicting key cultural contrasts such as aristocratic refinement with mob violence

O'Gorman, Frank, *Voters, Patrons and Parties: The Unreformed Electorate of Hanoverian England 1734–1832* (Oxford: Clarendon Press, 1989)
> Useful and clear explanation of English political corruption and reform in the second half of the eighteenth century

Speck, W. A., *Stability and Strife: England 1714–1760* (London: Edward Arnold, 1980)
> Historical overview of the political and legislative conditions which shaped English culture in the first half of the eighteenth century

Thomas, Keith, *Religion and the Decline of Magic* (London: Weidenfeld & Nicolson, 1971)
>An invaluable exploration of European cultural change, particularly as it pertains to religious conviction and ritual, from the medieval to the early modern period

Watts, Michael, *The Dissenters: From the Reformation to the French Revolution* (Oxford: Clarendon Press, 1978)
>Detailed and invaluable guide to the experiences of English dissenters over several tumultuous centuries; excellent historical context provided throughout

Willman, Robert, 'The Origins of "Whig" and "Tory" in English Political Language', *Historical Journal*, 17:2 (June 1974), pp. 247–64
>Clear contextual explanation of two key terms for scholars of eighteenth-century culture

Economic History

Brantlinger, Patrick, *Fictions of State: Culture and Public Credit in Britain, 1694–1994* (Ithaca: Cornell University Press, 1996)
>Excellent discussion of the formation of the Bank of England

Daunton, M. J., *Progress and Poverty: An Economic and Social History of Britain 1700–1850* (Oxford: Oxford University Press, 1995)
>Detailed and compendious economic overview of the period containing a wealth of statistical evidence and analysis

McVeagh, John, *Tradefull Merchants: The Portrayal of the Capitalist in Literature* (London: Routledge & Kegan Paul, 1981)
>Considers cultural development and the changing social status of mercantilism in the early modern period, employing both historical and literary sources of evidence

Literary Genres

Drama

Brown, Laura, *English Dramatic Form, 1660–1760: An Essay in Generic History* (New Haven: Yale University Press, 1981)
Thought-provoking analysis of the period's earlier drama within the context of contemporary politics and economics

Canfield, Douglas J. and Deborah Payne (eds), *Cultural Readings of Restoration and Eighteenth-century English Theater* (Athens: University of Georgia Press, 1995)
Invaluable collection of essays which explore the period's drama as a rich source of literary analysis, considering well-known plays and some lesser-known texts

Owen, Susan J. (ed.), *A Companion to Restoration Drama* (Oxford: Blackwell Publishing, 2008)
Useful reference guide for theatrical terminology, dramatic genre and cultural context for eighteenth-century English theatrical performances and texts

The Novel and Its Development

Armstrong, Nancy, *Desire and Domestic Fiction: A Political History of the Novel* (New York: Oxford University Press, 1987)
Considers the relationship between seventeenth- and eighteenth-century conduct literature for females and the development of the novel genre

Barnett, George L. (ed.), *Eighteenth-century British Novelists on the Novel* (New York: Meredith Corporation, 1968)
Useful collection of quotations from contemporary authors on the development of the genre

Bender, John, *Imagining the Penitentiary: Fiction and the Architecture of the Mind in Eighteenth-century England* (Chicago and London: University of Chicago Press, 1987)
Discussion of the genre's development in relation to contemporary notions of behaviour, the individual and authority

Further Reading

Davis, Lennard J., *Factual Fictions: Origins of the English Novel* (New York: Columbia University Press, 1983)
> Explores how the dialectic notion of 'fact' versus 'fiction' in novels emerges from the genre's (and early readers') relationship to earlier literary forms, such as newsbooks

—, *Resisting Novels: Ideology and Fiction* (New York and London: Methuen, 1987)
> Interrogates the genre's subconscious impact on readers and their cultural expectations; argues that closer analysis of novels reveals their underlying ideologies

Hägg, Tomas, *The Novel in Antiquity* (Berkeley and Los Angeles: University of California Press, 1983)
> Fascinating discussion of the origins of novel-type narratives in Classical Greek literature

Hunter, J. Paul, *The Reluctant Pilgrim: Defoe's Emblematic Method and Quest for Form in 'Robinson Crusoe'* (Baltimore: Johns Hopkins University Press, 1966)
> Concise analysis of narrative structure and thematic content within this seminal work of prose fiction; provides a valuable sense of the cultural context in which early novels must be read

—, *Before Novels: The Cultural Contexts of Eighteenth-century English Fiction* (New York and London: W. W. Norton, 1990)
> Detailed, compendious exploration of popular literary forms which preceded, or were contemporary with, early English novels

McKeon, Michael, *The Origins of the English Novel, 1600–1740* (Baltimore: Johns Hopkins University Press, 1987)
> Required reading for students of eighteenth-century literature and the novel; provides a detailed and extensive analysis of the genre's cultural development

Starr, G. A., *Defoe and Spiritual Autobiography* (Princeton: Princeton University Press, 1965)
> Considers the novels of Defoe within the structural and thematic context of popular religious and didactic literature (e.g. sermons and conversion narratives)

Watt, Ian, *The Rise of the Novel: Studies in Defoe, Richardson and Fielding* (London: Peregrine Books, 1963)
> Invaluable and still thought-provoking analysis of the development of 'economic individualism' in early novels

Poetry and Verse

Cohen, Ralph, *The Art of Discrimination: Thomson's 'The Seasons' and the Language of Criticism* (London: Routledge & Kegan Paul, 1964)
> Uses *The Seasons* as a primary focus for a wide-ranging exploration of the history of literary criticism

Davie, Donald, *A Travelling Man: Eighteenth-century Essays* (Manchester: Carcanet Press, 2003)
> Incisive and scholarly investigation of eighteenth-century culture and poetry with excellent individual essays on Goldsmith, Cowper, Johnson and the Augustan lyric

Fairer, David and Christine Gerard (eds), *Eighteenth-century Poetry: An Annotated Anthology* (Oxford: Blackwell, 1999)
> Comprehensive anthology incorporating well-known and lesser-known poets, valuable both as a source of primary material and critical analysis

Political and Social Satire

Hammond, Brean S., *Professional Imaginative Writing in England, 1670–1740* (Oxford: Clarendon Press, 1997)
> Provides valuable economic context for the 'marketing of the literary imagination' as well as a close discussion of genre, forms and the development of satire during the period

Pollard, Arthur, *Satire* (London: Methuen, 1970).
> Useful and accessible overview to eighteenth-century satire

Weinbrot, Howard D., *Eighteenth-century Satire: Essays on Text and Context from Dryden to Peter Pindar* (Cambridge: Cambridge University Press, 1988)
> Close analytical readings of key satirical texts from the seventeenth and eighteenth centuries

Thematic Surveys of the Long Eighteenth Century

Nationalism and Imperialism

Colley, Linda, *Britons: Forging the Nation, 1707–1837* (New Haven: Yale University Press, 1992)
> Thought-provoking consideration of how British national identity was formed during this period through the country's religious conflicts, overseas wars and colonial settlement, and the growth of trade

Wilson, Kathleen, *The Sense of the People: Politics, Culture, and Imperialism in England, 1715–1785* (Cambridge: Cambridge University Press, 1995)
> Valuable discussion of English regional politics and the influence of imperialism on the formation of national identity during this period

Gossip as a Social Phenomenom

Parsons, Nicola, *Reading Gossip in Early Eighteenth-century England* (London: Palgrave Macmillan, 2009)
> Focuses on gossip and scandal, and its political significance, as portrayed in literature during the reign of Queen Anne

Spacks, Patricia Meyer, *Gossip* (Chicago: University of Chicago Press, 1986)
> Reflective discussion of the social phenomenon, in gendered terms, which includes a valuable consideration of the theme within eighteenth-century literature

The 'Body Politic' and the Body

Archambault, P., 'The Analogy of the "Body" in Renaissance Political Literature', *Bibliotèque d'humanisme et renaissance*, 29 (1967), pp. 21–53
Useful background reading which contextualises use of the concept by Hobbes

Brown, Norman O., *Love's Body* (New York: Random House, 1966)
Fascinating, if now somewhat dated, exploration of metaphors of sexual desire and the body as applied to the wider context of eighteenth-century culture and literature

Baconian Thinking and Scientific Enquiry

Ford, Brian J., 'The Royal Society and the Microscope', *Notes and Records of the Royal Society of London*, 55:1 (January 2001), pp. 29–49
Useful and informative discussion of the early social history of the microscope

Haynes, Roslynn D., *From Faust to Strangelove: Representations of the Scientist in Western Literature* (Baltimore and London: Johns Hopkins University Press, 1994)
Broad cultural overview of the changing role, and cultural responses to, scientific investigation (including early reactions to the Royal Society)

Hunter, Michael, *The Royal Society and Its Fellows 1660–1700: The Morphology of an Early Scientific Institution* (Oxford: British Society for the History of Science, 1982)
Detailed analysis of the Society's early membership and its development as a key cultural institution in the early modern period

—, *Science and the Shape of Orthodoxy: Intellectual Change in Late Seventeenth-century Britain* (Woodbridge: Boydell Press, 1995)
Particularly useful investigation of the early cultural reception of the 'new philosophy' and the Royal Society

Peltonen, Markku (ed.), *The Cambridge Companion to Bacon* (Cambridge: Cambridge University Press, 1996)
A range of essays which gives a strong sense of the Baconian legacy inherited by the Royal Society as well as Baconian influences on literary culture

Moral Reformation, Sensibility and Sentiment

Barker-Benfield, G. J., *The Culture of Sensibility: Sex and Society in Eighteenth-century Britain* (Chicago and London: University of Chicago Press, 1992)
> Seminal work on the history and development of sensibility in eighteenth-century culture and literature

Hunt, Alan, *Governing Morals: A Social History of Moral Regulation* (Cambridge: Cambridge University Press, 1999)
> Early chapters provide a useful overview of eighteenth-century English moral reformation (including the Society for the Reformation of Manners)

Mullan, John, *Sentiment and Sociability: The Language of Feeling in the Eighteenth Century* (Oxford: Clarendon Press, 1988)
> Closely analyses the relationship between the eighteenth century's growing cultural predilection for sentiment, female virtue and the rise of the novel

Philosophical Contexts

Thomas Hobbes and John Locke

Goldie, Mark, 'The Reception of Hobbes', in J. H. Burns and M. Goldie (eds), *The Cambridge History of Political Thought 1450–1700* (Cambridge: Cambridge University Press, 1994), pp. 589–615
> Excellent overview of the contemporary influence and cultural legacy of Hobbes

— (ed.), *The Reception of Locke's Politics: From the 1690s to the 1830s* (6 vols, London: Pickering & Chatto, 1999)
> Invaluable reference work for closer investigation of Locke's cultural legacy from the publication of his *Essay Concerning Human Understanding* onwards

Miller, Benjamin, 'Hobbes: On Religion', *Political Theory*, 16:3 (August 1988), pp. 400–25
> Useful clarification of still-contested issues concerning the views of Hobbes

Aesthetics, the Sublime and the Road to Romanticism

Butler, Marilyn, *Romantics, Rebels and Revolutionaries: English Literature and Its Background, 1760–1830* (Oxford and New York: Oxford University Press, 1981)
> The first chapter provides an excellent introduction to the prevailing political and cultural atmosphere which characterised the last decades of eighteenth-century Europe

English Educational Reform

Ong, Walter J., *Ramus, Method, and the Decay of Dialogue* (Cambridge: Harvard University Press, 1958, reprinted 1974)
> Useful discussion of the writing and cultural influence of Petrus Ramus on educational reform, particularly in relation to the teaching of rhetoric

The Scottish Enlightenment

Daiches, David, Peter Jones and Jean Jones (eds), *The Scottish Enlightenment, 1730–90: A Hotbed of Genius* (Edinburgh: University of Edinburgh Press, 1986)
> Useful reference work for examining the profound influence and contribution of Scottish writers and thinkers on contemporary British culture

Key Debates

Female Authorship and Representation

Backscheider, Paula R. and John J. Richetti (eds), *Popular Fiction by Women 1660–1730: An Anthology* (Oxford: Clarendon Press, 1996)
> A valuable anthology of often-neglected works; includes writing by Behn, Manley, Haywood, Jane Barker, Penelope Aubin, Mary Davys and Elizabeth Singer Rowe

Further Reading

Ballaster, Ros, *Seductive Forms: Women's Amatory Fiction from 1684 to 1740* (Oxford: Clarendon Press, 1992)

> Detailed textual analysis of one of the key literary genres which preceded the popular novels of the 1740s, covering works by Behn, Manley and Haywood

Barash, Carol, *English Women's Poetry, 1649–1714: Politics, Community, and Linguistic Authority* (Oxford: Oxford University Press, 1997)

> Scholarly analysis of the political and cultural forces which motivated female poets in the earlier period of the long eighteenth century, plus close textual readings

Gallagher, Catherine, *Nobody's Story: The Vanishing Acts of Women Writers in the Marketplace, 1670–1820* (Berkeley: University of California Press, 1994)

> Considers the creative relationship between female authorial identity and the eighteenth-century cultural tendency towards authorial anonymity as it relates to specific contemporary texts

Jones, Vivien (ed.), *Women in the Eighteenth Century: Constructions of Femininity* (London and New York: Routledge, 1990)

> Fascinating collection of contemporary writing, thematically grouped, which provides a vivid insight into cultural notions of females and femininity during the long eighteenth century

Mendelson, Sara, *The Mental World of Stuart Women* (Brighton: Harvester Press, 1987)

> Presents, in the form of biographical case studies, explorations of the roles and identities of three eighteenth-century female authors (Behn, Margaret Cavendish and Mary Rich)

Spencer, Jane, *The Rise of the Woman Novelist: From Aphra Behn to Jane Austen* (Oxford: Blackwell, 1986)

> Presents a female authorial canon of English fictional literature which interrogates Watts's model of the 'rise' of the novel

Marriage and Property

Bonfield, Lloyd, *Marriage Settlements, 1601–1740: The Adoption of the Strict Settlement* (Cambridge: Cambridge University Press, 1983)
Detailed historical, legislative and economic overview of marriage in the early modern period

MacFarlane, Alan, *Marriage and Love in England: Modes of Reproduction 1300–1840* (Oxford: Basil Blackwell, 1986)
Offers diverse evidence of affectionate marriage through the centuries, thereby interrogating the prevailing scholarly depiction of wedlock as an economic transaction

Misogyny, Satire and the Female Body

Brown, Laura, 'Reading Race and Gender: Jonathan Swift', *Eighteenth-century Studies*, 23:4 (Summer 1990), pp. 425–43
Considers Swift's depiction of the commodification of the female body

Castle, Terry, *The Female Thermometer: Eighteenth-century Culture and the Notion of the Uncanny* (Oxford: Oxford University Press, 1995)
Explores, through readings of a range of texts, eighteenth-century representations of female sexual desire and how Freudian notions of phantasmagoria and the uncanny help to uncover patterns of psychic disturbance in the period's culture

Nussbaum, Felicity, *The Brink of All We Hate: English Satires on Women 1660–1750* (Lexington: University of Kentucky Press, 1984)
Overview of eighteenth-century satirical and misogynistic depictions of females in literature

Pollak, Ellen: *The Poetics of Sexual Myth: Gender and Ideology in the Verse of Swift and Pope* (Chicago: University of Chicago Press, 1985)
Close textual analysis of misogyny in the poetry of Swift and Pope

Trade, Consumerism and Cultural Difference

Brewer, John and Roy Porter (eds), *Consumption and the World of Goods* (London: Routledge, 1993)
> Superb exploration of the eighteenth century's 'explosion' in trade and consumerism, taking in a broad range of subjects and scholarly approaches

Kiernan, Victor, *The Lords of Humankind: European Attitudes to Other Cultures in the Imperial Age* (London: Serif, 1969, 1995)
> Somewhat dated but still relevant, and region-specific, overview of cultural difference that emerged during Europe's imperial expansion during the seventeenth and eighteenth centuries

McKendrick, Neil, John Brewer and J. H. Plumb, *The Birth of a Consumer Society: The Commercialisation of Eighteenth-century England* (Bloomington: Indiana University Press, 1982)
> Considers the growth of eighteenth-century consumerism as evident through economic, historical and other cultural sources

Slavery

Sadler, Nigel, *The Slave Trade* (Botley: Shire Publications, 2009)
> Brief but concise overview of British involvement in the transatlantic slave trade

Walvin, James, *Black Ivory: A History of British Slavery* (London: HarperCollins, 1992)
> Useful and informative general study with a wealth of historical background

The Coffee House

Ellis, Markman, *The Coffee-house: A Cultural History* (London: Weidenfeld & Nicolson, 2004)
> Lively and engaging exploration of the cultural significance of the coffee house from its origins through to the present day

Ellis, Markman (ed.), *Eighteenth-century Coffee-House Culture* (London: Pickering & Chatto, 2006)
> Compendious reference work which provides a useful sense of the coffee house's breadth of cultural influence during the eighteenth century and beyond

Print Culture

Anderson, Benedict, *Imagined Communities: Reflections on the Origins and Spread of Nationalism* (London: Verso, 1983, revised 1991)
> Highly influential and thought-provoking discussion of how readership influences cultural notions of belonging and exclusion

Clery, E. J., Caroline Franklin and Peter Garside (eds), *Authorship, Commerce and the Public: Scenes of Writing, 1750–1850* (Basingstoke and New York: Palgrave Macmillan, 2002)
> Helpful and accessible introduction to the history of eighteenth-century publishing and print culture through a series of collected essays

Eisenstein, Elizabeth L., *The Printing Press as an Agent of Change: Communication and Cultural Transformation in Early Modern Europe* (Cambridge: Cambridge University Press, 1979)
> Highly influential investigation of the cultural impact of print on European culture

Kramnick, Jonathan Brody, *Making the English Canon: Print-capitalism and the Cultural Past* (Cambridge: Cambridge University Press, 1998)
> Argues that the English canon (including Shakespeare, Spenser, Milton and Dryden) is first formed during this period

Raven, James, *Judging New Wealth: Popular Publishing and Responses to Commerce in England, 1750–1800* (Oxford: Clarendon Press, 1992)
> Close, scholarly analysis of the growth of the popular press in the second half of the eighteenth century

—, 'New Reading Histories, Print Culture and the Identification of Change: The Case of Eighteenth-century England', *Social History*, 23:3 (October 1998), pp. 268–87
> Interesting discussion of the obstacles to systematic analysis of eighteenth-century reading practice

Raymond, Joad (ed.), *News, Newspapers and Society in Early Modern Britain* (Portland: Frank Cass, 1999)
    Collected essays which consider the cultural impact of printed periodicals on English society from the beginning of the seventeenth to the end of the eighteenth century

Rogers, Pat, *Grub Street: Studies in a Subculture* (London: Methuen, 1972)
    Vivid depiction of an important and sometimes neglected aspect of eighteenth-century literary production

Rose, Mark, *Authors and Owners: The Invention of Copyright* (Cambridge: Harvard University Press, 1993)
    Valuable overview of the legal history of copyright and the notion of intellectual property

Politeness, Refinement and Gender

Carter, Phillip, *Men and the Emergence of Polite Society, Britain 1660–1800* (Harlow: Longman, 2000)
    Detailed exploration of the development of male social identity during the eighteenth century as a barometer of cultural change

McIntosh, Carey, *The Evolution of English Prose, 1700–1800: Style, Politeness and Print Culture* (Cambridge: Cambridge University Press, 1998)
    Charts the development of eighteenth-century English literature as a 'feminisation' of social and moral values, evinced by a mature and more refined prose style

Critical Approaches to Literature

Brown, Norman O., *Life Against Death: The Psychoanalytic Meaning of History* (Middleton: Wesleyan, 1959)
    Early but influential exploration of desire and erotic love as suppressed forces of human creativity; a useful starting-point for students interested in psychoanalytic literary criticism

Castle, Terry, *Masquerade and Civilisation: The Carnivalesque in Eighteenth-century English Culture and Fiction* (Stanford: Stanford University Press, 1986)
> Fascinating application of Bakhtin's notion of the 'carnivalesque' (state-licensed periods of public recreation or 'play') to eighteenth-century literature and culture

Eagleton, Terry, *The Function of Criticism: From the 'Spectator' to Post-Structuralism* (London: Verso, 1984)
> Invaluable Marxist history and critique of critical approaches to literature

Foucault, Michel, *The History of Sexuality*, Volume 1, trans. Robert Hurley (London: Penguin Books, 1978)
> Considers the social, political and economic forces which have shaped Western culture's attitudes towards sexuality in scientific terms

—, *Discipline and Punish: The Birth of the Prison*, trans. Alan Sheridan (New York: Vintage, 1979)
> Examines the development of the penal system (in France and, by extension, the Western world) in the modern age as an institution centred in notions of reform

Habermas, Jürgen, *The Structural Transformation of the Public Sphere*, trans. Thomas Burger and Frederick Lawrence (Cambridge: MIT Press, 1989)
> Considers the development of the European bourgeois public sphere with special significance attributed to the growth of literary culture

Holquist, Michael (ed.), *The Dialogic Imagination: Four Essays by M. M. Bakhtin*, trans. Caryl Emerson and Michael Holquist (Austin: University of Texas Press, 1981)
> Still the best source to consider Bakhtin's complex but valuable discussion of the novel as a cultural force in which disparate 'languages' or 'voices' co-exist

Kaul, Suvir, *Eighteenth-century British Literature and Postcolonial Studies* (Edinburgh: Edinburgh University Press, 2009)
> Recent consideration of postcolonial studies as applied to a range of well-known eighteenth-century texts; the introduction is highly informative regarding this field of critical study

Further Reading

Shklovsky, Viktor, *Russian Formalist Criticism: Four Essays*, trans. L. T. Lemon and M. J. Reis (Lincoln: University of Nebraska Press, 1965)
   Essays providing an overview of principles of Russian Formalism as they relate to European literature; the discussion of *Tristram Shandy* is particularly useful

Stallybrass, Peter and Allon White, *The Politics and Poetics of Transgression* (London: Methuen, 1986)
   Lively and engaging text which considers Habermas's theory of the public sphere in relation to modes of behaviour and identity within eighteenth-century culture

Index

Index

Index

Killigrew, Sir Thomas 61, 78
Knox, Vicesimus, *Essays, Moral and Literary* 318–21
Kramnick, Jonathan Brody 51, 300, 302

labour 220, 224
Lanham, Richard 178
law *see* English law
Lawson, Philip and Phillips, John 281
Lemmings, David 259, 264
Lennox, Charlotte 301, 321–4
L'Estrange, Sir Roger 14, 20
libertines 254–5 *see also* rakes
liberty 13–14, 25, 27, 41, 122, 205, 220, 224, 227, 276
libraries 317
Licensing Acts 14, 21, 89, 156, 311
Lillo, George, *The London Merchant* 70, 289*n*
Lipking, Lawrence 28
literacy 15, 248, 249, 306
literary criticism 24, 310, 318–21, 325–30
Locke, John 125, 176, 213, 216, 227
  and America 224–5
  association of ideas 172–3
  on civil equality 276
  as employee of Lord Shaftesbury 222
  Essay Concerning Human Understanding 100
  on power of individualism 217–21
  and rejection of patriarchal kingship 222
  return from exile 224
  on slavery 241*n*
  on state of nature 212, 213, 220–1, 224, 225
London
  'as the novel's protagonist' 163–4
  attractions in 129, 199
  chaos and filth in 316
  coffee houses in 313–14
  in *Evelina* 199–201
  expansion of 17, 194
  Great Fire of 16–17

Grub Street 302, 308
  moral reformation in 228
  social elite in 204
  urban corruption and 132, 194
Louis XIV, King of France 18
love sonnets 119
Lutz, Alfred 134, 239
luxury goods 101, 103, 112, 258, 283–94
Lygon, Richard, *History of the Island of Barbados* 278

Macaulay, Catherine 245
McCloskey, Susan 68
Mace, Nancy 165, 179*n*
McKendrick, Neil, Brewer, John and Plumb, J. H. 295–6
Mackenzie, Henry 202, 238
McKeon, Michael 153–4, 188
Magdalen Hospital for the Reception of Penitent Prostitutes 265–6
Mancini, Hortense 262–3
Mandeville, Bernard 265–7
Manley, Delarivier 183, 184, 251, 317, 326
Manners, Robert 146
Marlborough, John Churchill, Duke of 45
marriage 59, 62, 76–7, 79, 80–1, 83–4, 102, 182, 194, 199, 323
  clandestine 259, 261
  in comedy of manners 64–9
  contracts 226–7
  female virtue and 194
  forced 195, 196
  Hardwicke's Marriage Act 258–62, 264
  idealisation of companionate 264–5
  for love 261–2
  moral reformation and 252
Marxist literary interpretation 215, 333*n*
Mary II, Queen (joint monarch with William III) 20, 22, 89, 224
Mary of Modena (queen consort to James II) 18, 223, 262
Mazarin, Duke of 262
melodrama 200, 322
Melville, Herman, *Moby-Dick* 187*n*

Index

political 18, 31, 32, 33–40, 41, 42, 48, 92–8
Tom Jones 166–7, 169
Tristram Shandy 170–8
Savile, Sir Henry 234
scandal 72–4
scandal sheets 317
scholarship 45, 176
science 123–4, 130, 228–31
    Enlightenment 236, 237
    innovations 98–9
    rationalism 216
Scotland 19–20, 275
Scottish Enlightenment 236–40
sedition 21, 35, 37, 89
seduction 59, 71, 74, 80, 82, 105, 106, 145, 196, 204–8, 267
Seidel, Michael 38
Sekora, John 283
Seneca 48
sensibility 202, 251
sentimental literature 71, 202, 239, 251
sexual conduct 59, 79, 167
    changing attitude towards 71
    in *Clarissa* 195–6
    comedy of manners 64–5
    London's social elite 204
    male promiscuity 59, 196
    potential dangers 194
    stricter standards of 63
sexual desire 32, 47–8, 50, 253
sexuality 31, 250, 252–5, 265–7
Shaftesbury, Anthony Ashley Cooper, first Earl of (1621–83) 19, 34, 38, 89, 122*n*, 222, 223
Shaftesbury, Anthony Ashley Cooper, third Earl of (1671–1713) 238
Shakespeare, William 119
    The Taming of the Shrew 62
    Winter's Tale 154
Shammas, Carole 298*n*
Sharpe, Kevin 14
Sharrock, Roger 187, 189
Shenstone, William, Rural Elegance 138*n*

Sheridan, Richard Brinsley 79
    The School for Scandal 62, 71–7, 255, 282
Shklovsky, Victor 170, 172
Shoemaker, Richard 73–4
slave trade 25, 276–82
slavery 97, 130, 132, 225, 239, 328
Smith, Adam 237, 238–9
Smollett, Tobias 25, 320
social class 145–6, 162, 168
social conscience 25, 127–30
social contract 221, 224, 226–7
social elite 10, 62, 63, 94, 102, 110, 229
    divorce and 262–4
    Fielding's depiction of 168
    marriage transactions 260–1, 268
    sexual conduct 204 *see also* aristocracy
social hierarchy 8–10, 24, 27, 217, 286
social injustice 147, 239
social mobility 9–10, 27, 123, 132, 133, 286
social reform 229–31, 233, 236, 256, 265
Society for the Reformation of Manners 228, 265
South America 282
South Sea Company ('South Sea Bubble') 23, 282–3
Southerne, Thomas 327, 329, 330
Spacks, Patricia 70
Speck, W. A. 134
Spectator 278, 287, 313, 314, 318*n*
Spencer, Jane 84*n*
Spenser, Edmund 119, 301
spiritual biographies 183, 189–90, 214
Springborg, Patricia 226
stagecraft 61, 75, 80
Stallybrass, Peter and White, Allon 315, 316
Stamp Act (1712) 310
standing armies 283
state of nature 212, 213, 220–1, 224, 225
    see also Locke, John; Hobbes, Thomas
Statt, Daniel 254, 270*n*
Steele, Sir Richard 71*n*, 278, 287, 313

Index

The best books ever written

PENGUIN CLASSICS

SINCE 1946

20% discount on your essential reading from Penguin Classics, only with *York Notes Companions*

Rochester: Selected Works
John Wilmot
Edited with an Introduction and Notes by H. Frank Ellis
Paperback | 160 pages | ISBN 9780140424591 | 07 Oct 2004 | £9.99

The Life and Opinions of Tristram Shandy, Gentleman
Laurence Sterne
Edited by Joan New and Melvyn New
Paperback | 720 pages | ISBN 9780141439778 | 27 Mar 2003 | £8.99

Gulliver's Travels
Jonathan Swift
Edited with an Introduction by Robert DeMaria
Paperback | 336 pages | ISBN 9780141439495 | 30 Jan 2003 | £5.99

Evelina
Frances Burney
Edited with an Introduction by Margaret Anne Doody
Paperback | 560 pages | ISBN 9780140433470 | 31 Mar 1994 | £9.99

The History of Tom Jones
Henry Fielding
Edited by Thomas Keymer and Alice Wakely, with an Introduction by
Thomas Keymer
Paperback | 1024 pages | ISBN 9780140436228 | 28 Apr 2005 | £8.99

Oroonoko, the Rover and Other Works
Aphra Behn
Edited with an Introduction and Notes by Janet Todd
Paperback | 400 pages | ISBN 9780140433388 | 26 Nov 1992 | £8.99

To claim your 20% discount on any of these titles
visit **www.penguinclassics.co.uk** and use
discount code **YORK20**